# FROMMER'S
## *EasyGuide*
### TO
# ISRAEL

*By*
## Robert Ullian

*EasyGuides are* ✦ Quick To Read ✦ Light To Carry
✦ For Expert Advice ✦ In All Price Ranges

## FrommerMedia LLC

Published by
**FROMMER MEDIA LLC**

ISBN 978-1-62887-010-7 (paper), 978-1-62887-040-4 (e-book)

Editorial Director: Pauline Frommer
Editor: Craig Nelson
Production Editor: Heather Wilcox
Cartographer: Roberta Stockwell
Cover Design: Howard Grossman

For information on our other products or services, see www.frommers.com.

Frommer Media LLC also publishes its books in a variety of electronic formats. Some content that appears in print may not be available in electronic formats.

Manufactured in the United States of America

5  4  3  2  1

# CONTENTS

## ABOUT THE AUTHORS

**Robert Ullian** has been the author of editions of *Frommer's Israel* for 20 years and is the co-author of *Frommer's Venice Walking Tours* and *Frommer's Israel Past and Present: A Guide to Archeological Sites in Israel*. Educated at Amherst College and Columbia University, he has also written guidebooks on Morocco and Bali.

**Sadek Shweiki,** research assistant and multilingual translator, was born in Jerusalem and educated at Hampshire College, in Amherst, Massachusetts, and at the School for International Training in Vermont. He brings his personal knowledge of many cultures to this book.

## ABOUT THE FROMMER'S TRAVEL GUIDES

For most of the past 50 years, Frommer's has been the leading series of travel guides in North America, accounting for as many as 24% of all guidebooks sold. I think I know why.

Though we hope our books are entertaining, we nevertheless deal with travel in a serious fashion. Our guidebooks have never looked on such journeys as a mere recreation, but as a far more important human function, a time of learning and introspection, an essential part of a civilized life. We stress the culture, lifestyle, history and beliefs of the destinations we cover, and urge our readers to seek out people and new ideas as the chief rewards of travel.

We have never shied from controversy. We have, from the beginning, encouraged our authors to be intensely judgmental, critical—both pro and con—in their comments, and wholly independent. Our only clients are our readers, and we have triggered the ire of countless prominent sorts, from a tourist newspaper we called "practically worthless" (it unsuccessfully sued us) to the many rip-offs we've condemned.

And because we believe that travel should be available to everyone regardless of their incomes, we have always been cost-conscious at every level of expenditure. Though we have broadened our recommendations beyond the budget category, we insist that every lodging we include be sensibly priced. We use every form of media to assist our readers, and are particularly proud of our feisty daily website, the award-winning Frommers.com.

I have high hopes for the future of Frommer's. May these guidebooks, in all the years ahead, continue to reflect the joy of travel and the freedom that travel represents. May they always pursue a cost-conscious path, so that people of all incomes can enjoy the rewards of travel. And may they create, for both the traveler and the persons among whom we travel, a community of friends, where all human beings live in harmony and peace.

Arthur Frommer

# THE BEST OF ISRAEL

For a country the size of New Jersey, Israel is startlingly diverse. When you find yourself in the silent, haunting desertscape near the Dead Sea, spotting ibexes on cliffs that are dotted with inaccessible caves—like those in which the Dead Sea Scrolls lay hidden for more than 18 centuries—it can be hard to believe that less than 60 minutes away is the 19th-century East European ghetto world of Jerusalem's Orthodox Mea Shearim quarter. And a few blocks from Mea Shearim, you'll find the labyrinthine medieval Arab bazaars of the Old City, with calls to prayer from the city's minarets punctuating your wanderings. Hop into a sherut (shared taxi) to Tel Aviv, and in an hour you're in a world of glass skyscrapers, surf-boards, and bikinis on the beach. Travel 2½ hours to the north, and you can explore ruined Crusader castles in the green forests of the Galilee Mountains.

The Holy Land surprises visitors in other ways as well. Thirty-five years ago, the country was still an austere, no-frills society—Israelis lived with few luxuries, and this spartan life was part of the national ideology. Today, Israeli society is frenetically inventive, the country's economy is booming, the standard of living has skyrocketed, and many surveys rank Israel's per-capita income among the top 20 in the world. Israel is becoming a nation with a lively sense of style and a taste for the good life. Luxury and better-quality hotel accommodations have popped up all over the country, and visitors find an interesting array of restaurants, shopping opportunities, and sophisticated boutique wineries.

With the Israeli-Jordanian peace treaty, a journey to Israel can also easily include an excursion to the fabulous ancient Nabatean city of Petra in Jordan, camping with Bedouin in Jordan's wild Wadi Rum, or a stay at one of the excellent luxury spas on the Jordanian side of the Dead Sea.

But amid Israel's busy swirl of exoticism, ancient sites, markets, and crowded highways, you can still find young, idealistic kibbutzim and communities in the Negev, where new immigrants and old-timers are reclaiming the land from the desert as they learn how to live on it, appreciate its wonders, and make it truly their own.

# ISRAEL'S iconic EXPERIENCES

o **Visiting the Dome of the Rock and the Temple Mount (Haram Es Sharif):** Built by the early Islamic rulers of Jerusalem in A.D. 691 on the site of the Temple of Solomon, this shrine is one of the world's most beautiful structures and the centerpiece of this awesome, sacred compound. Take the time to experience the power of this extraordinary place on your own. See p. 71.

o **The Western Wall on the Eve of Sabbath:** Enter Jerusalem's Jaffa Gate before Shabbat and join the flow of worshippers making their way downhill through the bazaars and alleys of the Old City as they move toward the Western Wall. At the Wall, you'll feel the magnetism and charisma that this remnant of the ancient Temple possesses for millions in the Jewish world. See p. 70.

o **Twilight from a Rooftop in Jerusalem's Old City:** Find a high vantage point (the terrace of the Austrian Hospice, the roof of the Petra Hotel, or the roof of Papa Andreas's Restaurant) where you can watch over the Old City and listen to echoes of synagogue prayers, mosque chants, and church bells that usher in Jerusalem's aura of evening sanctity. See chapter 5.

o **Journeying into the Past at Mea Shearim:** This Hassidic Jewish quarter of Jerusalem is a surviving fragment of the ultrareligious world of East European Jewry that disappeared into the Holocaust. A walk through these streets offers insight into the powerful traditions that continue to make Israel unique. See p. 98.

o **An Evening Stroll Through Old Jaffa:** The beautifully restored Casbah of Old Jaffa is filled with galleries, shops, cafes, great restaurants, and vistas of minarets and Crusader ruins set against the sunset and the sea. It's a special Israeli mix of the ancient and the cutting edge. See p. 186.

o **Holy Week in Jerusalem:** Starting with the Palm Sunday procession into the Old City and continuing with the Stations of the Cross on Good Friday and the Easter Sunday rites of the Latin, Orthodox, Coptic, Ethiopian, and Armenian churches at the Holy Sepulcher Church, this is a time of passion and meaning for the thousands of pilgrims.

o **Yad VaShem Memorial & Holocaust Museum:** A visit to this complex of memorials and museums in Jerusalem that commemorates the six million Jews who fell victim to the Nazis is an act of contemplation about the dangers of hatred and indifference to suffering. No visitor can leave unaffected. See p. 92.

o **Circling the Sea of Galilee:** This gemlike, turquoise lake set amid the mountains of Galilee is Israel's greatest natural treasure and was the landscape of Jesus's ministry. The eastern and northern shores are less developed and better reveal the lake's poetry. Explore biblical sites and watch twilight fall over this magical body of water from a eucalyptus-shaded beach. Kibbutz Ein Gev is perfect for overnighting and idyllic swimming. Rent a car for a few days and freewheel through the Galilee's olive groves, wineries, ruined Roman-era synagogues, Crusader castles, ancient churches, and the walled Casbah of Akko beside the Mediterranean. See chapter 7.

# THE most evocative
# ANCIENT SITES & CITIES

Israel and neighboring Jordan are filled with ancient sites and cities from every part of their long histories. Some sites are famous places of pilgrimage; others were lost and forgotten until modern times. Now, dazzling physical monuments to the past are being recovered at a rapid pace.

o **City of David:** Just outside the present walls of Jerusalem, this is where most of Jerusalem was located from prehistoric to Old Testament times. Presently undergoing intensive, sometimes controversial, archaeological excavation, this area is now in the densely populated Arab neighborhood of Silwan. It is best visited on an organized tour or with a guide. See p. 74.

o **Capernaum, Tabgha & the Mount of Beatitudes:** This lyrically lovely corner of the Sea of Galilee was the center of Jesus's early ministry. It contains the sites of St. Peter's house, the Miracle of the Loaves and the Fishes, and the Sermon on the Mount. See chapter 7.

o **Masada:** Herod's dramatic desert palace, built on an almost inaccessible mesa/plateau in about 10 B.C., became the final stronghold of the First Jewish Revolt against Rome. Here, in A.D. 73, the last Jews to live under their own rule (until the 1948 creation of the State of Israel) committed mass suicide on the eve of their conquest by Roman armies. See p. 121.

o **Basilica of the Nativity** (Bethlehem, West Bank): The site of Jesus's birth, this is the oldest surviving church in the Holy Land; the Persians spared it during their invasion in A.D. 614 because, according to legend, they were impressed by a representation of the Magi (fellow Persians) that decorated the building. See p. 115.

o **Caesarea** (on the coast between Tel Aviv and Haifa): Built by Herod as the great harbor and seaport of his kingdom, this was the splendid capital of Roman Judea and Byzantine-era Palestine. The vast Roman and Crusader ruins include amphitheaters, a hippodrome, and Crusader forts that are all the more romantic with Mediterranean waves lapping at the ancient stones. See p. 199.

o **Zippori** (Sepphoris, near Nazareth): This cosmopolitan Jewish-Hellenistic city, close to Nazareth, was the capital of the Galilee in Roman times. Especially interesting because the area was probably familiar to Jesus, Zippori's highlights include a colonnaded street, a mosaic synagogue floor, and a masterpiece mosaic portrait of a Roman-era woman dubbed "the Mona Lisa of the Galilee." See p. 130.

o **Korazim:** Once hidden by mountains of thistles, this Roman-Byzantine-era Jewish town in the hills just northeast of the Sea of Galilee is a beautiful place with sweeping views of the lake. Houses and an ancient synagogue adorned with beautifully carved black basalt detailing still stand. See p. 145.

o **Petra:** One of the great wonders of the world, yet forgotten for a thousand years, this legendary 2,000-year-old Nabatean city carved from the walls of a hidden desert canyon is the highlight of excursion tours into Jordan. The entire Petra experience, including the trek into the canyon, has an air of adventure and mystery. Stays of 1 or 2 nights are recommended. See chapter 10.

# THE best WAYS TO EXPERIENCE ISRAEL LIKE A LOCAL

o **Watching the Sun Set over the Mediterranean:** Israel's entire coastline of white-sand beaches, cliffs, and bluffs faces directly west into the sunset. The Jewish Day traditionally begins with the marking of sunset. Take a half-hour and find a spot to watch the sun sink into the sea—it's a memorable way to unwind and reflect.

o **Going with the Flow on the Sabbath:** The idea that every living thing must be allowed to rest for one-seventh of its existence is one of Judaism's ancient precepts. In modern Israel, most businesses and public transportation cease on Shabbat and *everyone* relaxes, if not rests. Join the national aura of Sabbath calm: Keep your Sabbath itinerary slow and restful.

o **Wildflower-Watching in Late Winter:** After the winter rains, thousands of Israelis and travelers pour into the Galilee to enjoy the oceans of wildflowers and the famous wild irises near Netanya and the Gilboa hills that cover the normally parched landscape; it's a tradition akin to cherry-blossom viewing in Japan.

o **Sampling the Music Scene:** Israel possesses an oversupply of magnificent musicians; even smaller cities, such as Beersheba, are home to orchestras that would be the envy of world capitals. Check local tourist offices for information about concerts and festivals ranging from classical to jazz to traditional local music.

o **Noshing Your Way Through the Arab Bazaars of Jerusalem's Old City:** Sample this authentic food festival of treats while you wander: oven-fresh pita breads with local spices; *kanaffeh* (a scrumptious sweet cheese dessert that looks like pizza doused in honey); fresh figs or grapes sold straight from the baskets of country women; stuffed grape leaves, baklava, and sesame cookies with perfumed tea; or even a shepherd's liver-and-spleen sandwich!

o **Riding Public Transportation:** A busy, efficient network of inter- and intracity buses, shared taxis, and trains takes you everywhere (except during the Sabbath), and drivers and conductors are required to know English. This is a great way to travel, mix with Israelis, and get a feel for the fascinating and diverse populace.

o **Ask Questions Everywhere:** Israelis and Palestinians live with passion. They have lots to say, and most speak at least some English. Ask polite questions. Don't impose your own views—just listen to the answers you get. You'll hear a mosaic of feelings that reflect Israel's ancient traditions and modern complexities.

# ISRAEL'S best RESTAURANTS

o **Little Jerusalem at Ticho House** (Jerusalem): This restaurant is set in a 19th-century gardened mansion that was home to a legendary Jerusalem family. The food is fabulous! See p. 51.

o **Machneyuda** (Jerusalem): At the edge of the Market District, this favorite offers the country's most inventive (and luxurious) menu, lively spirit, and a joy-filled open kitchen where you can watch three master chefs at work. See p. 57.

o **Jerusalem's Machane Yehuda Market:** This enormous market for produce, spices, and exotic ingredients is dotted with tiny no-name, genuine eateries and a sprinkling of new boutique food shops and gourmet restaurants. Sip fresh almond milk, munch sweet grapes or a bag of fresh-from-the-oven *ruggele* pastry, and let the aromas, sights, and mountains of foods overwhelm you. See p. 109.

o **Catit** (Tel Aviv): There's no view here, but chef Meir Adoni has created a menu filled with the richest, most lavishly romantic dishes ever seen in Israel. The food is dreamlike, while the setting is quiet and charming. See p. 174.

o **Margaret Tayar's** (Jaffa): A breezy garden terrace by the sea, at the foot of the Casbah of Old Jaffa, is the location for long and talkative Mediterranean-style evening meals, where Jaffa's most legendary cook brings you creations and tidbits from her tiny kitchen. See p. 181.

o **Cordelia** (Jaffa): Located in a Crusader-era Jaffa building lit by hundreds of candles, Cordelia is food as theater and like nothing else in Israel. Chef Nir Zook's inventive menu is designed to surprise, amaze, shock, and please. See p. 180.

o **Decks** (Tiberias): With a setting that floats on the surface of the Sea of Galilee like a dream, Decks offers luxurious meats and fish expertly grilled over olive- and citrus-wood fires. As an extra, go on a complimentary postdinner disco cruise. Decks is kosher and a great choice for a memorable evening at moderate-to-expensive prices. See p. 140.

o **Helena** (Caesarea): With vistas of the sea, waves lapping at its terrace, and a great young chef designing its menu, this restaurant, set amid the ruins of Caesarea, may be the most romantic spot in Israel for a gourmet meal, especially when the sun sets over the Mediterranean. See p. 202.

# ISRAEL'S best HOTELS

o **David Citadel Hotel** (Jerusalem): Rival to the luxurious King David, this hotel is architecturally engaging and lively and offers a state-of-the-art spa along with excellent food services, including a great kosher sushi bar. Almost all the light, modern guestrooms offer Old City views. See p. 38.

o **Saint Mark's Lutheran Guest House** (Jerusalem): Simple, beautiful, affordable, and atmospheric, with tranquil gardens overlooking the main Arab bazaar, this is the best place to stay in the Old City. See p. 34.

o **American Colony Hotel** (Jerusalem): This atmospheric, gardened enclave was once a 19th-century pasha's villa. As an international meeting place between East and West Jerusalem, it attracts journalists, writers, and archaeologists and may be the most romantic spot in the Middle East (outside Rick's Café in the film "Casablanca"). The hotel's Saturday afternoon lunch buffet is famous. See p. 43.

o **Mount Zion Hotel** (Jerusalem): This lesser-known four-star standout features lovely gardens, interesting architecture, a large swimming pool, and the most dramatic vistas of the Old City, Hinnom Valley, and the Mount of Olives of any Jerusalem hotel. The Tower rooms and suites are very special. See p. 41.

o **Harmony Hotel** (Jerusalem): Located on a picturesque pedestrian street in the heart of West Jerusalem, the Harmony is a moderately priced boutique hotel that offers fresh style, attentive service, and pleasant extras, such as a free late-afternoon happy hour with snacks. See p. 35.

o **Jerusalem Inn Hotel** (Jerusalem): Just a short walk from the Old City and 1½ blocks from Zion Square, the bustling Ben-Yehuda, and Yoel Salomon malls, this small hotel offers near-budget rates and tidy, no-frills doubles with a touch of style. See p. 38.

o **Abraham Hostel** (Jerusalem): A great new concept in hostels, the Abraham offers guests a lively spirit of camaraderie and lots of tours, ideas, and advice on how to really experience Jerusalem and Israel. See p. 35.

o **Tel Aviv Sheraton Hotel & Towers** (Tel Aviv): The most fun of Tel Aviv's luxury hotels—right on the beach, but steps away from the city's restaurant and gallery district—feels like an urban resort. Food services are probably the best of any hotel in the country, topped off by the inventive (and kosher) Olive Leaf (p. 171). Direct Mediterranean views from many of the guestrooms, complete with dazzling sunsets, are a plus, as are the calm, well-run club-level lounges. See p. 163.

o **Efendi** (Akko): A romantic combination of luxury and authenticity, this beautifully restored villa/boutique hotel has helped turn exotic but undervisited Akko into an overnight destination. See p. 216.

o **Vered HaGalil Guest Farm** (Galilee): This country retreat, set among gorgeous gardens and vistas, offers rustic family bungalows, an attentive staff, and a great base for exploring the Galilee. It also offers beautiful horses and the best riding programs in Israel, and it lies within walking distance of the ruins of Korazim, a Roman-era Jewish village complete with an ancient synagogue. See p. 139.

# SUGGESTED ITINERARIES

Without a doubt, Jerusalem is the most fascinating place in Israel, so if you have a very limited amount of time, plan to spend much of it there. Distances are not great in Israel, and it is possible to get a quick taste of the desert, the Mediterranean coast, and even the Sea of Galilee on organized day trips from Jerusalem. But if you want to visit Eilat or get a real feel for the Galilee, then you're going to have to get on the road and move around the country. To help you make the most of your time, this chapter offers two itineraries. The first is for the time-dependent traveler who can spend only a week or two in Israel. The second is specifically designed for families. The chapter also includes a summary of each region in the country for those who prefer to plan their own itineraries.

## ISRAEL IN 2 WEEKS

This itinerary allows time to enjoy the beauty and variety of Israel's landscapes. You'll swim in four seas and have a solid block of time in which to explore Jerusalem, the jewel in the crown.

### Day 1: Tel Aviv & Jaffa

Head from Ben-Gurion Airport to a hotel close to the sea. Lots of sunlight will help get you into the rhythm of Israeli time. In the cool of the evening, explore the **Old City of Jaffa** with its medieval streets, galleries, and eateries overlooking the sea.

### Day 2: Tel Aviv

Spend at least a few hours at Tel Aviv's unique **Diaspora Museum** (p. 183). Swim as the sun plummets into the Mediterranean and then head to the Tel Aviv Port, recently recycled into a stylish seaside boardwalk, for an evening of people-watching, dining, shopping, dancing, and drinking.

### Day 3: Haifa

Head to Haifa next, but use it as a base for excursions. Consider spending the day touring the countryside, including the walled Arabic port city of **Akko**, famous for ancient bazaars and mosques. Near Akko, **Kibbutz Lohammei HaGetaot**, founded by survivors of the Holocaust, combines past tragedy with hope for the future: It contains an important **Holocaust Museum**, set amid the orchards and fields where the descendants of those few who survived have made their lives.

## Day 4: Freewheeling Through the Galilee

Move inland across the northern Galilee. Base yourself in the mystic, mountain-top city of **Safed** or at a kibbutz guesthouse. Visit the ancient ruined synagogue at **Bar'am** (the best preserved in Israel). Dine at a rustic spot, such as **Dag Al HaDan,** a trout-farm restaurant set amid streams, where the fish on your plate was alive and swimming while you were parking your car.

## Day 5: The Sea of Galilee

Circle the shoreline of this mysterious and lovely lake with its New Testament sites at Tabgha, Capernaum, Kursi, and the Mount of Beatitudes, where the Sermon on the Mount was given. The eastern shore south of Ein Gev has quiet, eucalyptus-shaded beaches.

## Day 6: More Galilee

While you're based at the Sea of Galilee, make your way south to Nazareth, famous for the **Church of the Annunciation** and **Nazareth Biblical Village,** with its replicas of buildings from the time of Jesus. Next day, check out the ruins of Zippori, a Hellenistic-era metropolis close to the then-tiny Nazareth of Jesus's childhood.

## Day 7: Galilee to the Dead Sea

Travel south through the Jordan Valley to visit the vast archaeological park of Roman-era **Bet She'an** or the Crusader castle ruins at **Belvoir.** Or make a short stop at the famous zodiac mosaic floor of the 5th-century **Bet Alpha Synagogue** at **Kibbutz Heftziba.**

## Day 8: The Dead Sea, Masada & Ein Gedi

Explore the legendary Herodian fortress of **Masada,** where the last Jewish resisters against Rome chose suicide over surrender; try to sink in the amazing Dead Sea. Indulge in the famous therapeutic mud, mineral, and massage treatments at one of the many Dead Sea spa/hotels or at the Kibbutz Ein Gedi Spa. Or hike the Ein Gedi Reserve, a canyon oasis where David hid from King Saul.

## Day 9: Eilat

**Snorkel** Eilat's coral reef with its exotic Indian Ocean fish or view the fish at the aquarium or from a glass-bottom boat. Enjoy Eilat's busy restaurant scene and nightlife. For kids, there are camel rides and the **Dolphin Reef** (p. 220), where you can watch wild dolphins leap in the distance.

## Day 10: Drive to Jerusalem

En route to Jerusalem (4 hr.), stop at **Timna Park**'s desert landscapes or look around **Kibbutz Lotan**'s inventive desert buildings and organic farm—you may want to overnight here to get the feel of a genuine, creative kibbutz. In Jerusalem, drop bags at your hotel, return the rental car, and take an evening walk to the **Jewish Quarter** of the Old City and the **Western Wall.**

## Day 11: The Old City

Get up early and go into the **Old City** to see the **Temple Mount.** The Temple Mount, with the magnificent **Dome of the Rock** and **Al Aqsa Mosque,** is open Sunday to Thursday 9 to 11am and sometimes in the early afternoon (hours vary; it may be open at 8am). It's a highlight of any journey to Jerusalem and should not be missed. Exit the Old City via the Damascus Gate and take a round-trip taxi to the **Mount of Olives,** which is best visited in the morning, when the sun will be behind you as you look (and photograph) west to the panorama of the Old and New cities. Afterward, explore the Old City bazaars; the **Crusader Church of St. Anne,** with its exquisite acoustics; and the **Holy Sepulcher Church.**

## Day 12: The New City

Go on **Egged Bus no. 99**'s Jerusalem Highlights tour, which takes you all over the city. Visit the **Israel Museum** or **Yad VaShem Holocaust Memorial & Museum** (or both).

## Day 13: More of New Jerusalem

Choose from the **Knesset,** with its Chagall panels; **Hadassah Hospital Ein Kerem,** with its world-famous Chagall stained-glass windows; and a host of small museum gems (see chapter 5). Take an excursion to bucolic **Ein Kerem** (p. 98), village of John the Baptist, or to **Mini Israel,** 45 minutes from Jerusalem, where you can see miniatures of almost every place you've visited (at twilight, the buildings' interior lights go on). Other choices for the late afternoon are a visit to West Jerusalem's **Machane Yehuda** produce market—colorful and filled with great places for falafel, mixed grill, hummus, and other treats. Walk over to **Mea Shearim** via Ethiopia Street and explore this 19th-century world of East European Jewry.

## Day 14: Your Favorites in Jerusalem

Browse the Old City—it's endlessly fascinating—or if you haven't done so, visit (or revisit) Yad VaShem or the Israel Museum. Choose a place with a view or special menu for your farewell dinner, and then finish your shopping before heading off to the airport.

# 8 DAYS IN NORTHERN ISRAEL WITH YOUNG KIDS

Israel is a kid-friendly country, and exploring it through a child's eyes will add new levels of meaning to your journey. The country is a tale of two halves. Southern Israel is filled with a plethora of attractions and sites geared to kids, from camel-trekking in the **Ramon Crater** to riding in glass-bottom boats above the coral reefs of Eilat to floating in **the Dead Sea.** Even archaeological sites, such as Masada, are filled with adventure and drama for young ones. Touring the northern part of Israel with a child, however, requires more careful planning. Only the most pious child will enjoy darkened holy places, the rubble of archaeological sites, and being hounded by shopkeepers in the Jerusalem bazaars trying to sell child-size crowns of thorns. So this itinerary is designed to help you navigate the northern spots without taxing you or your child's patience.

### Jerusalem Sightseeing

Tailor the Jerusalem suggestions in this tour to the days when sites are open. The Temple Mount is closed to visitors Friday and Saturday; much of West Jerusalem shuts for Shabbat. There are wonderful concerts, performances, and lectures (many in English); check the Friday editions of "The Jerusalem Post" or "Haaretz" for listings.

## Days 1 & 2: Jerusalem's Old City

Spend your morning in the Old City, exploring the bazaar and Jewish, Christian, and Islamic holy sites. Be sure to visit the Crusader-era **Church of Saint Anne** (p. 76), where groups and individuals of all religions are welcome to try out the exquisite acoustics with religious songs of any tradition. Check the Via Dolorosa between the fourth and fifth Stations of the Cross for shops selling simple Kanafeh (an ancient kind of sweet cheese pizza) at **Jaffar and Sons Pastry Cafe** (p. 49) on the Suq Khan es-Zeit Bazaar is always a big hit.

## Day 3: Jerusalem's New City

Visit the **Israel Museum** (p. 91). Children will especially enjoy the Children's Museum; the wall of Chanukah menorahs from all over the world in the Judaica Wing; and the Billy Rose Sculpture Garden filled with works by Picasso, Rodin, and others. For older kids, the **Bible Lands Museum** (p. 90), next to the Israel Museum, contains awesome, interactive computer explanations of scarabs and ancient inscriptions and brings ancient artifacts to life. Move on to the excellent **Tisch Family Zoological Gardens** (p. 105).

## Day 4: To the Galilee

Drive north through Jordan Valley. Stop to swim at Sachne, which has a water park for kids; check out Belvoir Crusader castle and **Hammat Gader** hot springs (p. 146), with its alligator farm, vast ruins of ancient baths, and a good Thai restaurant. Take a swim in the lake before dining at Ein Gev on incredibly fresh Saint Peter's fish.

### Kids' Activities

No matter where you travel with your kids, always read the Friday "Haaretz/ Herald Tribune" and "The Jerusalem Post" and check in with tourist information offices. Especially in summer, there's usually an array of street performers at night on Jerusalem's Ben-Yehuda Mall or Tel Aviv's beach promenade, puppet shows, and special museum exhibits and activities aimed at kids.

## Day 5: The Galilee

Swim in the lake at Ein Gev's beautiful beach, explore the nearby ruined Roman-era Jewish village of **Korazim** (p. 145), and then ride the quiet Galilee countryside on Vered HaGalil's beautiful horses. End the day on an evening party boat on the Sea of Galilee.

## Day 6: To Tel Aviv via Nazareth & Caesarea

Explore **Nazareth Village** (p. 127) for its replicas of biblical-era houses and synagogues and then head off to explore the vast seaside **Roman and Crusader ruins at Caesarea** (p. 199), which includes a great multimedia presentation. Check into a beachfront hotel in Tel Aviv before dining at **Margaret Tayar's** (p. 181) in Jaffa, which has acclaimed food and is *very* informal, so kids can prowl around between courses. Take an evening stroll through romantic Old Jaffa.

## Day 7: Tel Aviv

See the **Eretz Israel Museum**'s (p. 183) exhibitions of living crafts, planetarium, and ancient glass; there's a great museum shop for kids and adults. For older kids, move on to the **Diaspora Museum** (p. 183); for younger kids, try the wonderful drive-through **Safari Park** (p. 185), where children find the thriving giraffe herd fascinating. Take a late-afternoon Mediterranean swim.

# MORE kid-friendly picks IN ISRAEL

**Dan Caesarea** (Caesarea; p. 200)   Set amid vast, lush gardens, with an enormous pool and a kid size basketball court, this is a fun place to relax for a day or so while taking in the region. The nearby ancient ruins of Caesarea (p. 199) come alive with a modern, multimedia presentation.

**Dan Carmel Hotel** (Haifa; p. 209)   The energetic children's summer staff and evening entertainment captivate kids, and the swimming pool is deliciously warm by August. The Dan Hotels' children's clubs are excellent throughout the country.

**Kibbutz Shefayim Guest House** (north of Tel Aviv)   This place has a mobbed kids' water park and a swimming pool with artificial waves and a sandy bottom. Kids also like walking along the wild cliff-side paths overlooking the Mediterranean as they watch the sun set.

**Taybet Zaman Hotel and Resort** (Petra, Jordan)   The entire Petra experience is exciting for kids. The unique Taybet Zaman hotel, created from a traditional Bedouin village, is charming and itself an interesting place to explore.

## Day 8: Back to Jerusalem

Stop at **Mini Israel** (p. 116), located between Tel Aviv and Jerusalem, where kids can explore miniatures of virtually every landmark they have visited in Israel. Stop off in Jerusalem for last-minute shopping and a good-bye dinner in West Jerusalem. Head off to Ben-Gurion Airport for a late-night flight home or spend 1 more night in Jerusalem and fly home the next morning.

## The Regions in Brief

It doesn't take much time to get from one region of Israel to another (at some points, it's only 16km/10 miles wide), but you'll find the country is enormously varied. A quick review of the landscape will help you to decide where to spend your time.

**Jerusalem**   The jewel in the crown. The city is many worlds: modern and timeless; Jewish and Arab; religious and nonreligious. The walled, labyrinthine Old City has been named a World Heritage Site; in addition to being a perfectly preserved town with more than 4,000 years of history, it contains the great holy places of Judaism, Christianity, and Islam—the Temple Mount with the Dome of the Rock and the Al Aqsa Mosque, the Western Wall, and the Church of the Holy Sepulcher. Highlights of the New City include the remarkable Israel Museum, which houses the Dead Sea Scrolls, and Yad VaShem, the haunting Holocaust Memorial and Museum.

**The Dead Sea**   Easy to visit for a day by using Jerusalem as your base, the Dead Sea, the lowest point on the earth, is also a good place to visit for a few days as part of a jaunt into the Negev Desert. The almost impregnable Herodian Fortress of **Masada,** the most dramatic ancient site in the country, is perched on a plateau above the Dead Sea. It was here that the last Jewish resisters against Rome committed suicide rather than surrender. The beautiful canyon oasis of **Ein Gedi** is another attraction, as is the unique experience of trying to sink in the mineral-heavy Dead Sea. The southern Israeli shore of the sea is now lined with world-famous spas and hotels offering an array of therapeutic and beauty-treatment packages.

**The Negev**   The southern part of Israel (nearly two-thirds of the country) is desert and semidesert; it contains beautiful **nature**

**reserves** and is great for hiking and nature tours. This part of the country, least visited by tourists, is perhaps the most mysterious. Long famous for its coral reef and laid-back snorkeling and diving opportunities, **Eilat,** at the southern tip of the Negev, is a world unto itself—a mirage rising out of the sand, with dozens of new high-rise megahotels and fancy restaurants grouped on the city's few miles of Red Sea shoreline. The **Sinai Coast of Egypt,** a bit farther south and easily accessible from Eilat, offers reefs that are more spectacular, a landscape that is more dramatic and less developed, and hotels that are considerably less expensive.

**Tel Aviv**   Full of energy and verve (many wonder how it can be in the same country as Jerusalem), Tel Aviv has great restaurants, good beaches, and three inventive museums: the Diaspora Museum, the Eretz Israel Museum, and the Tel Aviv Museum of Art. From April to October, Tel Aviv is a good first stop in Israel—you can spend a day or two at the beach to recover from jet lag before plunging into the rest of the country.

**The Mediterranean Coast**   If you want to relax on the beach, get to know this area, also known as the Golden Coast. The ruined Roman- and Crusader-era city of **Caesarea** is the most dramatic archaeological site along the coast; farther north, the Old City of **Akko,** with its bazaars, cafes, and minarets beside the Mediterranean, is the most exotic site. **Kibbutzim** and moshav holiday villages, from Nahsholim, south of Haifa, right up to the northernmost coast, are good spots for a pleasant beach break from touring.

**Haifa**   Israel's third major city offers a spirit and face quite different from Jerusalem or Tel Aviv. It is a business and industrial city, but it's also beautifully laid out on a stepped mountain overlooking the harbor. It's really dazzling from the heights of Mount Carmel. The magnificent Baha'i Center is also

memorable, and Haifa makes a good urban base for exploring the northwestern part of the country.

**The Galilee**   Israel's northern region is filled with a lovely countryside of forested mountains and olive groves dotted with Israeli-Arab cities and towns, kibbutzim, and the remains of ancient ruined cities, synagogues, and churches. At the heart of the Galilee is the freshwater **Sea of Galilee,** a lyrically beautiful body of water made all the more special by its association with both New and Old Testament sites. The Galilee offers great hiking and nature trails, but it's also a good place to rent a car for a few days and freewheel.

**The West Bank/Palestinian Authority Areas**   This was a countryside of classic biblical landscapes and ancient sites, but 20 years of political turmoil and war have made the West Bank difficult to visit at the best of times and outright dangerous at the worst of times. As of press time, the governments of most Western countries advise against visiting this area until the political situation improves, so it's best to consider this area off limits when planning your itinerary, although visits with organized Christian tour groups to Bethlehem are popular when the political situation allows.

**Petra, Jordan**   Israel's neighbor offers dramatic, totally unspoiled landscapes and magnificent sites from ancient times, such as the legendary rock-hewn city of **Petra** in the southern part of the country. Luxury and moderate hotels here are a bargain compared to those in Israel. The less-developed Jordanian side of the Dead Sea is dotted with hot springs and now contains a number of relaxing spas and hotels that offer a variety of unique therapeutic and beauty treatments. **Wadi Rum,** south of Petra, offers opportunities for camping and hiking with Bedouin guides in one of the most dramatic desertscapes in the world.

# ISRAEL IN CONTEXT

**3**

srael lies on the tectonic plates where the continents of Africa and Asia, the East and the West, and the Heavenly and the Earthly all collide. No other place is quite like it.

Not only is Israel the birthplace of religions and ideas that lie at the heart of Western Civilization, but this tiny land encompasses incredible diversity on every level—deserts and forested mountains, awesome holy sites and hedonistic beaches, ancient walled cities and coral reefs in crystal-clear waters, medieval bazaars and sleek high-tech society. To millions of Jews, Christians, and Muslims, Israel is the Holy Land where Solomon reigned in all his glory, where Jesus taught and performed miracles, and where Muhammad visited during a miraculous night journey from Mecca. Yet amid this swirl of charisma, history, legends, and spiritual pull, Israel is also a modern, lively, innovative country that's fun and fascinating for visitors.

## Israel Today

In 2013, Israel celebrated its 65th anniversary as an independent country, but its identity and future are still in the process of being shaped. The country today has fulfilled its mission of becoming a haven where Jews from all over the world can live free from persecution. With its energetic spirit, high-tech and cultural achievements, innovative style, and endless absorption of new immigrants, Israel is clearly thriving. But Israel's security remains at risk, and with constant waves of immigration, the long-term identity of Israel is still a work in progress.

The population of Israel within its 1967 borders now stands at about 7,800,000: Approximately 5,700,000 Israeli citizens are Jewish; 1,850,000 are Arab Christians, Muslims, and Druze; and at least 300,000 are of other backgrounds or are international.

**Israel's Jewish population** comes from all over the world. **Israel's Arab citizens** form about 22 percent of the county's population. They are the descendants of Palestinian Muslims and Christians who remained in the newly formed State of Israel after the 1948 partition of British Mandate Palestine and Israel's War of Independence. These groups automatically became citizens of Israel when the state was created and now number close to two million. Israel's Arab population is centered in the Galilee, in mainly Arab cities, such as Nazareth, and in mixed Jewish/Arab cities, such as Haifa, Akko, and Jaffa. The **Druze** people and the once-nomadic **Bedouin** peoples of the Negev and the Galilee are also part of the Israeli-Arab tapestry. Israel's Arab citizens are not required to complete military service; however, most Israeli Bedouins and Druze serve voluntarily, and a large number have received citations for valor.

Additionally, in East Jerusalem, which Israel captured and annexed in 1967 following the Six-Day War, live approximately 300,000 **East Jerusalem Palestinians** who hold permanent Israeli/Jerusalem resident IDs and reside in the homes and neighborhoods where they lived before 1967. Most East Jerusalem Palestinians are not actual Israeli citizens, both by their own choice and the choice of the Israeli government. East Jerusalem Palestinians, unlike the Palestinians of the West Bank and Gaza, have complete freedom to travel, work, and study inside Israel. Also, along with thousands of foreign workers from Asia, large numbers of refugees from wars in Sudan, Somalia, and elsewhere in Africa have made their way into Israel, adding to the mix of peoples, foods, and cultures you'll encounter as you travel through the country.

# LOOKING BACK: ISRAEL'S HISTORY

Recorded Jewish history dates from the time of Abraham, between 2000 and 1800 B.C. Many elements of the patriarchal chronicles have been confirmed as accurate by recent archaeological discoveries, but other elements of this enormously distant past may never be historically documented. Modern scientific methods reveal that human beings have lived in the Holy Land since the Old Stone Age, some 100,000 years ago. But a history so deep and full of universal significance is almost impossible to grasp in its entirety. Here is an outline of the major periods and events up to the present.

**A BRIEF LOOK AT THE PAST**   In Israel's museums and at Israel's archaeological sites, you will encounter the following terms used to define the many time periods in Israel's long history.

**Late Stone Age** (7500–4000 B.C.): First villages appear, including Jericho; animal husbandry, irrigation, and pottery begin.

**Chalcolithic (Copper) Age** (4000–3200 B.C.): Copper is used in tools; towns grow; designs appear on pottery; a culture develops at Beersheba.

**Early Bronze (Canaanite) Age** (3200–2200 B.C.): Towns are fortified; temples and palaces are built.

**Middle Bronze (Canaanite) Age** (2200–1550 B.C.): The Age of the Patriarchs; Abraham travels; trade develops; the Hyksos invade Canaan and Egypt.

**Late Bronze (Canaanite) Age** (1550–1200 B.C.): Hebrews are enslaved in Egypt; the alphabet develops; the Exodus from Egypt occurs; the Ten Commandments are delivered on Mount Sinai; Hebrew tribes conquer the Promised Land.

**Early Iron Age** (1200–1020 B.C.): Period of the Judges; Philistine invasion.

**Middle Iron Age** (1020–842 B.C.): The united kingdom of Israel and Judah under King David (1000 B.C.) with Jerusalem as capital; between 960 and 950, King Solomon builds the First Temple; it is a golden age of Israelite culture and power.

**Late Iron Age** (842–587 B.C.): Period of the later kings and prophets; the Kingdom of Israel is destroyed in 701 B.C. The Kingdom of Judah is destroyed in 587 B.C. by Babylonians; the First Temple in Jerusalem is destroyed.

**Babylonian & Persian Periods** (587–332 B.C.): Jewish captivity in Babylon, followed by Persian permission to return to Jerusalem; the Second Temple is built in 515 B.C.; times of Ezra and Nehemiah; public reading of the Torah begins.

**Hellenistic & Maccabean Periods** (332–37 B.C.): Conquest by Alexander the Great, followed by Hellenistic dynasties; the Maccabean revolt and liberation of Judea.

**Roman Period** (37 B.C.–A.D. 324): Herodian dynasty; birth of Jesus, his ministry, and crucifixion; Jewish revolt against Rome; the Second Temple and Jerusalem are destroyed (A.D. 70); fall of Masada (A.D. 73); Bar Kochba revolt against Rome (A.D. 132–35).

**Byzantine Period** (A.D. 324–640): Galilee Jews revolt against Byzantine domination; Jerusalem Talmud is completed; Persian invasion and sack of Jerusalem (A.D. 614); birth and rise of Islam in the Middle East.

**Arab Period** (A.D. 640–1096): Jerusalem is conquered by Islamic armies (A.D. 638); Arab Empire capital is first at Damascus, later Baghdad; joint Christian-Muslim protectorate of holy places; Christian pilgrimage rights are curtailed.

**The Crusades** (1096–1291): First Crusade (1096–99); Crusader conquest of Jerusalem (1099); Crusader Kingdom established under Godfrey of Bouillon; Saladin recaptures Jerusalem for Islam (1187); the end of the Fourth Crusade (1202–04) sees the destruction of Crusader kingdom.

**Mamluk & Ottoman Turkish Period** (1291–1917): Mongols and Seljuks replace Arabs and Byzantines as rulers of the Holy Land; Ottomans conquer Palestine in 1517; Suleiman the Magnificent rebuilds Jerusalem's walls; thousands of Jews, expelled from Spain and Italy, find refuge in Ottoman Empire; Safed, in the Galilee, becomes a center for Jewish scholarship; Napoleon's campaign in Egypt and Palestine (1799); movement to re-create a Jewish homeland is led by Theodor Herzl (1860–1904), who publishes "The Jewish State"; first Zionist Congress is held in Basel (1897).

**THE BRITISH MANDATE**   The Balfour Declaration in 1917 announced British support for the creation of a "national home" for the Jewish people in Palestine. In 1920, after Great Britain had captured the region of Palestine from the Ottoman Empire at the end of World War I, the League of Nations granted the British a "mandate" to govern Palestine. In 1922, Great Britain separated Trans-Jordan (present-day Jordan) from British Mandate Palestine and established a separate Arab country.

Within Palestine, huge progress was made during the first 20 years of British administration. Hospitals and schools were established in both Jewish and Arab areas, and in Jewish areas, dazzlingly modern, planned communities, both urban and agricultural, were built; much desolate land was reclaimed for agricultural use. The Arab population resented British policies of the early 1920s, which encouraged Jewish immigration; almost immediately after the British Mandate took effect, political disorder erupted. The era of the British Mandate saw three-way disputes between British, Jewish, and Arab factions and Arab attacks on Jewish communities, especially in 1921 and 1929. Jewish immigration increased during the early Hitler years.

An Arab insurrection from 1936 to 1939 led the British in 1939 to severely limit Jewish immigration before cutting it off entirely. Thus, during World War II, Jews seeking to escape the Holocaust in Europe were denied refuge. After the outbreak of World War II, political tensions within Palestine diminished somewhat, and the area became a bustling Allied military base. However, the coming conflict was inevitable. In 1946, Arab and Jewish terrorism against the British began, the King David Hotel was blown up by a Jewish underground group at odds with David Ben-Gurion's more mainstream Zionist organization, and the cycle of violence reached new heights.

In November 1947, with Britain abstaining, the UN General Assembly voted to partition Palestine into two states—one Arab and one Jewish. On May 14, 1948, with the Jewish parts of Jerusalem under Arab siege, fighting widespread across Palestine, and 400,000 Arab Palestinian civilians fleeing their homes, the British Mandate ended in shambles, and the State of Israel was proclaimed. Arab armies from surrounding states invaded the fledgling nation but were pushed back, and the 1949 cease-fire lines left Israel in control of somewhat more territory than the UN partition had allotted. Only a few Jewish areas fell to Arab armies. The Palestinian State proposed for those areas that remained under Arab control did not come into being. The West Bank and East Jerusalem (including the Old City) were annexed by Jordan, although most of the international community did not recognize this act. Jordan granted citizenship to all Palestinians under its control, the only Arab nation to do so. Egypt occupied but did not annex the Gaza Strip. Its inhabitants were declared stateless.

**THE MAKING OF AN INDEPENDENT STATE**    In the beginning of the State of Israel's history, there was enormous exhilaration but also a grim determination. The double weight of the horrors of the Holocaust and the enormous casualties suffered in the War of Independence from 1948 to 1949 drove the country to protect every sand dune, to force life out of the desert, and to create a haven for any Jews who might again find themselves in danger. Life was austere. For years, food, clothing, razor blades, and paint were severely rationed, as the country struggled to survive as well as to feed and shelter the thousands of new immigrants who arrived each month. In less than a decade, the nation's population quadrupled as hundreds of thousands of Holocaust survivors and Jewish refugees from the Middle East arrived. Hundreds of thousands more were added in the 1960s as the Jewish communities of North Africa fled.

Slowly, with enormous effort, conditions grew more stable. Basic housing was built, uprooted people began to develop new identities, and although life was still spartan (the founding fathers refused to allow television stations to be established, claiming that the nation had more important things to attend to), the country began to flourish. Modern farming and irrigation, along with dedication, made the desert bloom, but even more important were Israel's developing industries (today, huge areas of hard-won agricultural land are being plowed for new cities and industrial zones).

**WARS & THE SEARCH FOR PEACE**    During the Suez War of November 1956, Great Britain and France invaded Egypt to secure the Suez Canal, which Egypt had nationalized, and Israel (in coordination with the British and French recapture of Suez) conquered Egypt's Sinai Peninsula and the Gaza Strip, hoping to put an end to 9 years of Egyptian attacks on southern Israel. In exchange for the stationing of a UN peace-keeping force on the Egyptian side of the Israeli-Sinai border, and with promises of freedom to send its shipping through the Red Sea to Eilat, Israel withdrew entirely from the Sinai Peninsula and Gaza in early 1957. Ten years of relative peace followed, punctuated by periodic sniper attacks on the Galilee from Syrian batteries on the Golan Heights and Israeli retaliations.

In May 1967, the UN peacekeeping force that had maintained security on the Israeli-Egyptian border for 10 years was unilaterally ordered out by Egypt's president, Gamal Abdel Nasser, in violation of international guarantees. At the same time, Nasser blockaded the port of Eilat on the Red Sea, economically strangling Israel, while Syria stood ready to attack the Galilee from the Golan Heights. For Israelis, only too aware that the nation was less than 16km (10 miles) wide and that the Jordanian army in East Jerusalem was aimed point-blank at Jewish West Jerusalem, the agony of these weeks, while the Israeli government tried to rally international support, was unbearable. The pace of propaganda against Israel throughout the Arabic world reached new pitches of frenzy, and Arab armies in Egypt and Syria mobilized to deliver what was claimed would be a crushing blow. The Israelis dug mass graves in the parks of Tel Aviv in preparation for the civilian casualties of an Arab invasion.

In the early morning of June 5, 1967, Israel made a preemptive strike against the air forces of Egypt and Syria. At noon, Jordan, despite diplomatic pleas that it stay out of the conflict, began to shell West Jerusalem. In the **Six-Day War** that followed, Israel swept to an unimaginable victory, conquering the Sinai Peninsula, the Gaza Strip, the Golan Heights, East Jerusalem, and the entire West Bank. The Arab world was left in a state of shock. Suddenly Israel was no longer a struggling state hanging on tenaciously to its hard-won independence. Land areas under its control more than tripled. Israel's patriarch, David Ben-Gurion, by then in retirement, warned that all the conquered areas must be relinquished immediately, but in the euphoria of the day, his words made little sense to most Israelis. Many believed that peace would finally develop.

As the years passed, however, the Arab world continued to refuse to recognize Israel diplomatically, and the plight of the Palestinian refugees scattered throughout the Middle East continued to be ignored by the world at large. In the absence of a peace agreement that would trade most land captured in 1967 for peace, the occupation of the West Bank and the Gaza Strip began to seem less temporary. The small political movement for Jewish settlement of the Occupied Territories began to grow, although at first the Israeli government officially opposed it. Resentment grew among the Palestinians under occupation.

The country experienced a sharp change in fortune in October 1973. The **Yom Kippur War,** an unexpected simultaneous attack against Israel launched by Egypt and Syria, had a sobering effect on the entire nation. In the first days of the attack, the Golan Heights were almost retaken by Syria, and Egyptian forces, crossing the Suez Canal, overwhelmed Israeli troops in Sinai. More than 2,500 young Israelis were killed in 1 month, losses proportionately higher than the casualties the United States sustained during the entire Vietnam War. Egyptian and Syrian casualties were enormous. Although the war ended with Israeli forces closer than ever before to Cairo and Damascus, the high cost in lives shook the nation's confidence and tarnished the images of its leaders. In a backlash, voters turned against the Labor Party, which had led the state since its founding, and elected a government dominated by the right-of-center Likud led by Menachem Begin.

In 1977, Prime Minister Begin quietly set in motion a series of events that resulted in Egypt's President Anwar Sadat making a dramatic visit to Jerusalem. This led to a peace treaty with Egypt in March 1979, ending 30 years of war between the two countries. Accordingly, Israel returned the Sinai to Egypt. With peace established, it remains open to tourists from Israel, although the current turmoil in Egypt makes travel to Sinai uncertain.

The hopes for a regional peace agreement that the Egyptian-Israeli settlement raised were not quickly realized. No additional Arab countries came forward to negotiate. The 1982 invasion of southern Lebanon put further strains on Israel's relations with its neighbors. Deteriorating relations with Palestinians in the West Bank and Gaza marked the 1980s, as more land was appropriated for Jewish settlements. In 1987, the Palestinian population of the West Bank and Gaza began daily commercial strikes and demonstrations. This uprising, the Intifada, continued through the early 1990s.

The 1990s brought a wave of almost a million immigrants from Ethiopia and the dissolving Soviet system and, in the summer of 1990, the Kuwait crisis. Israel was not a participant in the Allied coalition against Iraq in the Gulf War that followed, but

## dining BARGAINS

1. Look for weekday business lunch specials. In many restaurants, they go until 5 or 6pm. Remember—after the witching hour, when lunch turns to dinner, the price for the same dishes can double.

2. In Jerusalem, Tel Aviv, and Eilat, you'll find free tourist magazines and pamphlets loaded with coupons offering 10 percent discounts on many restaurants. Some of these places are quite good.

3. Amazingly, kosher restaurants are not all that easy to find in all parts of Israel. Check out **www.eluna.com**, a website that reviews tons of kosher choices all over the country. It also offers coupons and vouchers for dining spots.

4. Fill up at breakfast. Israeli hotels offer vast morning buffets, and if you're discreet, and your hotel dining room is big and busy, you should have no problem slipping a few treats into your daypack for later in the day.

Saddam Hussein declared that he would "incinerate half of Israel" with missile-borne chemical and bacteriological attacks if the Allied coalition moved against him. The United States asked Israel to refrain from retaliating if it came under attack and pledged that any Iraqi missile threat to Israel would be destroyed by American bombing within the first hours of war. Nevertheless, Israelis found themselves dashing for gas masks and sitting in makeshift sealed rooms, experiencing nightly Scud missile attacks for the entire 6 weeks of the Gulf War. Iraq's missiles turned out to be armed only with explosives instead of the chemical weapons Hussein had threatened, but the ordeal left its mark on Israeli society. Many Israelis came to believe it was worth taking risks to try to achieve peace. Others were more determined than ever to avoid any further concessions. The Oslo peace process began in 1991 and continued after President Bill Clinton arranged a White House peace process ceremony between newly elected Prime Minister Yitzhak Rabin and Palestinian leader Yasser Arafat in 1993.

**THE PEACE PROCESS STALLS**   Negotiating directly with Palestinians and moderate Arab governments, Israel began a planned withdrawal from parts of the West Bank and Gaza in 1994. In the same year, **a peace treaty was signed with the Kingdom of Jordan.** The assassination of Prime Minister Rabin by a Jewish opponent of the peace process in 1995 was a blow for those who hoped for lasting peace.

After the assassination of Prime Minister Rabin, a new, violent Palestinian Intifada erupted from 2000 to 2005. In 2005, Prime Minister Ariel Sharon evacuated all Israeli settlements in Gaza but suffered a massive stroke before he could outline further plans. Since then, the conflict has continued on a course of uncertainty, punctuated by rocket attacks on southern Israeli towns from Gaza and by Israeli retaliation.

# EATING & DRINKING

For the first half of Israel's existence, food was supposed to be simple and healthy. It was virtually anti-Zionist to be into the many ethnic cuisines that flooded the country from the far corners of the earth.

Today, Israel is in love with fine food as well as with good wines. The country is awash with young, imaginative Israeli chefs who are creating inventive haute cuisine menus rooted in ancient local food traditions and immigrant recipes including French,

# ISRAELI street food TIPS

Falafel and *shwarma* tucked into a pita with chopped salad and eaten on the run have become the national fast foods of Israel. To make sure you sample the best the country has to offer, here are a few tips:

- A quality falafel (spiced chickpea fritter) sandwich should contain at least four falafels and your choice of a number of fresh salads and condiment sauces.
- Buy from places with a big turnover and fresh, hot falafels. You should be able to see falafels being fried; if the oil is dirty or not constantly boiling, move on.
- A sandwich made with giant napkin-size Iraqi pita bread costs a half-shekel more and fills you up for most of the day.
- *Shwarma* (spiced turkey or lamb on a spit) should be freshly sliced from the spit. If the proprietor must turn on the flame to heat the spit, move on.
- Many stands offer hummus either as a separate sandwich choice or with falafel. Avoid it after 11am on a hot summer day.
- Falafel sandwiches, especially with lots of essential *techina* sauce, tend to be messy. Grab tons of napkins—*techina* stains are forever.

**3**

Eating & Drinking

ISRAEL IN CONTEXT

Mediterranean, nouvelle, and Asian traditions, often all blended. Tel Aviv is the foodie center, but elsewhere in the country, food standards have improves, too.

Strangely, amid all this elegance, fusion, and attention to quality, it's hard to find a good chicken soup in Israeli restaurants. Very few restaurants serve old-world Eastern European Jewish dishes. Instead, typical Israeli cuisine draws on Arabic traditions, such as the **meze,** a vast array of spiced salads and spreads that opens a lavish Middle Eastern–style feast. It includes the Arabic falafel and moves on to scrumptious *shwarma* (seasoned meat cooked on a spit) and kabobs, served with your choice of salads and sauces, all tucked into a pita sandwich. Palestinian *zataar* (a traditional mix of local spices that includes dried hyssop and salt) flavors food throughout the country. For travelers, big, often very shareable fresh salads are available in cafes everywhere. For kosher travelers, Israel offers a rare chance to sample excellent kosher Indian food as well as an array of kosher Italian, French, Chinese, and sushi dishes.

But a big chunk of the Israeli cuisine experience is just being there. A great lamb chop, a plate of ordinary pasta, a grilled lamb kabob, or even a falafel sandwich becomes a memorable meal if it's served on a starlit dock stretching into the Sea of Galilee or on a rooftop terrace in the heart of Jerusalem's Old City.

## Dining Customs

**THE SABBATH (SHABBAT)** On Friday afternoons and afternoons before holidays, kosher restaurants close around 2pm in preparation for Shabbat (the Jewish Sabbath), which begins at sunset. Most restaurants don't reopen until Saturday evening after dark. Depending on the volume of business, some restaurants may stay open beyond normal closing hours on Saturday night. A number of nonkosher restaurants remain open on Shabbat in the big cities.

Your hotel usually provides Saturday breakfast, but you will need to deal with Friday's dinner and Saturday's lunch. Most larger hotels serve kosher Friday-night meals

18

and Saturday lunches prepared before the Sabbath, but hotel dinners are expensive and bland, and you generally need to reserve these ahead of time, whether you're a guest of the hotel or not. By Saturday evening after the sun sets and Shabbat is over, restaurants will be open again, but in summer, the end of Shabbat comes quite late. If you're kosher and don't want to go to the expense of reserving Shabbat hotel meals, eat a hearty lunch on Friday and buy take-away supplies.

**KOSHER FOOD**     According to the rigorous regulations of kashrut, only peaceful, nonpredatory animals that chew their cud and have cleft hooves and birds that do not eat carrion may be used for food—and then, only if they have been killed instantly and humanely according to methods supervised by religious authorities. Only fish with fins and scales can be eaten, which means no shellfish or dolphins. Pork, too, is forbidden. Kosher restaurants that serve milk will not serve any food containing meat or poultry, although they are permitted to serve fish. This means that cheese lasagna must be meatless. In restaurants serving meat, your coffee will be served with milk substitute and desserts won't contain milk products.

A restaurant may maintain a kosher menu, but if it prepares and cooks food or does business on Shabbat, it will generally not be able to receive a kashrut certificate.

*Note:* Never bring your own food (such as a cookie or a piece of baklava) to a meal at a kosher restaurant, as this may contaminate the kashrut status of the establishment.

In many cases, kosher restaurants may be 5 to 10 percent more expensive than comparable nonkosher restaurants. If kashrut is not a concern, you can save a bit by seeking out nonkosher places. Glatt kosher and mehadrin (especially stringent supervision of kashrut) often mean an even higher price.

# WHEN TO GO

## Climate

Israeli has two seasons: winter (late Oct to mid-Mar), which is cool to cold and when the rains occur, and summer (Apr–Oct), which is warm to hot and virtually rain-free. Winter in Israel starts with showers in October and advances to periodic heavy rainfall from November to March. Swimming is out in the Mediterranean during this time, except during occasional heat waves, although at times you can swim in Eilat and the Dead Sea in the winter. The Israeli winter doesn't normally involve snow, except for on Mount Hermon on the Golan Heights.

During February and the beginning of March, the entire country turns green from the winter rains, and wildflower displays in the Galilee and Golan regions are truly spectacular. By late March, the flowers and the green fade. In the months that follow, the heat gathers intensity, reaching its peak in July and August. By September

Israel also experiences hot, dry desert winds at the beginning and end of the summer, although a *hamsin* can occur anytime from March to November. A *hamsin* (or *sharav*) heat wave means you must cut back on rushing around: Plan to be in air-conditioned museums, in the shadowy depths of a bazaar, or in the water during midday, and make sure you increase your water intake.

In winter, cold rain systems move in from the north. Because they are prevented from continuing south by the constant tropical highs over Africa, these storms can stall over Israel for days until they rain themselves out. Lots of warm socks, layered clothes (including a fleece liner), and a good raincoat and portable umbrella are necessary.

## Israel's Average Temperatures

| | | JAN | FEB | MAR | APR | MAY | JUNE | JULY | AUG | SEPT | OCT | NOV | DEC |
|---|---|---|---|---|---|---|---|---|---|---|---|---|---|
| JERUSALEM | °F | 43–53 | 44–57 | 47–61 | 53–69 | 60–77 | 63–81 | 66–84 | 66–86 | 65–82 | 60–78 | 54–67 | 47–56 |
| | °C | 6–12 | 7–14 | 8–16 | 12–21 | 16–25 | 17–27 | 19–29 | 19–30 | 18–28 | 16–26 | 12–19 | 8–13 |
| TEL AVIV | °F | 49–65 | 48–66 | 51–69 | 54–72 | 63–77 | 67–03 | 70 86 | 69 89 | 59 83 | 54–76 | 54–77 | 49–66 |
| | °C | 9–18 | 9–19 | 11–21 | 12–22 | 17–25 | 19–28 | 21–30 | 21–32 | 15–28 | 12–24 | 12–25 | 9–19 |
| HAIFA | °F | 49–63 | 47–64 | 47–70 | 55–78 | 58–76 | 64–82 | 68–86 | 70–86 | 68–85 | 60–80 | 56–74 | 48–65 |
| | °C | 9–17 | 8–18 | 8–21 | 13–26 | 14–24 | 18–28 | 20–30 | 21–30 | 20–29 | 16–27 | 13–23 | 9–18 |
| TIBERIAS | °F | 48–65 | 49–67 | 51–72 | 56–80 | 62–89 | 68–95 | 73–98 | 75–99 | 71–95 | 65–89 | 59–78 | 53–68 |
| | °C | 9–18 | 9–19 | 11–22 | 13–27 | 17–32 | 20–35 | 23–37 | 24–37 | 22–35 | 18–32 | 15–26 | 12–20 |
| EILAT | °F | 49–70 | 51–73 | 56–79 | 63–87 | 69–95 | 75–99 | 77–103 | 79–104 | 75–98 | 69–92 | 61–83 | 51–74 |
| | °C | 9–21 | 11–23 | 13–26 | 17–31 | 21–35 | 24–37 | 25–39 | 26–40 | 24–37 | 21–33 | 16–28 | 11–23 |

# Israel's Calendar(s)

Israel "officially" operates on two separate systems for determining day, month, and year: the Jewish calendar, dating from some 5,750 years ago, and the Gregorian calendar, used in most countries. Recognized, but "unofficial," are even more calendars, such as the Julian (Julius Caesar) calendar, which runs 13 days behind the Gregorian; and the Muslim era, which counts the years from A.D. 622, when the Prophet Muhammad led the Hegira from Mecca to Medina. These calendars disagree not only about dates but also about whether time is measured by the sun, the moon, or a combination of the two and when the year should start and end. (We know of at least three Christmases in Israel.)

**THE WEEKLY HOLIDAY SCHEDULE**   Israel is a confusing place when it comes to the weekly holiday schedule. Jews stop work at midafternoon on Friday; some Muslims stop at sundown on Thursday (although many shops remain open on Fri); most Christians are off all day on Sunday. In Tel Aviv, no buses run from late Friday afternoon until Saturday after sundown, although small private minibuses cover some of the main routes. In Jerusalem, buses run only in the Arab neighborhoods on Saturday; in Haifa, there's partial bus service on Saturday. In Eilat, there is no public transport on Shabbat. Throughout the country, some shops open just as others are closing for a holiday.

On Saturday, almost all shops throughout the country are closed (except in Israel's Arab communities, including cafes and Arab or Christian establishments in Jerusalem's Old City), as are nearly all transportation stops (only Haifa has limited municipal bus service at this time, and only taxis or small sherut companies operate in or between cities). Gas stations are mostly open on Shabbat, because few are located in religious neighborhoods. Most admission-free museums are ordinarily open for part of Shabbat; entrance tickets, when required, must sometimes be bought from private-duty guards outside the museum entrance. Precise hours for the duration of Shabbat, which vary according to the time of sunset, are listed in the Friday "Jerusalem Post."

There is a growing list of exceptions: In Tel Aviv, many restaurants, cafes, discos, and theaters close on Friday afternoon for a few hours but reopen on Friday night; Haifa has always had a quiet alternative Friday nightlife; and in Jerusalem, a number of cinemas and nonkosher restaurants remain open; recently the pub area around Jerusalem's Russian Compound has begun to boom, and Friday nights are busy.

Most Israelis are not Sabbath-observant and love to travel on their day off, so if you drive on Saturday, you'll find the roads to beaches and parks quite busy. About the only people who will try to stop you are the ultrareligious Jews. Many streets in religious areas are blocked with boulders; most ultra-Orthodox neighborhoods in Jerusalem and Bnei Brak, near Tel Aviv, have official permission to close their streets to traffic. Don't even think of trying to drive in such areas—you can be stoned and your vehicle damaged, and you will have no help from the police.

**HOLIDAYS** If awards were given for having the maximum number of holidays a year, Israel would win. Israeli holidays will affect your visit in several important ways. First, hotels and campsites fill to capacity, and rates rise by as much as 20 percent. Next, transportation and restaurant service may be curtailed or completely suspended, and places of entertainment may be closed. On the other hand, a holiday is a special occasion, and you won't want to miss the events that may take place. To keep your wits amid all these openings and closings read the following information carefully.

# Israel Calendar of Holidays & Events

Here's a general guide to when holidays and festivals occur in Israel. Keep in mind that a Jewish holiday that generally falls in March may some years fall on a late date in February, because Jews follow a lunar-based year. Note also that not all Jewish holidays are subject to Sabbath-like prohibitions and closings. Holidays when things close down are indicated by an asterisk (*). **Note: The celebration of each holiday commences at sundown on the evening before the date listed and ends at sundown of the last day shown.**

For updated information about holidays, special events, and festivals, check with your nearest IGTO office. In North America, call the Israel Tourism Information Center at ℂ **888/77-ISRAEL** (477-235) or visit www.goisrael.com.

## JANUARY/FEBRUARY

**Israeli Arbor Day (Tu b'Shevat):** Thousands of singing and dancing schoolchildren traipse off to plant trees all over the country. Synagogues and some restaurants have special Tu b'Shevat dinners.

## MARCH

**Purim (Feast of Lots):** Recalling how Queen Esther saved her people in Persia (5th c. B.C.), this is an exciting time when folks, especially children, dress up in fancy or zany (sometimes irreligious) costumes, have parties, parade in the streets, give food baskets, spray shaving cream at passersby, and make merry. In Jerusalem and Safed, Purim is celebrated 1 day later than in the rest of the country.

## APRIL

**Passover (Pesach)*:** The commemoration of the ancient Israelites' Exodus from Egypt. Because the Israelites left in haste, before the bread in their ovens could rise, no bread, beer, or other foods containing leavening are obtainable for 7 days (8 days outside Israel). Many restaurants simply shut down for this period. The first night of the holiday is devoted to a Seder, a family meal and ritual recalling the Exodus of the ancient Israelites from Egypt. (**Note:** In the Diaspora, the Seder is held on both the first and second nights of Passover; however, inside Israel, the Seder is held only on the first night.) Many hotels and restaurants have special Seders for tourists. The first and last days of this holiday are Sabbath-like affairs, which means the country more or less closes down. During the half-holiday days of Passover week, many shops, museums, and services are on reduced schedules. As schools are closed, Israelis travel during this week. Reservations at hotels, B&Bs, and kibbutzim are impossible to get unless you book well ahead, and rates are the highest of the year.

**Holocaust Memorial Day (Yom Ha-Shoah)*:** This marks the time of the year in 1945 when the concentration camps in Europe were liberated and the Holocaust came to an end. It also marks the Warsaw

Ghetto Uprising in 1943. All places of entertainment are closed. As the day begins (like all Jewish days, at nightfall), most restaurants are closed, although public transportation continues, and most shops and businesses are open. At 10am on Yom Ha-Shoah, a siren sounds throughout Israel, and a period of silence is observed in memory of the six million Jews who perished. A memorial ceremony is held at Yad VaShem in Jerusalem.

**Memorial Day*:** One week after Yom Ha-Shoah, the nation remembers its war dead. Restaurants and places of public entertainment are closed, but transportation companies operate, and most shops are open. Again, at 11am, a siren sounds, and a period of silence is observed. Throughout the country, memorial services are held.

**Independence Day:** The day after Memorial Day, Israel commemorates the day in 1948 when the British Mandate ended and the State of Israel was proclaimed. It is celebrated with house parties and municipal fireworks.

**Jacob's Ladder Country, Folk, and Blues Festival (usually at Kibbutz Nof Ginosar):** This important event is held in the Galilee for 3 days in mid-May. All types of music from contemporary and classic folk to Celtic are offered. For information, call ✆ **04/696-2231** or visit www.jlfestival.com.

**Lag b'Omer:** Ending 33 days of mourning, this is a happy celebration for the Hassidim, who head to the Meiron tomb of the mystical Rabbi Shimon Bar Yochai in Galilee to sing and dance around bonfires. There are also pilgrimages made to the tombs of other great rabbis. Children around the country sing, dance, and light bonfires.

**Shavuot (Pentecost)*:** A summer harvest celebration and a special favorite of agricultural settlements, this is often marked by plays, entertainment, and children dressed in white and wearing floral crowns. Because it also recalls the receipt of the Ten Commandments, it is observed as a religious holiday. Dairy foods, such as blintzes and cheesecakes, are traditionally prepared. At

synagogues as well as at the Western Wall, the Torah is studied throughout the night.

**Abu Gosh Music Festival:** This is a new festival held in the Arab-Israeli village of Abu Gosh, in the hills west of Jerusalem. Classical and religious music is performed in the village's two churches; there are also street performances and arts and crafts. It's held each year at Shavuot and Succot.

**Israel and Jerusalem Festivals of the Performing Arts:** In late spring, two festivals featuring extraordinary music groups and theater and dance companies come from all over the world to perform. Exact dates at www.goisrael.com.

**White Nights:** This is Tel Aviv's annual late-June, all-nighters' festival, featuring rock concerts, free architectural tours, parties at local bars, dancing on the beach, art-gallery receptions, outdoor videos, and special dinner deals. Visit www.goisrael.com for information.

**Tel Aviv Gay Pride Week:** A growing festival it includes a major parade, dozens of events, and thousands of visitors from Israel and abroad. Visit www.gaytlvguide.com.

**Israeli Folkdance Festival (Karmiel, in the Galilee):** Jewish ethnic dancers come from around the world for this festival. Early July.

**Jerusalem International Film Festival:** Increasingly prestigious, with offerings from around the globe, this festival takes place at the Jerusalem Cinémathèque. For more information, call ✆ **02/672-4131** or visit www.jer-cin.org.il. First 2 weeks in July

**Jerusalem Arts and Crafts Festival:** Held in the Sultan's Pool in the valley outside the western walls of the Old City, the contemporary Israeli craft booths are not usually of a high level, but the large International Craft Section is excellent. Performances by Israeli musicians take place every night. Late July.

**Ramadan:** During the holy month of Ramadan, Muslims do not eat or drink during daylight hours, but at night many parties are held. Most places serving food in Arab communities are closed during the day; Islamic sites and mosques are closed to non-Muslims during the entire month.

**Eid Al Fitr:** The biggest holiday in the Islamic year is celebrated the day Ramadan ends and for 2 or 3 days immediately following. On Eid Al Fitr, most Muslim-owned shops are closed.

**Tisha b'Av:** The fast day on the ninth day of the Jewish month of Av is a time set aside to remember the destruction of the First and Second Temples, which by ominous coincidence were destroyed on the same calendar day in the years 586 B.C. and A.D. 70. Entertainment facilities and many restaurants are closed.

**Red Sea Jazz Festival (Eilat):** This acclaimed international jazz festival is held in Eilat. Visit www.redseajazzeilat.com for information.

## SEPTEMBER/OCTOBER

**The Jerusalem International Chamber Music Festival:** Held at the YMCA Concert Hall and produced by the Jerusalem Symphony Orchestra, this festival offers an array of internationally famous musicians performing classical chamber music. For information, check out www.jcmf.org.il.

**Rosh Hashanah (Jewish New Year)\*:** The start of the High Holy Days is a 2-day religious festival, not an occasion for revels but rather for solemn contemplation and prayer. Almost everything in the Jewish sectors close.

**Yom Kippur (Day of Atonement)\*:** On the 10th day of the Jewish year, the High Holy Days culminate in the most solemn of Jewish holidays. Places of worship are crowded, but the large synagogues reserve seats for tourists, and some of the larger hotels organize their own services. Yom Kippur is a fast day, but hotel dining rooms serve guests who wish to eat. Everything comes to a standstill; even TV and radio stations suspend broadcasting.

**Succot (Feast of Tabernacles)\*:** This 7-day holiday recalls how Moses and the children of Israel dwelled in "booths" (or "succot")

as they left Egypt to wander in the desert. Observant families have meals and services in specially built, highly decorated yet simple huts located in gardens or on balconies. Succot is also a harvest festival and thus an agricultural and kibbutz favorite. On the first and last days of Succot, Sabbath-like restrictions are observed.

**Simchat Torah\*:** As Succot ends, Jews rejoice as they complete the yearly cycle of reading the Torah (the first five books of the Bible); street festivities in Jerusalem and Tel Aviv mark this day. Cantors read the final verses of the Torah in synagogues around the country and then immediately start again.

**Eid Al Adha:** The second-biggest Islamic holiday commemorates Abraham's near-sacrifice of his son. Animals are sacrificed, big family feasts are held, children receive gifts and new clothes, many shops in Arab neighborhoods are closed, and mosques are closed to tourists.

## NOVEMBER

**Olive Festival:** In recent years, both Jewish and Arab communities in the Galilee have come to mark the November olive-harvest period with at least a dozen local festivals of traditional foods, music, crafts, and dance. Check with the Nazareth and Akko tourist information offices for the best options.

## DECEMBER

**Chanukah:** Celebrates the victory of the Maccabees over Syrian Greeks and the consequent rededication of the Temple in 164 B.C. For 8 days, this history-based holiday is marked by the nightly lighting of the eight-branch menorah.

**International Choir Concerts:** These take place in Bethlehem on Christmas Eve (December 24). The Christian Information Centre (www.christusrex.org) inside Jaffa Gate has information about these programs and security conditions in Bethlehem.

**Liturgica (Jerusalem):** A week of choral music organized by the Jerusalem Symphony Orchestra in late December. For program information, visit www.jso.co.il.

# SETTLING INTO JERUSALEM

Planning your trip to Jerusalem needn't cause you undue *tsuris* (that's the Yiddish word for "stress"). This chapter covers the best ways to navigate the city and introduces you to the city's most authentic and evocative restaurants and hotels, places that truly wouldn't exist outside the Holy Land. With these suggestions in hand, the practical issues involved in your stay should go smoothly and allow you to concentrate on sightseeing (covered in chapter 5), which is really the reason you've come to Israel. But having a nice place to stay and great meals surely adds to the overall experience.

**4**

## ORIENTATION
### Arriving

**BY PLANE**   Ben-Gurion Airport is the country's international arrivals center. It's a 45-minute drive west of Jerusalem and a 25-minute drive in the opposite direction to Tel Aviv. There are a number of options to get from Ben-Gurion into Jerusalem.

**Sherut**   A popular, reasonably priced way to get to Jerusalem from Ben-Gurion Airport is by these 8 to 10 passengers vans with a fixed per-person rate (NIS 65, baggage included). The sherut stand, run by **Nesher Sheruts,** is to the left as you exit the arrivals area of the terminal building. Confirm that the destination of the Nesher van is Jerusalem, give your luggage to the driver, and climb in. When all the seats are claimed, the van will take off. For no additional charge, the driver must take you from the airport to the doorstep of the hotel or residential address of your choice anywhere in Jerusalem. If your hotel is in the Old City, a sherut will generally take you *near* but not *inside* the Jaffa Gate or Damascus Gate. Depending on conditions, sheruts may not serve addresses deep inside East Jerusalem.

**Sherut from Jerusalem to Ben-Gurion Airport**   For the return trip to the airport, your hotel will be glad to make an appointment for **Nesher Sheruts** to pick you up (let the hotel know about 2 days before your departure). If you want to make your sherut reservation in person, the office of **Nesher Taxis and Sheruts** (© **02/625-7227**), known for its extremely reliable airport service, is upstairs at 23 Ben-Yehuda St., near King George Street. The company picks up passengers round-the-clock, 7 days a week. Be sure to specify **sherut** rather than a **special,** which means a much more expensive private taxi. *Note:* If you need transportation to the airport on the Sabbath, you must make your reservation by Thursday—although sheruts run during Shabbat, the Nesher office is closed on Shabbat and is not available for reservations in person or by phone. If you are with a group of three or four people, it could pay to take a taxi.

**Private Taxi**   The fixed-price rate for a **private taxi** is NIS 280. There is a higher tariff for the Sabbath, holidays starting at 4pm on Fridays (or the eves of holidays) and weekday nights after 9pm. If you happen to have three or four people in your party (standard taxis take only up to four passengers, and the fourth passenger is at the driver's discretion), the cost for this most convenient option is really little more than that of a sherut. Agree on a definite price ahead of time. Taxi drivers do not expect tips, but if you have a number of heavy bags, the driver may quote a slightly higher fare. If your driver doesn't charge extra for help with bags, offer a tip of NIS 10.

**Rental Car**   All major car-rental companies have offices at Ben-Gurion Airport. Traffic, road construction, and parking problems make having a rental car in Jerusalem more hindrance than help.

**BY TRAIN**   On weekdays, 20 trains a day arrive from Tel Aviv at Jerusalem's Malha Station, on the far western edge of the city. From there, you must take a municipal bus into the center of town. Trains are slower and less frequent than buses, but the route is a bit more scenic. Officially the trip takes 1½ hours; the fare from Tel Aviv to Jerusalem is NIS 25, with small discounts for students and children up to age 10; kids under 10 are free. For current schedules and fares, visit www.rail.co.il.

**BY BUS**   There is direct, scheduled bus service from most major cities to Jerusalem. Between Tel Aviv and Jerusalem, buses leave as soon as they are full; the trip takes 1 hour, and the fare is NIS 22. Most buses arrive and depart from Jerusalem's **Central Bus Station,** at the western entrance to the city, right on Jaffa Road. From there, you can easily pick up municipal buses to all parts of West Jerusalem.

**To Bethlehem, West Bank:** Arab-owned buses run (as far as the Crossing Point from Jerusalem into Bethlehem) from a bus station across the street and a block east of the Damascus Gate. At press time, bus no. 22 went to the Bethlehem crossing. Returning from Bethlehem, you can request to be let off near Jaffa Gate or the New Gate (if you are staying in West Jerusalem). Fare is NIS 6.

**BY CAR**   Route 1 (Hwy. 1) is the main road to Jerusalem from Tel Aviv and Ben-Gurion Airport; it runs right into Jaffa Road, the main street in downtown West Jerusalem. You know you've reached the western entrance to the city when you go under the new **Chords Bridge,** a highly sculptural structure shaped like a white harp in the sky, over which the new Jerusalem Light Railroad passes. Signs at the city entrance direct you to the downtown center, via a slightly circuitous route, as private cars are barred from most of Jaffa Road. If you're going to hotels on Herzl Boulevard, or points in the extreme western part of the city, follow signs for Herzl Boulevard/Government Center. The newer, often less-busy Hwy. 443 from Tel Aviv runs parallel to and north of Route 1 and leads to the northern part of Jerusalem. Parts of it traverse territory lined by high cement security walls, so you don't see much of the landscape. If you're coming from the coast north of Tel Aviv, this is the fastest route.

**From the Sea of Galilee, the Dead Sea, or Eilat and the Negev:** The most direct way is via Route 90, which follows the Jordan Valley. From Route 90, turn onto Route 1 just south of Jericho and make the steep ascent up to Jerusalem. At the edge of the city, follow signs to the "Centre." This route takes you to the northern walls of the Old City, approaching Damascus Gate. Keep right if you're heading for the center of West Jerusalem, and left for East Jerusalem.

# GETTING connected IN JERUSALEM

**Downtown West Jerusalem**'s Ben Yehuda-Jaffa Road-King George Street triangle is a free Wi-Fi hotspot, expanding outward in all directions for several blocks and filled with Wi-Fi-friendly cafes, restaurants, and small hotels. Cafes, indoors and out, welcome anything that connects. Same with the **German Colony**'s many eateries along its main drag, Emek Refaim Street.

**Inside the Walled City of Jerusalem,** wireless connections (including cell phones) are not great. The best (and possibly the cheapest) choice is **Mike's**

**Centre Internet Cafe,** right in the center of the Old City above the venerable **Abu Assab Orange and Carrot Juice Shop,** 172 Suq Khan es-Zeit St. (the main thoroughfare running from Damascus Gate south; ✆ **02/628-2486**). It offers private, air-conditioned booths and discount plans and is open daily 9am to 10pm. It also offers unique advantages, such as freshly squeezed orange, grapefruit, and carrot juice (the best in town) to keep you alert and healthy while surfing. You can even get your laundry done here while you browse the Web.

Parking is difficult in Jerusalem. Many hotels have limited or no parking facilities. There are parking garages in downtown Jerusalem, outside Jaffa Gate on Mamilla Street, and on Mamilla Street under the David Citadel Hotel. Metered streets and resident-parking-only streets are scattered throughout the center of town; there are also non-meter streets, where you must purchase a ticket in advance from a kiosk or sidewalk ticket machine and display it with the appropriate time marked. Parking is free after 7pm and during the Sabbath. In Jerusalem, it is much easier to use public transportation or taxis. The Old City is only accessible by foot.

## Visitor Information

A **Ministry of Tourism** information desk (✆ **03/971-1145**) is located in the arrivals hall of Ben-Gurion International Airport. The staff provides city maps and brochures (which you must buy) and answers questions. A hotel reservations desk nearby can also help you find a room for the night.

In the Old City, a **Tourist Information Office** lies just inside Jaffa Gate, a few steps down on the left (✆ **02/627-1422**; Sun-Thurs 8am-5pm and Fri 8am-1pm). This office sells maps and booklets, but a shelf offers free maps and tourist brochures as well. Look for the Jerusalem Menus booklets, with its discount coupons. The office also rents a recorded walking tour of the Old City for NIS 50/day plus security deposit.

The **Christian Information Centre,** at the far end of the square inside Jaffa Gate (✆ **02/627-2692**; www.cicts.org; Mon-Fri 8:30am-5:30pm, Sat 8:30am-noon), offers all kinds of useful information about tours, Christian hospices, group tours to Bethlehem (on the West Bank), and religious services.

If you're surfing the Web, the **Ministry of Tourism** site is www.goisrael.com, and the **Municipality of Jerusalem** site is www.jerusalem.muni.il.

**PUBLICATIONS** The **"International New York Times"** contains the entire daily English-language edition of **"Ha'aretz,"** Israel's most respected newspaper (www.haaretz.com). The Friday "Ha'aretz" contains a detailed Weekend Section on events in Jerusalem and throughout the country. "The Jerusalem Post" (www.jpost.com) has a daily listing of city events, but the Friday (weekend) edition is your best bet. Another source of information is the free monthly "Events in the Jerusalem Region," prepared by the Tourist Information Office and available at various tourist office locations and in many hotel lobbies.

## City Layout

To get around Jerusalem easily, it helps to understand how the city has grown. In the mid-1800s, Jerusalem was still a walled medieval city—a tortuous maze of semi-ruins with sewage running down the streets. After the mid–19th century, Christian pilgrims and Zionist settlers began to create neighborhoods outside the city walls. From 1948 to 1967, Jerusalem was further divided when modern West Jerusalem remained under Israeli jurisdiction while the Old City and downtown East Jerusalem became part of the Kingdom of Jordan. Although the city has been united under Israeli control since 1967, Jerusalem is still three different cities in one: the Old City, the newer Israeli city of West Jerusalem, and the newer Arab city of East Jerusalem.

Due east of the Old City, the Kidron Valley lies between ancient Jerusalem and the long ridge known as the Mount of Olives (*Et-Tur* in Arabic). On the slopes of the mount is the Garden of Gethsemane. Farther down the valley, south of the Old City walls, is the Arabic town of Silwan, where the earliest settlement of Jerusalem developed more than 5,000 years ago. This is where the Jerusalem of King David was located in ancient times; today, it is a densely inhabited East Jerusalem neighborhood.

## The Neighborhoods in Brief

### THE OLD CITY

The Old City is easily defined: It is the area still enclosed within the grand walls built by the Ottoman Turkish Sultan Suleiman the Magnificent in 1538. The Old City is divided into four quarters: the **Muslim Quarter,** the **Christian Quarter,** the **Armenian Quarter,** and the **Jewish Quarter.** Seven gates provide access through the massive walls; two of these are important for visitors. The **Jaffa Gate** (*Sha'ar Yafo* in Hebrew, *Bab el-Khalil* in Arabic), at the end of Jaffa Road (*Derech Yafo*), offers the main access to the Old City from West Jerusalem. **Damascus Gate** (*Sha'ar Shechem* in Hebrew, *Bab el-Amud* in Arabic) offers the main access from East Jerusalem (if you get lost in the Old City's labyrinthine alleys, just ask for either gate).

The great Jewish, Christian, and Muslim holy sites are mostly found in the Old City. Except in the Jewish Quarter, the dominating motif here is Arab: The food is Arabic, the language is Arabic, and customs are Eastern.

### WEST JERUSALEM

Extending far to the south and west, and encroaching on the east, of the Old City, this modern Israeli city is a huge area of residential, commercial, and industrial development punctuated by high-rise hotels and office blocks. The "New City" (as it's sometimes called) includes the Knesset and the government precinct on the western edge of town; Ramat Gan, one of Hebrew University's two large campuses; the Israel Museum; and, in a distant western area beyond the neighborhood called Ein Karem, the Hadassah Medical Center. Broad avenues twist and turn along the tops of the Judean Hills to connect West Jerusalem's outlying quarters with the century-old downtown area.

**Downtown West Jerusalem** is centered on Zion Square (*Kikar Ziyon*), where Jaffa Road intersects with Ben-Yehuda Street. A few short blocks west of Zion Square is King George V Avenue (known as King George St., or *Rehov Ha-Melech George*), which joins Ben-Yehuda Street and Jaffa Road to form a **Downtown Triangle.** Many of the hotels, restaurants, and businesses of interest are in or near this triangle. **Ben-Yehuda Street** is now a bustling pedestrian mall filled with souvenir, jewelry, and Judaica shops; cafes; and places to grab a quick snack. Evenings, especially in good weather, Ben-Yehuda becomes a mecca for younger travelers and young Israelis. A more quaint pedestrian mall network, centering on **Yoel Salomon Street,** runs off Zion Square at the foot of Ben-Yehuda Street. This area is known as **Nahalat Shiva.** Its renovation has transformed Jerusalem's evening ambience from that of a quiet mountain town to a lively, Mediterranean-style city where people like to stroll and rendezvous in cafes. This small enclave of old West Jerusalem is being preserved, but other 19th-century neighborhoods in West Jerusalem are slated for demolition and will be replaced by large office blocks. Many of Nahlat Shiva's most charming cafes and eateries have moved to the new, multistory **Mamilla Shoping Mall** that leads up to the Jaffa Gate. In South Jerusalem, the areas around the **Cinematheque** and the renovated Ottoman-era **First Train Station in Abu Tor** as well as the gentrified **German Colony** neighborhood are also filled with cafes and dining spots, some of which are open during Shabbat.

EAST JERUSALEM

Not as modern and sprawling as its western counterpart, downtown East Jerusalem is nevertheless a bustling modern cityscape lying north of the Old City. Its compact business, commercial, and hotel district starts right along the Old City's north wall on **Sultan Suleiman Street,** which runs from Damascus Gate to Herod's Gate and then downhill to the Rockefeller Museum. **Nablus Road** (*Derech Shechem* in Hebrew) runs northeast from Damascus Gate to the American Colony Hotel; **Saladin Street** (*Sallah ad-Din* in Arabic), the area's chief shopping thoroughfare, starts at Herod's Gate and meets Nablus Road near the American Colony Hotel. The triangle formed by these streets encloses the heart of downtown East Jerusalem. This area is quiet at night and is only beginning to recover economically from the years of the Intifada.

# GETTING AROUND

**BY BUS**   Due to construction of the new Light Rail System, many local bus routes are being changed or detoured. Routes often no longer follow the same streets in both directions, and because of circuitous one-way traffic streets, the return bus route may you far from your original starting point. To find the right bus to your destination, consult with the Tourist Information Office inside Jaffa Gate, or go to www.jet.org.il/Web/En/Lines/Buses/Default.aspx. Many bus lines do not intersect with the Light Rail.

Bus drivers make change, sell single and monthly passes, and speak English.

A single full-fare city bus ticket costs NIS 6.60, but this fare is almost certain to rise. *Tip:* If you pay for a normal, single fare, *keep the receipt the driver gives you until you exit the bus.* Occasionally you may be asked to produce it as proof that you've paid.

There is a rambling city bus station near Damascus Gate on Nablus Road for destinations in East Jerusalem and surrounding Arabic communities.

## Using the Jerusalem Light Rail

With its space age, shining silver cars, and its clanging bells reminiscent of San Francisco's antique cable cars, the new **Jerusalem Light Rail** is a great way to see and get around the city. The route glides from the outer southwestern neighborhoods of the city; then along Downtown Jerusalem's main thoroughfare, Jaffa Road; then near the Old City's Damascus Gate; and then northeastward with stops in the Palestinian neighborhoods of Shuafat and Beit Hanina. Finally, it travels to the extreme northeastern Israeli neighborhood of Pisgat Ze'ev. The Light Rail line intersects with bus lines that take you to all other areas of the city.

Trains arrive at frequent intervals. Digital signs on each train alternately flash the direction of the train and the name of each stop. Buy a ticket from the automated

Jerusalem's special **Red Double-Decker 99 Tourist Bus** leaves four times daily from in front of Safra Square on Jaffa Road, Sunday to Thursday, starting at 9am. It stops at 29 major sites throughout the city and is a great way to sit back and get a feel for Jerusalem. Audio descriptions of the route and sites are available in eight languages. The fare for the **All City Circle Route** (approx. 2 hr.; no getting off the bus) is NIS 60. **All-Day Passes,** allowing multiple stop-offs, are NIS 80, but you have to coordinate reentering the bus with the route schedule. Tickets can be bought at many hotels (your hotel can also make a reservation for you); for further information, go to www.egged.co.il and click "English."

machines at each stop and enter the next train. **Once aboard the train, you must immediately validate your ticket on the validation machine.** From the time validated on your ticket, you have 90 minutes during which you can use your ticket to transfer to any connecting bus line along the Light Rail's route. Inspectors make random checks of passengers. Failure to be in possession of a time-validated ticket results in a fine of NIS 160, and pleading ignorance is no excuse. The single fare on the Light Rail is NIS 6.60 (just like the bus), but expect this fare to rise in the future.

**BY TAXI** Private taxis take you throughout the city and charge higher night and Shabbat rates. The standard initial drop is approximately NIS 10. By law, the meter (ha-sha-on) must be turned on, and you will be given a printed receipt (ka-ba-lah) at your destination, but when taxi drivers see a foreigner, many ask for a set price before starting. Except during the most terrible rush-hour traffic jam, you'll always do better with the meter. (But on a rainy Fri night, if the driver claims his meter is broken, you may not want to argue.) In central Jerusalem, a daytime ride should not be much more than NIS 30 to NIS 40, higher after 9pm and on Shabbat. Taxi drivers do not expect tips; at most, if your driver claims to have no change, round off the fare to the nearest shekel. Your driver may charge extra if he assists you in dragging baggage into or out of a building. If he doesn't charge for this, a tip of a few shekels is warranted.

**ON FOOT** Central Jerusalem and the Old City are compact and easy to walk. However, it's hard to get to museums and the Knesset area at the western side of town on foot, as distances are far, and pedestrian facilities along access roads are not good.

# [FastFACTS] JERUSALEM

**Airport Transportation** Call

**Area Code** The telephone area code is **02.**

**Consulates** See chapter 11.

**Currency Exchange** Banking hours are 8:30am to noon or 12:30pm Sunday through Friday and on Sunday, Tuesday, and Thursday from 4 to 5pm. **Money-changers,** which are legal, can be found in the Old City, inside Damascus and Jaffa gates; they are generally open daily from 9am to 5 or 6pm. In West Jerusalem, **Change Point,** a convenient money-changing office, has branches on the Ben-Yehuda Mall near Zion Square that are open Sunday through Thursday from 9am to 8pm and on Friday from 9am to 1pm.

Conveniently, **ATMs** connected to the major international networks can be found almost everywhere, with a large concentration at Zion Square and on the Ben-Yehuda Mall. You must use ATMs with the Cirrus, Sum, PLUS, or other international connection networks indicated or ones specifically indicating that foreign ATM cards can be used.

**Drugstores** "The Jerusalem Post" lists under "General Assistance" the names and addresses of duty pharmacies that stay open nights and on Shabbat.

**Emergencies** To call the **police,** dial ☎ **100.** Dial ☎ **101** for Magen David Adom (Red Shield of David), Israel's emergency first-aid ambulance service. Magen David Adom has a clinic in Romema, near the Central Bus Station, and a **mobile intensive-care unit** (☎ **02/652-3133**) on call 24 hours a day. For medical emergencies requiring hospitalization, dial ☎ **102.**

**Events Information** For details on special performances and events in Jerusalem, call the **city hot line** (☎ **02/531-4600**) or visit **www.jerusalem.muni.il**.

**Hospitals** Hospital emergency rooms are open daily, 24 hours. Bring your passport and a means to pay the fees. In central Jerusalem: **Bikur Holim Hospital,** Strauss Street near Jaffa Road (☎ **02/646-1111**). At the western edge of the city: **Sha'arei Tzedek Hospital,** Sderot Herzl, Bayit VeGan

(☎ **02/655-5111;** emergency room ☎ 02/655-5508). **Hadassah Hospital,** Ein Kerem (☎ **02/677-7111**). For information on possible Blue Cross–Blue Shield coverage at Hadassah Hospital, Ein Kerem, call ☎ **02/677-6029.**

**Libraries** The **American Cultural Center Library** (☎ **02/625-5755**) is on Keren Hayesod Street, between Agron Street and the Dan Panorama Hotel. It's open Sunday through Thursday from 10am to 4pm.

**Luggage & Storage Lockers** Bags are best stored at your hotel. Be prepared for a security check before storing.

**Post Office** Jerusalem's Central Post Office (☎ **1-700-500-171**) is at 23 Jaffa Rd., near the intersection with Shlomzion HaMalka Street. General hours for all services are Sunday to Thursday from 7am to 7pm; limited services (telephone and telegraph) are available nights and on Shabbat. East Jerusalem's post office is opposite Herod's Gate at the corner of Saladin Ibn Sina and Sultan Suleiman streets.

The Old City's post office is a few steps from Jaffa Gate, past the Citadel of David and next to the gate of the Christ Church Anglican Hospice.

**Religious Services** The **Christian Information Centre** (☎ **02/627-2692**),

inside Jaffa Gate on Omar Ibn El-Khattab Square, has a list of all Christian services. The center is open Monday through Saturday from 8:30am to 1pm, closed Sunday and holidays. "This Week in Jerusalem," available free at major hotels, lists Reform, Conservative, and Orthodox Jewish synagogues. Because of security regulations, which vary according to the level of warnings from week to week, independent Muslim tourists who do not have Israeli IDs or advance security clearance may not be allowed into the Al Aqsa compound on Friday (when only Muslims are allowed onto the Temple Mount for Fri prayers) unless they are with an official group.

**Safety** Jerusalem is a low-crime city, but be aware of pickpockets in the crowd crushes of the Old City. Political demonstrations in West Jerusalem are passionate but usually safe. Avoid demonstrations in East Jerusalem or in the Old City. Keep alert at all times. *Get away from and report any unattended or suspicious objects immediately.*

**Telephones** Information is ☎ **144.** Collect calls are ☎ **142.**

**Toilets** In the Old City, signs reading WC or OO indicate public restrooms. In West Jerusalem, restaurants and cafes are your best option.

# WHERE TO STAY

Moderately priced hotels are in short supply, especially in Jerusalem. And the pricing system is something of a joke. Official "rack rates" (aka published rates; it's what this chapter lists) for hotel rooms are fantasies—except during important Jewish holidays. So look for discounts wherever you can! The 11th commandment now reads: You shall not pay full price at a hotel.

So when are the important, rate-raising holidays? Jerusalem's hotels are busiest at Passover and Easter, in September or October during the Jewish high holidays (Rosh Hashanah, Yom Kippur, Succot, and Simchat Torah), and at Christmas. Many hotels consider July and August to be the regular season.

*Note:* All official hotel prices in Israel are quoted in U.S. dollars. Foreign travelers are expected to pay by credit card or foreign cash; if you pay the equivalent amount in shekels, you must also pay an additional value-added tax (VAT) of 18 percent.

## The Old City

The advantage to staying in the Old City is that you feel the rhythms and hear the sounds of this extraordinary (and largely car-free) place—the calls to prayer from the minarets, the medley of bells from the city's ancient churches. You'll watch the bazaars come to life in the morning and slowly close down for the night. You won't come across any high-rise (or even low-rise) luxury hotels in the Old City, just a few inexpensive-to-moderately priced hotels, hospices, and hostels.

The crime rate in the Old City, as in all of Jerusalem, is low, but the streets here (except for parts of the Jewish Quarter) are deserted at night and can seem intimidating. So you'll need a spirit of adventure and an enjoyment of labyrinths and casbahlike alleyways for this to be the right part of town for your base. You'll also need a good pair of walking shoes, because it will most likely be a trek from your hotel to the nearest gate, where you'll be able to catch taxis and trams to the rest of the city. *Tip:* Wi-Fi and cellphone connections are not always dependable inside the Old City.

### NEAR JAFFA GATE
#### Inexpensive

**East New Imperial Hotel** ★   With a fabulous, impossible-to-miss location just steps inside Jaffa Gate, the New Imperial was the last word in luxury when it opened in the 1880s: The ground floor courtyard was once an elegant, gated private bazaar for fastidious 19th-century guests. By today's standards, guest rooms are very simple and creaky, but this is an interesting bottom budget choice for those who don't want a hostel or the constraints of a Christian guesthouse. It's true that some of the rooms are so tiny that you may have trouble fully opening your luggage if you place it next to the bed. But others are roomier, and some even feature atmospheric, rough stone walls. Other pluses include friendly management, headed by Mr. Walid Dajani, and dynamite views from the roof. A/C, TV, and fridge are available in some rooms, and extras like hair dryers can be ordered. Rooms at the back avoid the noise of the Jaffa Gate area.

Jaffa Gate. © **02/628-2261.** www.newimperial.com. 32 units. $90–$100 double. Rates include breakfast. **Amenities:** Dining room, free Wi-Fi and Internet lounge.

**Gloria Hotel** ★★   One of the best value deals in town, this is a pleasant, well-run hotel with modern facilities, located on a quiet street just inside Jaffa Gate. Public areas are spacious, with touches of local color in the decor; the breakfast buffet/dining area offers views of the Tower of David and of West Jerusalem. Many guest rooms

# Old City Attractions & Accommodations

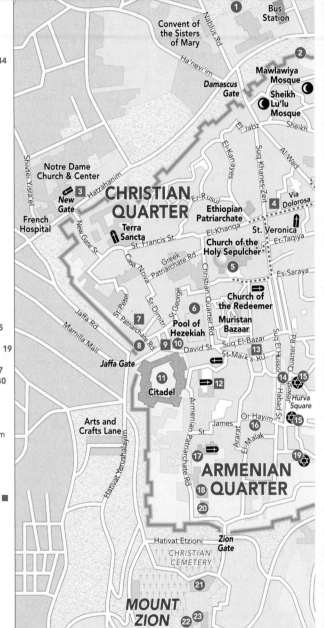

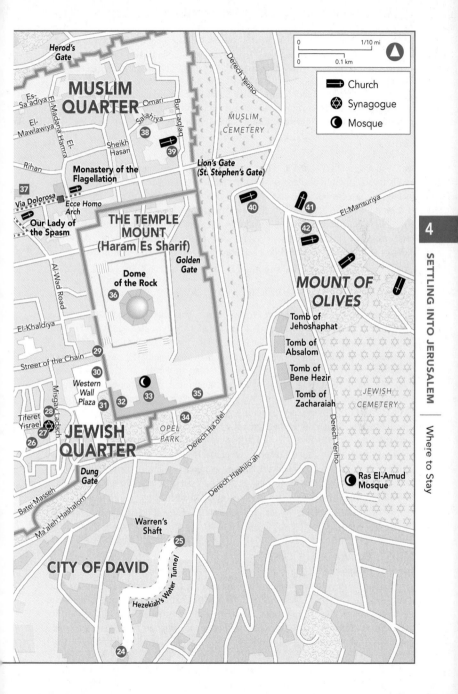

were renovated in 2013 and all offer good heating and air-conditioning, quality beds, and bathroom facilities—items that can be hard to find inside the Old City. Some are located in the 22-room annex across the street from the main building. The staff here is especially impressive, a cheery, helpful group of people who are extremely knowledgeable about Jerusalem, and—wonder of wonders!—can often set up free parking for guests. The downside? A long staircase up to the lobby (from which there is an elevator to higher floors) could be a consideration for those with mobility issues.

Latin Patriarchate St. About 80 ft. inside Jaffa Gate, turn left onto Latin Patriarchate St. ✆ **02/628-2431.** www.gloria-hotel.com. 100 units. $170–$200 double. Discounts in off season. Rates include breakfast. Bus to Jaffa Gate. **Amenities:** Wi-Fi, A/C, TV, dining room, bar, limited free parking.

**Saint Mark's Lutheran Guest House** ★★    This tranquil, atmospheric enclave, a 5-minute walk from Jaffa Gate, is hidden behind a lovely walled garden and features terraces that overlook the Dome of the Rock and the rooftops of the Old City's bazaars. So yes, it's in a splendid location (made even better by being off a quiet street). Who cares that many of the rooms are closet-size (some are larger; ask to move if you're unhappy), are decorated with mass-produced motel furniture, and have tiny bathrooms with showers only? This still counts as one of the best bargains in the city. An unusually generous breakfast is served in a lovely, stone-walled dining hall and included in the nightly rate. Visitors of all backgrounds are welcome, so don't worry if you're not Lutheran, or even Christian. Two quirks you should know about: The guesthouse, unlike most in the city, quotes its prices in euros. And Saint Mark's lies up an obscure staircase street off the David Street bazaar, so phone for directions before arrival. If you're traveling with a lot of luggage, it may be wise to arrange for a baggage porter to meet you at Jaffa Gate. Payments are accepted in cash only.

St. Mark's Rd. ✆ **02/626-8888.** www.luth-guesthouse-jerusalem.com. 23 units. Regular season (June 16–Sept 14 and winter except Christmas and Easter) $160 double. Rates include breakfast. Any bus to Jaffa Gate. **Amenities:** Dining room, lounge, garden, use of kitchen, nonsmoking rooms, free Wi-Fi.

## NEAR DAMASCUS GATE
### Inexpensive

**Al Hashimi Hotel and Hostel** ★    A traditional-style Middle Eastern inn built some 300 years ago, but redesigned in 2006, the Al Hashimi is set around a handsome interior atrium. It boasts spectacular views eastward toward the Dome of the Rock and the rooftops of the Old City, especially from its panoramic terrace. In fact, we've met guests who spent more time on that lovely terrace than they did in their guest rooms. That may be because this is a terrifically social inn, one that attracts both Muslim and non-Muslim guests (it's in the Muslim quarter), people of all ages and nationalities, and has a staff savvy and friendly enough to make sure that everyone gets acquainted.

The other reason for all the terrace time may be the ultracompact (read: tiny) size of most of the guest rooms. In its defense, rooms are kept spotlessly clean and boast quality mattresses and decent showers (in the small attached bathrooms). Spacious VIP rooms can be secured for higher rates. With any size room, make sure you're facing away from the bazaar, as it can get quite noisy.

Four small warnings: Reservations can be held with a credit card, but actual payment is cash only. And if you have heavy baggage, phone ahead from Damascus Gate so that a porter can be arranged. Finally, alcohol is not allowed on the premises, and unmarried couples are not allowed to room together here.

73 Suq Khan es Zeit. *©* **054/547-4189.** www.hashimihotel.com. 40 units plus dorm beds. $90–$130 double. Rates include breakfast. **Amenities:** Free Wi-Fi.

## West Jerusalem
### ZION SQUARE, JAFFA ROAD & BEN-YEHUDA MALL
Step out of your hotel and it's a short walk to the Old City and the heart of the New City's downtown shopping-and-restaurant district. The area is noisy, and in summer, discos add to the roar of traffic.

### Moderate
**Arthur Hotel ★★**   Opened in 2013, this is a new Atlas Hotel, modeled after the Harmony (see below). It offers similar style, boutique service, and amenities but is located on a pedestrian-only street that offers no direct car or taxi access. Guests with baggage can be dropped off at the rear entrance of the Harmony Hotel and shuttled over to the Arthur by golf cart. A rear-facing room helps minimize street noise.

13 Dorot Rishomim St. Hotel is off Ben Yehuda Pedestrian Mall. *©* **02-623-9999.** www.atlas.com. il. 54 units. $200–$250 double. Rates include breakfast. **Amenities:** Business center, nonsmoking rooms, fridge, free Wi-Fi, limited pay parking.

**Harmony Hotel ★★★**   In the past few years, Israel's moderate-range Atlas Hotel Chain has developed new standards for style, up-to-the-minute amenities, helpful staff, and all kinds of guest-pampering extras, such as free late-afternoon happy hours with snacks and refreshments. Its Harmony Hotel is a wildly popular property, located on a charming pedestrians-only street just off Zion Square. Public areas are pleasant and include a library stocked with coffee-table books. Guest rooms are not the largest but are sleek and chic, with zebra print chairs, fluffy white duvets, and, in the suites, actual working fireplaces. Double-glazed windows and summer air-conditioning help block out street noise in this busy area (ask for a rear-facing room). For religious guests, a special elevator is programmed to run on Shabbat.

6 Yoel Salomon St. *©* **02/621-9999.** www.atlas.co.il. 60 units. $200–$270 double. Rates include breakfast. **Amenities:** Business center, nonsmoking rooms, fridge, free Wi-Fi, limited pay parking. GPS: 14 Shamai St., Jerusalem. Light Rail to King George St.

### Inexpensive
**Abraham Hostel ★★★**   The biblical Abraham wasn't just the founder of monotheism—he was the world's first backpacker, according to Maoz Innon, the irreverent owner of this funky, fun hostel/hotel. He hopes to extend "biblical hospitality" to his guests, and no, that doesn't have dirty connotations. What it means is that much is free here, from Wi-Fi to walking tours of the city to breakfast. It also means, we think, that the spirit of communalism that enlivened the Israel's first kibbutzim is alive and well at the Abraham. Guests and staff cook up Shabbat dinners together and engage in passionate conversations in the Abraham's bar and numerous friendly lounges. Sound too

# alternative ACCOMMODATIONS

**Christian hospices or guesthouses** are a good alternative to hotels—Jerusalem abounds with them, and guests of all faiths are welcome. Guesthouses were originally built to accommodate the pilgrims who began to arrive in great numbers in the 1880s. Many are housed in atmospheric 19th-century complexes with evocative Jerusalem architecture and style. The atmosphere is, of course, sedate; better hospices are like extremely well-run small hotels, with comfortable private rooms with bathrooms. Depending on denomination, decor may include a crucifix over the bed, a Byzantine-style icon, or a framed photo of the pope. **St. George's,** Jerusalem's Anglican guesthouse (p. 44), has a bar, but most do not. *Tip:* Unmarried couples can forget about sharing a room at most Christian guesthouses. You might be able to fudge separate last names on passports, but no visible wedding ring means no double room.

**Bed-and-breakfast accommodations** in a private home or apartment are an interesting alternative to hotel stays. Prices are considerably lower than hotels, and hosts are often senior citizens with lovely, spacious (by Israeli standards) homes and a genuine interest in meeting visitors from abroad.

A room in an apartment that has its own private bathroom could be about $80 for a single and $130 for a double, with breakfast and service included. A small studio or private flat would start about $120 for two people; long-term rates are available. Unique places with private entrances, gardens, views, and especially nice decor, or accommodations for families, could be much more.

**Good Morning Jerusalem,** 17 Ezrat Israel St., Jerusalem (✆ **02/623-3459;** www.accommodation.co.il), is a bed-and-breakfast and holiday apartment rental agency. With listings all over Israel, including in Jerusalem, it will reserve accommodations for you and try to match your requirements. (The office cannot vouch for the kashrut standards of any particular household and accepts the claims of its participating hosts.) The office is open Sunday to Thursday from 9am to 5pm and Friday from 9am to 1:30pm. With advance notice, the office can make arrangements to meet travelers or facilitate nighttime arrivals.

**Home Accommodation Association of Israel** (www.bnb.co.il) is an affiliation of 24 homeowners, many with distinctive properties and locations. You deal directly with the property owners: The website includes contact information, photos, and descriptions for each property.

A final resource for private B&B stays (and entire apartment rentals): the massive, international website **AirBnB.com.** It offers a number of choices in Jerusalem, and the hosts tend to be younger than those who work with the agencies listed above.

touchy-feely? Guests don't have to partake of any of this. In fact, they don't even have to stay in dorm rooms here (despite the word "hostel" in the name). In addition to communal rooms, there are also sleek private doubles (with bendy wall lamps for reading in bed, high-quality linens, and lots of light). Group and family rooms also available. *Note:* the hostel doesn't only do beds; its brilliant "Hop On Hop Off Bus Routes," operated by the affiliated Abraham Tours (p. 241), lets guests travel at their own speed to many normally hard-to-access areas in Israel.

67 Hanevi'im St. at Davidka Sq. ✆ **02/650-2200.** www.abraham-hostel-jerusalem.com. 72 units. Dorm bed NIS 80–NIS 110; private double NIS 300–NIS 400. Rates include breakfast. **Amenities:** Bar, tour programs, billiards room, A/C, free Wi-Fi. Light Rail to Machane Yehuda/Davidka Sq.

# West Jerusalem Accommodations & Dining

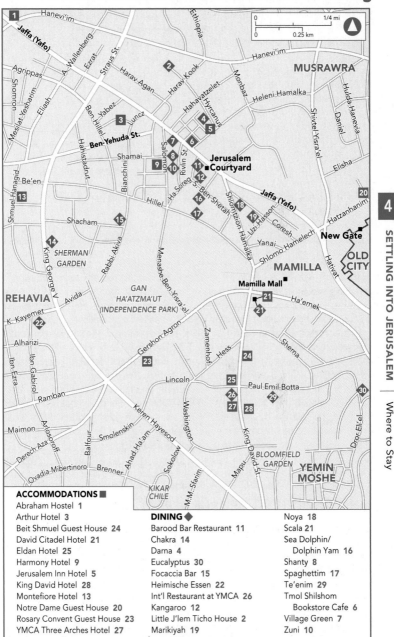

0                    1/4 mi
0          0.25 km

**MUSRAWRA**

**Jerusalem**
■**Courtyard**

**MAMILLA**

**Mamilla Mall**■

**REHAVIA**

*GAN*
*HA'ATZMA'UT*
*(INDEPENDENCE PARK)*

*SHERMAN*
*GARDEN*

**New Gate**

**OLD**
**CITY**

*BLOOMFIELD*
*GARDEN*    **YEMIN**
            **MOSHE**

*KIKAR*
*CHILE*

**ACCOMMODATIONS** ■
Abraham Hostel **1**
Arthur Hotel **3**
Beit Shmuel Guest House **24**
David Citadel Hotel **21**
Eldan Hotel **25**
Harmony Hotel **9**
Jerusalem Inn Hotel **5**
King David Hotel **28**
Montefiore Hotel **13**
Notre Dame Guest House **20**
Rosary Convent Guest House **23**
YMCA Three Arches Hotel **27**

**DINING** ◆
Barood Bar Restaurant **11**
Chakra **14**
Darna **4**
Eucalyptus **30**
Focaccia Bar **15**
Heimische Essen **22**
Int'l Restaurant at YMCA **26**
Kangaroo **12**
Little J'lem Ticho House **2**
Marikiyah **19**

Noya **18**
Scala **21**
Sea Dolphin/
  Dolphin Yam **16**
Shanty **8**
Spaghettim **17**
Te'enim **29**
Tmol Shilshom
  Bookstore Cafe **6**
Village Green **7**
Zuni **10**

# family-friendly HOTELS

Traveling with kids in tow? Try the following hotels, which either offer savings for families or swell amenities for the little ones.

**David Citadel Hotel** (p. 38)   This is the luxury choice for families, as it boasts both a heated, outdoor pool (open year-round) and a whimsical children's playroom that your kids will find difficult to leave. The Citadel's super-size rooms are perfect for large groups, and the staff is particularly attentive to the needs of young guests.

**King David** (p. 39) and **Dan Jerusalem** (p. 43)   Members of the same chain, each allows up to two children to stay free in a room with their parents; the only charge is for breakfast.

**Ramat Rachel** (p. 42)   The Rachel not only offers a large swimming pool but also has playground facilities on the property, plus basketball and tennis courts. When school is out, the staff here offer specialized kids' activities.

**The Mount Zion Hotel** (p. 41) You're likely to meet local families, always a plus, at this hotel's roomy, in-season pool area, which also includes a children's pool. A number of its rooms are extra-large and can easily accommodate families.

**Jerusalem Inn Hotel** ★★   A great budget find, this recently renovated hotel is extremely well located: on a small taxi- and car-accessible street (rare for this area) just a 3-minute walk from Zion Square. Most rooms and bathrooms are Lilliputian—are you seeing a pattern among Jerusalem hotels?—but the large windows or sliding doors to balconies that all rooms have make them feel less cramped. Plus the in-room safes, glass-enclosed showers or tubs, plasma TVs, and cushy beds (and bedding) are all above the quality usually found in this price range. Loaner laptops, offered by the bright, helpful young Israeli staff, are a terrific perk. Yes, the lack of an elevator is a minus; if you have heavy baggage or accessibility problems, you may want to ask for the roomy ground-floor VIP rooms. And late-night noise can sometimes be a problem in this central area. But the small rooftop patio and an upgraded breakfast buffet added in 2013 mean the positives outweigh the negatives here. And there's even a small pay parking lot across the street—a small miracle in Jerusalem!

7 Hyrcanos St. (from Hanevi'im St., turn onto Helena HaMalka St., then left on Hyrcanos). ✆ **02/625-2757.** www.jerusalem-inn.com. 27 units. $99–$170 double; $150–$210 suite and new deluxe room. Rates include breakfast. **Amenities:** Free Wi-Fi. Light Rail to King George or Safra Sq.

## KING DAVID/KING GEORGE STREET AREA

This area is also central, although a bit farther from the Light Rail line on Jaffa Road. You can easily walk from here to the Old City.

### Very Expensive

**David Citadel Hotel** ★★★   Feeling lucky? You will be when you check into this horseshoe-shaped hotel (designed by architect Moshe Safdie of Yad Vashem fame). It is filled with every luxury imaginable and lies just a short stroll from the Old City. Rooms are opulent in the extreme, large and bright and outfitted with Fendi furnishings and superbly comfortable beds swathed in Frette linens. Almost all have balconies, many with dramatic views. The pampering continues in the hotel's award-winning spa; at its many inventive restaurants (which include the fabulous **Scala** [p. 58] as well as a kosher sushi bar); and in each and every interaction with the staff, a group of *menches* (Yiddish for "good people") who bend over backward to make sure that all requests are accommodated. This may sound like an adults-only type of place, but the Citadel is wonderfully family-friendly, thanks to those large rooms (with alcove rooms, for those sharing digs with their kids); the hotel's large, all-season, heated pool; and its dedicated, whimsical, and well-equipped playroom.

7 King David St. (at the corner of Mamilla St.). © **02/621-1111.** www.thedavidcitadel.com. 384 units. $600–$800 standard double. In-building underground parking (fee). **Amenities:** Restaurant, dining room, terrace cafe, sushi bar, bar, children's activities, concierge, health club, rooms for those w/limited mobility, children's pool and heated outdoor pool, room service, sauna, nonsmoking rooms, spa, steam room, gym, synagogue, Wi-Fi (fee). Bus: 6, 18, or 21.

**King David Hotel** ★★★   Built in 1930 during the British Mandate, the King David has outlasted the British Empire and continues to sail on, refined and majestic. Its Egyptian-esque Art Deco lobby still draws gawkers, as does its lushly gardened pool area, made famous in the film "Exodus" (it's where Paul Newman romanced Eva Marie Saint). For world leaders visiting the city, there's no other choice for digs. Surprisingly, though, the rooms are not in the least old-fashioned. In fact, a number of them were combined in the late 1990s to offer more space to guests (although some remain small). Today, all boast fine wood furnishings, handsome heavy draperies, top-quality bed linens, and shiny wood parquet or thickly carpeted floors. Outside the guest rooms, the hotel's many modern-day conveniences include tennis courts, a working synagogue, a small fitness center/spa, a shopping arcade, and the most lavish, over-the-top breakfast buffet in all of Israel. *Tip:* You don't have to be a millionaire to stay here (despite the rack rates listed below). Many air/hotel packagers and tour companies use the King David, and their guests pay far less than the guests who book with the hotel directly (although they're usually relegated to the smaller rooms or ones that don't have the iconic views of the Old City). Parent company Dan Hotels sometimes offers off-season discounts; check the website.

23 King David St. © **02/620-8888.** www.danhotels.com. 237 units. $600–$800 standard double with street view; $800–$1,100 deluxe double with Old City view. Rates include breakfast. Limited parking (fee). **Amenities:** Restaurant, dining room, cafe, fitness center and spa, outdoor pool, room service, sauna, nonsmoking rooms, synagogue, tennis court, Wi-Fi (fee). Bus: 6, 18, or 21.

## Moderate

**Eldan Hotel** ★   This modern hotel is affiliated with Israel's largest car-rental company, which means you can get a small discount if you rent an Eldan vehicle; the Eldan Rental office is in the hotel, so pick-up and drop-off couldn't be easier. And just like a decent rental car, the hotel runs smoothly, although you'll likely forget what it looks like the moment you check out. That being said, it's superbly located (right across from the King David Hotel), clean, and comfortable and boasts tubs in most of the bathrooms, a nice perk. In 2013, the fifth-floor rooms were refurbished, so ask for them (they're also quieter than rooms on lower floors).

24 King David St. © **02/567-9777.** www.eldanhotel.com. 76 units. $170–$250 double. Rates include breakfast. Limited free parking. **Amenities:** Restaurant, dining room, bar, fitness room, Internet, room service, nonsmoking rooms, free Wi-Fi. Bus: 6, 18, or 21.

**Montefiore Hotel** ★★   This cheery hotel, built in the 1990s, has more of a Western vibe than others in its price category, for all the good and the bad that implies. Rooms are a hair larger than one usually gets at this price point and feature more color: navy blue rugs, happy bubble-patterned coverlets, toast-colored curtains. Rooms that face Shatz Street on higher floors tend to be the quietest picks, unless you get one near the squeaky elevator (ask to move if that happens). We very much like the location, right on a pedestrian street just 1½ blocks from the intersection of King George Street and the Ben-Yehuda pedestrian mall. A very good breakfast buffet was instituted in 2013. Because the hotel is on a pedestrian, taxis can't drop you off at the door, but it's only a half-block downhill from Shmuel HaNaggid Street. Call ahead for arrival info and possible help with baggage. Parking is difficult here. In late fall and winter, there are often fabulous room deals, so do surf the Internet.

7 Schatz St. 🕜 **02/622-1111.** www.montefiorehotel.com. 47 units. $140–$180 double. Rates include breakfast. **Amenities:** Restaurant, dining room, free Wi-Fi and use of laptop. Bus: 4, 8, 9, or 19.

**YMCA Three Arches Hotel ★**   When locals need to house visiting relatives and friends, this unpretentious yet historic property is the one they often pick. That may be partly because it's so famous: Completed in 1933 and designed by Arthur Loomis Harmon (architect of the Empire State Building), the building is a beaut, with a magnificent lobby that mixes Art Deco and Islamo-Byzantine touches; and a famed observation tower. Plus, guests can use the 1930s-style indoor swimming pool and modern fitness room at no extra charge. But their choice likely also has to do with the prices, which are usually more-than-reasonable for digs this well located (it's just across the street from the King David hotel). So although the rooms are nothing to write home about—they tend to be small but clean and with adequate air-conditioning—most who stay here are pleased with the experience. Friendly service and good, although nonkosher, on-site eating options add to the value.

26 King David St. 🕜 **02/569-2692.** www.ymca3arch.co.il. 56 units. $160–$250 double (higher on major Christian and Jewish holidays). Rates include continental breakfast. Limited free parking. **Amenities:** Restaurant, dining room, cafe, fitness room, Internet desk, library/lounge, indoor pool, room service, nonsmoking rooms, fridge in some rooms, free Wi-Fi. Bus: 6, 18, or 21 to King David St.

## Inexpensive

**Beit Shmuel Hostel and Guest House ★**   Designed by acclaimed architect Moshe Safdie (he also did the David Citadel Hotel), this sprawling, contemporary cultural and educational center is run by the World Union for Progressive (Reform) Judaism. The complex boasts excellent views of the Old City and a network of terraces, gardens, and courtyards. At night, the college campus–like area bustles with activity—lectures, concerts, art exhibits, you name it. As for Beit Shmuel's hostel, it contains rooms with private bathrooms that can be arranged for two to six people; better rooms in the Beit Shimshon Guest House wing can handle up to four guests. We'll be blunt: The rooms are worn from heavy use. But we still recommend Bet Schmuel for all the cultural perks it offers. Visitors of all faiths and ages are welcome. Phone ahead to make arrangements if you need wheelchair access. Reserve far in advance, as this is a popular place to lodge.

13 King David St. (the entrance is around the corner from Koenig St.). 🕜 **02/620-3473** or 620-3456. www.beitshmuel.com. 50 units. $115–$165 double in hostel; higher on Jewish and school holidays. Rates include breakfast. **Amenities:** Dining room, Wi-Fi, no TV or phone in hostel rooms. Bus: 6, 18, or 21 to 1st stop on King David St.

**Rosary Convent Guest House and Hostel ★★**   This hidden gem is centrally located in a quiet garden around the corner from the high-rise Jerusalem Leonardo Plaza Hotel and across the street from a Supersol supermarket. Most of the rooms were renovated in 2013 (including new bathrooms) and they are airy, with high ceilings, heating, and air-conditioning, and are roomy enough to fit three beds (there are no double beds here, just singles). Everything is spotless, homemade breads and jam grace the table at breakfast, and the Rosary Sisters are especially helpful to guests. The gate to the convent closes at 10pm, but you can arrange to be let in later. Reservations need to be made by phone; call between 9am and 2pm Jerusalem time.

14 Agron St. ☏ **02/625-8529** or 02/623-5581. 23 units, most with private bathroom. $130 double. Rates include breakfast. Cash only. Bus: 4, 7, 9, 14, or 19.

## FARTHER WEST: EIN KEREM
### Inexpensive
**Notre Dame de Sion Convent Guest House Ein Kerem** ★ Not to be confused with the Notre Dame de Sion Guest House in the Old City, this is one of the most special places to stay in the Jerusalem area. It's set in a walled convent with its own orchards and gardens in the charming village of Ein Kerem (birthplace of John the Baptist), a half-hour municipal bus ride from downtown Jerusalem. Not all guests are religious; many travelers come for the poetry and romance of the place. The convent itself is a lovely ensemble of atmospheric, stone buildings; rooms are very simple but spotless, and many share a balcony, a huge plus in a setting this lovely. Rates are slightly higher on weekends; for reservations (which are essential), you must phone between 9am and 2pm Jerusalem time.

Ha-Oren St., Ezor "D," Ein Kerem. ☏ **02/641-5738** or 02/643-0887. www.sion-ein-karem.org. 34 units, 23 with private bathroom, 8 with shared bathroom. Sun–Thurs NIS 400 double; Fri–Sat NIS 450 double. Rates include breakfast. **Amenities:** Dining room, chapel for meditation and prayer, gardens. Bus: 17 from downtown Jerusalem to Ein Kerem.

# South Jerusalem

South of the King David Street area, it's about a 30-minute walk or short bus ride from the city center. The area is convenient to the many cafes, shops, and restaurants in the German Colony. You are also close to the dramatic Cinematheque complex and the renovated First Train Station in Abu Tor.

## EXPENSIVE
**Mount Zion Hotel** ★ Set in a series of architecturally intriguing 19th- and early-20th-century Jerusalem stone buildings to which a modern complex has been added, the entire hotel is built on a cliff-side overlooking the dramatic Hinnom Valley and the sprawling walls of the Old City. (It's about a 10-min. walk from here to the Jaffa Gate.) The pool area and gardens are exquisite, rivaling those of the King David Hotel. We wish we could say the same for the rooms, many of which are in serious need of a renovation. They're not dirty, but you will see scuff marks on some walls, frayed towels, and the like. An exception are the executive and junior suites in the Citadel wing; the views from their private terraces are dazzling. Beyond the views and outdoor areas, the hotel's top draw is its 19th-century *hammam* (a heated, Turkish-style bathing pool/steam room), a wonderful place to relax after a long day of sightseeing.

17 Hebron Rd. (the hotel is just south of the landmark B'nei Brith overhead bridge spanning Hebron Rd.). ☏ **02/568-9555**. www.mountzion.co.il. 140 units. $240–$400 double; $350 and up Citadel double; $400 and up junior and executive suites. Rates include breakfast. Extra charge for Old City–view rooms. Free limited parking. **Amenities:** Dining room, lobby bar/cafe, fitness room, Jacuzzi in garden (fee), large outdoor pool, sauna (fee), spa, Turkish steam room (fee), fridge (in some rooms), kitchenette (suites only), Wi-Fi (fee). Bus: 7, 8, 21, or 48.

## MODERATE
**Dan Boutique Hotel** ★ Planned originally as a residential hotel, the Dan Boutique has all the class and comfort that are the hallmarks of this hotel chain (think cushiony beds, decor in serene tans and taupes, well-trained staff, a generous breakfast buffet) but because of its original architecture, rooms come in a wide variety of sizes

and arrangements, which can make it a good choice for families and large groups. The better rooms (some of which have balconies) are on floors five to eight; these include 14 roomy suites. The worst are the ground-floor rooms; they get a "lovely" view of the parking lot. Nearby bus stops take you all over the city. Look for off-season specials.

31 Hebron Rd. (just north of Havaselet St.). © **02/568-9999.** www.danhotels.com 126 units. $200–$250 double. Rates include breakfast. Limited free parking. **Amenities:** Dining room, cafe, bar, fitness center, synagogue, Wi-Fi ($15/day). Bus: 7, 8, 21, or 48.

**Ramat Rachel Hotel** ★   The only kibbutz guest accommodations accessible via Jerusalem's city buses, the Ramat Rachel may be the top choice in the area for families with very active children. Along with an Olympic-size outdoor pool and an indoor pool for rainy days, the resort—and it's much more of a resort than a hotel—offers night-lit tennis and basketball courts and a playground, along with organized children's activities. There are refurbished, less-expensive older rooms in addition to 60 newer rooms; all are comfy by kibbutz standards, and some even have balconies with killer views of the desert and Bethlehem in the distance (the hotel is set on a hill). Meals are glatt kosher, and all hotel facilities are wheelchair-accessible. The kibbutz is heavily booked in summer and Jewish holidays, and the pool is filled with locals on weekends. *Note:* The bus into town runs on schedule but is not that frequent, so this is a better choice for travelers who have cars (there's ample free parking).

Kibbutz Ramat Rachel. © **888/669-5700** in the U.S., or 02/670-2555. www.ramatrachel.co.il. 164 units. $180–$300 double; extra on Jewish holidays. Discounts available through Kibbutz Hotel Chain/ITC 7-day packages (see chapter 11). Rates include breakfast. Free parking. **Amenities:** Dining room, cafe, bar, airport transfers (fee), children's center, health club and spa, Jacuzzi, 7 rooms for those w/limited mobility, playground, Olympic pool and indoor heated pool, sauna, nonsmoking rooms, lit tennis and basketball courts, free Wi-Fi. Bus: 7.

## INEXPENSIVE

**Little House in Baka** ★   Not so "little," this extremely friendly hotel is set in a landmark, early-20th-century mansion in one of the city's outer neighborhoods. It gets a lot of repeat business thanks to its affordable rates and genial staff, who make guests feel like family. That familial ambience continues in the guest rooms, which are nowhere near luxurious but are tidy, comfortable, and pleasant, with art on the walls of the kind your great-aunt might pick. The house offers 13 singles (a rarity in Jerusalem) and an annex with family rooms and suites. Double rooms in the basement are less expensive but not too inviting. The location is on busy Derekh Hebron (ask for a room in the back if you want quiet), with relatively frequent buses into the center of town. It's within walking distance to gentrified streets and eateries of the German Colony; there's also an excellent on-site restaurant. If this popular place is full, the management also runs the nearby **Little House in the Colony** and the **Little House in Rehavia.** Both are on the same website and offer similar accommodations. For reservations, be sure to specify which Little House you're asking for. Food is kosher mehadrin.

Hebron Rd. (at Yehuda St.). © **02/673-7944.** www.o-niv.com/bakah. 33 units. $135–$170 double; add $20 on weekends; $200 double Jewish holidays. Rates include breakfast. Free on-street parking. **Amenities:** Dining room, cafe/bar, limited room service, free Wi-Fi. Bus: 8.

**Saint Andrew's Church of Scotland Guest House** ★★   The flag of St. Andrew's waves from the tower of this guesthouse, welcoming visitors. It's a cheery sight, as are the gardens that surround this hillside lodging; stand in their midst or on St. Andrew's sun porch, and you'll be treated to postcard-perfect views of Mount Zion and the Old City. St. Andrews offers spotless, recently renovated guest rooms (bright white usually, with cool tile floors and top-quality beds), a lounge/library, and a dining room where guests can have free tea and coffee all day. The location is a block away from cafes and eateries at the Cinematheque and the new First Station complex as well as a few steps to buses all over town. Staff is congenial, and there's a ground-floor special-access room and free, gated parking for guests.

Church of Scotland. © **02/673-2401.** www.scotsguesthouse.com. 20 units. $150–$200 double; add $20 for room with 2 beds. Rates include breakfast. Free parking. **Amenities:** Dining room, lounge, free Wi-Fi. Bus: 4, 8, or 48 along King George V Ave. or Keren Hayesod St.; or 6, 18, or 21 from Central Bus Station or Jaffa Rd.; First Station/Khan Theater stop.

# North Jerusalem
## EXPENSIVE
**Dan Jerusalem** ★  If you're looking for a good deal at a major hotel and are willing to stay in a somewhat out-of-the-way neighborhood, you'll find real bargains at the vast Dan Jerusalem, nestled on the lower slopes of Mt. Scopus. Built in the 1980s, with an impressive contemporary design by an award-winning Israeli architect, the hotel was recently taken over by Dan Hotels, which has done extensive renovations of the 130 executive rooms in the King David Wing and a lighter, but much-needed, updating of most of the standard rooms. Pluses include sweeping views of the Old City in the distance, very good breakfasts, top service, a large pool and extensive sports facilities, and a free hotel shuttle service that runs to the Old City and West Jerusalem. But there are real downsides to staying here, such as the lack of interesting nearby streets for strolling and the hefty fees for Wi-Fi. And if you're assigned to one of the rooms that haven't yet been upgraded, you'll likely want to ask to be moved (some are very tired). Light Rail to downtown is 2 long blocks away; at night, most take taxis.

32 Lehi St. © **02/533-1234.** www.danhotels.com. 503 units. $210–$250 standard double. Rates include breakfast. **Amenities:** Restaurant; dining room; cafe; bar; free parking; floodlit basketball, volleyball, tennis courts; in-season children's activities; fitness center and spa (fee); Internet (fee); playground; outdoor swimming pool; room service; free shuttle to downtown Jerusalem; synagogue, Wi-Fi ($20 per computer in room; free in 4th-floor lobby). Light Rail to Ammunition Hill.

# East Jerusalem & the East/West Jerusalem Seam
The atmosphere in East Jerusalem is Palestinian, and the genuine helpfulness and hospitality found in many of East Jerusalem's hotels are well known. As a rule, East Jerusalem hotels are somewhat less expensive than those in the western part of town. Be forewarned, however, that the area is relatively dead at night and that many of the cheaper East Jerusalem hotels, not listed here, can be run-down and smoky.

## EXPENSIVE
**American Colony Hotel** ★★★  Few cities anywhere are as rich in history, so it should come as no surprise that Jerusalem's hotels have scintillating stories attached to them. The American Colony was originally constructed for a Turkish pasha and his harem of four wives and later became a commune or "colony" for a cult of messianic American and Swedish Christians (hence the name). It was transformed into a hotel in 1902 by Plato von Ustanov, grandfather of British film star Peter Ustinov. In 1917, when British troops arrived at the city during World War I, a white bed sheet from the hotel was used to signal Jerusalem's surrender. Famous past guests include Lawrence of Arabia, Bob Dylan, John Le Carre (who wrote a novel while staying here), and Winston Churchill, among others. But even if you didn't know the history, you could tell this was a storied place by gazing at the exquisite painted wooden ceilings, tracing

the patterns on the colorful Armenian tile that coat the public areas, or walking through the walled courtyards. Those lucky enough to stay in one of the pasha rooms or suites in the original 19th-century building are surrounded by fine antiques. More affordable but still spacious (deluxe) rooms and smaller economy rooms are available in the newer, less-exotic wings. Within each room category there's variation, so try to see different rooms, if possible, before settling. If you decide *not* to stay here, consider coming by for the **Saturday luncheon buffet in the Arabesque Room** (p. 60; food is not kosher), a Jerusalem tradition. A state-of-the-art swimming pool was added to the hotel's famous gardens in 2013.

Nablus Rd. ✆ **02/627-9777.** www.americancolony.com. 92 units. $280–$445 standard (deluxe) double; up to $850 for pasha rooms and suites in main building. Rates include breakfast and use of business center. Limited free parking. **Amenities:** Restaurant, dining room, cafe, bar, babysitting, concierge, fitness center with Jacuzzi and sauna, outdoor pool and children's pool, coded high-speed Internet access for added security (fee), Wi-Fi (free for guests paying rack rates). Bus: 27.

## MODERATE

**Jerusalem Hotel ★★**  A special, boutique hotel, the Jerusalem is known as the affordable, more personal version of the legendary, nearby American Colony Hotel. Set in an old Jerusalem mansion with Middle Eastern architecture, exposed stone walls, and hand-crafted furnishings, the hotel is located 1 long block from Damascus Gate. You enter through a walled, vine-covered garden restaurant that's heated in winter and is a rendezvous spot for Israelis, Palestinians, and in-the-know internationals. The restaurant is famous for live, traditional Arabic music on Friday nights, with diners and waiters often dancing in the aisles. Depending on conditions, the management can arrange tours to Bethlehem and the West Bank. Ask for a room away from the restaurant, as it can get loud, but that's about the only negative as rooms are quite handsome, with colorful, exotic coverlets, heavy wood furnishings, exposed stone walls, and arched windows. This is a Christian-owned hotel, so alcohol is served.

Nablus Rd. (entrance at 4 Antara Ben-Shadad St. on a side street facing the north side of the Egged East Nablus Rd. Bus Station). ✆ **02/628-3282.** www.jrshotel.com. 15 units. $190–$235 double; off season as low as $100. Rates include breakfast. **Amenities:** Restaurant, dining room, free Wi-Fi in public areas and in rooms. Bus: 27. Light Rail to Damascus Gate.

**St. George Landmark Hotel ★★**  Originally built in the 1960s, the St. George was totally redesigned in 2012 after a long closure. Everything, from the relatively spacious guest rooms, to the rooftop terrace and pool, double-glazed windows, and free Wi-Fi, is new and, in the case of the decor, quite handsome. Alas, views could not be added to most of the rooms, but the vista from the rooftop terrace is breathtaking. Up there you'll also find the **Turquoise** Lebanese restaurant (p. 60), presided over by a master chef trained in Israel's finest restaurants. It serves the best traditional Arabic cuisine in the city (other in-house dining here is simply average). When booking a room, ask for one in the back, as they're quieter. Families may want to consider the generous, but not too pricey, minisuites. The hotel is an easy walk to Damascus Gate.

Amir ibn al Aas St. (between Nablus Rd. and Saladin St.). ✆ **02/627-7232.** www.stgeorge landmark.com. 130 units. $200–$250 double. Rates include breakfast. **Amenities:** Business center, concierge, restaurants, rooftop pool and terrace, free Wi-Fi.

## INEXPENSIVE

**St. George's Cathedral Pilgrim Guesthouse ★**  Centered around a green and tranquil English garden, this Anglican/Episcopal establishment is welcoming to all travelers. In fact, we'd say that the service is what makes St. George's special: The tireless staff dispense savvy travel and dining advice from morning until night, always with a smile. Guest rooms, as you might imagine, are somewhat monastic, but they can vary in shape and size, so ask to see a few before you check in. All have air-conditioning, thankfully. If you like quiet, try for a room away from the bar or the street. The cavelike lounge (open in the evenings until midnight) is an unusual extra and contributes to the congenial, mildly English ambience.

20 Nablus Rd. (at Saladin St.). 🕿 **02/628-3302.** stgeorges.gh@j-diocese.org. 24 units. $150–$180 double. **Amenities:** Dining room, lounge, bar, Internet desk, A/C, free Wi-Fi. Bus: 27.

# WHERE TO EAT

Jerusalem has a huge selection of restaurants, dairy bars, lunch counters, snack shops, delicatessens, and cafes.

**In the Old City and East Jerusalem,** you'll find mostly Middle Eastern cuisine, including numerous snack stands and inexpensive Arab eateries. Pork is prohibited for Muslims and Jews, but you will find pork, shellfish and alcohol (forbidden to Muslims) in East Jerusalem restaurants catering to tourists or Christian Jerusalemites. There are no kosher restaurants in East Jerusalem or in the Old City except in the Jewish Quarter. Most Old City restaurants open daily from late morning to 5 or 6pm.

**In West Jerusalem,** the dining scene is quite different. There's not much authentic, ethnic dining, but West Jerusalem has an oversupply of French/Mediterranean restaurants overseen by talented, inventive chefs. These meals are not cheap, but almost all restaurants offer **incredible business lunch specials** from noon until 5 or 6pm that make them very affordable, at least at that time of day. You'll find pedestrian streets that are wall-to-wall eateries, but some of the best dining choices are in quiet, slightly out-of-the-way streets and in old Ottoman-era mansions surrounded by walled gardens. Almost every restaurant or cafe has a security guard at its entrance (and many add a small security charge that's worth the peace of mind).

## The Old City
### NEAR JAFFA GATE
#### Inexpensive
**Armenian Tavern** ★ ARMENIAN   Specializing in tasty home-style Armenian dishes flavored with traditional spices and sauces, this restaurant can be hard to find. Make the effort. You descend a steep flight of stairs to an atmospheric Crusader-era room decorated with hand-painted Armenian tiles. Soft Greek and Armenian music adds to the atmosphere. Frankly, we could—and often do—make a meal of the appetizers here, particularly the small, traditional meat pies, salads, and soups (try the pepper salad and the cucumber-and-yogurt salad). Israeli beer and a good selection of wine are served, and a $10 minimum order is required.

79 Armenian Orthodox Patriarchate Rd. (after entering Jaffa Gate, turn right at the Tower of David [Citadel]; continue straight; restaurant is on the right, down a flight of stairs). 🕿 **02/627-3854.** Reservations necessary Fri–Sat evenings. Main courses NIS 40–NIS 85. Tues–Sun 11am–10:30pm.

**Papa Andreas** ★ MIDDLE EASTERN   We'll be frank: The magnificent views of the Dome of the Rock are why you choose this rooftop terrace restaurant—it's a truly memorable spot for a meal. As for the menu, it offers standard Middle Eastern cuisine as well as a few Western-style dishes, such as pizza and pasta. Service is friendly, and you can usually linger over tea and baklava in the twilight amid evening prayer calls. There's also a large indoor dining room, but we'd suggest eating elsewhere if it's too

# Citywide Jerusalem Accommodations & Dining

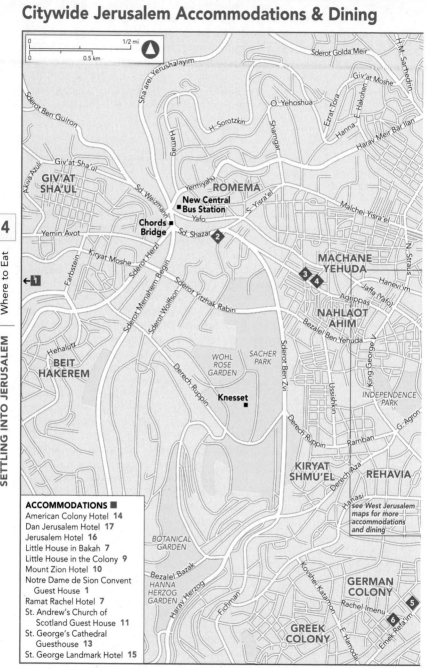

0    1/2 mi
0    0.5 km

Sderot Golda Meir

H.M. Sanhedrin

Giv'at Moshe

Sderot Ben Guiron

Sha'arei Yerushalayim

O. Yehoshua

Ezrat Tora

E. Hakohen

H. Sorotzkin

Hanna

Shamgar

Harav Meir Bar Ilan

Hamag

Giv'at Sha'ul

Akiva Azuli

**GIV'AT SHA'UL**

Sd. Weizmann

Yermiyahu

**ROMEMA**

S. Yisra'el

Malchei Yisra'el

N. Straus

**New Central Bus Station**

**Chords Bridge**

Yafo

Yemin Avot

Sd. Shazar

**2**

**MACHANE YEHUDA**

Hanevi'im

Kiryat Moshe

Sderot Herzl

**3** **4**

Jaffa (Yafo)

Farbstein

**1**

Sderot Menahem Begin

Sderot Yitzhak Rabin

Agrippas

**NAHLAOT AHIM**

Sderot Wolfson

Bezalel Ben Yehuda

King George V

Hehalutz

**BEIT HAKEREM**

Ussishkin

**INDEPENDENCE PARK**

**WOHL ROSE GARDEN**

**SACHER PARK**

Sderot Ben Zvi

Derech Ruppin

G. Agron

**Knesset**

Derech Ruppin

Ramban

**KIRYAT SHMU'EL**

**REHAVIA**

Derech Aza

Hanasi

see West Jerusalem maps for more accommodations and dining

**ACCOMMODATIONS** ■
American Colony Hotel **14**
Dan Jerusalem Hotel **17**
Jerusalem Hotel **16**
Little House in Bakah **7**
Little House in the Colony **9**
Mount Zion Hotel **10**
Notre Dame de Sion Convent Guest House **1**
Ramat Rachel Hotel **7**
St. Andrew's Church of Scotland Guest House **11**
St. George's Cathedral Guesthouse **13**
St. George Landmark Hotel **15**

**BOTANICAL GARDEN**

Bezalel Bazak

**HANNA HERZOG GARDEN**

Harav Herzog

Eichman

Kovshei Katamon

Rachel Imenu

E. Hamodai

**GERMAN COLONY**

**5**

**6**

Emek Refa'im

**GREEK COLONY**

**4**

SETTLING INTO JERUSALEM | Where to Eat

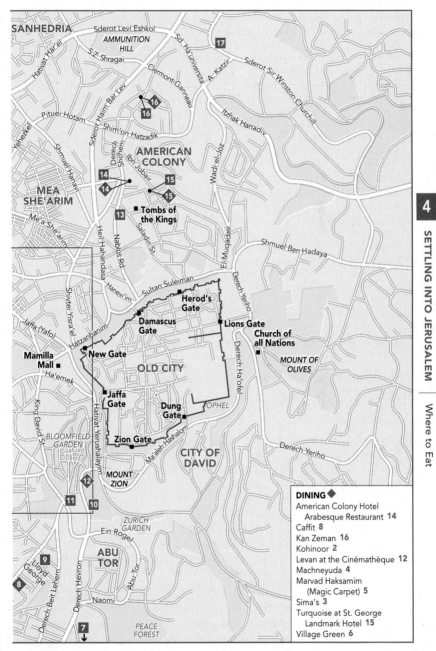

SANHEDRIA

Sderot Levi Eshkol

AMMUNITION HILL

S.-Z. Shragai

Clermont-Ganneau

17

Sd. Ha'universita

A. Katzir

Sderot Sir Winston Churchill

Pituei-Hotam

16

Shim'on Hatzadik

Itzhak Hanadiv

Hatvat Ha'el

Yehezkel

Shmuel Hanavi

Sderot Haim Bar Lev

Derech Shchem

Ibn Jubair

AMERICAN COLONY

Wadi el-Joz

MEA SHE'ARIM

14

15

15

Me'a She'arim

13

Tombs of the Kings

Saladin St.

El-Muqadasi

Shmuel Ben Hadaya

Heil-Hahandasa

Nablus Rd.

Hanevi

Sultan Suleiman

Herod's Gate

Damascus Gate

Lions Gate

Church of all Nations

Derech Yeriho

Shivtei-Yisra'el

Jaffa (Yafo)

Hatzanhanim

New Gate

Mamilla Mall

Ha'emek

OLD CITY

MOUNT OF OLIVES

King David St.

Hatvat Yerushalayim

Jaffa Gate

Dung Gate

Derech Ha'ofel

OPHEL

BLOOMFIELD GARDEN

Zion Gate

Ma'aleh Hashalom

CITY OF DAVID

Derech Yeriho

12

MOUNT ZION

11

10

ZURICH GARDEN

Ein-Rogel

ABU TOR

Lloyd George

9

8

Derech-Beit-Lehem

Abu-Tor

Derech-Hevron

Naomi

7

PEACE FOREST

DINING ◆
American Colony Hotel
  Arabesque Restaurant **14**
Caffit **8**
Kan Zeman **16**
Kohinoor **2**
Levan at the Cinémathèque **12**
Machneyuda **4**
Marvad Haksamim
  (Magic Carpet) **5**
Sima's **3**
Turquoise at St. George
  Landmark Hotel **15**
Village Green **6**

4 SETTLING INTO JERUSALEM | Where to Eat

47

# JERUSALEM'S top EATERIES

**Best for Special Occasions: Noya** (p. 53), run by a chef with golden hands, Noya offers generous portions of scrumptious, often inventive foods (the salt-baked chicken is to die for). The Business Lunch here is one of the best values in town. And it's kosher, so everyone can enjoy it. **Adom** (p. 59), a creative Mediterranean restaurant, is a close second with a menu that ranges from fine Galilee lamb to crab ravioli in Roquefort cheese sauce. As you may have guessed, Adom is not kosher.

**Best for Eye Candy:** In the Old City, **Papa Andreas** (p. 45) serves a Middle Eastern menu with a breathtaking view of the Dome of the Rock. It has no peer in this neighborhood. In the New City, **Lavan at the Cinematheque** (p. 60) has a terrace that overlooks a dazzling panorama of the Old City. Its food is of a higher quality than Papa Andreas', although we've found that we can linger longer over a meal in the Old City, which

is important when you've come for the views.

**Best Festive Atmosphere: Jerusalem Hotel** (p. 44), but that only holds for its special Friday dinners, which feature live Arabic and Middle Eastern music and lots of dancing (the waiters perform, but the customers usually end up joining the action, too).

**Best for Foodies:** Located near the city's food market, **Machneyuda** (p. 57) offers Jerusalem's most inventive, upscale menu (sweetbreads with chutney, labneh, and cornichons, anyone?). The tasting menu is highly recommended so that you can see the brilliant range of the chefs here.

**Best for Traditional Jerusalem Cuisine:** Presided over by the popular Moshe Basson, **Eucalyptus** (p. 50) offers a true taste of the city. Not only does Basson reconstruct authentic traditional recipes, he also loves to explain them to guests.

**4**

Where to Eat

SETTLING INTO JERUSALEM

cold for the roof; you come here for the view. The restaurant and terrace require a climb up four long flights of stairs.

64 Aftimos St., Muristan Bazaar, Christian Quarter. ℂ **02/628-4433.** Reserve if you want a table with a great view. Main courses NIS 39–NIS 85. Daily 9am–9pm.

## IN THE BAZAARS & NEAR DAMASCUS GATE

Although there are not many restaurants in this area, you can find plenty of Arabic pastry shops, simple eateries grilling whole chickens (which can be carved and packed in aluminum foil for takeout), and fresh juice bars. Wander from Damascus Gate along Suq Khan es-Zeit Street, which bears to the right at the fork.

### Inexpensive

**Abu Assab Refreshments ★★** FRESH JUICES    For decades, this little counter with three tiny tables has served up the best freshly squeezed orange, grapefruit, and carrot juice in town at very fair prices. You can't miss it in the main Suq Khan es-Zeit bazaar halfway from Damascus Gate to the Cardo. Cash only.

Suq Khan es-Zeit Bazaar. No phone. NIS 8–NIS 15. Sat–Thurs 9am–5pm, Fri 9am–3pm.

**Abu Shukri ★** HUMMUS    There's only one Abu Shukri, although the hummus here is so famous that other places as far away as the town of Abu Ghosh (p. 114), in the hills West of Jerusalem, have taken on the name, hoping to cash in on the legend. Abu Shukri has been immortalized in the pages of "The New York Times," "Condé Nast Traveler," and even "Playboy." Decor is nonexistent, and it's a good idea to bring

a supply of napkins, but the hummus is heavenly. It's served plain or with your choice of a dab of *fool* (brown beans), whole white garbanzo beans, or roasted pine nuts (a gourmet extra). You can also add a plate of chopped salad and falafel, grilled kabobs, or *kubbe* (fried cracked wheat dumpling stuffed with ground meat). Lots of pita to sop up your hummus is included in the price. Make sure to ask for it to be served heated: Cold pita is an insult to the meal. Sorry, cash only here.

63 Al Wad Rd. (near the 5th Station of the Cross, where the Via Dolorosa and Al Wad Rd. meet). ✆ **02/627-1538.** Main courses NIS 20–NIS 40. Daily 8am–4:30pm (sometimes later on Sat).

**Amigo Emil ★★** INTERNATIONAL/ARABIC   Located on the edge of the Christian Quarter, this spotless, pleasantly decorated place, set in an ancient structure, is a good choice for a tranquil break while exploring the bazaars. The menu is wide-ranging. You can order a fresh omelet, pasta, spicy chicken wings, an assortment of Middle Eastern salads, chicken breast stuffed with feta and herbs, or the highly recommended California/Arabic-style wraps and sandwiches. Great espresso is served, as are local treats, such as *karabij halab* (a crunchy biscuit with marshmallow cream made by the owner's family) or freshly squeezed tangerine juice. There's a wine and beer list, a bonus in the Old City. Major credit cards are accepted.

El Khanka St. Bazaar (left side as you go downhill; from David St., near Jaffa Gate, turn left onto Christian Quarter Rd.; at the end, turn left onto El Khanka). ✆ **02/628-8090.** Main courses NIS 32–NIS 70. Mon–Sat 10am–9pm.

**Families Restaurant ★** MIDDLE EASTERN   This spot, deep in the market, serves the best *shwarma* (seasoned meat cut from a spit) in the bazaar—you can order it in a pita sandwich or as a more expensive *shwarma* platter, or have it wrapped in flat, fluffy *laffa* bread. Whatever you choose, stay at the counter at the front of the restaurant while your *shwarma* is being prepared so that you can point out which of the wide range of salads and toppings you would like added to your order. We don't advise trying to eat a *shwarma* sandwich while walking in the crowded bazaar, so grab a table in the large, arched-ceiling dining room that dates from Crusader times. No alcoholic drinks. Cash only.

Suq Khan es-Zeit Bazaar (coming from the direction of Jaffa Gate, it will be on the right about 30m/98 ft. after the turn for Via Dolorosa). No phone. Main courses NIS 30–NIS 40; *shwarma* sandwich NIS 18. Daily 8am–6pm.

**Jaffar and Sons Pastry Cafe ★** ARABIC PASTRY   And this is the top place in the Old City for sampling *kanafeh,* a rich traditional Middle Eastern dessert made of mildly sweet cheese, grains, and pistachios baked in a very light honey syrup. You'll see flat, orange-colored slices of *kanafeh* in Jaffar's window being cut on large pizzalike trays. Purchase a ticket at the cashier's counter for an order of *kanafeh,* take a seat at a table (drinking glasses are communal—you'll probably prefer bottled soft drinks or water), and your order will soon be delivered. Decor is plain (think polished gray walls and Formica tables), but this is an authentic place filled with locals enjoying this much-loved treat. You can order takeout, but *kanafeh* is best fresh from the oven. Cash only.

Suq Khan es-Zeit Bazaar (from Damascus Gate, bear right at the fork in the road, and continue into the narrow bazaar; Jaffar is the 2nd large pastry shop with glass windows on the right). No phone. Items NIS 14. Daily 9am–5pm.

## THE JEWISH QUARTER

This part of the Old City is home to a number of kosher fast-food spots on Jewish Quarter Road, where you can have a bowl of soup (usually made from powder), a slice

## SABBATH dining

Kosher restaurants usually close by 2 or 3pm on Friday for Shabbat. The following nonkosher restaurants, described in detail in this chapter, have Friday evening or Saturday afternoon hours and provide a good variety of choices.

**In downtown West Jerusalem:** Barood (p. 51), Focaccia Bar (p. 52), the restaurant at the King David Street YMCA (p. 58), Spaghettim (p. 52), and Zuni (p. 53).

**In South Jerusalem:** Adom (p. 59) and Lavan (p. 60) at the Cinémathèque.

**In East Jerusalem:** Restaurants are open on Shabbat.

of kosher pizza, or a bagel at a shop at the Seven Arches, near the Burnt House. On Jewish Quarter Road you'll also find two (nonkosher) old-fashioned Arabic-style bread bakeries where you can buy warm, freshly baked pita and big sesame rolls, which are tasty to snack on as you explore the Old City. Ask the baker for a tiny, free package of *zataar* (local spices) to flavor the bread in Middle Eastern style.

**Keshet** ★ VEGETARIAN/DAIRY   With friendly management and freshly made food, this is the preeminent kosher choice in the Old City. It serves nongreasy potato latkes (pancakes), tasty quiches, salads, soups, omelets, and even fish dishes. There's cozy indoor seating (blessedly air-conditioned in summer) as well as outdoor tables overlooking bustling Hurva Square. Fresh fruit drinks and alcohol (including Golan wines) are served.

Tiferet Israel St. (in the corner of Hurva Sq.). © **02/628-7515.** Main courses NIS 40–NIS 65. Sun–Thurs 9am–7pm in summer, to 5 or 6pm in winter; Fri 9am–2pm.

## West Jerusalem

### AROUND MAMILLA MALL & JUST OUTSIDE JAFFA GATE
### Moderate

**Eucalyptus** ★★ JERUSALEM HOME-STYLE   Chef/owner Moshe Basson, who grew up on the southern edge of Jerusalem, has a stockpile of traditional family recipes and knows the wild herbs and plants that grow around the city like the back of his hand. His original little neighborhood eatery has now moved to this romantic, candle-lit spot in a picturesque enclave just outside the walls of the Old City. The menu includes an array of traditional soups, which you can sample in tiny espresso cups; local appetizers, such as stuffed sage leaves and figs stuffed with chicken in tamarind sauce (a favorite, and quite filling); or highly recommended medleys of small tapas-style salads and spreads. Main courses include such specialties as *ingria,* a sweet-and-sour meat and eggplant casserole, and *malouba,* a chicken/rice casserole served with great ceremony. When Moshe is present, he loves to explain the ingredients and preparation of his dishes, and hearing him do so is one of the delights of dining here. Traditional desserts (interesting but not lavish) are on offer, and sometimes complimentary samples of local *arak* (licorice liquor) are available. There's indoor and outdoor seating, and reservations are recommended.

14 Hativat Yerushalayim, Artists' Colony Hutzot Hayotzer (outside Old City, across the road and downhill from Jaffa Gate). © **02/624-4331.** Reservations recommended. Main courses NIS 80–NIS 140; tasting menus NIS 170–NIS 225. Sun–Thurs noon–11pm, Sat after Shabbat–11pm.

**4**

Where to Eat

SETTLING INTO JERUSALEM

## ZION SQUARE AREA: JAFFA ROAD, BEN-YEHUDA & YOEL SALOMON PEDESTRIAN MALLS

### Expensive

**Darna** ★★★ MOROCCAN   Owner Ilan Sibony, who came to Israel from Morocco in his youth, spared no effort or expense to create this charming, intimate Moroccan restaurant that offers food prepared according to standards of *kashrut.* The spiced barley and lamb soup served with dates or the *mezes* of interesting Moroccan salads (different from the local Palestinian and Israeli *mezes*) are wonderful ways to start a feast here. You also can't go wrong with the pastilla, a sweet phyllo pie of Cornish hen mixed with spices and delicate layers of egg white, almonds, and cinnamon. The choice of main courses is equally difficult, as all are scrumptious, from the traditional clay-pot cooked tagines (casseroles) of lamb, baked with dried fruits and vegetables, to chicken baked in olive and lemon sauce, to various couscous dishes. Unusual specialties include a rich but light *tagine* of brains with lemon, saffron, and egg. Service? It's downright graceful. For two people, soups, the *meze, pastilla,* and one main course should be adequate. This is one of the best dining experiences in Israel, so reservations are recommended.

3 Hyrcanos (Horkanos) St. (near Helene HaMalka St.). ✆ **02/624-5406.** Main courses NIS 100–NIS 170; business lunch NIS 80. Glatt kosher. Sun–Thurs 12:30–3:30pm and 6:30pm–12:30am, Sat after Shabbat–midnight. Light Rail to stop closest to Zion Sq.

### Moderate

**Barood Bar Restaurant** ★★ CONTINENTAL/SEPHARDIC   Barood is a great choice for a Friday night or Saturday afternoon meal, when few West Jerusalem restaurants are open. Late on Friday and Saturday nights, it's also a pleasant, low-key bar for drinks and meeting people (the bar offers a vast range of a drinks). There's occasional live music, and in good weather, tables are set up in the vine-covered Jerusalem Courtyard. As for the food, it's quite different from what you'll get at most other Israeli restaurants, featuring a daily changing menu of home-style choices, such as pork spareribs with a rosemary barbecue sauce, Balkan/Sephardic leek stew with meat and plums, or plates of crispy fried calamari.

Jerusalem Courtyard (enter through arch at 31 Jaffa Rd.). ✆ **02/625-9081.** Main courses NIS 60– NIS 100; complete lunch specials Sun–Thurs noon–5pm from NIS 55. Mon–Sat 12:30pm–1am. Light Rail to Safra Sq.

**Little Jerusalem Restaurant at Ticho House** ★★★ VEGETARIAN/DAIRY/ FISH   The food at this restaurant is among the very best in Jerusalem and lives up to its location in the historic, much-loved home of Abraham and Anna Ticho (p. 94). They were Jerusalem icons, famous for hosting lively evenings with artists, politicians, musicians, scientists, and philosophers. You'll feel like you, too, are one of their favored guests when you dine here, because every dish is prepared in a way that includes special, surprising twists. That's despite the fact that they seem, on the surface, to be fairly standard: salads, crepes and quiches, various sorts of pasta and fish. But the salads will be superfresh, the pastas innovative, and the fruits of the sea perfectly prepared. Don't be shy about bringing kids, as there's a children's menu. And if you're on a diet, ask for the low-calorie menu (also quite delish). You can dine inside Ticho House itself or in the large garden terrace. Four nights a week after 8:30pm, there are themed programs of live music (check the Ticho House website for the weekly schedule). Always call ahead for reservations. In the daytime, check out the special exhibits upstairs.

Abraham Ticho St. (off Ha Rav Kook St.). ✆ **02/624-4186.** www.go-out.com/ticho. Main courses NIS 45–NIS 98; light meals or brunch NIS 40–NIS 60. Sun–Thurs 10am–midnight, Fri 10am–2pm, Sat after Shabbat–11:45pm. Light Rail to King George St.

## Inexpensive

**Focaccia Bar ★★ ECLECTIC/MEDITERRANEAN**   A very popular place (especially on Shabbat) filled with travelers, families, and young Jerusalemites, Focaccia Bar serves pizzas and focaccias baked in a traditional brick *taboon* oven. But there's much more on the menu, ranging from heaping stir-fried salads laced with chicken or goose breast to excellent calamari or seafood pasta in a spicy Indian-style coconut sauce. The setting is a 19th-century Jerusalem stone cottage with a large dining garden (covered and heated in winter). Good wines and desserts round out the menu. Reservations are useful here, especially for Shabbat. *Tip:* In 2013, a kosher version of Focaccia Bar with an inventive menu opened in the German Colony at 35 Emek Refaim St. (✆ **02/538-7132**). It offers a similar menu but is closed for Shabbat.

4 Rabbi Akiba St. (off Hillel St.). ✆ **057/944-3123** or 02/624-2273. Main courses NIS 40–NIS 80. Daily 10am–2am.

**Kangaroo ★★ GEORGIAN/RUSSIAN**   Hidden on a quaint pedestrian street, this charming, family-run restaurant serves authentic, home-style Georgian cuisine. The food is rustic, hearty, and intricately spiced with complex sauces, laced with finely ground walnuts and herbs. The menu ranges from dumpling-filled soups to hefty meat pies and rich lamb stews that are especially great in winter. But an absolute must is *khachapuri*, a cheese-and-egg puff-pastry dish that's rich, delicate, and made on the spot. With a soup and salad, a *khachapuri* is a good choice for a lighter meal or lunch. There's an outdoor terrace for summer dining.

Ma'a lot Nahalat Shiva St. (btw. Yoel Salomon and Rivlin sts.). ✆ **02-625/0618.** Main courses NIS 45–NIS 80. Sun–Thurs noon–10pm, Fri noon–3pm. Light Rail to King George St.

**Shanty ★★ INTERNATIONAL**   This intimate pub is loved by locals for its well-stocked bar and trendy, imaginative menu that interprets dishes from all over the world. It's a place where you can linger and talk over a slow meal of fabulous spiced sweet potato soup and *pad Thai* noodles, baby-back ribs, or a generous, lightly stir-fried Mediterranean salad loaded with herbs, spices, and chunks of succulent chicken. There's a wide range of tapaslike dishes and appetizers and even a few desserts to accompany conversation. It's tricky to find but definitely worth the effort.

4 Nahalat Shiva. (On Yoel Salomon St., turn into the alleyway to the side of the Ceramics gallery at 11 Yoel Salomon. At the end of the alley, turn left into the courtyard. The security guard for Shanty, Mike's Place, and Tmol Shilshom Bookstore Cafe is at the end of the courtyard.) ✆ **02/624-3434.** Main courses NIS 38–NIS 90. Daily 7pm–after midnight.

**Spaghettim ★ ITALIAN**   Serving spaghetti and pasta with all kinds of interesting tomato, olive oil, or cream-based sauces, this is an affordable choice that has the added benefit of being open on the Sabbath. Dishes are filled with generous amounts of fresh herbs and vegetables; but more unusual choices are also recommended, such as spaghetti and chicken in an Indian-style coriander sauce. The mint-filled Panzanella salads and a loaf of freshly baked house bread (extra charge) are worthwhile additions to any meal. The restaurant is located in a spacious, contemporary room inside Beit Agron, the modern Journalists' Center. Whole-wheat pasta and nonpasta dishes are available for those who want a healthy choice.

Inside Beit Agron, 35 Hillel St. ✆ **02/623-5547.** Main courses NIS 45–NIS 100; 10 percent student discount. Daily noon–midnight.

**Tmol Shilshom Bookstore Cafe ★★ VEGETARIAN**   A Jerusalem institution, thick with atmosphere, this is one of the best vegetarian choices in town. It's also an

Saturday night is big for dining out in Israel, but think twice before booking a top table at a kosher restaurant, because you won't find restaurants at their best. Many kosher restaurants prepare food on Thursday, when they receive their last batch of fresh fish and vegetables before the weekend, so their staff won't have to work on the Sabbath. If you're going to splurge at a top restaurant, do it midweek.

unofficial social club, a place where people come during off-hours to sit and talk over coffee or a glass of wine. Many stay through dinner so they can order steaming bowls of soups, salads, a slice of hefty lasagna, or *shakshuka* (a spicy Jerusalem home-style tomato-and-egg casserole). The daily menu ranges from excellent fillet of Denis from the Red Sea served on a bed of couscous to homemade bread with lox and cream cheese. Fabulous cakes and Ben & Jerry's ice creams are added pluses; recently, the chef has been printing out her recipes for such treats as crispy quinoa cakes as an added incentive to stop by. Set in a 19th-century house with rooms lined with used books, the cafe sponsors a program of readings and talks in Hebrew and English on some nights, music on others. Check the monthly schedule of events.

5 Yoel Salomon St. (in rear courtyard of Yoel Salomon St.; enter from alley at 11 Yoel Salomon St., next to Ceramics Gallery; cafe is at far left and upstairs). ✆ **02/623-2758.** www.tmol-shilshom.co.il. Main courses NIS 40–NIS 90. Sun–Thurs 9am–after midnight, Fri 9am–1pm, Sat after Shabbat.

**Village Green** ★ VEGETARIAN   A small, self-service *mehadrin* kosher cafeteria, Village Green offers up top-quality salads and hot choices, such as spaghetti, brown rice, steamed vegetables, and ratatouille (sold by weight). You'll also find delicious, hearty soups, tofu and buckwheat burgers, lasagnas, and veggie pies. The staff speaks English and is very helpful. A second branch with more dining space is located in the German Colony at 5 Rachel Imenu St. (✆ **02/650-0106**).

19 Emek Refaim. ✆ **02/566-0011.** Full meal NIS 30–NIS 70. Sun–Thurs 9am–10pm, Fri 11:30am–3pm. Light Rail to Safra Sq.

**Zuni Restaurant/Café/Bar** ★ FRENCH/INTERNATIONAL   This stylish, pub-like space in the upstairs rooms of an old stone building on the Yoel Salomon pedestrian street is conveniently open 24/7. It's good for a late morning brunch, soup, coffee, sandwich, quiche, or a late evening talk and drink. After 5pm, more ambitious dishes are served, such as seafood risotto and a grilled breast of chicken with a green salad on the side. There's nothing too exotic, but the round-the-clock hours are unique.

15 Yoel Salomon St. ✆ **02/625-7776.** Main courses NIS 60–NIS 130. Lunch (until 5pm) is 30 percent off the regular menu price. Daily 24 hr. Light Rail to Safra Sq.

## OFF & ON SHLOMZION HAMALKA STREET

**Shlomzion HaMalka Street,** running south for 2 blocks from Jaffa Road to David Street, is lined with very stylish restaurants and bars. Restaurants here pride themselves on their friendly vibe. Late on Thursday, Friday, and Saturday nights, the establishments of the street sometimes morph into a wall-to-wall party.

### Moderate

**Noya** ★★★ CONTINENTAL/MODERN ISRAELI   A triple threat, Noya is elegant, affordable, and kosher, which in this town is an unbeatable combination. It also

# coffee & PEOPLE-WATCHING

Jerusalem's cafe life is thriving. All over town, you'll find happily caffeinated customers at bustling cafes, downing cup after cup, arguing, laughing, and living a life that's downright Parisian. The draw ain't just brewed beans: Customers at these places accompany their java with giant, eminently shareable salads as well as quiches, pasta dishes, soups, sandwiches, and rich desserts. *Tip:* If you *just* want coffee, make sure there are no minimum charges.

Here's where to go if you'd like to join the scene:

o A great cup of coffee, probably the best in town, can be found 2 blocks south of Ben-Yehuda Mall, at **Aroma,** on the corner of Hillel and Rabbi Akiva streets. It's a busy counter with a few tables, but it's a Jerusalem institution, serving inexpensive sandwiches as well and open 24/7. Other branches are at 34 Emek Refaim St. in the German Colony and on Jaffa Road.

o **Cafe Rimmon,** at the lower end of Ben-Yehuda Mall, is an ideal spot for watching Jerusalem life pass by. Here, gaping is more important than imbibing.

o **Hillel Espresso Café** offers an abundance of sidewalk and indoor tables and is known for its excellent salads, sandwiches, quiches, and desserts. It's located in Jerusalem's free Wi-Fi access zone, so tables tend to be dotted with laptops.

o **Tmol Shilshom Bookstore Cafe** is located a block to the east, on the corner of Jaffa Road and Helene HaMalka Street, at 5 Yoel Salomon Mall (p. 52). Tmol Shilshom is a most atmospheric retreat. Its walls are lined with books, and its patrons seem unusually scholarly as they sip coffee, write letters, and read.

o **El Dorado** (128 Saladin St.) is East Jerusalem's trendiest coffee shop, owned by a family that has procured coffee for generations. People actually dress up to sip coffee here.

o Directly across the street from Damascus Gate is the upstairs section of a modern cafe called **Seasons,** which offers a panoramic view of the Old City along with java.

offers a raft of well-prepared, sometimes unusual meat dishes, such as salt-baked chicken and entrecote steak stuffed with lamb. Vegetarians and those who eat fish are well taken care of, too, with such options as stuffed sardines in olive and pepper sauce or root vegetable raviolis. And the focaccia here is legendary. If you're an early-bird type, know that the excellent lunch special is served all the way until 5pm, making it one of the best deals in town.

3 Shlomzion HaMalka St. (off Jaffa Rd.). ☏ **06/625-7311** or 057/944-3403. Main courses NIS 60–NIS 190; complete lunch specials until 5pm NIS 60–NIS 80; complete dinner specials NIS 105–NIS 145. Sun–Thurs noon–midnight, Fri noon–3pm.

**Sea Dolphin (Dolphin Yam)** ★★ FISH/SEAFOOD   Top-quality fresh seafood is not the norm in Jerusalem, except at really expensive restaurants. Moderately priced Sea Dolphin is the exception to that rule, owned by a family that's been bringing fresh fish to Jerusalem for decades. Included in the price of your main course is a (bottomless) *meze* of 10 Middle Eastern salads and appetizers, but there are also good seafood soups and seafood appetizers you can add a la carte. You can order your fish fried, baked, or grilled (your waiter will suggest which would be best for your choice). There's a selection of intriguing sauces, but you might ask for the sauce to be served on the side so you can savor a true taste of the sea. A few meat and vegetarian options are served, and there's a good selection of lunchtime specials.

9 Ben Shetah St. ⓒ **02/623-2272.** Reservations recommended. Main courses NIS 65–NIS 120; lunch specials (Sun–Fri noon–5pm) NIS 60–NIS 80. Daily noon–midnight. Light Rail to Safra Sq.

## Inexpensive

**Marakiyah ★★** SOUP   Loved by students, artists, musicians, and travelers of all stripes, the Marakisyh, with its attic-sale decor, looks like an eatery in San Francisco or New York's East Village. "Marak" means soup, and this little local institution started out as a soups-only eatery that has expanded over the years to include great *shak-shouka* (a spicy tomato-and-egg casserole) and a few other simple additions. Soups come with lots of bread and pesto; the choices are all vegetarian and vary each night, but standards include sweet potato; lentil with wine; spicy Yemenite tomato, onion, and cheese; and tomato with anise. Teas, coffee, wines, and beer are served. There's often live music Monday and Wednesday nights after 10pm. The staff is mostly students and always helpful. Cash only.

4 Koresh St. (behind the Jaffa Rd. Central Post Office). ⓒ **02/625-7797.** Soup and bread NIS 30; half-liter of wine NIS 20. Sun–Thurs 7pm–3am, Sat after Shabbat–3am. Light Rail to Safra Sq.

# WEST OF KING GEORGE V AVENUE
## Moderate

**Chakra ★★★** ECLECTIC   Chef Ilan Garousi's mastery of wildly varied cooking techniques, his deep understanding of spices, and his endless energy combine to give this sleek restaurant a menu that's inventive, cosmopolitan, and absolutely delicious (it also changes with the seasons). Expect scrumptious seafood dishes cooked and served in copper pans, Stroganoff of beef filet in cream sauce, or his herb and goat cheese *capelletti,* an unofficial signature dish. The choices are so tempting that Chakra offers a tasting menu for NIS 230 per person (minimum of two people), an assortment of other prix-fixe menus, and Saturday luncheon specials. The alcohol and wine list are as extensive as the food choices. Chakra is usually busy, but the atmosphere is party-like. Come with friends so you can sample and share. Reservations are necessary, because this is one of Israel's best restaurants at any price.

41 King George St. ⓒ **02/625-2733.** www.chakra-rest.com. Main courses NIS 75–NIS 125. Daily 7pm–after midnight, Sat 12:30–4pm. Light Rail to King George St.

## Inexpensive

**Heimische Essen** EAST EUROPEAN JEWISH   Traditional East European home-style restaurants are hard to find in Jerusalem, but this neighborhood take-away place, with a few tables on the side, fits the bill. Not to be confused with a New York–style deli, Heimische Essen doesn't do pastrami. Instead, it specializes in matzo ball soup, baked chicken, Sabbath *cholent* (casserole), potato kugel, gefilte fish, and other home-cooking classics. And there are days when an old-fashioned, nourishing meal of a bowl of soothing chicken soup can be a godsend. Luncheon specials drop the price for that meal; the take-away option can be useful on Friday before Shabbat.

19 Keren Kayemet St. (Keren Kayemet St. is off King George, halfway between Ben-Yehuda and Aza [Gaza] sts.). ⓒ **02/563-9845.** Main courses NIS 40–NIS 60. Sun–Thurs 11am–9pm, Fri 9am–2pm. Light Rail to King George St.

# street MEALS

Want to grab a quick bite, on the run? Here are some suggestions:

**Falafel**   You can find this dish almost everywhere, but we're partial to the **Yemenite falafel counter** on the corner of Agrippas Street and the wide, uncovered pedestrian street of the Machane Yehuda market (on your right as you walk up Agrippas St. from King George; it's the first broad market street past the covered market area). It serves well-spiced falafel and all kinds of salads, pickled vegetables, sauces, and condiments. For a bit extra, you can ask for your falafel to be wrapped inside an enormous Iraqi pita instead of a regular pita, which makes for a very filling meal. Best of all, you can carry your sandwich across Agrippas Street and through one of the entrance portals to the old Nahalat neighborhood, where you'll find a small playground with benches. There, under the scrutiny of the local cats, you can sit down and enjoy your meal (but bring your own napkins!). For added flavor, slice a few little plum or cherry tomatoes from the market into your sandwich.

A second, and similarly nameless, choice sits on the corner of Agrippas and King George streets, where you'll find a large and very busy **falafel and shwarma place**. Here you'll have to eat standing on the sidewalk like a normal Israeli (hopefully you've acquired the local skill of not dripping sauce all over yourself or having your sandwich land in the gutter). The falafels are solid, and turnover is fast, which ensures freshness. It's open until 10pm or later from Sunday to Thursday (until 2pm Fri).

**Shwarma   Moshiko's,** at the lower end of the Ben-Yehuda Mall, makes Jerusalem's finest *shwarma* sandwiches, hands down. The quality of the meat is tops. Portions, spicing, and accompanying salads are excellent. And if you can nail down one of Moshiko's outdoor tables, you can people-watch while you nosh without running the risk of losing half your sandwich on the ground.

Prefer a bit more heat in your meat? The **Gate Cafe,** just inside the Damascus Gate, on an upstairs covered terrace on the left, serves fabulous, extra-spicy hand-built *shwarma*, a kind of *shwarma* not made on a spit. It's different, authentic, and quite memorable.

## Moderate

**Kohinoor ★★★ KOSHER INDIAN**   With a relaxed but elegant ambience, this kosher branch of Tel Aviv's famous Tandoori Restaurant is a treat for all visitors, offering an exceptional chance for kosher travelers to sample one of the world's great cuisines. Start your meal with zafrani lassi, a refreshing chilled drink normally based on Indian "yogurt" and fruit, but here based on soy, as meat is served on the menu. All traditional cream-based sauces are brilliantly recreated using nondairy ingredients. There are examples of many regional cuisines here, including rich South Indian dishes with spicy coconut milk sauces, exotic vegetarian village dishes, and meat dishes with lamb (no beef is served). You can have a simple meal or a banquet fit for a maharajah. Dishes tend to be moderately spiced, but if you prefer fiery traditional Indian seasoning, just let the staff know. You may also want to ask the staff if you can take home a menu, as the explanations of how each dish is made on it could serve (almost) as a recipe book. Reservations recommended.

**Bagels** You may be surprised to find that the doughy rounds we're used to in the United States taste far more breadlike in Israel. But that doesn't mean they're not tasty, especially those at **Bagel Corner,** 41 Jaffa Rd. (ⓒ **02/624-4115;** Sun–Thurs 24 hr., Fri until 2pm, Sat after Shabbat), right at Zion Square. It sells a wide variety of freshly made bagels, ranging from onion and garlic to whole-wheat and cheese, for approximately NIS 5 each. As in the U.S., they can be "supersized" with the addition of various types of cream cheeses, lox, and other fillings. In the Jewish Quarter of the Old City, you can pick up your bagels at a similar shop, set right beside the Seven Arches, near the Burnt House Museum.

**Burekas** (phyllo-dough pastries) The block of shops on Haneviim Street opposite Havatzelet Street includes a bakery with a sidewalk window counter where you can order flaky, fresh-from-the-oven, potato, spinach, or cheese *burekas,* as well as miniature cheese or fruit Danish-style pastries. You can find *burekas* throughout the city, but they're always more of a treat when fresh.

The **Machane Yehuda market** is another good place for freshly baked *burekas,* as is the **English Bakery,** on Jaffa Road opposite Zion Square.

**Stuffed Breads** The Middle Eastern answer to pizza, these piping hot breads are stuffed with savory cheeses and herbed vegetables. Tops for this treat is **Samboosak Bakery/Café,** on Jaffa Road next to the Coffee Bean on the corner of Helene HaMalka Street.

**Ice Cream & Frozen Yogurt** Ah, where should we start on this one? There are so many choices. You might try **Dr. Lek,** at the end of Yoel Salomon near Hillel Street. This local chain made its name by flavoring its ice creams with organic ingredients, such as dates, mangoes, and Bourbon vanilla pods from Madagascar. At the corner of Lunz and Ben-Yehuda streets, you'll find **a popular place** (no name, but you won't be able to miss it) that offers a choice of 25 kinds of fruits, nuts, and chocolates that staff can whip into a fresh frozen yogurt for you on the spot. Finally, **Aldo Ice Cream,** 21 Ben-Yehuda St., 40 Jaffa Rd., and 46 Emek Refaim St., in the German Colony, uses ingredients prepped in Italy but made fresh daily (without preservatives) in Israel. It's a chain, but a good one, with shops throughout Israel.

Jaffa Rd. (in the Crowne Plaza Hotel). ⓒ **02/658-8867.** Main courses NIS 40–NIS 90; all-you-can-eat lunch buffet (Sun–Thurs noon–3pm) NIS 69. Sun–Fri noon–3:30pm, Sun–Thurs 6pm–midnight, Sat after Shabbat–midnight. Light Rail, or any bus to Central Bus Station.

## AGRIPPAS STREET & MACHANE YEHUDA

Walk a few blocks up Agrippas Street, and you'll find yourself surrounded by no-frills restaurants and hole-in-the-wall spots serving generous portions of grilled meats, shashlik (chunks of meat on a skewer), and kabobs (ground meat on a skewer). Don't be afraid to try semi-nameless holes-in-the-wall. Any place that survives in this competitive market area has to be good!

### Expensive

**Machneyuda Restaurant** ★★★ MODERN ISRAELI Named for the way locals pronounce Machane Yehuda Market (and with a decor that purposefully looks like a market warehouse), this is the hottest upscale restaurant in Jerusalem. The creation of three talented young chef/owners, it's a loud, bustling place—so not the choice if you're hoping for an intimate, romantic meal. But if you're interested in modern gastronomy, try to nab seats at the bar overlooking the kitchen so you can watch the three chefs working, joking, and (when we were there last) dancing around at their stations. The menu is written on a board each day and always features what's freshest at the market, often in zany concoctions. On our last visit, we were lucky enough to try an appetizer of Blue Fin fish with watermelon, purple foie gras, and sea bream on fresh buffalo yogurt with Swiss chard; and a special market stew that bubbled all-day long until it was meltingly tender. First and main courses are a must if you really want the experience here; don't worry, portions are not huge. Although the restaurant is not kosher, it's closed on Shabbat. Make reservations well in advance.

10 Beit Yaacov St. © **02/533-3442** or 053/809-4897. www.2eat.co.il. Main courses NIS 80–NIS 180. Sun–Thurs 12:30–4pm and 6:30pm to last customer, Fri 11:30am–3:30pm, Sat after Shabbat to last customer.

### Inexpensive

**Sima's** ★ MIDDLE EASTERN    Sima's is legendary throughout Israel for its fabulous seasoned *me'orav Yerushalmi* (Jerusalem mixed grill), an *a la plancha* combination of succulent pieces of lamb, chicken, and organ meats served on a platter, with chips, salad, olives, and pickles. There's also a less-expensive NIS 38 sandwich inside a large pita (order a small tomato salad on the side to add to the sandwich). When Sima's is busy, you must order a platter meal rather than a sandwich to qualify for table service. To our mind, Sima's secret spice recipe is unequaled, but **Sami's**, its slightly less-legendary next-door competitor, has its own committed following. If Sima's is too crowded, don't feel too put out if you end up at Sami's. Cash only.

82 Agrippas St. No phone. Main courses NIS 40–NIS 70. Sun–Thurs 9am–11pm, Fri 9am–1pm, Sat after Shabbat–midnight. Light Rail to Machane Yehuda.

## NEAR THE YMCA & KING DAVID HOTEL
### Expensive

**Scala Chef Kitchen & Bar** ★★ CONTEMPORARY MEDITERRANEAN    Chef Oren Yerushalmi trained at Tel Aviv's legendary Catit Restaurant, and he's combined Catit's lavishness with his own unique and fearlessly complex touch. The main courses are exquisitely presented and strong on intricate taste constructions, such as pan-seared sea fish fillets on roasted eggplant with za'atar (Arabic spices), wrapped in pasta with fresh tomato and special herbed olive oil. Meat dishes have a rustic feel, such as a winter stew of lamb tongue, meats, and legumes or melt-in-your-mouth short ribs. The decor is understated, and service is intelligent and discrete. Carefully chosen boutique Israeli wines are offered by the glass and bottle. Reservations are necessary.

In the David Citadel Hotel, 7 King David St. © **02/621-1111** daytime, or 621-2030. www.thedavid citadel.com. Main courses NIS 100–NIS 180. Sun–Thurs 6pm–11pm; bar opens at 5:30pm.

### Moderate

**International Restaurant at the YMCA** ★ CONTINENTAL    We'll be blunt: The food here is solid but not exceptional. People generally come for a light bite so they can enjoy the ambience and the panoramic view of Jerusalem from the YMCA's landmark tower. The dining terrace is lovely, but the indoor dining room, with its Islamic Art Deco style and Ottoman-Turkish fireplace, is over-the-top fabulous. I'd say it looks like a set from a film about the British Mandate. Reservations are recommended in the evenings.

26 King David St. © **02/623-1154.** Main courses (which include side dishes) NIS 65–NIS 110. Daily 8am–midnight. Bus: 6 or 18.

**Te'enim Vegetarian Cuisine** ★ VEGETARIAN   Located in the Zionist Confederation House (just behind the King David Hotel, with fine views of the Old City walls), this is Jerusalem's gourmet all-vegetarian restaurant. Chef Patrick Melki, who comes from the south of France, can make his carefully chosen ingredients sing with purity, but his menu also includes an array of special dishes from different parts of the world, each served on a different day of the week. Desserts are worthwhile here and run from an unusual eggplant and honey creation to sorbets.

In the Zionist Confederation House, 12 Emile Botta St. (from King David St., follow Emil Botta St. past parking lot; look for sign on right to Zionist Confederation House). ℰ **02/625-1967.** Main courses NIS 45–NIS 70. Sun–Thurs noon–11pm. Bus: 6 or 18.

## South Jerusalem
### NEAR THE CINAMATHEQUE, FIRST TRAIN STATION & GERMAN COLONY
### Moderate

**Adom** ★★★ FRENCH/MEDITERRANEAN   Long a favorite nonkosher option, in 2013 Adom moved from its cozy, atmospheric downtown site to a new, upscale designer location in the renovated Ottoman-era First Train Station. And with this move, the ambience and food changed, too. The seasonally changing chef menu is still among the best in town, although a bit less daring and unique than it used to be. However, it's still a more-than-worthwhile choice. Standouts to look for include a heavenly gnocchi with porcini and chestnuts; pasta and calamari in curry and apple sauce; seaweed risotto with calamari and split blue crab; and a special housewarming gift to Adom from Meir Adoni (creator of Catit, Tel Aviv's most legendary gourmet eatery) in the form of his own recipe for veal sweetbreads. In winter, the palate-warming chestnut soup appetizer reappears on the menu and must be tried. After 10pm, when Adom becomes more of a wine bar and pick-up spot, a menu of tapas-style dishes and half-portions becomes available. The bar is excellent, as are desserts.

4 Remez St. (in the First Train Station complex). ℰ **02/624-6242.** Reservations recommended. Main courses NIS 65–NIS 140. Sun–Fri 6:30pm–after midnight, Sat 1pm–after midnight.

### Inexpensive

**Caffit** ★ VEGETARIAN CAFE   As the grandparent of the many vegetarian eateries in the gentrified German Colony, Caffit has a panache that keeps locals, travelers, and Jerusalemites from other parts of town coming from early morning to after midnight. The excellent dairy menu is made up of hefty herbed salads, sweet potato pancakes with sour cream, quiches, pastas, and crepes as well as dinner courses, such as pan-fried fish. A selection of wines and alcohol is served. Caffit is such an institution that it was invited to open a branch (ℰ **02/648-0003**) in Jerusalem's Botanical Gardens. Both restaurants offer the same menu.

35 Emek Refaim St. ℰ **02/563-5284.** Main courses NIS 40–NIS 100. Sun–Thurs 7am–2am, Fri 7am–2pm, Sat after Shabbat. Bus: 4 or 18.

**Marvad Haksamim (Magic Carpet)** ★ ISRAELI   This popular place has been serving up traditional home-style food in generous portions for great prices since 1948. Decor is absolutely no-frills, and the food makes no pretense to gourmet standards, but the wide-ranging menu comprises dishes that draw from Israel's multiethnic melting pot. Start with warm, flaky Yemenite *salouf,* a flat bread, served with traditional tomato puree dip, and then go on to a Kurdish dumpling soup, East European liver blintzes, a Viennese-style chicken schnitzel, a Middle Eastern plate of grilled lamb or chicken kabobs (the chicken is better), or a Moroccan couscous, all served with side orders of veggies, potatoes, pasta, or salad. At lunch or dinnertime, there's often a line, but turnover is fast and the wait is seldom long. Takeout is available.

42 Emek Refaim St. ℭ **02/567-0007.** Main courses NIS 45–NIS 90. Sun–Thurs 10am–11pm, Fri 10am–3pm. Bus: 4 or 18.

### Inexpensive
**Lavan at the Cinémathèque** ★★ ITALIAN/MEDITERRANEAN    You have to be exceptional *and* affordable to be the restaurant of Jerusalem's world-class Cinémathèque. Lavan fits this bill and comes with dramatic views of the Old City walls to boot. The menu is dotted with toothsome salads, focaccia, cheeses, and sandwiches to be snacked on by film buffs. But people mostly come to enjoy the extraordinary panorama and to try the delicious, seasonally changing dinner choices—yam soup, lamb and walnut ravioli, veal fillet with wild mushroom risotto, or a finely prepared fillet of salmon were some recent choices. There's a schedule of live music some nights, a full bar, and tempting desserts to accompany after-show conversations. *Tip:* Call ahead to reserve a view-rich terrace table. Advance arrangement must also be made for those who cannot climb the Cinémathèque's many access stairs.

Hebron Rd. (at the B'nei Brit Overhead Pedestrian Bridge). ℭ **02/673-7393.** www.jer-cin.org.il. Main courses NIS 60–NIS 120; light meals NIS 45–NIS 70. Daily 10am–after midnight. Bus: 6, 7, 8, 21, 38 or 48 to the old First Train Station, or 4 or 18 and ask for the stop nearest the Cinémathèque.

## EAST JERUSALEM
### Expensive
**American Colony Hotel Arabesque Restaurant** ★ CONTINENTAL/MIDDLE EASTERN    The American Colony hotel, looking like a vision from "Masterpiece Theater," has been used as the locale for numerous films. The generous half-Continental, half–Middle Eastern **Saturday luncheon buffet** at the hotel's Arabesque Room is a Jerusalem institution that offers nonguests the chance to experience the hotel's romantic, old-timey ambience without actually staying here. A delicious, fresh whole chilled salmon is often the centerpiece of this all-you-can-eat spread that stretches across many tables. For other meals, the Arabesque Restaurant can only be considered average. Reservations are needed for the Arabesque Room, especially for the Saturday buffet.

Off Nablus Rd. ℭ **02/627-9777.** Main courses NIS 80–NIS 150; Sat buffet NIS 187. Daily noon–3pm and 6:30–10:30pm. Bus: 27.

### Moderate
**Turquoise Lebanese Restaurant** ★★★ MIDDLE EASTERN    The highly refined recipes of Lebanese-style cooking are considered to be the *haute cuisine* of the Arabic world, and that's what's on offer at Turquoise, open since 2012. Talented Chef Kamal Hashlamon is at the helm (he trained at Mul Yam, Tel Aviv's famed seafood restaurant), and he has created a menu that's both sophisticated and traditional. In addition to Kamal's exquisite but more familiar hot and cold *meze* and salad dishes (including a marvelous *tabbouleh*), look for such choices as *kibbe nayeh* (a kind of steak tartar made with bulgur and spearmint) or *bathenjan,* a delicious hot appetizer of eggplant, fried bread, Lebanese country yogurt, and tahini touched with lemon and pomegranate, to which pieces of seasoned lamb can be added. Main courses include unusual oven-baked meat and chicken dishes, grilled meats, and scrumptious home-style dishes, such as lamb meatballs in a minty tomato sauce. With its sweeping vistas of Jerusalem from its location on the gardened rooftop terrace of the St. George Landmark Hotel,

this is one of those rare restaurants where the food matches the superb views. Reservations are recommended.

In the St. George Landmark Hotel, 6 Amr Ibn Al A'as St. © **02/627-7332.** Meze and first courses NIS 20–NIS 60; main courses NIS 70–NIS 125. Daily 1–10:30pm. Light Rail to Damascus Gate. Taxi is best if coming from West Jerusalem.

### Inexpensive

**Kan Zeman** ★★ MIDDLE EASTERN   Kan Zeman shines on Friday evenings, when popular singers accompany live Arabic music and diners pack every table. Local families with kids, young East Jerusalem couples, tourists, waiters, and cooks often dance in the aisles, and the whole place rocks well into the evenings. Monday nights offers quieter, more traditional live music without vocalists. But even if you can't make it on those evenings, this charming, vine-covered garden restaurant (it's heated in winter) rewards customers. The menu is a moderately priced mix of Continental and Middle Eastern dishes, all expertly cooked; the house specialty is a deliciously seasoned chicken *shwarma* (NIS 45), served with freshly chopped salad. In 2013, a special Ramadan menu was inaugurated, with traditional lamb, chicken, and vegetarian dishes cooked in clay pots and local *tagine* stews, all available most nights of the year with advance request. Reservations are required for music nights, as is a minimum dinner order. As the restaurant is Christian-owned, alcohol is served.

In the Jerusalem Hotel, 4 Antara Ben Shadad St. (on a side street off Nablus Rd., facing the north side of the Egged East Bus Terminal). © **02/628-3282.** Reservations required Fri night. Main courses NIS 38–NIS 100. Daily 11am–11pm. Light Rail to Damascus Gate.

# JERUSALEM NIGHTLIFE

Israel has long been known for the high quality of its musicians, and the recent wave of Russian immigrants has led to an even greater embarrassment of riches. Classical music lovers will discover new and remarkable artists performing everywhere, from concert halls and clubs to street corners and pedestrian malls. Also watch for **English Theater productions** listed in the Friday editions of "The Jerusalem Post" and "Haaretz" newspapers.

*Note:* Jerusalem's two main **ticket agencies** are **Klaim,** 12 Shamai St. (© 02/622-2333; www.klaimonline.co.il), and **Bimot,** 8 Shamai St. (© 02/624-0896; www.bimot.co.il/eng).

*Additional Note:* To find out what's going on in town, look in the Friday edition of "The Jerusalem Post," "Haaretz," and in the monthly **"Calendar of Events,"** which you can pick up free at the Tourist Information Office. If you have a student card, bring it; at times, you may be given a discount.

## Performance Centers

**Beit Shmuel/Center for Progressive Judaism** ★ PERFORMING ARTS VENUE   Performances here offer the best in contemporary and popular Israeli singers and musicians, ethnic music, readings and lectures, and dance and theater performances. In summer, concerts are held in the outdoor courtyard; always bring something warm to put on, because Jerusalem can get downright chilly at night. Shama'a St. (off King David St.). © **02/620-3455** or 02/620-3456. www.beitshmuel.com. Bus: 6, 18, or 21.

**Bible Lands Museum** ★★★ PERFORMING ARTS VENUE   Famous for a wide range of Saturday evening concerts, the Bible Lands Museum often includes wine and cheese in the admission price. You'll need a taxi to get here before buses start running. Museum Row, 25 Granot St. © **02/561-1066.** www.blmj.org. Bus: 9 or 17.

**Israel Museum** ★★★ PERFORMING ARTS VENUE  The museum is host to a wide range of concerts, performances, films, and exotic cultural and international events. Museum Blvd. ✆ **02/563-6321** for the box office. www.imj.org.il. Bus: 9 or 17.

**Jerusalem Performing Arts Center (Jerusalem Theatre)** ★★★ PER-FORMING ARTS VENUE  Located near the corner of Chopin (in the Rehavia District near the president's house), this modern complex houses the Jerusalem Theater (Sherover Theater), Henry Crown Auditorium, and the smaller, more intimate Rebecca Crown Hall. Original Israeli plays and Hebrew translations of foreign classics and modern works are performed in the theater's main hall. The theater also hosts performances of the **Jerusalem Symphony Orchestra** and the **Israel Chamber Ensemble,** and the Israel Philharmonic performs here. From October through early June, the Henry Crown Auditorium hosts the free **Etnacha Concert Series,** produced by Israel Radio's classics station. 20 David Marcus St. ✆ **02/560-5755.** www.jerusalem-theatre.co.il. Bus: 15.

**Mount Zion Cultural Center** ★ PERFORMING ARTS VENUE  Saturday nights, after Shabbat, the center often hosts Klezmer music concerts and Hassidic-style dancing and music starting around 8pm in winter, 9pm in summer. This section of Mount Zion houses yeshivas and Jewish outreach programs; many of the participants are students, but all are welcome. Call for information; prices vary by event. Outside Zion Gate (near King David's Tomb). ✆ **02/671-6841.** Bus: 1 or 38.

**Targ (Ein Karem Music Center)** ★ PERFORMING ARTS VENUE  Located in the rustic village of Ein Kerem, at the far western edge of Jerusalem, this center hosts Friday late-morning/early-afternoon concerts as well as other events. Allow at least 1½ hours by public transportation from downtown Jerusalem. 29 Ma'ayan St. ✆ **02/641-4250** or 02/561-7075. Bus: 17.

**Ticho House** ★★ PERFORMING ARTS VENUE  A block away from Zion Square, Ticho House maintains a busy schedule, including readings, events for children, and Friday morning concerts. Harav Kook St. ✆ **02/624-5068.** Light Rail or any bus to Zion Sq.

**Train Puppet Theater** ★★ PERFORMING ARTS VENUE  Jerusalem has become a center for puppetry, interestingly enough. Inventive performances are held here year-round. In August and October, Jerusalem hosts International Puppet Theater Festivals. Many performances will be understandable to English-speaking children. Liberty Bell Park. ✆ **02/561-8514.** www.traintheater.co.il. Bus: 4, 14, or 18.

**YMCA** ★ PERFORMING ARTS VENUE  Concerts and performances of Israeli music and folk dancing are held here throughout the year, usually on Monday, Thursday, and Saturday evenings. As there are no reserved seats, come early to nail down a spot. Always call to verify schedules and performances. 26 King David St. ✆ **02/569-2692.** www.ymca.org.il. Bus: 6, 18, or 21.

## More Entertainment

**Son et Lumière** ★ LIGHT SHOW  During the warmer months, a sound-and-light show combined with multimedia presentations about the history of Jerusalem is featured in the Citadel of David at Jaffa Gate. Performances are in English at 8:45pm from April to October, but check on times and tickets in advance. Be prepared for the chill created by the stone fortress and the night breezes. In summer, there are also special night concerts and performances at various venues inside the Old City. Check with the Tourist Information Office for details. Jaffa Gate. NIS 35.

**Sultan's Pool** ★★★ PERFORMING ARTS VENUE  Major outdoor classical, rock, and jazz concerts are held in this dramatic setting in warm weather; a typical

Jerusalem Nightlife

SETTLING INTO JERUSALEM

month might include concerts by the likes of Sting or Bob Dylan or a performance of the opera "Carmen." In a valley beneath the Old City walls between Jaffa Gate and Mount Zion.

## Clubs & Bars

Israelis (especially Jerusalemites) are not really a drinking people—an evening at a cafe over a meal or wine and snacks are more the local style. Try **Rivlin Street** (where some of the ever-changing bars offer small dance floors) or the neighboring **Salomon Street Mall,** in the heart of the cafe/pub scene near Zion Square.

**The American Colony Hotel Bar** in East Jerusalem is atmospheric, visited by locals and travelers in the know. You can also have drinks and tasty food at the hotel's gardened **Courtyard Cafe/Bar.**

**Barood** ★★ This is a friendly, authentic little place with an amazingly well-stocked bar and excellent food (p. 51) ranging from Sephardic-style snacks to major meals. Live music some nights. Open Monday to Saturday 12:30pm to 1:30am. Jerusalem Courtyard, off 31 Jaffa Rd. ✆ **02/625-9081.**

**Casino de Paris** ★ Hidden in the "Georgian Enclave" of Machane Yehuda's Produce Market, this sleek spot is named for and built into the site of a legendary British Mandate–era officers' watering hole known for sleazy romance and intrigue. Now serving the local gentrified population, the bar is kosher and serves imaginative snacks. Open Sunday to Thursday noon to very late, and Saturday after Shabbat. 3 Machane Yehuda (in the "Georgian Market" section). ✆ **02/650-4265.**

**Mike's Place** ★★ A friendly expat hangout with live folk, jazz, and blues performances every night (no cover charge), Mike's is a central spot that draws Americans, Internationals, and Israelis for beer and wine, talk, music, and a well-worn pool table. Food is pub-style and kosher. 33 Jaffa Rd. (at the corner of Rivlin St., behind Village Green Restaurant). ✆ **052-381-4861.** www.mikesplacebars.com.

**Mona Bar Restaurant** ★★ This rustic restaurant inside the Jerusalem Artists' House has a cozy fireplace on cold winter nights and a well-stocked bar that attracts journalists, politicians, Jerusalem personalities, and savvy internationals. Mona serves top-quality meals and snacks very late into the night. Mona was recently taken over by the owners of the acclaimed **Machneyuda Restaurant** (p. 57). Open Saturday to Thursday 7pm to midnight. 8 Shmuel Ha Naggid St. ✆ **02/622-2283.**

**Uganda** ★ A gathering point for Jerusalem's student and 20-something alternative crowd, this tiny spot has no decor except a sense of irony, plus a basic stock of drinks and excellent hummus. The name comes from the fact that the British once considered offering Uganda as an alternative to a Jewish Homeland in Palestine. Open daily noon to very late. 4 Aristobulus St. (off Helene HaMalka St.). ✆ **02/623-6087.** www.uganda.co.il.

## Films

West Jerusalem shows the latest European and American films, almost always in the original language with Hebrew subtitles.

**The Jerusalem Cinémathèque** ★★★ (✆ 02/672-4131; www.jer-cin.org.il) offers a dramatic location and features nightly screenings of classics, the best of the current international scene, rarely shown international films, and the experimental and arcane. The Cinémathèque is located near the old railway station. Go to the traffic intersection between the railway station and Hebron Road. Walk down the slope to the northeast, toward the Old City, and soon you'll come to the Cinémathèque, built into the hillside below the Hebron Road (bus no. 8, 21, 48, 4, or 18).

# EXPLORING
# JERUSALEM

**J**erusalem has been a holy city for 3,000 years, far eclipsing the length of time that any other place has carried such a title. It is also a holy city for all three major religions of the Western world: Judaism, Christianity, and Islam. In the past 150 years, Jerusalem has slowly expanded from a mysterious, charismatic walled city in the Judean mountains to a modern metropolis spread across the surrounding hills. It's a complicated Chinese box of exotic communities, ancient traditions, and rivalries, plus the highest hopes and aspirations of humanity. There is no place on earth like it.

The city invites exploration. Jerusalem's sacred sites and dramatic vistas are filled with exoticism and meaning. In 1 day, you may find yourself wandering the Old City's bazaars; awestruck by the golden, shimmering Dome of the Rock on the Temple Mount; overwhelmed by the site of the Crucifixion; or by Yad VaShem, the memorial and museum dedicated to the six million Jews who fell victim to the Nazis. Later you'll stop in your tracks, mesmerized by the evening calls to prayer echoing through the streets of the Old City.

Although the ancient grandeur of Jerusalem long ago vanished in the ravages of warfare and time, the city's mystique has expanded far beyond anything that could have been dreamed of in ancient times. The most awesome holy places of Judaism, Christianity, and Islam have come to dot the Old City and its nearby hills. During the centuries of the Crusades, Jerusalem was the shimmering vision that moved the armies of Europe and Islam. But for almost 700 years after the Crusades ended, the actual city of Jerusalem existed mostly as a shadowy, forgotten backwater, slowly falling into ruin and decay. Not until the 19th century did the city again begin to come alive and reemerge from behind its walls to spread across the surrounding hills.

During the years of the British Mandate (1918–48), the modern incarnation of Jerusalem developed as a religious center, tourist attraction, and university town in a remarkably beautiful mountain setting. Nineteen years of division by war, barbed wire, and minefields (1948–67) brought Jerusalem's gentle renaissance to a temporary halt. However, with the city's reunification in 1967, Teddy Kollek, the city's world-renowned former mayor, began a modern, ongoing crusade to make sure that Jerusalem would not merely exist or even thrive but would absolutely shine.

Jerusalem today is a busy place where the old and new mix and clash. A state-of-the-art light-rail tram, opened in 2012, glides from points all over the biblical Judean Hills and continues along the Old City walls and the middle of downtown West Jerusalem's main thoroughfare, Jaffa Road. New high-rise construction is going on everywhere.

The city is at a crossroads politically and socially as well as physically. Will it someday be a shared capital for Palestinians and Israelis? Will the religious Jewish community become the demographic and ruling majority in West Jerusalem, and, if so, what will happen to the museums, parks, entertainment, and cultural institutions created by the city's secular community over the past 50 years? Should developers be allowed a free hand to Manhattanize Jerusalem, or should limits be placed on the future growth of the city? Optimists believe that city planners and real-estate developers will find a way to turn a mysterious walled holy city into a fast-paced holy megalopolis. For now, in many ways, the city walks a tightrope between its legend and the rapidly encroaching world of the 21st century.

# THE OLD CITY

The Old City is enclosed by a 12m-high (39-ft.) wall built in 1538 by Suleiman the Magnificent, the greatest of the Ottoman Turkish sultans (some portions of the wall are actually built on ruins of earlier walls more than 2,000 years old). The existence of this wall, which gives unity and magnificence to the Old City, is something of a miracle. According to legend, Sultan Suleiman, who never visited Jerusalem, had a dream that he would be devoured by lions unless he rebuilt the walls that had lain in ruins around Jerusalem since the Crusader wars of the early 13th century. So disturbing was this dream that he sent his architects from Istanbul to reconstruct Jerusalem's walls. Either through ignorance or because the architects hoped to keep some of the building funds for themselves, the new walls did not include the southern part of Mount Zion, which had been inside Jerusalem's defenses in earlier times. When the sultan learned of the architects' omission, he had them beheaded.

There are eight gates in the Old City fortress wall. The most famous gates are:

○ **Jaffa Gate** (in Hebrew, Sha'ar Yafo; in Arabic, Bab al Khalil), the main entrance into the Old City from West Jerusalem and approached from a promenade that runs from the end of Jaffa Road along the Old City walls or via the new, multilevel Mamilla Shopping Mall.

○ **Damascus Gate,** in the northern wall of the Old City, entered from Ha-Nevi'im Street or Nablus Road and the main entrance into the Old City from the Arab New City. Israelis call Damascus Gate Sha'ar Shechem; the Arabic name is Bab-el-Amud. On some maps it is also called Nablus Gate.

○ **Dung Gate,** in the southern wall of the Old City, closest to the Western Wall and now accommodating taxis and buses.

○ **Zion Gate,** in the southern wall of the Old City and leading directly to the Jewish Quarter. It bears the scars of the battle by Israeli forces to relieve the besieged Jewish Quarter in 1948.

○ **The Lions' Gate** (St. Stephen's Gate), in the eastern wall of the Old City, which leads to the Mount of Olives.

○ **Golden Gate,** or the Gate of Mercy, on the eastern side of the Old City and in ancient times the most magnificent of the city gates. According to tradition, this will be the gate through which the Messiah will enter Jerusalem; however, it has been walled up for many centuries.

The Old City itself is divided into five sections: the **Christian Quarter,** the **Armenian Quarter,** the **Muslim Quarter,** the **Jewish Quarter,** and **Temple Mount** (Mount Moriah), the latter including the Western (Wailing) Wall, the Dome of the Rock, and Al Aqsa Mosque. The Dome of the Rock and the Al Aqsa Mosque were built from A.D.

691 to 720, 600 years after the Temple was destroyed by Rome. Throughout the Islamic world, this complex is called **Haram es Sharif,** or the Noble Sanctuary.

## The Jaffa Gate ★

This is the traditional entrance into the Old City from the western part of the New City. The citadel tower, beside the Jaffa Gate, is known as the **Tower of David ★**, although historically this fortress was only first developed 800 years after King David died. Three massive towers built by Herod on the foundations of Hasmonean fortifications originally stood on this spot. Just to the south, close to the protection of the garrison in the Jaffa Gate's tower, would have been Herod's palace. After the destruction of Jerusalem by the Romans in A.D. 70, the foundations of the towers guarding the Jaffa Gate were among the few structures not deliberately obliterated on orders from Rome. They were left standing to show there had once been a city that had been no pushover to subdue. Each of the subsequent rulers of Jerusalem, from Romans and Byzantines to Muslims, Crusaders, and Ottoman Turks, has rebuilt the fortifications beside Jaffa Gate, although none have come close to the scale of Herod's three towers. The Ottoman Turks built a mosque here, and its minaret still dominates the complex.

The **Tower of David Museum of the History of Jerusalem ★★**, Omar Ibn el Khattab Square (✆ **02/626-5310** 24-hr. information line; www.towerofdavid.org.il), now fills the citadel, hosting well-chosen, often very exciting temporary art and history exhibits, performances, and tours. Although some of the permanent exhibits look like illustrations from a school textbook, they are useful teaching tools. The structure of the citadel itself, with its great views of the New and Old Cities, is fascinating. The courtyard of the citadel is also used for concerts and performances of plays by contemporary Israeli writers. From April to October, a **Night Spectacular** show that narrates Jerusalem's history in 40 minutes is presented in English on Saturdays at 9pm and on Mondays and Wednesdays at 9:30pm. Bring warm clothes for evening performances. If the special performances and events are scheduled, look for bundled admission packages to the museum, the performance, and the sound-and-light show. Admission is NIS 30 to the tower and NIS 50 for the Night Spectacular; a combined ticket is NIS 65, and there are small discounts for children and students. The museum is open Sunday through Thursday 10am to 4pm (Sun–Wed until 5pm; Thurs until 7pm in July and Aug) and Saturday 10am to 2pm; open Friday 10am to 2pm only in July and August. **Guided tours in English** are Sunday through Thursday at 11am. **Tour reservations** can be made at ✆ **02/626-5347.** Tour is not included in the admission fee.

A breach in the city walls beside Jaffa Gate was made for the visit of Kaiser Wilhelm II of Germany and his entourage in 1898. Here, the leader of the British forces, General Allenby, liberating Palestine from Ottoman rule, entered Jerusalem in 1917. Today, this breach allows automobiles to enter the area of the Old City just inside the Jaffa Gate, and the **Tourist Information Office** is located here.

If you head straight into the **bazaar** (the *suq*) from the Jaffa Gate, you'll enter David Street, bustling with shops selling religious crafts and souvenirs, maps, and household items.

If your first destination is the **Church of the Holy Sepulcher,** proceed straight down David Street and take the first left, which is called Christian Quarter Road. Follow this road until you come to St. Helena's Road, a stepped bazaar on the right that will lead you down to the entrance to the church.

If the **Western Wall and the Temple Mount** are your first goal, continue straight along David Street. It makes a quick jog to the right and then to the left in the heart of the covered bazaar, where it changes its name to Street of the Chain (Silsileh, in Arabic). Follow the street downhill as the bazaar continues. Eventually, turning right on a small side street marked Ha-Kotel leads to the Western Wall. Just to the right of the Western Wall, a long, curved ramp leads to the Mograbi Gate, the only gate non-Muslims can use to enter the Temple Mount.

## Armenian Quarter ★

As you pass Omar Ibn el Khattab Square, just before you descend the steps into David Street, you'll see a road heading off to the right, past the moat and the Tower of David. This is the Armenian Patriarchate Road, leading into the Armenian Quarter, a walled world unto itself, centered around Armenian religious structures and home to much of Jerusalem's Armenian community. Around A.D. 300, Armenia became the first nation to adopt Christianity, predating Emperor Constantine's conversion of the Roman Empire by several decades. From that time, there has always been an Armenian presence in Jerusalem.

Follow the Armenian Patriarchate Road, look left for an entrance into the walled Armenian Quarter, and follow the signs.

**Saint James Cathedral ★★** is the most important site in the Armenian Quarter. Entered through the Armenian Monastery on Armenian Patriarchate Road, it dates from the 11th and 12th centuries and is built on the site of earlier churches. It commemorates the place where James the Elder, son of Zebedee, was put to death by order of Herod Agrippa I in A.D. 44 (Acts 12:2). The cathedral also contains the tomb of James, the oldest brother of Jesus and first bishop of the Jerusalem Christian community. This James was the author of the Epistle of James and was stoned to death in A.D. 62. The cathedral, with its rich interior of hanging lamps, censers (for burning incense), and ceremonial objects, may be visited for services daily from 3 to 3:30pm.

*Tip:* The intricacies of the secluded Armenian Quarter are difficult to explore on your own. Aram Khatchadourian (P.O. Box 14003, Old City, Jerusalem; ✆ **050/735-1859**), a licensed guide and member of Jerusalem's Armenian community, gives full- or half-day private walking tours of the quarters of the Old City.

## The Jewish Quarter ★★★

Take a detour through the Jewish Quarter on your way to the Western Wall and Temple Mount. By doing so, you'll save an uphill walk, as the wall lies well below most of the quarter.

The Jewish Quarter lies directly west of the Temple Mount and sits on a higher hill than the Temple Mount itself. With the exception of the sacred Temple Mount, the entire original city of Jerusalem from the time of David (1000 B.C.) was outside the walls of the present Old City, just downhill and to the south. Over the centuries, ancient Jerusalem spread northward, up the slope. By the time of King Hezekiah, around 700 B.C., much of the uphill area now occupied by the Jewish Quarter had become a new addition to the city, surrounded by the Broad Wall. But the wall and its many towers were not strong enough to keep out Nebuchadnezzar of Babylon, who conquered and laid waste to Jerusalem in 586 B.C.

Jews returned to rebuild Jerusalem after the Babylonian Captivity, but it took centuries for the city to regain its former size. In the late Second Temple period, Jerusalem again expanded uphill, and the area that is now the Jewish Quarter was inhabited once more and developed into an aristocratic and priestly residential neighborhood. The main market street of Herodian Jerusalem developed at the bottom of the Tyropoeon

(Cheesemakers') Valley, which separates the heights of the present Jewish Quarter from the Temple Mount. The market street continued northward to the Damascus Gate. For thousands of religious pilgrims to make their way to the Temple Mount without becoming entangled in the crush of the market, two massive pedestrian staircases and overpasses were constructed above the market street. By the A.D. 1st century, Jerusalem had expanded northward, beyond the present Old City's northern wall. A new, bustling Upper Market developed where the present Suq Khan es-Zeit market leads toward the Damascus Gate. The original City of David, the oldest part of town, came to be known as the Lower City.

Jerusalem was again leveled in A.D. 70 by Roman armies (the remains of houses burned in that conflagration have been uncovered in what is now the Jewish Quarter); 65 years after the Romans destroyed Jerusalem, they (and later their Byzantine successors) rebuilt the city. You can visit several recently uncovered vestiges of Roman/Byzantine times in the Jewish Quarter, including the ruins of the gigantic **Nea Church** and the southern end of the city's colonnaded north-south thoroughfare, the **Cardo Maximus.** Jews were forbidden to reside in Jerusalem during the long Byzantine period, which began in A.D. 326, and many Jewish inhabitants of the area allied themselves with the then-pagan Persians, who conquered and occupied Jerusalem from A.D. 614 to 629. The Byzantines returned in A.D. 629, followed quickly by the Muslims, who conquered Jerusalem in A.D. 638. Under their more tolerant rule, a permanent Jewish community was reestablished in the northeast quadrant of the Old City, on the site of the present Muslim Quarter. The Crusaders conquered Jerusalem in 1099 and celebrated their triumph by massacring most of the city's Jewish population as well as thousands of Muslims and local Christians.

In 1267, after the Crusaders were driven from Jerusalem, a small Jewish community reestablished itself in the ruins of what is now the Jewish Quarter. This area has been the center of the Jewish community in the Old City ever since.

The Jewish Quarter's most recent destruction came during and after the 1948 war with Jordan, when all the synagogues and most other buildings in the quarter were severely damaged and over the next 2 decades fell into almost total ruin; many were systematically demolished. Since the Israeli conquest of the Old City during the 1967 war, the quarter has been rebuilt and revitalized. Although some original buildings have been carefully re-created, and many new structures were designed to blend in with them, the basic nature of the current Jewish Quarter is quite different from the impoverished, densely populated neighborhoods that existed here before 1948.

Following St. James Road (a left turn off Armenian Patriarchate Rd.) to where it becomes Or Hayim Street, you'll come to the **Old Yishuv Court Museum,** 6 Or Hayim St. (© **02/628-4636**). This small museum displays artifacts and crafts typical of Ashkenazi and Sephardic communities in the Jewish Quarter from the middle of the 19th century to the end of Turkish rule in 1917. Admission is NIS 15, and it's open Sunday to Thursday from 10am to 2pm.

The **Cardo Maximus** is a recently excavated A.D. 2nd- to 6th-century street that was Roman and Byzantine Jerusalem's main market and processional thoroughfare, once bordered by stately columns and lined with portico-shaded shops. The original street is said to have been laid out by the Roman emperor Hadrian (A.D. 117–38) when he rebuilt the city as Aelia Capitolina after the Bar Kochba Revolt of A.D. 132 to 135. In late Byzantine times, the Cardo was extended southward and served as the processional route between the **Holy Sepulcher** and the **Nea,** Jerusalem's two largest churches of that era.

The southern portion of the Cardo is open to the sky; the rest is beneath the modern buildings of the Jewish Quarter. At the end of Or Hayim Street, the Cardo's imposing columns, found by archaeologists, have been re-erected. As you walk northward along the reconstructed Cardo, where modern tourist shops have been installed, you can see on your right the walled-up facades of Crusader-era shops built into the arches. In this restored section, you can look down well-like structures that reveal how far above the original level of the land the city has risen in its constant rebuilding on the ruins of each wave of destruction. You'll also see fragments of the city's defensive walls dating from the First Temple period, around 700 B.C.

Parallel to the Cardo is the Jewish Quarter Road. Many Jewish Quarter buildings from other times are today recalled by only a single arch, doorway, or minaret. You can inspect the haunting arches, altar, apse, and ruined cloister from the once-lost **Crusader Church of Saint Mary of the Teutonic Knights** (1128) on Misgav Ladach Street. If you enter the ruins, walk back to the apse, where the windows frame a wonderful view of the Temple Mount. Across from the entrance to the church is a small covered square known as **Seven Arches.** In the pre-1948 Jewish Quarter, Seven Arches was the heart of a lively market packed with vegetable vendors and customers. To the west, you'll see the minaret from the **Omar Sidna Mosque,** and beside it is the rebuilt (2010) **Hurva Synagogue,** which was once the Great Synagogue of the Jewish Quarter. The name, meaning "ruin," recalls its difficult and unfortunate history. The original Hurva was built in the 17th century with Ottoman permission but was soon destroyed by Ottoman decree. In the 1850s, a new synagogue was authorized and built. Heavily damaged in the 1948 war, it was demolished after the Jordanians captured the Jewish Quarter. In the decades after 1967, when the Israelis recaptured the Old City, there were a number of movements and plans (including one by visionary American architect Louis Kahn) calling for a new Hurva Synagogue. From 1967 until 2010, the site of the Hurva was marked only by a simple arch, in memory of the Great Synagogue of Jerusalem. The new Hurva, with its landmark dome matching the arch of the original synagogue, is as close as possible to the design of the one that was destroyed in 1948.

Between the minaret and the Hurva is the **Ramban Synagogue** of Rabbi Moshe Ben-Nachman, who helped reconstitute the Jewish community of Jerusalem in 1267, after it had been obliterated by the Crusaders. You'll also want to take a look at the complex of **Four Sephardic synagogues ★** named for Rabbi Yochanan Ben-Zakkai, whose school, according to tradition, occupied this site during the Second Temple period. One of the four is named for the rabbi himself and another for Eliyahu Ha-Navi (Elijah the Prophet); the other two are the Central Synagogue and the Istanbuli Synagogue. During Muslim rule, no church or synagogue was allowed to exceed the height of the nearest mosque, so to gain headroom, the floors of these synagogues were laid well below ground level. The synagogues are open Sunday to Thursday from 9:30am to 3:45pm and Friday from 9:30am to 1pm. Admission is NIS 12.

The **Tiferet Israel (or Yisrael) Synagogue** (Ashkenazi, or Eastern European Jewish) was founded by Nisan Bek and inaugurated in 1865. Dedicated to the Hasidic Rabbi Israel Friedman of Ruzhin (the synagogue's name means "Glory of Israel"), it was destroyed after the War of Independence and was restored after 1967.

Moving eastward across the Jewish Quarter in the direction of the Western Wall, you can visit two remnants of the neighborhood's elegant Herodian past.

The **Herodian Quarter Wohl Archaeology Museum ★** (✆ **02/628-3448**) contains archaeological excavations, done in the 1970s, of the wealthy residential quarter of Herodian Jerusalem. It includes remains of a palatial mansion with painted faux marble walls, mosaic floors, an atrium pool, ritual bath installations, and elegant classical furnishings and stone water jugs. Only the lower portions survive from what is estimated to have been a multistory structure of 557 sq. m (6,000 sq. ft.). The grandeur of the mansion has led some to suggest it may have been the residence of a high priest. Admission is NIS 20; a combined ticket with Burnt House (see below) is NIS 35. The entrance is on Hakara'im Street. It's open Sunday to Thursday from 9am to 5pm and Friday 9am to 1pm.

The **Burnt House ★** (*①* **02/628-3448**) is a remnant of the destruction of Jerusalem by the Romans in A.D. 70. The wealthy Upper City, site of the present Jewish Quarter, held out for a despairing month after the Lower City and the Temple Mount fell. From these heights, the inhabitants of the Upper City stood on their roofs and watched with horror as the Temple went up in flames. When the Romans finally decided to storm the Upper City, they found little resistance; much of the population was dead or near death from disease and starvation. The Burnt House chillingly brings to light the day when the Romans burned the Upper City. In the 1970s, when archaeologists excavated what had been the kitchen or workroom of this building, they found the forearm bones of a young woman amid the debris. As diggers continued to excavate the area of the room that lay where the arm pointed, they uncovered a wooden spear, almost as if the young woman had been reaching for this weapon when she met her death. Most tantalizing of the household artifacts found on this site is a set of weights marked with the name "Bar Kathros," a priestly family mentioned in the Talmud (and also in an ancient folk song as one of the wealthy families that oppressed the poor). Historians know the House of Bar Kathros was responsible for the manufacture of incense for the Temple. The excavated house, now preserved beneath modern buildings, offers a brief slide-show about the site. The entrance to the house is marked on a modern door in Seven Arches off Misgav Ladach Road (ask if you have difficulty finding the door). The house is open Sunday to Thursday from 9am to 5pm and Friday from 9am until noon. Admission is NIS 20; a combined ticket to Burnt House and Herodian Quarter Wohl Museum is NIS 35.

## The Western Wall ★★★

This is known in Hebrew as the *Kotel Ha-Ma'aravi.* It was formerly called the "Wailing Wall" by European observers because for centuries, Jews came here to mourn the loss of their temple. It is the holiest of Jewish sites, a remnant of the monumental Herodian retaining wall that encloses and still supports the Temple Mount.

For centuries, the Wall stood 18m (59 ft.) above the level of the earth and 27m (89 ft.) long, towering over a narrow alley 3.6m (12 ft.) wide that could accommodate only approximately a hundred densely packed worshipers. In 1967, immediately after the Six-Day War, the Israelis bulldozed the Moors Quarter facing the wall to create a plaza that could accommodate tens of thousands of pilgrims. They also made the wall about 2m (6½ ft.) higher by digging down when building the plaza and exposing two more tiers of the Wall's ashlars (squared stones) that had been buried by accumulated debris for centuries. At the southern end of the Wall, away from the area reserved for prayer and worship, archaeologists (since 1967) have uncovered spectacular remains from various periods.

At the prayer section of the Western Wall, grass grows out of the upper cracks. The lower cracks of the chalky, yellow-white blocks have been stuffed with bits of paper containing prayers. Orthodox Jews can be seen standing at the wall, chanting and swaying. Visitors of all religions are welcome to approach the Wall and pray silently beside it (both Pope John Paul II and the Dalai Lama prayed here as pilgrims). Men who would like to go to the Wall must wear a hat or take a head covering; if you don't have a yarmulke, sun hat, or baseball cap, you can take one, at no cost, from a box beside the entrance to the prayer area. Women may borrow shawls and short-skirt coverings, but it is best to come with a longish skirt and long sleeves. A separate section at the extreme right of the Western Wall is reserved for women, who are not allowed into the men's section in keeping with Orthodox Jewish tradition. On some days, you may encounter a number of professional beggars, who can make a visit to the Wall difficult. Giving charity at a time of pilgrimage is an ancient Jewish tradition, but many travelers find it best to avoid the Western Wall charity seekers and instead make a donation to an organized charity at a later time. Services are held here daily; no photography or smoking is permitted on the Sabbath and some Jewish holidays.

The exposed lower courses of the Western Wall are composed of enormous rectangular ashlars, or carefully carved stones, each dressed only with the recessed borders typical of Herodian-era stonework. The sides of these monumental ashlars have been carved with such precision that they rest perfectly against and on top of each other, without mortar. Over the millennia, the fine straight lines and margins of some of the ashlars have eroded.

The Wall was built by King Herod just before the time of Jesus and is part of a structure that retains the western part of the Temple Mount and the vast, artificial ceremonial plaza Herod created on the Temple Mount itself. These retaining (as well as defensive) walls surround the western, southern, and eastern sides of the Temple Mount. The largest of the ashlars is 3.6m (12 ft.) high and 14m (46 ft.) long and weighs approximately 400 tons. According to Josephus, the Roman Jewish historian, construction of the walls took 11 years, during which time it rained in Jerusalem only at night so as not to interfere with the workers' progress.

In the right-hand corner of the women's prayer area, beside a protruding newer building, you can see an area of the Wall composed of small, rough stones. These stones block a fragment of a Herodian-era door to the Temple Mount, today called **Barclay's Gate** after the 19th-century American who first identified it. South of the earthen ramp leading up the Temple Mount, you'll see a fragment of large stonework protruding from the upper reaches of the Wall. This is **Robinson's Arch,** all that remains of a great stairway, set on arches, that passed over the busy market street at the foot of the Western Wall and led directly onto the southern side of Temple Mount.

The Western Wall is actually much higher and longer than the portion you can readily see today. For an idea of how high the original construction was, and what the level of the earth was 2,000 years ago, enter the doorway located between the men's restrooms and the public telephones on the plaza's northern side. Both men and women can enter (on weekdays, by request) this dark passage of vaults, chambers, and pitfalls (now rendered safe by lamps, grates, and barriers). Inside, the continuation of the Wall is clearly visible. Shafts have been sunk along the Wall to show its true depth. The arches in this artificial cavern date from various eras, ranging from Herodian (37 B.C.–A.D. 70) to Crusader (1100–1244). The platform is behind a prayer room filled with Orthodox worshipers. The prayer room is off-limits to women, except in the viewing area.

A special walk into recently excavated tunnels alongside the entire Western Wall can be arranged by making an appointment with the **Western Wall Heritage Foundation** (✆ **02/627-1333;** www.thekotel.org). Admission is NIS 28; special tours are extra. Book ahead online if possible.

## Temple Mount (Haram es Sharif)—Dome of the Rock ★★★

Take the rising pathway to the right of the Western Wall, which leads to the Temple Mount, one of the most historic and sublime religious sites in the world. In the Islamic world, this is the Haram es Sharif, the Noble Sanctuary, and one of its crowning architectural achievements. After David conquered Jerusalem, he purchased the flat rock at the top of Moriah from Araunah the Jebusite, who had used it as a threshing floor. Some historians theorize that the name Araunah, a dialect variation of the name Aaron, may indicate that Araunah was a Canaanite priest, and the site a Canaanite holy place. The Bible (2 Chron. 3) relates that "Solomon began to build the house of the Lord at Jerusalem on Mount Moriah." The more modest Second Temple (Solomon's was destroyed by Nebuchadnezzar in 586 B.C.) was originally built by returnees from the Babylonian Captivity between 525 and 515 B.C., and later, shortly before the time of Jesus, Herod enlarged and rebuilt it into the most massive religious complex in the eastern Roman Empire. The vast Temple Mount you see here is an artificially created, flat, stone-paved platform, about 12 ha (30 acres) in area, built by Herod to accommodate vast numbers of pilgrims in ancient times. Herod's temple complex was destroyed by the Romans in A.D. 70. All structures on the Temple Mount today, including the Dome of the Rock and the Al Aqsa Mosque, are Islamic holy places and religious institutions built after the Muslim conquest of A.D. 638.

There is no charge to enter the Temple Mount compound. You must not, however, wear shorts or immodest dress in the compound. (If your outfit is too revealing, guards may be willing to provide you with long cotton wraps, or they may ask you to return another time.)

There is an admission fee of NIS 38 to go inside the two mosques and the Islamic Museum, but they have been closed to non-Muslims since 2000. If the buildings are again open to foreign visitors, we highly recommend that you invest in the combined admission ticket, which may be purchased from a stone kiosk between Al Aqsa and the Dome of the Rock.

**Al Aqsa Mosque ★★**, the third-holiest place of prayer in the world for Muslims (after Mecca and Medina), is the first large edifice you'll come to. Completed in approximately A.D. 720, it is among the oldest mosques in existence and also among the most beautiful—a vast broad basilica originally nine naves wide (it was rebuilt somewhat smaller after the Crusades). It was in front of the graceful porticos of the Al Aqsa that King Abdullah I of Jordan was assassinated in 1951 by gunmen who believed he was attempting to create a basis for eventual peace in the area. He died here in the presence of his then-15-year-old grandson, the late King Hussein of Jordan.

*Note:* Although at press time the interiors of Al Aqsa and the Dome of the Rock are closed to visitors, the following information is provided in case they are reopened.

A mosque is a sacred enclosure open to air and light (as opposed to the dark interiors of pagan-era temples). Because a mosque is a sacred precinct, you must remove your shoes before entering. This tradition is very ancient, going back to the time when Moses, approaching the Burning Bush in the Sinai, heard the voice of God telling him to take off his shoes. You must also leave handbags and cameras outside, so you might want to come with a partner who can watch these things for you. Try to stash your wallet and identification papers in a pocket.

After passing through the portico, you will enter a broad, open hall with chandeliers, its floor covered with Oriental rugs. The mosque's lofty ceilings, supported by a forest of varied columns, are embellished with early Islamic and Byzantine design. Up front, past rows of great marble pillars, is a wood-partitioned platform reserved for the Jordanian royal family. The extraordinary wooden-stair pulpit of the Al Aqsa Mosque, one of Islam's great artistic treasures for more than 7 centuries, was commissioned by Saladin for the rededication of Al Aqsa as a mosque after the Crusader occupation. Originally built by master artisans from Syria, it was destroyed when a mentally disturbed Australian tourist set fire to Al Aqsa in 1969, and it has been painstakingly

Visitation hours for the Temple Mount are constantly subject to change. Tourists can only visit the Temple Mount/ Haram es Sharif Sunday to Thursday 7:30 to 11am (10am in winter) and 1:30 to 2:30pm. Hours can change, so it is best to always check beforehand and arrive at least an hour ahead of closing time. Although visitors may walk around on the Temple Mount, take photographs, and enjoy the vistas, for now entry into the Dome of the Rock, the Al Aqsa Mosque, and the Islamic Museum is not permitted. The Temple Mount is always closed to non-Muslims on Friday and Saturday and is either totally closed or, depending on circumstances, open for very limited hours during the entire holy month of Ramadan. Non-Muslims may not bring prayer books or engage in public or private prayer on the Temple Mount.

reconstructed by craftspeople retrained in techniques that have not been used for hundreds of years. A separate women's prayer chamber, in blue, is at the right. As you enter Al Aqsa, you face south, in the direction of Mecca. **Mihrabs,** or prayer niches on the southern wall, remind worshipers of the *qibla,* or direction they must face during prayers, which are performed five times a day. Unlike most churches and synagogues, mosques contain no pews or chairs. Visitors are invited to view the architecture and design details of the building; however, they are requested not to engage in any prayers.

Leave Al Aqsa, reclaim your shoes and belongings, and turn right. You will only be permitted to walk to the end of the building, but at the far end of the vast pavement is a corner in the city walls. Some say this is the "pinnacle of the Temple" where Satan took Jesus to tempt him (Matt. 4:5). In the distance, you can get a marvelous view of the Mount of Olives and the Kidron Valley.

A stairway leads to the so-called **Solomon's Stables,** perhaps first misidentified by the Crusaders. Today, these subterranean chambers are popularly believed to have been the stables for King Solomon's thousands of horses. The "stables" are actually the substructure supporting this portion of Herod's vast, artificially created ceremonial platform that is the present surface of the Temple Mount. To add to the confusion about the site, many Muslims believe the "Solomon" referred to is the Ottoman Sultan Suleiman (Solomon) the Magnificent, who rebuilt the walls that surround the present Old City and did extensive repair work on the Dome of the Rock during his reign in the mid-1500s. (For security reasons, this area will most likely be closed to visitors.)

Heading straight across Temple Mount Plaza toward the Dome of the Rock, you'll pass **El-Kas,** the fountain where Muslims perform their ritual ablutions before entering the holy places. It is equipped with a circular row of pink marble seats, each of which has a faucet. The fountain is not for use by non-Muslims.

The exterior walls of the dazzling **Dome of the Rock ★★★** are covered with a facade of Persian blue tiles, originally installed by the Ottoman Sultan Suleiman the Magnificent in the mid–16th century. In 1994, under the auspices of Jordan's King Hussein, the great dome was completely reconstructed and regilded with 80kg (176 lb.) of 24-karat gold. The Dome of the Rock is reached by climbing the broad ceremonial stairs that lead to a decorative archway and a raised center portion of the Temple Mount complex. The Dome of the Rock's interior is every bit as lavish and intricate as

5

EXPLORING JERUSALEM | The Old City

the outside. Plush carpets line the floor, and stained-glass windows line the upper ceiling.

Everything in this beautiful Muslim sanctuary, built in A.D. 691, centers on the rock that occupies the middle of the shrine. According to Islamic tradition, this rock is the spot from which the Prophet Muhammad ascended to view paradise during the Night Journey described in the 17th Sura of the Koran. Tradition holds that when the Prophet rose, the rock tried to follow, and although it failed, the cave beneath the rock was formed. Footprints of Muhammad are pointed out on the rock.

Next to the rock, a few strands of the Prophet Muhammad's hair are kept in a latticework wooden cabinet. A stairway leads under the rock to a cavelike chamber; according to tradition, this is the Well of the Souls, where it is said the souls of all the dead are gathered. Glass partitions have been erected to stop pilgrims from eroding the sacred rock—for centuries, it was chipped away by the faithful who wanted to bring home a memento.

Jewish tradition holds that on this rock occurred the supreme act of faith that stands at the foundation of the Jewish religion: Abraham's near-sacrifice of Isaac. Genesis 22 relates how Abraham, in approximately 1800 B.C., followed God's instructions to go to Moriah and sacrifice Isaac, his beloved son. At the final moment, the voice of God intervened and ordered Abraham to lower his knife. Approximately 900 years later, around 960 B.C., the Temple of Solomon was constructed either on or beside this rock. For the next millennium, the First and Second Temples were located on this site.

From the flat courtyard surrounding the two mosques, you have a wonderful view. To the south are the **Valley of Jehoshaphat** (Valley of Kidron) and the **UN Government House** (Mount of Contempt) on the hill. To the east are the lower slopes of the **Mount of Olives;** the **Russian Magdalene Church,** with its many onion-shaped golden domes; and the **Tomb of the Virgin.** Midway up the Mount of Olives is a large, modern, white structure with many levels of arcades that seem built into the side of the slope. This is the vast **Mormon Center,** constructed in the 1980s and considered to be one of the most beautiful examples of contemporary architecture in Jerusalem. On the crest of the Mount of Olives, above the Church of Mary Magdalene, you'll see the high-steepled **Russian Monastery** and the **Dome of the Ascension,** marking the site from which Jesus is traditionally believed to have ascended to heaven. Farther to the right and a bit downhill is the gray, tear-shaped dome of Dominus Flevit, which commemorates the spot where Jesus wept as he saw a vision of Jerusalem in ruins. Indeed, from the time of the city's destruction in A.D. 70 until the building of the Dome of the Rock in A.D. 691, Jews traditionally stood near this spot and viewed the actual ruins of the Temple Mount. To the right, on the southern crest of the ridge, is the modern Seven Arches Hotel, built during Jordanian times on the ancient Jewish cemetery of the Mount of Olives.

Your combined entrance ticket also admits you to the **Islamic Museum,** in the southwest corner of the Temple Mount complex, to the right of the Al Aqsa Mosque. The museum is filled with architectural details, including capitals and carved stonework from earlier structures on the Temple Mount as well as ornamental details from earlier periods of the Al Aqsa Mosque's existence.

# Dung Gate, Silwan (the City of David) & the Jerusalem Archaeological Park ★★

The gate in the city wall near the Temple Mount is Dung Gate, which leads downhill to the Arab neighborhood of Silwan, the site of Jerusalem and the ancient City of David as it existed around 1000 B.C. Until the medieval era, Silwan was encompassed within the walls of Jerusalem; only when the walls of the city shrank to their present configuration and the city wall separated Silwan from the rest of the city was the Dung Gate built. For centuries, the gate was just a small doorway in the wall, but in recent years it has been widened to accommodate cars and buses. Jerusalemites claim that the gate is named for the debris from each consecutive destruction of Jerusalem that was dumped out into the valley below. Silwan today is as crowded as in ancient times—its houses now climb the sides of a steep cliff at the edge of the Mount of Olives. Silwan is where the original settlement of Jerusalem developed in prehistoric times beside the **Gihon Spring.** Its streets are where the prophets walked and the events of First Temple Jerusalem took place.

By the 2nd century B.C., the growing city of Jerusalem was expanding uphill and north-ward onto the site of the present Old City. The newer Upper City was the more affluent part of town; the older Lower City was densely populated and poor. In the centuries after the Roman destruction of Jerusalem in A.D. 70, the population of Jerusalem had so greatly decreased and the technology of warfare had progressed to such a point that the original City of David was no longer militarily defensible. It was left outside the walls of the city and by medieval times had sunk to the status of a small, sporadically settled village known as Silwan. So completely forgotten was the site of the original city that until late in the 19th century, most historians and visitors believed the Jerusalem of the First Temple period had been located on the site of the present Old City.

Since the 1950s, extensive archaeological excavations have been made of the area; however, dramatic claims that specific sites and structures from the time of David and Solomon have been identified require further academic assessment.

In Silwan you can visit the underground water tunnel and the collection **Pool of Siloam** (in Hebrew, Shiloah) built by King Hezekiah in 701 B.C. (and rediscovered in the late 19th c). This remarkable structure hid Jerusalem's water supply from the Assyrians and saved the city from destruction.

At the southern end of Silwan (which takes its Arabic name from the biblical pool of Siloam), just beyond where the walls of old Jerusalem would have been, are ancient overgrown gardens of pomegranates and figs still watered by the **Gihon Spring.** These gardens, originating in prehistoric times, most likely occupy the site of the gardens of the kings of Judah and may be the site of the walled gardens that inspired the Song of Songs. It was to a tent beside the Gihon Spring that David initially brought the Ark of the Covenant, the pivotal first step in Jerusalem's transformation into a holy city. Here the ark rested until the Temple of Solomon was built to house it. The Bible also records that King David was buried inside this city; if so, his tomb should be somewhere in Silwan rather than at the site on Mount Zion that has been venerated since at least medieval times. Normally, under Judaic law, burials are not permitted within the walls of a city, but the Bible records that an exception was apparently made for King David. Archaeologists are still searching for evidence of the Davidic burial site, but the Lower City was extensively quarried for building stone in the centuries after the Roman destruction, and the true location of David's tomb, legendary for its powers, remains one of Jerusalem's mysteries.

You can enter daily from 9am to 5pm for free and follow the paths along the steep hillside past the excavation site. However, under current political conditions, it is best to visit this area with an organized tour. **Sandeman's Tours** (www.newjerusalemtours. com) offers a variety of escorted Old City walking tours, including a free introductory 2-hour tour; ask at the tourist office for information. **Archaeological Seminars Ltd.** (© **02/627-3515**) and **SPINI** (© **02/625-2357;** fax 02/625-4953) lead guided tours of the City of David. See "Organized Tours," later in this chapter, for more information.

# THE JERUSALEM ARCHAEOLOGICAL PARK

**The Southern Wall of the Temple Mount and the Davidson Center ★★**

HISTORIC SITE   The Jerusalem Archaeological Park just outside the southern wall of the Temple Mount offers an opportunity to explore the monumental ruins of the Herodian Temple Complex and later Byzantine/Islamic structures that have been uncovered here during the past 3 decades.

When the Temple was in existence (before A.D. 70), the southern wall of the Temple Mount was the main route for approaching the Temple. A broad staircase, mentioned in Talmudic writings, ended in a broad esplanade, which was wide enough to provide access to the two sets of gates that once existed, fragments of which can still be seen. From the gates, pilgrims would have proceeded through tunnels that dramatically emerged onto the surface of the sacred enclosure not far from the Temple building itself. Visitors to the park can now stand on the Broad Stairs (the gates are blocked by later construction, but traces are still visible) and walk on the Herodian market street that ran along the western side of the Temple Mount. They can also explore the ruins of Herodian-era shops along the market street (they were part of the complex, and rents may have gone toward the upkeep of the Temple Mount) and see where the great staircase to the Temple Mount once stood, supported by a series of arches that spanned the market street below. The excavations have also uncovered Byzantine-era structures that once stood beside the partly destroyed southern wall of the Temple Mount and the impressive walls of early Islamic palaces (ca. A.D. 8th c.) that took their place.

**The Davidson Exhibition Center ★★**   This complex offers a chance to take a virtual tour of the Temple Mount, as archaeologists believe it might have appeared to a pilgrim in Herodian times (late 1st c. B.C. until the Roman destruction of Jerusalem in A.D. 70). Located in the ruins of an early-8th-century Islamic palace uncovered by archaeologists at the foot of the Temple Mount, the Davidson Center contains a small museum with artifacts found at the site as well as videos and computer information on the Temple Mount's history. The video and digital re-creation of the Herodian Temple Mount are interesting, but there are a number of anachronistic and questionable details (see if you can spot them). There are 1-hour audio tours of the center (which is already relatively self-explanatory) and of the archaeological park (worthwhile for those who want to understand all the intricate details). Private guides can be booked in advance for NIS 180 per person, but a map and the recorded audio tour of the site, available at the Davidson Center, are sufficient for most visitors.

Entrance from near inside of Dung Gate. ℭ **02/627-7550.** www.archpark.org.il. NIS 30 adults; NIS 16 students, children, and seniors. Sun–Thurs 8am–5pm, Fri 8am–2pm; closed Sat and Jewish holidays. Bus: 1, 2, 38, or 99.

## The Muslim & Christian Quarters

**Church of Saint Anne and the Pools of Bethesda ★★** CHURCH   Sixty meters (197 ft.) inside the Lion's Gate, on your right, is a wooden doorway leading to a hidden garden enclave where you'll find this beautiful 12th-century Crusader church, erected in honor of the birthplace of Anne (Hannah), the mother of Mary. It is built next to the Bethesda Pool, the site where Jesus is believed to have healed a paralytic. The pool would have been used by Herodian-era Jewish pilgrims for ritual purification before entering the northern gate of the nearby Temple Mount. The ruins of a small Crusader-era church can be seen amid the excavations of the ancient pool.

As the Church of St. Anne is just a few hundred feet east of the Sanctuaries of the Flagellation and the Condemnation, at the beginning of the Via Dolorosa, you might

# THE hidden WALL

For centuries, the small stretch of the Western Wall of the Temple Mount used for Jewish prayers was the only part of the Herodian Temple Mount complex that non-Muslims could actually approach and touch. The once-important southern wall of the Temple Mount was largely hidden by accumulated earth and debris and by later buildings that rose and fell with each successive wave of history. Now excavations have made the southern wall and extreme southern part of the Western Wall accessible all the way down to the Herodian street level. At a quiet time of day, when no tour groups are trudging through, you can sit in the shade of an ancient shop doorway and contemplate the charisma and enormity of the Herodian ashlars. Wild capers grow out of the monumental walls. If you look up near the extreme southern end of the Western Wall where the level of earth would have been centuries ago, you can see a large ashlar on which, probably in the Byzantine era, archaeologists believe a Jewish pilgrim to the ruined Temple Mount carved the Hebrew words from Isaiah 66:14: "And when you see this, your heart shall rejoice, and your bones shall flourish like an herb." For 1,500 years, this visitor's message lay hidden and forgotten in the earth.

want to visit it before following the Stations of the Cross. Saint Anne's acoustics, designed for Gregorian chant, are so perfect that the church is virtually a musical instrument to be played by the human voice. Pilgrim groups come to sing in the church throughout the day, and you, too, are welcome to prepare a song of any religion—only religious songs are permitted. The church's acoustics are most amazing when used by a soprano- or a tenor-range solo voice. *Tip:* If you want to try the acoustics, "Amazing Grace," sung with pauses between the lines to allow for the echo, will sound truly powerful in this 900-year-old church; so will "Silent Night."

Lion's Gate (Saint Stephen's Gate). Admission NIS 10. Mon–Sat 8am–noon and 2–5pm (until 6pm in summer).

## VIA DOLOROSA ★

This is the **Way of the Cross,** traditionally believed to be the route followed by Jesus from the Praetorium (the Roman Judgment Hall) to Calvary, which was the scene of the Crucifixion. Over the centuries, millions of pilgrims have come here to walk the way that Jesus took to his death. Each Friday at 3pm, priests lead a procession for pilgrims along Via Dolorosa (starting at the First Station of the Cross in the Monastery of the Flagellation at the tower of Antonia, not far from the Lion's Gate). Large wooden crosses are carried by some of those in the procession and prayers are said at each of the 14 Stations of the Cross. The Via Dolorosa begins in the Muslim Quarter, in the northeast corner of the Old City, and winds its way to the Church of the Holy Sepulcher in the Christian Quarter.

The Sanctuary of the Condemnation, where Jesus was scourged and judged, marks the first Station of the Cross. It's open daily from 8am to noon (also 2–6pm Apr–Sept and 1–5pm Oct–Mar). As you leave the sanctuary to follow the Via Dolorosa, keep in mind that each Station of the Cross is marked by a small sign or a number engraved in the stone above the spot. Paving stones on the Via Dolorosa itself have been set in a semicircular pattern to mark those stations directly on the street. Other stations are behind closed doors; knock and a guardian, monk, or nun will probably be there to open up for you. There's a restroom opposite Station 3.

The following is a quick guide to the Stations of the Cross:

**Station 1:** Jesus is condemned to death. **Station 2:** Jesus receives the cross (at the foot of the Antonia). **Station 3:** Jesus falls for the first time (Polish biblical-archaeological museum). **Station 4:** Jesus meets his mother in the watching crowd. **Station 5:** Simon the Cyrene helps Jesus carry the cross. **Station 6:** A woman named Veronica wipes Jesus's face; his image remains on her cloth. **Station 7:** Jesus falls for the second time (at bazaar crossroads). **Station 8:** Jesus consoles the women of Jerusalem. **Station 9:** Jesus falls for the third time (Coptic Monastery).

The five remaining Stations of the Cross are inside the Church of the Holy Sepulcher (see below). **Station 10:** Jesus is stripped of his garments. **Station 11:** Jesus is nailed to the cross. **Station 12:** Jesus dies on the cross. **Station 13:** Jesus is taken down from the cross and given to Mary. **Station 14:** Jesus is laid in the chamber of the sepulcher and from there is resurrected.

**Church of the Holy Sepulcher ★★★** CHURCH   After the Roman emperor Constantine converted to Christianity and made it the religion of Rome in A.D. 326, his mother, Queen Helena, made a pilgrimage to the Holy Land and located what was believed to be the tomb from which Jesus rose. According to tradition, further excavation near the tomb uncovered the True Cross, revered as the most sacred relic of the Christian world until it was carried off by the Persians in A.D. 614. It was over this tomb that Constantine began the construction of the first Holy Sepulcher Church around A.D. 328, a complex of classical structures that was enlarged 200 years later by the Byzantine emperor, Justinian. Fire, earthquake, a 7th-century Persian invasion, and an 11th-century Muslim caliph destroyed much of the great, classical church, but the Crusaders rebuilt it in the 12th century—a mixture of Byzantine remnants and medieval Frankish reconstruction that was far less grand than the original. The church has been restored many times and is currently undergoing structural renovation. In 1997, the renovated interior of the great dome covering the sepulcher was unveiled. It is bright, fresh, and, to some visitors, a bit incompatible with the antiquity of the place. Its design motifs had to be neutral, avoiding incorporating any of the special artistic traditions of the six rival branches of Christianity that control different areas of the building.

The church is divided among the six oldest Christian sects: Roman Catholic, Armenian Orthodox, Greek Orthodox, Egyptian Coptic, Ethiopian, and Syrian Orthodox. Each denomination has its own space—right down to lines drawn down the middle of floors and pillars—and its own schedule of rights to be in other areas of the church at specific times. The decor, partitioned and changed every few feet, is a mixture of Byzantine and Frankish Crusader styles. As the Protestant Reformation developed more than a thousand years after the building of the church, there is no specifically Protestant section.

You can observe the final Stations of the Cross inside the church—the marble slab at the entrance is the Stone of Unction, where the body of Jesus was prepared for burial; the site of Calvary is on the second floor; and the early-19th-century marble tomb edifice encloses the actual cave of the sepulcher.

If you're in Jerusalem during Easter Week, you can attend many of the fascinating services based on ancient Eastern church traditions that are held at the church. Most notable are the Service of the Holy Fire, the dramatic pageant called the Washing of the Feet, and the exotic midnight Ethiopian procession on the part of the church under Ethiopian jurisdiction—the roof. No admission fee, and modest dress is required. Admission inside the church at this time is by invitation only, but the ceremonies can be viewed outside on closed circuit TV.

**Lutheran Church of the Redeemer ★ CHURCH** Kaiser Wilhelm II of Germany made a pilgrimage to Jerusalem in 1898 to dedicate the Church of the Redeemer, a Protestant church just outside the gates to the Church of the Holy Sepulcher. Ottoman-Turkish permission to allow construction of a Protestant church at such a prestigious location symbolized the growing alliance between Germany and the Ottoman Empire, one that would continue through World War I. The church has become a **venue for concerts** and performances of organ music; **the view** from the tower (no elevator, and a steep climb of more than 200 steps) is exceptional.

Btw. Muristan Bazaar and Suq Khan es-Zeit Bazaar. ℂ **02/627-6111.** Admission to tower NIS 5. Mon–Sat 9am–1pm and 2–5pm. English services Sun 9am.

## DAMASCUS GATE & THE BAZAARS ★

The Damascus Gate, the largest and most magnificent of all the entrances to the Old City, is the main route into the Old City from East Jerusalem. Once you are inside the gate, cafes, shops, and market stalls line a wide-stepped entrance street going downhill, Whether you take **El-Wad Road** (the Valley Road) to the left or **Suq Khan es-Zeit** (the Market of the Inn of the Olive Oil) to the right, the way becomes very narrow and confusing. Unlike the markets near the Jaffa Gate, which cater primarily to tourists, this part of the bazaar is an authentic market used by the people of East Jerusalem. You'll see stalls of spices and coffees, craft shops, bread bakeries, shops selling sneakers and children's wear, tiny one-chair barber establishments, and more.

Suq Khan es-Zeit eventually becomes the covered **Suq El Attarin,** or Bazaar of the Spices, now mostly a clothing bazaar. In other centuries, this covered market was lined with open sacks of cumin, cocoa, sesame, pepper, sumac, saffron, and all kinds of beans, dried herbs, medicines, and vegetables. Parallel and to the right of this central market street is the covered Suq El-Lahamin (the Butchers' Bazaar), its pavement often slippery with puddles of blood.

If you continue walking straight, eventually Suq El Attarin will cross David Street, and soon thereafter it becomes the recently excavated and renovated Cardo (the main street of Roman and Byzantine Jerusalem), which runs through the restored Jewish Quarter. Here you will find modern, Jewish-owner tourist shops. The area, incidentally, is well patrolled by police officers.

## THE OLD CITY RAMPARTS ★★

A good place to explore is the walk on the **Old City Ramparts.** You can enter the wall route at Jaffa Gate. The views are thrilling, but an entire circuit of the walls (about 4km/2½ miles) is no longer permitted, because part of the route skirts the Temple Mount. Underneath the present Damascus Gate, the Roman-era gate, to the left and below, has been excavated. Within this classical, triple-arched gate (which may have been extant in Jesus's time) there's a small museum (closed at press time) displaying laser reconstructions of the original gate and worth a quick visit if it's open.

*Note:* It's not a great idea for anyone to walk alone on the ramparts at any time of day. The ramparts are at times patrolled by groups of unruly local kids and unsavory illegal "guides." The circuit involves many ancient, irregular stone stairs, and although some have guardrails, this is *not* a place for young children or anyone not sure-footed.

The entry ticket costs NIS 18 for adults (discounts for children) and is good for 2 days (3 days if you buy on Fri). The ramparts are open Saturday to Thursday from 10am to 4pm and Friday 9am to 2pm.

Thanks to the making of the film "Schindler's List," the story of Oskar Schindler, a German businessman who fervently worked to save the lives of Jewish slave laborers during the Holocaust, has become world famous. His final resting place, arranged by those who owed their lives to him, is in a graveyard on Mount Zion. Exit the Zion Gate, turn left, cross the road, and continue downhill around to the right to a Catholic cemetery (many of the graves have Arabic inscriptions). The grave of the often puzzling but heroic Oskar Schindler is in the lower tier, marked by the many stones that visitors leave on it (a Jewish tradition).

## STREET OF THE CHAIN ★

Perpendicular to the Suq El Attarin–Cardo market is the Street of the Chain, which runs gently downhill to the **Gate of the Chain,** the most important entrance to the Haram es Sharif, or the Temple Mount. This was the great residential street of medieval Islamic Jerusalem. It starts out as a typical market passageway, but as you get closer to the Haram, you'll begin to notice (hidden behind shop displays) monumental, richly ornamented doorways of Mamluk period mansions and buildings decorated with carved stonework in "stalactite" patterns over the entryways. You can only surmise this area's affluent past; like much of the Old City, the neighborhood is overcrowded and has not yet benefited from preservation and renovation programs.

# Mount Zion ★★

This important location can be easily spotted as you approach the walls of the Old City from the west or the south. The building with a round, squat tower is the Dormition Abbey, and near this site is King David's Tomb, with the Room of the Last Supper (Coenaculum) above it. To reach **King David's Tomb** from inside the Old City, walk out Zion Gate, proceed down a narrow alley bounded by high stone walls, and turn left. Although this place has been venerated as the site of David's burial, the tradition can only be traced back to early medieval times; many believe the tomb would have been located in the ancient City of David, south of the present Old City. The building is open daily, including the Sabbath, from 8am to 5pm and until 2pm on Friday. Men should cover their heads; modest dress and headscarves are advisable for women.

Near King David's Tomb (in fact, in the same building) are a doorway and flight of stairs leading to the **Coenaculum (Upper Room) ★**, where Jesus sat with his disciples to celebrate the Passover Seder, the Last Supper. Again, the room's authenticity is based on many centuries of veneration; however, some question this tradition. It is open daily from 8:30am to 4pm.

In the cellar of a building near King David's Tomb is a sign indicating the entrance to the **Chamber of the Holocaust ★**, an eerie room lit by candles and dedicated to the memory of the six million Jews slain by the Nazis. The chamber, a private memorial and museum, is filled with artifacts from the Holocaust. It's open Sunday to Thursday from 9am to 4pm and on Friday until 1pm. There is no admission fee.

Close by is the graceful **Dormition Abbey ★** (✆ 02/671-9927), completed in 1910 by the German Benedictine Order on the spot where, according to tradition, Mary fell asleep before her burial and assumption into heaven. Inside the church, you'll find an elaborate golden mosaic, a crypt containing interesting religious artwork, and a statue of Mary surrounded by chapels donated by various countries. From the tower of the church, there's a fabulous panoramic view. It's open daily from 8am to noon and 2 to 6pm. The Dormition Abbey at times is a dramatic venue for public concerts.

# AN EASY WALKING TOUR OF THE OLD CITY

| | |
|---|---|
| **Start:** | **The Jaffa Gate** |
| **Finish:** | **The tour has three options: The first takes you to the Jewish Quarter and the Western Wall, the second to the Islamic shrines and mosques on the Temple Mount, and the third to an unusual Christian enclave on the roof of the Church of the Holy Sepulcher.** |
| **Best Times:** | **Sunday to Wednesday 8am to 3pm** |
| **Worst Times:** | **Shabbat, Muslim holidays, Friday, or after 3pm when the Dome of the Rock is closed** |

This meandering walk gets you to some major sites, offbeat vista points, and authentic eateries, but the Old City is a vast, intricate Chinese box of experiences, as unplanned and exotic as the 4,000-year history of Jerusalem itself. One way to enjoy the texture of this sublime hodgepodge is simply to plunge in and wander, chancing upon hummus parlors and holy sites, ancient bakeries and antique Bedouin embroideries. Learn a bit of Jerusalem's history and local lore as you move along.

The first part of the walk takes you to the Cardo, where the walk divides into three possible options. Begin at:

## 1 Jaffa Gate

Before you enter Jaffa Gate, which is the traditional entrance to the city for visitors from the West, check out the stones from many eras that make up the present Old City wall, which was erected by order of the Ottoman-Turkish sultan Suleiman the Magnificent in 1538. Some stones have been dressed with carefully cut flat borders surrounding a raised, flat central area (the boss) in the style of King Herod's stonecutters and probably date from 2,000 years ago. You will see this style again in the monumental stones of the Western Wall, which Herod constructed to surround the original Jerusalem Temple site. You'll notice other kinds of stones with flat borders and rougher raised bosses. These are in the pre-Herodian style of the Hasmoneans (the Maccabees), who were the last Jewish rulers of Jerusalem until modern times. You'll also see rough ashlars of the Byzantine era as well as the virtually undressed stones of Crusader and medieval times. In each of the upper corners of the closed decorative archway to the left of the Jaffa Gate, notice stones carefully carved into a leaf design, which are believed to have come from a long-destroyed Crusader church. The walls of Jerusalem, like the city itself, are composed of stones used again and again, just as many of the legends and traditions of the city reappear and are reassembled by each successive civilization.

Inside the gate, on the left, is:

## 2 The Tourist Information Office

Here you can pick up free maps, information, and tourist publications.

# Old City Walking Tour & Sites

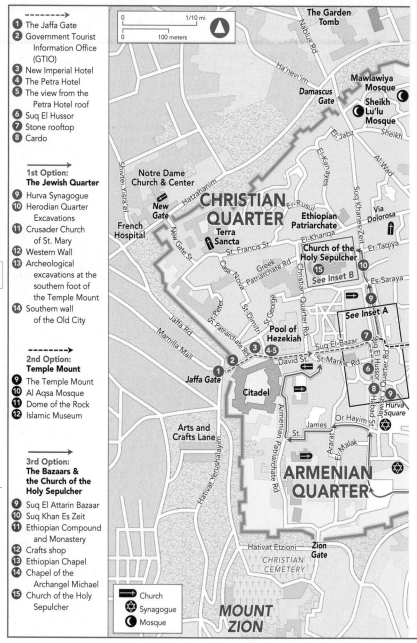

1. The Jaffa Gate
2. Government Tourist Information Office (GTIO)
3. New Imperial Hotel
4. The Petra Hotel
5. The view from the Petra Hotel roof
6. Suq El Hussor
7. Stone rooftop
8. Cardo

**1st Option:**
**The Jewish Quarter**

9. Hurva Synagogue
10. Herodian Quarter Excavations
11. Crusader Church of St. Mary
12. Western Wall
13. Archeological excavations at the southern foot of the Temple Mount
14. Southern wall of the Old City

**2nd Option:**
**Temple Mount**

9. The Temple Mount
10. Al Aqsa Mosque
11. Dome of the Rock
12. Islamic Museum

**3rd Option:**
**The Bazaars & the Church of the Holy Sepulcher**

9. Suq El Attarin Bazaar
10. Suq Khan Es Zeit
11. Ethiopian Compound and Monastery
12. Crafts shop
13. Ethiopian Chapel
14. Chapel of the Archangel Michael
15. Church of the Holy Sepulcher

5

EXPLORING JERUSALEM | An Easy Walking Tour of the Old City

82

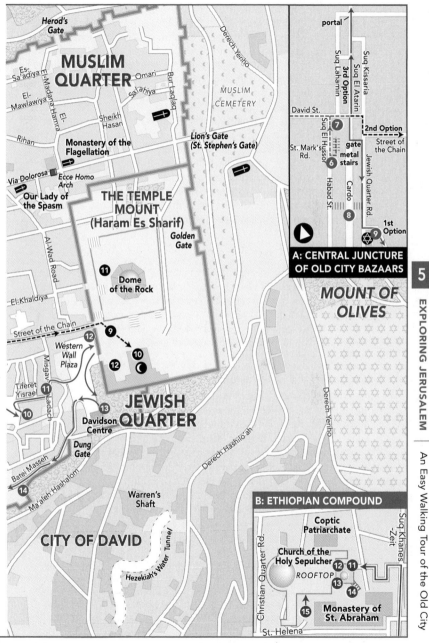

Herod's Gate

MUSLIM QUARTER

Es-Sa'adiya

El-Mawlawiya

El-Madana Hamra

Rihan

Omari

Sa'ahiya

Bur Laqlaq

Sheikh Hasan

Derech Yeriho

MUSLIM CEMETERY

Monastery of the Flagellation

Lion's Gate (St. Stephen's Gate)

Via Dolorosa

Ecce Homo Arch

Our Lady of the Spasm

THE TEMPLE MOUNT (Haram Es Sharif)

Golden Gate

Al-Wad Road

11

Dome of the Rock

El-Khaldiya

Street of the Chain

9

Western Wall Plaza

12

12

10

11

Misgav Ladach

Tiferet Yisrael

JEWISH QUARTER

10

13

Davidson Centre

Dung Gate

Batei Masseh

Ma'aleh Hashalom

14

Warren's Shaft

CITY OF DAVID

Hezekiah's Water Tunnel

Derech Hashilo'ah

Derech Yeriho

MOUNT OF OLIVES

**A: CENTRAL JUNCTURE OF OLD CITY BAZAARS**

portal

Suq Kissaria

Suq El Atarin

Suq Lahamin

3rd Option

David St.

7

2nd Option

Street of the Chain

St. Mark's Rd.

Suq El Hussor

6

gate metal stairs

Cardo

Habad St.

Jewish Quarter Rd.

8

9

1st Option

**B: ETHIOPIAN COMPOUND**

Coptic Patriarchate

Church of the Holy Sepulcher

ROOFTOP

Christian Quarter Rd.

Suq Khanes Zeit

12

11

13

14

Monastery of St. Abraham

15

St. Helena

Enter the archway on the left to the arcade of:

## 3 The New Imperial Hotel

Built in the 1880s, this was, in its time, the most luxurious hotel in Jerusalem. In the 19th century, the now largely deserted arcade was a private bazaar for hotel guests, where the beggars, lepers, cripples, and "riffraff" of Jerusalem could be neatly excluded. Slightly uphill and in the center of the arcade is a broken streetlamp mounted on a cylindrical stone that was uncovered when the foundations for the New Imperial were dug. The Latin lettering "LEG X" records a marker for the camp of the Tenth Legion Fretensis, which conquered and destroyed Jewish Jerusalem in A.D. 70. The Roman Jewish historian, Flavius Josephus wrote that after the Temple and the buildings of Jerusalem were systematically razed and the surviving inhabitants led off to slavery, death, and exile, the Tenth Legion encamped beside the ruins of the Jaffa Gate for 62 years to guard the ruins against Jews who might try to filter back to reestablish the city. The discovery of this marker in proximity to the Jaffa Gate confirms Josephus's account. The once-elegant New Imperial, as it drifted into seediness, became a spot for romantic assignations during the British Mandate period. Characters played by Humphrey Bogart and Ingrid Bergman would have felt right at home.

Next door is the:

## 4 Petra Hotel

The first modern hotel built in the Old City in the 1870s, the once-elegant Petra, now reduced to the status of a hostel, is popular with backpackers. Herman Melville and Mark Twain may have stayed in an earlier structure on this site (the old Mediterranean Hotel) during their visits to what was then a decrepit warren of ruins filled with lice-covered beggars and crazed religious fanatics. Neither Melville nor Twain found Jerusalem a pleasant place to stay.

Enter at the far right as you face the building, climb the stairs to the second-floor lobby of the Petra, and ask the person at the desk for permission to see:

## 5 The View from the Petra Hotel's Roof

Be sure to show this book at the desk in the lobby on the second floor and ask for permission to see the roof. Admission is about NIS 10 per person, but if you're in a group, try to bargain. From the lobby, climb two more long flights of stairs and emerge from the creaky wooden attic stairs onto the roof with its strange series of curved stone domes. Turn left, go up a few steps, turn left again, and you will face one of the Old City's great panoramas—perfectly aligned, with the golden Dome of the Rock (site of the First and Second Temples) in the exact center of the vista, with the roofline of the city spread out below you. This is where photographers come for postcard views. The roof used to be a quiet, contemplative spot, but guests of the hostel at times make the roof into a wall-to-wall sleeping bag encampment in summer.

As you look eastward toward the Temple Mount, you'll see the Mount of Olives across the horizon behind the Dome of the Rock. In ancient times, this now-barren ridge was a natural olive grove, and its cultivation was one of the sources of ancient Jerusalem's wealth. The green area of the ridge, just behind the Dome of the Rock, is the Garden of Gethsemane (Gethsemane is the anglicized version of the Hebrew word for "olive press"), where Jesus was arrested after the Last Supper. This is the western side of the Mount of Olives ridge. On the eastern side, out of view, is the site of the village of Bethany where Lazarus, who was raised from the dead by Jesus, and his sisters, Mary and Martha, lived. Jesus may have been making his way to their house after the Passover dinner at the time of his arrest.

The Dome of the Rock was built in A.D. 691. According to legend, the saintly warrior Omar Ibn El Khattab, who conquered Jerusalem for Islam in A.D. 638, was greeted by Sophronius, the Christian archbishop, at the Jaffa Gate. Sophronius surrendered the city peacefully to Omar and then offered to lead the new ruler on a tour of his conquest. The first thing Omar Ibn El Khattab asked to see was "the Mosque of Suleiman," or the place where Solomon's Temple had once stood. The vast ceremonial platform surrounding the site of the ancient Jewish temple was one of the few architectural landmarks of Herodian Jerusalem that the Romans had found too difficult to eradicate when they destroyed the city in A.D. 70. Three hundred years later, as Christianity triumphed over Roman paganism, the Temple Mount was one of the places in the city left purposely in ruins (perhaps symbolically) by the Byzantine Christians. By the time of the Muslim conquest, the Temple Mount had become the garbage dump for Jerusalem and the surrounding area. Omar Ibn El Khattab was so saddened by the sight of the ancient holy place defiled and in ruins that he removed his cloak and used it to carry away debris. Sophronius prudently followed Omar's example. Later, Muslim authorities ordered the most beautiful building possible to be placed over the Temple Mount's sacred rock. The silver-domed Al Aqsa Mosque, on the southern edge of the Temple Mount, also commemorates this event.

Just below the Petra's roof is a large, empty, rectangular area, the Pool of Hezekiah, misnamed centuries ago for the Judean king whose hidden water system saved ancient Jerusalem from Assyrian onslaught in 701 B.C.; the pool is actually a disused reservoir for a water system constructed in Herodian and Roman times. To the north, you'll see the great silver dome of the Church of the Holy Sepulcher, built over the site venerated for almost 2,000 years as the place of Jesus's crucifixion and entombment. In the far distance, beyond the walls of the Old City, on the northern part of the Mount of Olives, the small modern city is the complex of the Hebrew University and Hadassah Hospital on Mount Scopus. To your right (south), inside the walls of the Old City, are the domes of the Armenian Cathedral of Saint James, the roofs of the Armenian and Jewish quarters of the Old City; to the south, beyond the hill of Abu Tor (believed to have been the Hill of Evil Counsel the site of the Blood Acre purchased for a potters' field with Judas Iscariot's 30 pieces of silver) lies Bethlehem, the birthplace of King David and Jesus.

Leave the Petra Hotel and continue down David Street to:

## 6 Suq El Hussor

This former basket bazaar, which once sold the big, traylike olive-twig baskets older Palestinian women sometimes still balance on their heads, filled with grapes, fruits, and vegetables, is now a small covered street of ordinary shops, but it leads to a great view.

About 18m (59 ft.) on the left side of Suq El Hussor, you'll notice an open metal staircase. Climb up the staircase, and you'll be on:

## 7 The Stone Rooftop of the Covered Markets

Here you'll discover a different world above the bustling labyrinths of the bazaars. The broad rooftop area straight ahead covers the exact center of the Old City, where the four quarters meet. At the right time of day, if you listen carefully, you will hear emanating from the large dome on your right the unmistakable sound of a game of billiards; this dome at the very heart of the Holy City covers a billiard parlor. In Crusader times, this large structure housed the city's bourse or exchange. From this rooftop, you can clearly see the architectural distinctions among the four quarters of the walled city: the orange-tile-roofed Christian Quarter to the northwest; the dome-roofed Muslim Quarter with its many television antennas to the northeast; the new stonework of the Jewish Quarter to the southeast, rebuilt by the Israelis after they reoccupied the Old City in 1967 (this area is devoid of antennas; its inhabitants receive cable); and, to the southwest, the older stone buildings of the Armenian Quarter. Again, through the maze of TV antennas, you get an interesting chance to photograph the lavish Dome of the Rock.

Descend the metal staircase and backtrack on Suq El Hussor to David Street. Turn right onto David Street. The next right on David Street leads to:

8 The Cardo
The restored and renovated section of Roman and Byzantine Jerusalem's main market street is now filled with stylish modern shops.

At this point you have three choices for the rest of your tour.

**THE FIRST OPTION: THE JEWISH QUARTER**  You could easily wander the streets of this beautifully reconstructed area for a number of hours.

Walk south on the Jewish Quarter Road to the:

9 Hurva Synagogue
This site was home to the Jewish Quarter's main synagogue from the 16th to the mid–20th centuries, but it has been destroyed a number of times since its original construction. Most recently, it was blown up during the Jordanian occupation of the Old City after the War of Independence in 1948. In 2010, it was rebuilt almost exactly as it stood before it was destroyed. For more on this site, see p. 69.

10 TAKE A BREAK 💺
A slice of kosher pizza, a falafel, a light meal, and a wonderful Arabic sesame bread fresh from the bakery oven (with a packet of local spices) are available on the section of the Jewish Quarter Road beyond the Hurva Synagogue.

Walk across the square behind the synagogue, and you'll see signs for the:

11 Herodian Quarter
The present Jewish Quarter, on a hill opposite the Temple Mount, was the aristocratic residential part of Jerusalem in Herodian times. During the 1970s, intensive archaeological excavations were carried out here while the Jewish Quarter was being rebuilt. The ruins of large mansions were found with facilities for *mikvot* (ritual baths) and with mosaic floors ornamented by simple geometric designs (in strict keeping with the Mosaic commandment against graven images).

Take Tiferet Israel Street, which runs from the northeastern corner of the big square to the end, where you will come upon the:

12 Crusader Church of Saint Mary
In the extensive ruins of this Crusader-era church, once hidden beneath buildings from later times, explore the ruined cloister and the basilica, with a view of the Temple Mount and the Mount of Olives framed in the window of the central apse.

Turn right at the church and make a left to the great staircase, which descends down to the:

## 13 Western Wall

The Herodian retaining wall for the western side of the Temple Mount was built by Herod the Great more than 2,000 years ago. It's a remnant of the outer court-yard of the Jerusalem Temple and the holiest place of prayer in Jewish tradition. See p. 70.

Between the Western Wall and the Dung Gate, you can enter the area of:

## 14 Archaeological Excavations

Set at the southern foot of the Temple Mount, these excavations are accessed through the Davidson Exhibition Center (p. 76), which shows video programs depicting what the Jerusalem Temple would have been like in the years before its destruction in A.D. 70. Self-guided audio tours take you to various points along the southwestern and southern walls of the Temple Mount, where you can study the grandeur of this structure away from the crowds at prayer at the Western Wall.

From the excavations, take the road inside the city wall uphill to the:

## 15 Southern Wall of the Old City

Here you'll find a lovely view into the valley below, which was the site of the original City of David 3,000 years ago.

You will see a parking lot inside the city walls; cross it and turn right into a pathway that becomes Habad Road; follow Habad Road to the far end. Or Hayim Street is a left turn off Habad Road; continue uphill until the road ends at the Armenian Patriarchate Road. A right turn onto this road gets you back to the square inside the Jaffa Gate. Alternatively, at the edge of the parking lot at he end of Habad Road is a stop for Bus 38 that takes you back to West Jerusalem's New City.

**SECOND OPTION: THE TEMPLE MOUNT**   From the Cardo, if it is not a Friday and not after 11:30am, continue straight onto where David Street seems to end.

Turn right and then quickly take the first left, a continuation of David Street called the Street of the Chain. Continue down this road to the great green door (the Gate of the Chain) at the end, which leads directly onto the:

## 16 Temple Mount

The Temple Mount (in Arabic, Haram es Sharif) is open for visitors until 3pm. Give yourself ample time to walk around the ceremonial plaza and enjoy the views of the Mount of Olives. At press time, the Al Aqsa Mosque, the Dome of the Rock, and the Islamic Museum on the Temple Mount were not open to the public, but if entering them is again permitted, non-Muslims must buy admission tickets (approx. NIS 38, and well worth the fee) from a small stone kiosk to the right of the Al Aqsa Mosque to gain admission to both mosques and the museum. It is permissible to take photographs outdoors on the Temple Mount, but you cannot bring a camera into mosques or shrines.

Walk diagonally to the right after entering the Gate of the Chain to the southern end of the Temple Mount to:

## 17 Al Aqsa Mosque

This is the main Islamic prayer hall on the Temple Mount (p. 72).

In the center of the Temple Mount is the:

## 18 Dome of the Rock

You can't miss its lavish exterior tiles and its golden dome (p. 73).

At the southwest corner is the:

## 19 Islamic Museum

This museum houses a collection of Islamic artifacts from earlier periods on the Temple Mount.

**THIRD OPTION: THE BAZAARS & THE CHURCH OF THE HOLY SEP-ULCHER**   This walk begins at the intersection of David Street and the Cardo.

Turn left into the narrow, covered:

## 20 Suq El Attarin Bazaar

The Spice Market was covered during the time of the Crusaders, who perhaps could not bear the blazing summer sun of the region. It's actually an additional segment of the Cardo, once the great Roman north-south market and ceremonial street. The Roman Cardo, originally broad and colonnaded, evolved over centuries into the present warren of narrow, parallel bazaars (including the Butcher's Bazaar, with its dangling skinned sheep heads and gutters of blood, parallel just to the left). Suq El Attarin becomes Suq Khan es-Zeit and runs all the way north to the Damascus Gate. El Attarin is now mostly populated by clothing and sneaker shops.

Follow this covered market street until you exit from the covered portion, through a nondescript portal, and continue straight ahead. The next section of the street, no longer roofed over but covered by shop awnings, is:

## 21 Suq Khan es-Zeit (the Market of the Inn of the Olive Oil)

Probably since Herodian-Jewish times, this area has been a major food market—the Frankish Crusaders called this the *Malcuisinat,* or the Street of Bad Cookery, unhappy with the many Middle Eastern specialties sold here. You will notice pastry shops displaying mysteriously radiant mountains of baklava arranged on top of glowing lightbulbs and flashlights; the peanut baklava filling is sometimes dyed green to approximate the more costly pistachio. There are also chewy rolled pancakes filled with nuts or sweet cheese, served in a honey syrup; other shops sell dried fruits or dark globs of fruit- and nut-filled nougat. There are also hibachis cooking kabobs, *shashliks,* and rotisserie chicken to go. Any of these places are good bets for snacks.

## 22 TAKE A BREAK 🍵

**Abu Assab Refreshments,** a busy Old City landmark, sells fresh orange, grapefruit, and carrot juice and is the least expensive and best of its kind in town. It's a good place to stave off dehydration and fill up on vitamins, and you can order the juices straight or in any combination. Upstairs, Mike Abu Assab, the British-educated manager, runs the best Internet and phone center in the Old City, if you want to check your e-mail.

A short way along the same side of the street is a stone staircase. Climb the staircase to the top, turn left, follow the lane to the end, turn right, and follow the street around through the Coptic Convent and onto the:

## 23 Ethiopian Compound & Monastery

It's located on the Church of the Holy Sepulcher's roof with the protruding dome in the center. Through slits in the windows of the dome, you will be able to glimpse the **Chapel of Saint Helena** inside the Holy Sepulcher Church below; you'll even be able to smell the church incense and, at times, hear services and prayers.

The Ethiopians use this roof area each year on the Saturday midnight eve of Easter Sunday for one of the city's most exotic religious processions. The Ethiopian patriarch, with a great ceremonial African umbrella, circumambulates the dome, followed by monks beating ancient drums—so large that they must be carried by two men—and by chanting white-robed pilgrims. The procession then retires to a leopard-skin tent (nowadays made of canvas in a leopard-skin pattern) to chant and pray through the night. This very moving ceremony is open to the public, and many Jerusalemites make it a point to attend each year.

The Ethiopian compound is spread across the sprawling segments of the roof of the Church of the Holy Sepulcher. Note that on this ancient roof entire trees and gardens grow, among them the olive trees (or offshoots of olive trees) in which Abraham supposedly found the ram he offered in sacrifice after God freed him from the commandment to sacrifice his son, Isaac. Beside the expanse of the roof surrounding the dome are the living quarters of the tiny, walled, fortresslike monastery. Visitors may not enter this monastery compound, but you can look into the lane at the entrance to the monastery: The low, round-walled buildings and trees offer a distinctly African feeling. For centuries, the Church of the Holy Sepulcher has been divided among the six oldest factions of Christianity, and in the most recent division, the Ethiopian Church, with roots dating from the A.D. 4th century, got the roof. Both Ethiopian monks and a lay community have inhabited this location for centuries (you can often smell the wonderful spicy cooking of the communal kitchen). Note the church bells hanging in the ruined Gothic arches of the Crusader-era church structure to the right and above the tiny main street.

To the left of the doorway into the monastery lane, you will find the community's well, with a shaft running down through the Holy Sepulcher Church (running water has obviated the need for the well, but the Ethiopians still have the right to a certain amount of water from it each day).

Opposite the well is a small, sometimes open door leading to a:

## 24 Crafts Shop

It's usually closed, but at times you can find Ethiopian crafts and hand-painted icons for sale.

From this door continue around the corner to the large, ancient wooden door leading to the:

## 25 Ethiopian Chapel

This structure was probably built in medieval times. Here, if a monk is in attendance, you will be shown crucifix-shaped holy books written in ancient Ge'ez (the sacred language of Ethiopia), and you will have time to take in the paintings (unfortunately done by European religious painters rather than by traditional Ethiopian religious artists) that depict the queen of Sheba visiting King Solomon in approximately 940 B.C. Charmingly, the artist decided to depict an anachronistic group of 18th-century Polish Hasidic Jews among King Solomon's entourage. The royal Ethiopian family is said to have descended from the traditionally believed union of the queen and King Solomon (one of the emperor of Ethiopia's titles was "the Lion of Judah"), and in 1935, when Emperor Haile Selassie was forced to flee Mussolini's invasion of his country, he took up residence in Jerusalem, "the land of my fathers." There is a tray for contributions at the back of the chapel.

Continue to the rear of the chapel and down the staircase to the:

## 26 Chapel of the Archangel Michael

In this ancient chapel, with its carved and inlaid wood paneling, the community of Ethiopian monks gathers in late afternoon for prayers (around 4pm in winter; 5pm during daylight saving time, depending on how long sunlight is). Visitors are allowed to sit on the bench in the rear of the chapel outside the wrought iron fence and listen to the traditional Ethiopian chanting, which is extremely beautiful.

The ancient wooden door of the chapel leads outside to the main entrance plaza in front of the:

## 27 Church of the Holy Sepulcher

Now that you've seen the roof, you are ready to journey through the very special interior. (See p. 78 for a detailed description of the church.) After visiting the church, make your way back through the bazaars to David Street and the Jaffa Gate.

# WEST JERUSALEM ATTRACTIONS

## Museums

**The Bible Lands Museum** ★★ MUSEUM   This is a museum for people who appreciate beauty. Just next to the Israel Museum, the Bible Lands Museum concentrates on archeological treasures from Middle Eastern areas beyond the land of Israel. It was founded by Dr. and Mrs. Elie Borowski, who donated their world-famous collection of ancient Near Eastern artifacts. In the words of Dr. Borowski, a noted Near Eastern scholar and cousultant to museums, "Each of the objects [in the museum] has its time in history, its location in space, its meaning in religion and daily life, and last but not least, its beauty and artistry."

The collection's treasures include priceless **Assyrian ivories** from Nimrud (ca. 800 B.C.), with an iconic, delicately carved winged griffin grazing on foliage; the A.D. 4th-century **sarcophagus of Julia Latronilla,** decorated with elaborately sculpted depictions of scenes from the life of Jesus (among the earliest known representations of Jesus); and more simple, charming objects, such as an Egyptian cosmetics container in the shape of a swimming girl (ca. 1550 B.C.). The Bible Lands Museum also houses mysterious objects, like an A.D. 1st-century Roman painted linen shroud with the ethereal image of a woman covering its length (think: the controversial Holy Shroud of Turin). A fascinating gallery is devoted to cylinder seals and scarabs; lively, kid-friendly computer/video programs explore these minute works of art and offer detailed explanations. There are also constant visiting exhibitions. *Tip:* The museum hosts a wonderful program of **Saturday evening classical and popular concerts** (including wine and cheese). Concerts begin at 9:30pm, but the museum opens at 8:30pm for selected visiting. For programs, check the website.

25 Granot St. (beside the Israel Museum). © **02/561-1066.** www.blmj.org. Admission NIS 40, students NIS 20. Sun–Tues and Thurs 9:30am–5:30pm, Wed 9:30am–9:30pm, Fri 9:30am–2pm, Sat 10am–2pm. Closed holidays. English tours daily 10:30am. Call ahead for a schedule of additional English-language tours. Bus: 9 or 17.

**Israel Museum** ★★★ MUSEUM   Israel's national museum would be a treasure-trove even if it *didn't* house the Dead Sea Scrolls. But because they are the main reason people visit, we'll start our discussion with those ancient scrolls, which are 1,000 years older than the oldest previously known copies of the Hebrew Bible. Located in an area titled **the Shrine of the Book,** the exhibit that houses them not only displays pieces of the scrolls, with translation and fascinating commentary on the passages shown, but tells the story of their discovery. And what a story it is! They were discovered by chance in 1947 by Bedouin shepherds in a cave near the Dead Sea, where they were apparently hidden in advance of the Roman invasion of A.D. 67. They contain the only surviving biblical scrolls from the time when the Temple still stood in Jerusalem plus so-called extra-biblical writings that didn't make it into the canon.

The Shrine of the Book also exhibits some of the fascinating, precious personal possessions hidden in the Dead Sea caves by refugees who did not survive to retrieve them. Archeologist Yigal Yadin's beautifully photographed book "Bar Kochba" brings the stories behind these discoveries to life. *Tip:* In a recent initiative, the museum has made a number of the Dead Sea Scrolls in its collection available in their entirety on the Israel Museum website, providing an amazing opportunity for readers of Hebrew as well as a chance for others to examine the innate beauty and restrained grace of this sacred world heritage treasure in its most ancient form.

The museum holds far more than these precious scrolls (although they are, arguably, the "Mona Lisa" of the place), so don't just see the scrolls and bolt! You'll want to dedicate a good half-day to touring here.

The museum is divided into five main sections: The vast **Archeology Wing** contains the world's largest and most dramatic display of Israeli archeological finds. The **Judaica Wing** displays the world's most comprehensive, dazzling collection of Jewish cultural and religious objects, gathered from communities ranging from the Caribbean and Italy to Russia, Morocco, Iran, and India. The pavilions of the **Fine Arts Complex** house carefully chosen collections of Impressionist and 20th-century art as well as galleries of beautifully displayed Primitive, pre-Columbian, and Asian art. The 20-acre **Billy Rose Sculpture Garden,** designed by Japanese-American artist Isamu Noguchi, displays a 100-piece collection of works by Israeli and international artists ranging from Rodin to Picasso to Henry Moore. Near the sculpture garden, a very popular, intricate **Scale Model of Herodian Jerusalem,** created in the 1960s and constantly updated according to archaeological finds, is nestled against the landscape of the Jerusalem hills; elsewhere, other works of art and archeological treasures dot the museum's grounds.

**Also not to be missed:** the **ancient mosaic floors of Israeli synagogues, churches and villas,** filled with stories and messages about the cultural and religious worlds of their creators; the new indoor **"Synagogue Route,"** lined with intact interiors of synagogues transported from their original sites in places as varied as Cochin, India, and the Italian Veneto; the wall of exotic antique Hanukkah menorahs from all over the world; or the costumes, furnishings and **model rooms of Jewish homes in various countries.**

And beyond the permanent exhibits, there's an ever-changing array of exciting temporary exhibits: In 2013–14, the museum showed the mysterious "I Am Gabriel" scroll on stone, a little known extra-biblical text from the time of the Second Temple, along with Christian, Jewish, and Koranic texts pertaining to the Angel Gabriel. The museum also hosts programs of international and Israeli concerts, dance performances, theater, and film. Check them out—they're often the hottest tickets in Jerusalem!

There's so much to see in the museum that a visit of many hours should be planned. Look into a special discount "return visit" ticket so that you can come back another day. Fortunately, the museum contains **a stylish cafe and a more elegant, expensive restaurant called "Modern,"** featuring a daytime menu of contemporary Israeli food. Both choices make meals in the museum a pleasure. All food services are kosher. A large, imaginative **museum shop** featuring well-designed reproduction items is filled with good ideas for gifts and special mementos. Parents should know that a lively, innovative **Children's Wing** is available and engages both kids and their parents, often with interactive exhibits of ancient through modern art.

Ruppin St. ℂ **02/670-8811.** www.imj.org.il. Admission NIS 50, students NIS 37, children NIS 25, free for children under 17 Tues and Sat. Sat–Mon and Wed–Thurs 10am–5pm, Tues 4pm–9pm, Fri and holiday eves 10am–2pm; call for special hours on certain holidays. The cafe and restaurant are closed on Shabbat. Bus: 7, 9, 14, 35, or 99.

**L. A. Mayer Memorial Museum of Islamic Art ★ MUSEUM** Even those who know nothing about Islamic arts will find themselves moved by this extraordinary collection of ceramics, illuminated manuscripts, jewelry, textiles, carpets, and artwork. It truly is eye candy of the first degree. As well, the museum is world famous for its gallery of clocks, including the Salomons collection of antique and Breguet watches from Paris. Be sure to save time for the changing exhibits of contemporary Islamic art, which often features the work of local artists (in 2012–13, a one-woman show of the Galilee painter Fatma Abu Rumi dazzled visitors). Only parts of the museum's inventory are on display at any one time, but the museum is always a worthwhile stop.

2 Ha-Palmach St. ℂ **02/566-1291.** Admission NIS 40, discounts for children and students. Sun–Mon and Wed 10am–3pm, Tues and Thurs 10am–7pm, Fri 10am–2pm, Sat 10am–4pm. Bus: 9, 19, or 22.

**Sir Isaac and Lady Edith Wolfson Museum ★ MUSEUM** Hidden on an upper floor of Hechal Shlomo, this museum displays a changing array of exceptional Jewish ceremonial objects, drawn from the famous Wolfson Collection of Judaica. Until recently, a much greater number of the museum's antique Hanukkah menorahs, Kiddush cups, and scribal arts were exhibited, but this remains a small and worthwhile quick stop. The collection also includes works of contemporary Judaica by such craftspeople as Oded Davidson and Danny Azoulay, whose workshops can be visited in downtown Jerusalem.

In Heichal Shlomo, King George St. ℂ **02/623-7908.** Admission NIS 15. Sun–Thurs 9am–3pm. Bus: 4, 7, 8, 9, or 48.

# Memorials

**Mount Herzl ★★ CEMETERY** Mount Herzl is the cemetery for Israel's most heroic war dead and for many of its leading citizens, including Golda Meir, Levi Eshkol, and Yitzhak Rabin. But the memorial that, arguably, draws the most visitors is that of Theodor Herzl, who envisioned and worked for the founding of Israel until his death in 1904. A large, black monolith marks Herzl's interment, and the on-site **Herzl Museum** (ℂ **02/632-1515;** www.herzl.org) explores the life and work of the founder of modern Zionism with an inventive new 1-hour video production. It also contains a replica of Herzl's Vienna study with his own library and furniture.

Accessed on Herzl Blvd. in the Bet Ha-Kerem section. Apr–Oct daily 8am–6:30pm (Nov–Mar until 5pm). Free admission to the park and cemetery; museum admission NIS 25. Museum Sun–Wed 9am–6pm (last tour 5pm), Thurs 9am–7pm, Fri 9am–12:15pm. Bus: 14, 18, 20, 21, 27, 33, or 99. Light Rail to Har Herzl.

**Yad VaShem Memorial and Holocaust Museum ★★★ MEMORIAL/ MUSEUM** A biblical verse was the inspiration for the name of Israel's most heart-rending memorial: "And to them I will give within my temple and its walls a memorial and a name better than sons and daughters; I will give them an everlasting name that will not be cut off." The words "Yad Vashem" are the "memorial" and "name" of that verse. This intensely affecting monument and museum of the Holocaust is an effort to create a place and a name for those six million Jewish lives who fell victim to the Nazis—lives that were allowed no place of refuge on earth and whose persecutors hoped to erase even the memory of their existence.

The memorial campus is vast, spreading across a hill overlooking mountains on the edge of Jerusalem, and with a number of different memorials. Start your visit with the **Holocaust Museum,** built in 2005; it fills a long, tunnel-like structure, an agonized trail of personal possessions, diaries, photographs, and videos of Holocaust victims. Audio testimonies of survivors help reveal the history of the Holocaust on a very personal level (this museum replaces a smaller, more simple exhibit originally built in the 1960s).

Next, head to the large, empty, tomblike **Hall of Remembrance,** which an eternal flame shedding light on a stone floor containing plaques with the names of the many death camps and places of murder; and the moving **Avenue of the Righteous Among the Nations,** planted with trees in tribute to each individual gentile who helped save Jewish lives. Many of these heroes and their families suffered torture and death at the hands of the Nazis. Among those honored here are the courageous friends who tried to save the family of Anne Frank, as well as thousands of others in every corner of Europe who acted with equal bravery and humanity.

Yad VaShem's **Hall of Names** should be your next stop. It collects and preserves more than three million pages of testimony about the actions that were undertaken against the Jewish people during World War II, as well as the names, photographs, and personal stories of thousands of Holocaust victims. Visitors to Yad Vashem are asked to contribute any information they many have so that every possible victim may be remembered. Other memorials include the **Valley of the Destroyed Communities,** commemorating over 5,000 Jewish communities that were wiped from the face of the earth; and a haunting memorial to more than 1.5 million murdered **Children of the Holocaust.** In addition, there are research archives, an education center, and temporary exhibits: In 2013, an extraordinary exhibit of portraits created by Jewish artists living in the shadow of death, shed special light on those who struggled to live, create, and be remembered in the face of unimaginable horror.

After the Western Wall, Yad VaShem is the most visited site in the country. It demands a good amount of time to see (a minimum of 2 hr.) and is a place not recommended for young children.

On Har Ha-Zikaron. © **02/675-1611.** www.yadvashem.org.il. Free admission. Sun–Thurs 9am–4:45pm, Fri 9am–1pm; Hall of Names Sun–Thurs 10am–2pm, Fri 10am–1pm; archives and library Sun–Thurs 9am–3pm. Closed Sat and Jewish holidays. Light Rail or Bus: 10, 13a, 16, 20, 23, 24, 26, 26a, 27, 27a, 28, 28a, 33, 25, 39,. or 99 to Mt. Herzl. Free shuttle from Mt. Herzl goes to Yad VaShem. Car park at Yad Vashen NIS 28.

## Churches & Monasteries

**Rechov Ha-Nevi'im (Street of the Prophets)** was the "Christian street" of 19th-century West Jerusalem, and still has a variety of churches and missionary societies. From Zion Square, in the heart of downtown Jerusalem, cross Jaffa Road and go up the hill on Ha-Rav Kook Street. Opposite the intersection of Ha-Rav Kook and Ha-Nevi'im streets is the entrance to the narrow, high-walled **Ethiopia Street,** with its 19th-century stone mansions. Here you'll find the splendid **Abyssinian (Ethiopian) Church.** The elegant building with the Lion of Judah carved into the gate above the courtyard is the spiritual home of the Coptic Ethiopian clergy. The lion symbolizes the meeting of the Queen of Sheba (an Ethiopian empress), and King Solomon, from whom she received the emblem, according to legend. The interior of the century-old circular church is filled with a wonderful array of icons and paintings; although none are in the Ethiopian tradition, many were chosen for their charm and native beauty. Bungalows for clergy and pilgrims from Ethiopia surround the church enclave.

**Notre Dame de France,** built in 1887, is at Zahal Square, just opposite New Gate in the Old City walls. The monumental buildings of the complex, on the old border between East and West Jerusalem, were badly damaged during heavy fighting in the 1948 war. Part of the complex, restored in the 1970s, contains a restaurant, a hotel, and a Roman Catholic pilgrimage center.

**Saint Andrew's Church of Scotland,** its interior decorated with Armenian tiles, was built by the people of Scotland in 1929 and was dedicated by General Allenby, whose army liberated Jerusalem from the Ottoman Empire in 1917. This Presbyterian Church is situated on a scenic hilltop near Abu Tor and the old Jerusalem railroad station.

The **Russian Orthodox Holy Trinity Cathedral** is just off Jaffa Road. This white, multidomed architectural gem in the Renaissance style was constructed after the Crimean War for pilgrims of the Russian Orthodox faith.

The **Monastery of the Cross,** in the Valley of the Cross outside Rehavia, was built in the 11th century and is now maintained by the Greek Orthodox Church. According to tradition, this medieval, atmospheric monastery is located on the spot where the tree stood from which the True Cross was made. The monastery is open Monday to Friday from 9am to 4pm. Admission is NIS 5. Bus 9 or 17.

There are also a number of interesting churches and monasteries in Ein Kerem (see below), and in Abu Ghosh (p. 114).

## More Attractions

**Beit Ticho (Ticho House)** ★ HISTORIC SITE   Loved by Jerusalemites, both for its beauty and its history, Ticho House was built in 1880 as a private villa for the Aga Rashid Nashashibi. Around 1924, it became the home of artist Anna Ticho and her husband, Dr. Abraham Ticho, a legendary ophthalmologist who maintained his surgery there. The building is now officially a downtown branch of the Israel Museum, complete with a dandy museum gift shop. There's a permanent exhibit of Anna Ticho's controlled, powerful charcoals and drawings of the wild Israeli landscape, as well as visiting exhibitions arranged by the museum. Upstairs, Dr. Ticho's consulting office is preserved, filled with his international collection of antique Hanukkah lamps. Especially moving are the notes to Dr. Ticho, preserved under glass on his desk, from members of the Arab, Jewish, and British communities after he was seriously wounded during the political unrest of 1929. When the Tichos were alive, their home was a center for meetings, discussions, and private concerts. In that tradition, Ticho House now hosts poetry and fiction readings, intimate theater and music performances, and a Friday morning concert series. We highly recommend the cafe/restaurant on site (see p. 51) and taking a stroll through the gardens here.

Off Harav Kook St. ✆ **02/624-5068.** Free admission (donation requested). Exhibit rooms Sun–Mon and Wed–Thurs 10am–5pm (Tues until 10pm), Fri 10am–2pm. Restaurant Sun–Thurs 10am–midnight, Fri 10am–3pm, Sat after Shabbat.

**Chagall Windows at Hadassah Ein Kerem Medical Center** ★★ LANDMARK   The largest medical center in the Middle East, the Hadassah Hebrew University Medical Center stands on a hill several miles from downtown Jerusalem. The

Israel's older branch of Hadassah Hospital is on Mount Scopus, overlooking Jerusalem's Old City. The Mt. Scopus branch, opened in 1938 in an ultramodern building designed by Erich Mendelssohn, was funded by the contributions of Hadassah members throughout the world: It was the pride of the Jewish community during the British Mandate and the embodiment of a dream to bring quality medical care to all in Jerusalem "without regard to nationality or religion." By chance, at the time of the cease-fire at the end of Israel's War of Independence in 1948, the Hadassah Hospital on Mount Scopus became a small, Israeli-held military bastion in the middle of Jordanian-controlled East Jerusalem, protected by international agreement but cut off from Israeli-held West Jerusalem.

A new Hadassah Hospital was built in Ein Kerem at the far western edge of Jerusalem, where it would be relatively safe in case fighting broke out again. Marc Chagall created 12 jewel-like stained-glass windows depicting the Twelve Tribes of Israel for the synagogue of the new Hadassah in Ein Kerem—windows so special he claimed he dreamed them while he worked. Ironically, when the Six-Day War erupted in 1967, one of the first places hit by Jordanian bombardment was the new hospital. When Chagall learned that his windows had been shattered, he promised to return and make them "more beautiful than ever." He more than succeeded.

Today, the original Hadassah on Mount Scopus is again open, and both Hadassah hospitals serve all the people of Jerusalem.

center contains a medical school, nursing school, hospital, dental and pharmacy schools, and various laboratory buildings. The hospital's synagogue contains Marc Chagall's 12 jewel-like stained-glass windows depicting the blessings that Jacob, on his deathbed, bestowed to each of his 12 sons (Gen. 49:1–27). The sons of Jacob became the founders of the Twelve Tribes of Israel.

Call for information on new Bus Routes to Hadassah, for holiday visiting hours, complete 5-hour tours of the medical center, or for the short tour of the Chagall windows.

Ein Kerem. ℗ **02/677-6271.** www.hadassah-med.com/English. Admission and tour of Chagall windows NIS 18. Sun–Thurs 8am–12:45pm and 2–3:45pm. Bus: 19 or 27 from Jaffa Rd.; 19 from Jaffa Gate, Agron St., King George V Ave., or Bezalel St.

**Hebrew University, Givat Ram Campus** ★ CULTURAL INSTITUTION Located on two Jerusalem campuses, Hebrew University is one of Israel's most dramatic accomplishments with more than 18,000 students. Built to replace the university's original campus, which was cut off from West Jerusalem from 1948 to 1967, the Givat Ram campus now functions in tandem with the Mount Scopus campus, which was reclaimed in 1967 during the Six-Day War.

Outsiders visit here for the spectacular architecture, particularly of the Belgium House Faculty Club, La Maison de France, the physics building, and the huge Jewish National and University Library (partly inspired by LeCorbusier's Villa Savoye in Poissy, France) at the far end of the promenade. And don't miss the mushroom-shaped synagogue behind the library and the futuristic gym. The synagogue, with its dome supported by eight arches, was designed by Heinz Rau (one of the designers of Brasilia) and the Israeli architect David Reznik; Reznik's imprint dots the city—he

5

EXPLORING JERUSALEM | West Jerusalem Attractions

95

designed the Dan Jerusalem Hotel and co-designed the Mormon Center on Mount Scopus.

You can stop for lunch in the cafeteria of the administration building, or at the cafeteria in the Jewish National and University Library, which contains a vast stained-glass window depicting images of Jewish mysticism.

Givat Ram campus (West Jerusalem). ℭ **02/688-2819.** Free university tours Sun–Thurs 11am from Visitors Center in the Sherman Building. Bus: 9, 24, or 28 to modern Givat Ram campus.

### Jerusalem Artists' House and Old Bezalel Academy of Arts and Design ★ COMMERCIAL GALLERY

This Turkish-era mansion, hidden in a walled garden, was an early home of Jerusalem's famous Bezalel Art School (now part of Hebrew University). Inside holds exhibition rooms and a gallery where the works of more than 500 select artists are sold (if you buy, they'll pack and ship your purchases). Note the beautifully carved outside doors, the crenellated roof, and dome, all icons of this Jerusalem landmark.

12 Shmuel Ha-Nagid St. ℭ **02/625-3653.** Free admission. Daily 10am–1pm, Sun–Fri 4–7pm. Bus: 4, 7, 8, 9, or 19.

### The Knesset (Parliament) ★★ LANDMARK

This modern landmark—called by some West Jerusalem's Acropolis, by others an airport terminal without a runway—houses magnificent mosaics and tapestries by Chagall, as well as Knesset sessions that run the gamut from funereal to the most rowdy in the democratic world. Visitors are allowed to watch the proceedings, so call ahead to check the parliamentary schedule. The entryway, a grillwork of hammered metal, is the work of Israeli sculptor David Polombo, who did the dramatic doors at Yad VaShem. Important note: **You must have your passport with you,** and you will be subject to a careful security search when you enter.

Outside the Knesset are the Wohl Rose Garden, and a large, seven-branched menorah (the symbol of the State of Israel), given as a gift from the British Parliament to the people of Israel in 1956. *Tip:* The Knesset may not be the mother of parliaments, but it now has a dress code for visitors: no sandals, jeans, collarless T-shirts, shorts, or bare midriffs. Ben-Gurion himself would not have passed muster on certain days.

Government Quarter—Kiryat Ben-Gurion, Kaplan St. ℭ **02/675-3417.** Free guided tours Sun and Thurs 8:30am–2:30pm; viewing of Knesset sessions Mon and Thurs 4–9pm, Wed after 11am. Closed Jewish holidays. Bus: 9, 17, 24, 28, or 99.

### Russian Compound ★ HISTORIC SITE

Once this 19th-century series of structures surrounding the beautiful Russian Orthodox Holy Trinity Cathedral was the world's largest "hotel"; it could accommodate 10,000 Russian pilgrims at one time (until World War I, Russians composed the largest block of pilgrims in the Holy Land). Today, this neglected but architecturally striking enclave serves as a prison. Around the back, near the entrance to the prison, a low iron fence surrounds a monumental Herodian-era column, abandoned in the process of being carved directly from bedrock—it apparently cracked, and its size has led to speculation that it may have been meant to adorn The Temple complex. Sadly, much of the charming Russian-style neighborhood around the prison is being demolished to make way for office blocks.

Off Jaffa Rd. (near Zion Sq.).

### Sanhedrin Tombs ★ CEMETERY

Go up Shmuel Ha-Navi, off Shivtei Israel Street, to northeast Jerusalem's beautiful public gardens of Sanhedria. Here are the Tombs of the Sanhedrin or the Tombs of the Judges, where the judges of ancient

Israel's "Supreme Court" (during the 1st c. A.D., before the Romans destroyed Jerusalem and banned Jewish residence in the area) are buried. The three-story burial catacomb is intricately carved from rock.

Sanhedria. Free admission. Gardens daily 9am–4 or 5pm; tombs Sun–Fri 9am–4 or 5pm. Bus: 2 from Jaffa Gate.

**Supreme Court Building** ★ LANDMARK   In a country starved for good modern architecture, the new Supreme Court Building, opened in 1992, is a major hit with Israelis and visitors alike. The contemporary design of the building incorporates traditional Middle Eastern motifs of domes, arches, and passageways, all set up to create interesting interplays of shadow and light. Call for the current schedule of English tours that highlight the building's design and the traditions of the court.

Next to Knesset. ✆ **02/675-9612.** Sun–Thurs 8:30am–2:30pm; free tours in English Sun–Thurs at noon. Bus: 9, 17, 24, 28, or 99.

**YMCA** ★★ LANDMARK   The YMCA was built in the early 1930s with funds donated by James Jarvie, an American philanthropist. Designed by the architectural firm that did New York City's Empire State Building, the building is an interesting mixture of Art Deco, Byzantine, and Islamic styles. On the first floor you'll find a replica of the London room in which the YMCA was founded in 1844. The 46m (151-ft.) **YMCA Tower** (Mon–Sat 9am–2pm) offers one of the most dramatic panoramas of the city. Notice the six-winged bas-relief seraph that ornaments the center of the tower's facade; the tower also houses the only carillon in the Middle East. Concerts played on the tower bells, especially at midnight on New Year's Eve, are among the city's little-known pleasures. Built by Christian, Jewish, and Muslim workers and artisans, the YMCA is a meeting place for all the city's communities. The complex includes a swimming pool, tennis courts, sports facilities, lecture and concert halls, a gymnasium, a restaurant, and one of the best-located moderate budget hotels in Jerusalem (see p. 40).

24 King David St. ✆ **02/625-7111.** Free admission; small donations for tower entrance. Tours Mon–Sat 9am–3pm. Bus: 5, 6, 18, or 21.

# West Jerusalem Neighborhoods Worth a Visit

## YEMIN MOSHE ★

In the 1850s, British philanthropist Sir Moses Montefiore, with the help of Judah Touro from New Orleans, built the nucleus of this residential quarter, the first outside the walls of the Old City, in an effort to bring indigent Jews from the Old City into a more healthful environment. The project included a now-famous windmill for grinding flour. Despite its magnificent view and graceful architecture, the neighborhood remained poor for more than a century.

Today, Yemin Moshe is a picturesque, beautifully restored neighborhood—an architectural treasure and one of the most elegant addresses in town. There are no shops, but the views are spectacular. It's a fascinating place for an early evening or winter afternoon stroll (don't attempt it at noon in summer unless you enjoy heatstroke). **Note:** The steep pedestrian-street staircases of Yemin Moshe may make visiting here a bit difficult for some.

Down one of the first flights of stairs is the **Yemin Moshe Windmill,** which houses an exhibit room dedicated to Sir Moses Montefiore, a famed 19th-century Jewish philanthropists and proto-Zionist. It's open Sunday to Thursday from 9am to 4pm, and until 1pm on Friday. Admission is free. Below the windmill is the original row of **old stone buildings (Mishkenot Sha'ananim),** the first Jewish houses built outside the walls of the Old City since ancient times. Ornamented by Victorian ironwork porches, the buildings are now used as residences by visiting artists and diplomats.

A **replica of the Liberty Bell in Philadelphia** stands in the center of Jerusalem's **Liberty Bell Garden,** across King David Street from the windmill. You may wonder why a copy of the Liberty Bell has been made into the centerpiece of a Jerusalem park. The words inscribed on the American original were spoken by one of Jerusalem's most famous inhabitants, the Prophet Isaiah, more than 2,500 years before the Declaration of Independence: "Proclaim liberty throughout the land, and to all the inhabitants thereof." It was with these words that Israel's independence was announced in 1948.

## MEA SHEARIM ★★

This area, a few blocks north of Jaffa Road, is populated by Hasidic and ultra-Orthodox Jews of East European origin. It is a world unto itself, and a visit here is like going back in time to an era of religious Eastern European Jewry that existed before the Holocaust. A number of residents here speak only Yiddish in conversation, as Hebrew is considered too sacred for daily use. Some don't even recognize the laws of the Israeli government, believing that no State of Israel can exist before the coming of the Messiah.

Architecturally, Mea Shearim has the feel of an 18th-century Polish neighborhood, the more so because of the traditional dress and lifestyle of its residents. Visitors to this area are requested to dress modestly (no shorts, short skirts, uncovered arms or shoulders for women; slacks for men). Men and women are advised not to walk in close proximity (certainly not hand in hand), and visitors are advised to stow away cameras and to be very discreet in taking photographs. No inhabitant of Mea Shearim will voluntarily pose for snapshots, and there have been incidents in which improperly dressed visitors have been spat upon or stoned.

## GERMAN COLONY & BAKA ★

About 1.6km (1 mile) south of downtown West Jerusalem, these two picturesque neighborhoods are filled with overgrown gardens and are undergoing a process of gentrification. For many years after 1948, the old cottages and mansions (built at the start of the 20th c. by German Protestants and affluent Arabic families) housed Israelis from exotic places such as Kurdistan and Morocco, but more recently, members of Jerusalem's American, British, and Latin American immigrant communities have been moving in. **Emek Refaim Street** (a southern continuation of King David St.) is the German Colony's main artery and is lined with shops and eateries; a walk down **Yehoshua Ben Nun Street,** which runs parallel to Emek Refaim 1 block to the west beginning at **Rachel Immenu Street,** gives you a better idea of the neighborhood's interesting old residential buildings. For those who like architecture, the quiet back streets of this neighborhood are good places to meander by bike or on foot.

## REHAVIA-TALBEYEH ★

A turn to the west from King George V Avenue, at either the Jewish Agency compound or the Kings Hotel, will bring you into Jerusalem's most prosperous residential section. Rehavia's glory is its collection of 1930s International Style apartment buildings and houses made of Jerusalem stone, many of which are, sadly, being razed in order to build high-rises. Talbeyeh, just to the south, is filled with elaborate villas and mansions built mainly by Jerusalem's Arab Christian community in the 1920s and 1930s. Abandoned when their original owners fled in 1948, these houses are now inhabited by Israelis. **Hovei Zion Street** is lined with examples of these gracious homes.

Sights in the area include the **prime minister's residence,** at the corner of Balfour and Smolenskin, at the southern edge of Rehavia. And in Kiryat Shmuel, is **Bet Ha-Nassi,** the residence of the president of Israel. You can look through the gates, but except for receptions, neither building is open to the public.

## EIN KEREM ★

This ancient village, in a deep valley at the western edge of Jerusalem, is traditionally regarded as the birthplace of John the Baptist. Now incorporated into Jerusalem, you can reach it in less than 30 minutes by bus no. 17 from King George Street or Jaffa Road. The lanes and gardens of Ein Kerem (Well of the Vineyard) are lovely; the old

Arabic-style houses have been grabbed up and renovated by some of the city's most successful and famous inhabitants; and high above the area, on the crest of the mountains, is the vast Hadassah–Ein Kerem Medical Center (not accessible from Ein Kerem itself). Ein Kerem contains a number of 19th-century European churches, convents, and monasteries. Most important is the **Church of Saint John** in the center of town, marking John the Baptist's birthplace (daily 6am–noon and 2–5pm); on request you can see the grotto beneath the church with its Byzantine mosaic. On Ma'ayan Street, you'll find the **Church of the Visitation** (daily 8–11:45am and 2–5pm), commemorating the visit of Mary to her cousin Elizabeth, the mother of John the Baptist. It was often depicted in medieval and early Renaissance paintings as a scene in which the two expectant women touch each other's stomachs, and according to legend, the two infants jumped for joy inside their mothers' wombs when Mary and Elizabeth met. Below the Youth Hostel off Ma'ayan Street is a mosque and minaret marking the well from which Mary drew water; farther along the ridge is the Russian Convent, known as the **Moscobiyah,** a fascinating enclave of 40 Jerusalem stone buildings scattered among a wooded area of pines and cypresses. The nuns live in small, ocher-painted houses reminiscent of wooden cottages in Russia. You can make an appointment to visit by calling ✆ **06/625-2565** or 02/541-2887. Bring a snack or canteen along, or you can pick up something in the grocery at the center of town. Restaurants here look appealing, but meals are expensive and nothing special. The times for return to Jerusalem should be posted at the bus stop in the center of Ein Kerem; you may have to wait in downtown Jerusalem for up to 30 minutes until the infrequent bus no. 17 to Ein Kerem picks you up.

# EAST JERUSALEM ATTRACTIONS

You can probably cover the major sights of East Jerusalem in a half-day. **Saladin Street** leading northward from the Old City walls is a modern thoroughfare of clothing shops, appliance stores, and restaurants.

**The Garden Tomb ★** RELIGIOUS SITE   This 1st-century tomb, discovered in 1867, resembles the biblical description of the tomb of Jesus. In 1883, the very "Kiplingesque" General Gordon (later to die in the siege of Khartoum) visited Jerusalem on his way to Egypt, and in a fit of pique over the exclusion of Protestant services from the Church of the Holy Sepulcher, had a vision that this site outside the Damascus Gate was the real tomb of Jesus. The tomb was finally excavated in 1891, and whether it is the correct place or not, it did meet some of the specifications: close to the site of the Crucifixion, outside the walls of the city, hewn from the rock, a tomb made for a rich man, and situated in a garden. As late as the early 20th century, the nearby hill that Gordon identified as Golgotha (Calvary), or according to the New Testament, "the Place of the Skull," was indeed eerily shaped like a skull, but construction and quarrying have obscured this impression. Despite doubts about General Gordon's claims, the garden is a tranquil place for prayer and reflection.

To get here, head up Nablus Road (Derech Shechem), opposite Damascus Gate. Look for the side street named Conrad Schick Street on the right.

Conrad Schick St. ✆ **02/628-3402.** Free admission (donations accepted). Mon–Sat 8am–12:15pm and 2:30–5:15pm; Protestant service in English Sun 9am. Bus: 27.

**Rockefeller Archaeological Museum ★★** MUSEUM   Located across the road from Herod's Gate, this museum is filled with local ancient and archeological objects uncovered by expeditions during the first half of the 20th century. The museum's treasures range from Stone Age artifacts to dramatic architectural elements from the Church of the Holy Sepulcher, the Al Aksa Mosque, and from the 8th century early Islamic Palace of Hisham in Jericho. Named for John D. Rockefeller, whose bequest of $2 million in 1927 financed the museum's construction, the building is itself a Jerusalem landmark; its 1930s Art Deco/Byzantine/Islamic design gives it the feel of a locale for an Indiana Jones film. Now a part of the Israel Museum, the Rockefeller's galleries were recently updated and the building's elegant reflecting pools, surrounded by a cloister garden, have also been carefully restored.

Sultan Suleiman St. ℰ **02/628-2251.** www.english.imjnet.org.il. Admission NIS 26. Discount joint admission to Israel Museum available. Sun–Mon and Wed–Thurs 10am–3pm, Sat 10am–2pm. Bus: 1 or 2.

**Tombs of the Kings** ★ HISTORIC SITE   Behind the neo-Gothic Saint George's, on the left side as you head down Saladin Street, is a gate marked "Tombeau des Rois." About 6m (20 ft.) down a stone stairway, you'll see a hollowed-out courtyard with several small cave openings. Inside one tomb visitors will find four sarcophagi, covered with carvings of fruit and vines. Despite the name, the tomb is for the family of Queen Helena of the Mesopotamian province of Adiabene, who converted to Judaism in Jerusalem around A.D. 50.

Saladin St. Admission NIS 5. Mon–Sat 8am–12:30pm and 2–5pm. Bus: 27.

**Zedekiah's Cave** ★ HISTORIC SITE   Follow the Old City walls to the east of Damascus Gate, and you'll soon come to the entrance leading under the walls into Zedekiah's Cave, or Solomon's Quarries, which tradition calls the source of the stones for Solomon's Temple. Because of this, the cave is of special importance to the worldwide **Order of Masons,** which claims spiritual descent from the original builders of the First Temple. Jewish and Muslim legends claim secret tunnels in the caves extend to the Sinai Desert and Jericho. The quarries got their name because King Zedekiah was supposed to have fled from the Babylonians through these tunnels in 587 B.C., only to be later captured near Jericho. An illuminated path leads you far back into the caves under the Old City. *Note:* The cave is often closed during regular hours. Do not enter unless a guard selling official admission tickets is at the gate.

Near the Damascus Gate. ℰ **02/627-7550.** Admission NIS 15. Sun–Thurs 10am–4pm. Bus: 27.

# Mount Scopus, Mount of Olives & Valley of Kidron ★★

The northern half of the long, high Mount of Olives ridge just east of the Old City is called **Mount Scopus**—Har Hatsofim, which means "Mount of Observation." It was here that the Roman armies of Titus and Vespasian camped in A.D. 70 and observed the city under siege as they planned their final attack. The southern part of the ridge is the Mount of Olives. The deep Valley of Kidron/Valley of Jehoshaphat separates the ridge from the Old City. Traditionally, many believe this will be the site of the Last Judgment.

For Hebrew University Mount Scopus campus, take bus no. 4A, 9, or 28 from downtown West Jerusalem. Other parts of the Mount of Olives best reached by foot from the Old City's Lion's Gate, or by taxi.

**The Commonwealth War Cemetery** ★ CEMETERY   At the northern end of Mount Scopus is the final resting place for 2,472 Christian and Jewish soldiers who died fighting in the British Army during World War I. A memorial also honors 1,000 Muslim and Hindu soldiers, buried in separate graveyards in South Jerusalem. Open Monday through Saturday, 10am to 4pm.

East Jerusalem Attractions

EXPLORING JERUSALEM

About 90m (295 ft.) from the crest of the ridge is **Mount Scopus Hadassah Hospital;** at the crest is **Hebrew University on Mount Scopus,** which opened in 1925, and is now one of the largest institutions of higher learning in the Middle East. The university is mostly housed in a modern, fortresslike megacomplex designed by David Reznik. The design reflects the university's past experience, when from 1948 to 1967 it was a besieged Israeli enclave surrounded by then-Jordanian-controlled territory. From the Harry S. Truman Institute (a pink stone building), there's a sweeping view of both the New and Old cities. Tours are conducted Sunday to Friday at 11am from the Sherman Building.

**Visfas:** The road skirting the ridge of the Mount of Olives proceeds past the high-towered Augusta Victoria Hospital, the Arab village of Et-Tur, the Mount of Olives, the Jewish Cemetery, and the Seven Arches Hotel. The best views of Jerusalem are from Hebrew University on Mount Scopus, or from the Jewish graveyard on the Mount of Olives, and the Seven Arches Hotel. For optimum viewing and photographing, come in the morning, when the sun is behind you.

### Central Part of the Mount of Olives ★★

Here you'll find six churches and one of the oldest Jewish cemeteries in the world. It was this cemetery that religious Jews had in mind when they came to die in the Holy Land through the start of the 20th century. Start down the path on the right, and you'll come to the Tombs of the Prophets, believed to be the burial place of Haggai, Malachi, and Zechariah, but identified by archaeologists as tombs of prominent and noble families from the time of the Hasmoneans (Maccabees) in the 1st century B.C.

Farther up the road, on the southern fringe of Et-Tur, stands the **Mosque (and Chapel) of the Ascension** (ring the doorbell for admission), marking the spot where Jesus ascended to heaven. Interestingly, this Christian shrine is under Muslim control. Muslims revere Jesus as a prophet. However, they do not believe Jesus to be the son of God, nor do they believe that Jesus died on the cross.

Just a few steps away is the **Church of the Pater Noster** that was built on the traditional spot where Jesus instructed his disciples in the Lord's Prayer. Tiles along the walls of the church are inscribed with the Lord's Prayer in 44 languages. The Carmelite Convent and Basilica of the Sacred Heart are on the adjoining hill.

From up here you can see a cluster of churches on the lower slopes of the Mount of Olives. All can be reached either from here or from the road paralleling the fortress wall, diagonally opposite Saint Stephen's Gate (Lion's Gate).

If you head down the path to the right of the Tomb of the Prophets, you'll come to **Dominus Flevit** (daily 8am–noon and 2:30–5pm), which is a relatively contemporary Franciscan church that marks the spot where Jesus wept over his vision of the future destruction of Jerusalem. Next, the Russian Orthodox **Church of Saint Mary Magdalene,** with its Muscovite-style onion-shaped domes of gold, was built in 1888 by Czar Alexander III (Tues and Thurs 10–11:30am). Call ✆ **02/628-4371** or surf to www.jerusalem-mission.org/convent_magdalene.html for more information.

The Roman Catholic **Garden of Gethsemane** (Apr–Oct daily 8:30am–noon and 3pm–sunset; in winter daily 8:30am–noon and 2pm–sunset) adjoins the **Basilica of the Agony (Church of All Nations);** it's in the courtyard where Jesus is believed to have prayed before his arrest. The church's gold mosaic facade (which shines gloriously in late-afternoon sun) shows God looking down from heaven over Jesus and the peoples of the world. The church was built by people from 16 different nations in 1924. Next door, past beautifully tended gardens of ancient olive trees and bougainvillea, is the **Tomb of the Virgin,** which is a deep underground chamber housing the tombs of Mary and Joseph. The tomb is open daily 8am to noon and 2:30 to 5:30pm.

# Citywide Jerusalem Attractions

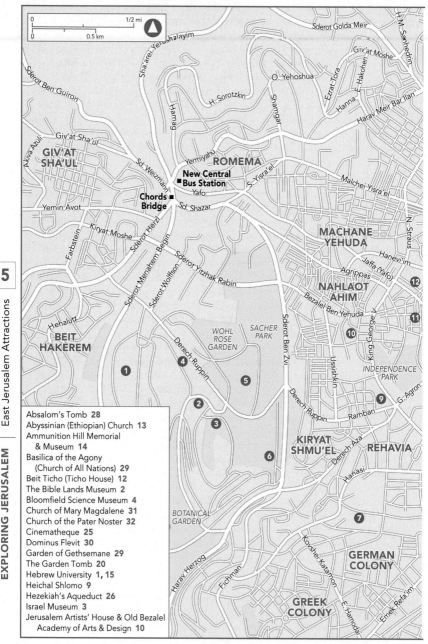

Absalom's Tomb **28**
Abyssinian (Ethiopian) Church **13**
Ammunition Hill Memorial
   & Museum **14**
Basilica of the Agony
   (Church of All Nations) **29**
Beit Ticho (Ticho House) **12**
The Bible Lands Museum **2**
Bloomfield Science Museum **4**
Church of Mary Magdalene **31**
Church of the Pater Noster **32**
Cinematheque **25**
Dominus Flevit **30**
Garden of Gethsemane **29**
The Garden Tomb **20**
Hebrew University **1, 15**
Heichal Shlomo **9**
Hezekiah's Aqueduct **26**
Israel Museum **3**
Jerusalem Artists' House & Old Bezalel
   Academy of Arts & Design **10**

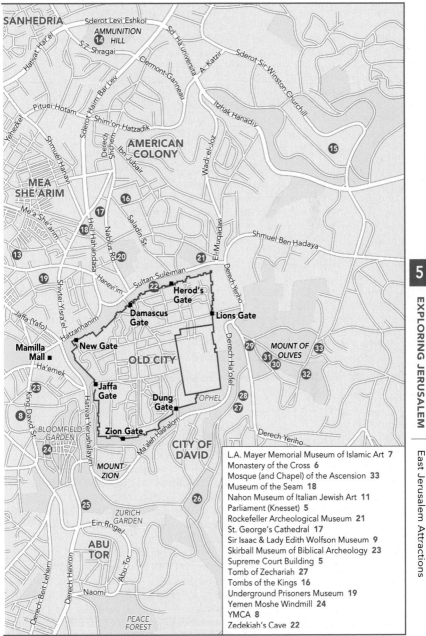

SANHEDRIA

Sderot Levi Eshkol
AMMUNITION
**14** HILL
S.Z. Shragai

Clermont-Ganneau

AMERICAN
COLONY

MEA
SHE'ARIM

Me'a She'arim

MAMILLA
Mall ■

**13**

**19**

**16**

**17**

**18**

**20**

**21**

Saladin St.

Shmuel Ben Hadaya

Sultan Suleiman
**22**
Herod's
Gate
Damascus
Gate ■ Lions Gate

New Gate

OLD CITY

**29**
**31** MOUNT OF
OLIVES
**30**
**32**
**33**

Jaffa
Gate

Dung
Gate ■

OPHEL

**28**
**27**

**23**

**8**

BLOOMFIELD
GARDEN
**24**

Zion Gate ■

CITY OF
DAVID

MOUNT
ZION

**25**

ZURICH
GARDEN
Ein Rogel

ABU
TOR

Naomi

**26**

PEACE
FOREST

L.A. Mayer Memorial Museum of Islamic Art **7**
Monastery of the Cross **6**
Mosque (and Chapel) of the Ascension **33**
Museum of the Seam **18**
Nahon Museum of Italian Jewish Art **11**
Parliament (Knesset) **5**
Rockefeller Archeological Museum **21**
St. George's Cathedral **17**
Sir Isaac & Lady Edith Wolfson Museum **9**
Skirball Museum of Biblical Archeology **23**
Supreme Court Building **5**
Tomb of Zechariah **27**
Tombs of the Kings **16**
Underground Prisoners Museum **19**
Yemen Moshe Windmill **24**
YMCA **8**
Zedekiah's Cave **22**

# THE PEOPLE'S princess

Among the thousands of people who have found their final resting place on the Mount of Olives, one of the most recent and unusual is Princess Alice of Greece, mother of Prince Philip, Duke of Edinburgh, and mother-in-law of Queen Elizabeth II. Born in Windsor Castle in 1885, the great-granddaughter of Queen Victoria, Princess Alice at an early age was diagnosed as being almost totally deaf. Carefully trained in lip reading, she was fluent in both English and French; later in life she also mastered Greek.

In 1903, Princess Alice married Prince Andrew, son of King George of Greece, and devoted her life to helping others. During the 1912 Balkan War, she worked as a nurse close to the battlefront, caring for sick and wounded Greek soldiers. During this time, both the princess and King George stayed in the home of the family of Haim Cohen, in the northern Greek city of Trikkala, near the war zone. Alice was fascinated by the family's warmth and traditions. The princess's friendship continued when Cohen later became a member of the Greek Parliament. By the late 1930s, the Greek royal family was no longer in power, but Princess Alice remained in Athens, wearing the habit of a nun as she became increasingly committed to a life of religion and charitable work.

In 1943, during the Nazi occupation of Greece, Princess Alice learned that the widow and children of Haim Cohen were desperately trying to escape deportation to the death camps in Poland. At the risk of her life, and with the help of two servants, Princess Alice hid her Jewish friends on the grounds of the royal palace in Athens for 13 months until Greece was liberated. Princess Alice died at Buckingham Palace in 1969, and in 1988, in accordance with her dying wish, was reinterred at the **Church of Saint Mary Magdalene** on the Mount of Olives. In 1994, Prince Philip and his sister, Princess Sophie, traveled to Jerusalem to receive Yad VaShem's Medal of Honor of Righteous Among the Nations, awarded to their late mother. A tree in memory of Princess Alice has been planted at Yad VaShem.

**Kidron Valley** ★    The Valley of Kidron is between the Mount of Olives and the Old City walls. It runs south, between Mount Ophel (where David built his city) and the Mount of Contempt. Just under the wall here, roughly in front of Al Aqsa Mosque, are two tombs: **Absalom's Tomb** and the **Tomb of Zechariah.** At one time, religious Jews would throw stones at Absalom's tomb (Kever Avshalom) in condemnation of Absalom, who rebelled against his father, King David. Modern scholars attribute Absalom's Tomb and its neighboring structures to Herodian times—they're Jerusalem's only relatively intact structures from before the Roman destruction in A.D. 70.

The Valley of Kidron is also known as the Valley of Jehoshaphat. The Book of Joel records that the last judgments will be rendered here.

About 180m (591 ft.) down the valley is the **Fountain of the Virgin,** in the Arab neighborhood of Silwan. Water from the spring (the Gihon) anointed Solomon king and served as the only water source for ancient Jerusalem. During the Assyrian invasion that wiped out the northern Kingdom of Israel (8th c. B.C.), Jerusalem's King Hezekiah constructed an aqueduct through which the waters of the Gihon could be diverted and hidden inside the city, an extraordinary engineering feat at the time. Today, no one knows exactly how the tunnel diggers, working from each end of the project, were able to link up deep inside the city's bedrock This tunnel saved ancient Jerusalem and the surrounding Kingdom of Judah from oblivion and changed the course of world history, **Hezekiah's Aqueduct** is still there (underneath the ruins of a church commemorating the spot where Mary once drew water to wash the clothes of Jesus). It's about 480m (1,575 ft.) long, and the depth of the water is from .5 to 1m (1⅔ ft.–3⅓ ft.). The walk (currently in escorted tour groups only) takes about 40 minutes; take a flashlight or a candle and a bag to keep valuables dry with you. You can walk through from Sunday to Thursday between 8:30am and 3pm, on Friday and holiday eves until 1pm. Entrance is free, but give the caretaker a tip. It is best to visit Silwan and Hezekiah's tunnel with a tour group (see "Organized Tours," below, for information). Beside the **Gihon Spring** lie the ruins of the oldest part of Jerusalem: The City of David (see "Dung Gate, Silwan & the Jerusalem Archaeological Park," earlier in this chapter).

# ESPECIALLY FOR KIDS

The **Train Puppet Theater** in Liberty Bell Park offers programs (in Hebrew, but none-theless interesting) for children and hosts an International Puppet Theater Festival every other year in August. Call ✆ **02/561-8514** for information, or check the listing in Fri-day's "Jerusalem Post." Also see "Jerusalem After Dark," later in this chapter. The **Israel Museum**'s lively **Children's Wing** has extremely engaging exhibits, many of them hands-on including workshops in recycled materials. Also on site:a library of children's books you can sit and read together. See "Museums," earlier in this chapter.

**The Time Elevator ★ TOUR** This is a 30-minute, multimedia, semi-virtual-reality history of Jerusalem, presented in an auditorium refitted with special chairs and a floor that provides special motion effects. It's not good for younger children or for those who do poorly on roller-coaster rides. The presentation itself is interesting, but expensive for what you get. Still some kids really enjoy it (we don't recommend it to those without children in tow). The show is repeated about every 40 minutes.

Beit Agron, Hillel, and Rivlin sts. ✆ **02/624-8381**, ext. 4. www.time-elevator-jerusalem.co.il. Admission NIS 54. Sun–Thurs 10am–8pm, Fri 10am–2pm, Sat 10am–6pm.

**The Tisch Family Zoological Gardens ★ ZOO** A beautifully landscaped site at the western edge of the city, the Tisch Zoo boasts a state-of-the-art open design that blends into the surrounding countryside. Emphasis is on creatures mentioned in the Bible or native to Israel, but there are also many animals, large and small, from the far corners of the world (the giraffe herds are world famous). Kids enjoy the friendly waterfowl and the camel encampment (camel- and pony-ride facilities are planned). There is a refreshment facility on the grounds. The zoo is at its best late in the day or in cooler weather, when the animals are most active. Prepare for a 10-minute walk from the bus stop. A Zoo Train takes you through the high points of the park, but accompanying explanations are generally in Hebrew. The Zoo train does not operate on Shabbat. Admission ends an hour before closing time.

Manahat, Jerusalem. ✆ **02/675-0111**. www.jerusalemzoo.org.il. Admission NIS 49 adults, NIS 38 children 3–18, free for kids under 3 years old. Sun–Thurs 9am–7pm (until 5pm in winter); Fri 9am–4pm; Sat and holidays 10am–6pm (5pm in winter). Bus: 26, 33, or 99. Light Rail stop to Malcha.

# ORGANIZED TOURS

As a general rule of thumb, make certain that your tour guide is officially licensed by the Ministry of Tourism. The licensing process is an extremely rigorous one, so those who get one tend to be guaranteed to be well-versed in Israeli history. Also, on any guided tour that includes holy places, you must dress modestly. This means no shorts (men or women), no sleeveless shirts or blouses, and women should have a head covering handy.

**BUS TOURS**   The red, double-decker **Jerusalem Circular Line Egged bus no. 99** (📞 *2800; www.egged.co.il) offers a 2-hour tour that passes the most-visited sights in the city, from the Mount of Olives to Yad VaShem, making it useful, especially for visitors with disabilities. The bus leaves from in front of Safra Square at 10am, Sunday to Friday; there are no Saturday buses. A single tour ticket is NIS 60; all-day excursion NIS 80; discounts for children. There are earphone cassettes at each seat with channels for route descriptions in English and seven other languages. It is always wise to check with the Egged website for the latest information on bus no. 99's timetable and route and about bookings.

**GUIDED WALKING TOURS**   Free, and usually quite interesting, walking tours of the Old City are offered by an outfit called **Sandeman's New Jerusalem Tours** (www.newjerusalemtours.com). They leave from in front of the **Tourist Information Office** at Jaffa Gate (📞 02/628-0382) daily at 9am, noon and 2:30 every day (except Fridays for the 2:30) tour. Since the guides are relying entirely on tips for the payment, they do their best to present their information in a compelling fashion. The 2-hour tour covers all four Old City quarters. The Jaffa Gate office also rents recorded, self-guided walking tours for the Old City for approximately NIS 60 per day.

For a more in-depth tour, various commercial concerns run programs that emphasize the city's history and archaeology. Most of these are 3-hour excursions in small groups with other visitors—but remember, you'd need a long, very full day to really get an idea of all the city's quarters and traditions. **Archaeological Seminars Ltd.,** 34 Habad St. in the Jewish Quarter (📞 02/586-2011; www.archesem.com), will guide you through the Jewish Quarter, Temple Mount, the Temple Mount excavations, the City of David (Ophel), or the Christian and Muslim quarters of the Old City. Tours run Sunday to Thursday and begin at NIS 200 plus VAT for a private half-day itinerary. For information on schedules, various itineraries, and the chance to "Dig for a Day" at an archaeological site, phone or stop at the office.

**Zion Walking Tours** (📞 02/627-7588), another recommended firm, will show you the historical and archaeological highlights of the Old City or the Mount of Olives. Half-day tours depart from the Tower of David and run from approximately $35 per person. **Walking Tours Ltd.** (📞 02/652-2568) also offers 3- to 4-hour itineraries for around the same price.

# OUTDOOR PURSUITS & SPORTS

**CYCLING**   Jerusalem is a hard city to bike in, with steep hills, insane traffic, and drivers who traditionally ignore cyclists (or worse). That being said, if you just gotta pedal push, bikes can be rented at Rochim Bikes, 88 Agrippas St. at the corner of Mani Street (📞 02/623-2598). Day rates start at NIS 40. The staff can offer advice, warnings, and news of local biking activities. The **Jerusalem Bicycling Club** (📞 052/253-1667) organizes mountain bike tours, usually starting very early on Saturday mornings. Call ahead for details and biking and rental advice. The Nitzan Bicycle Shop, 137 Jaffa Rd. (📞 02/625-2741) rents bikes and sometimes organizes bicycle tours starting from the shop at 9pm on Tuesday nights.

**JOGGING**   Jerusalem, with its many hills, is not the easiest place for unplanned jogging. The **Tayelet** (Promenade) in southern Jerusalem overlooking the entire city offers traffic-free pathways and a dramatic site (bus no. 8). The roads and pathways in the Bloomfield Gardens, just above Yemin Moshe, are also good options. Jogging in these places at night is not advised.

**SWIMMING**   In summer, reserving a hotel with a pool can be a good investment. However, there are public pools across the city (note: They get *packed* on especially scorching days). One of the most reasonably priced, if you're going for more than a quick dip, is the vast country club pool at **Kibbutz Ramat Rachel** (✆ **02/670-2555**) located at the southern end of Jerusalem's comparatively infrequent Number 7 Bus line. Adults NIS 70; children up to 10 are NIS 50. It's open from 6am to 9pm in summer only. If you decide to go by taxi, or have limited time, an in-town pool at a hotel would be a better choice.

The more expensive option is to pay the visitors' rate to use a pool at one of the city's hotels. In central Jerusalem, the **Inbal Hotel** (✆ **02/675-6666**) has a covered pool open year-round. The **David Citadel Hotel** (✆ **02/621-1111**) has a large, heated outdoor pool open year-round, with direct water access from indoors. Admission policies range up to NIS 190 Adults; NIS 110 child in summer. Prices are higher Friday and Saturday. Most hotel pools are open 10am to 6pm, and many fall under the chilly shadows of surrounding buildings, especially in late afternoon.

# THE SHOPPING SCENE

Jewelry, Judaica, and local Israeli crafts and art objects are the most worthwhile buys in Jerusalem. Many shops in the Ben-Yehuda area, as well as in the Jewish Quarter of the Old City, sell modern menorahs, mezuzahs, dreidels, candleholders, and embroidered yarmulkes, as well as objects for Passover, Succot, Shabbat, and synagogue services. *Tip:* It is possible to try to bargain a bit at most tourist shops in West Jerusalem.

Most of our listings are for places where you can find handmade items and purchase them directly from the artisans who make them. Merchants are generally cooperative about packing your purchases securely for shipping or for the plane ride home.

## Shopping A to Z
### ART
**Israel Museum Gift Shops** ★★   An exciting selection of posters is on sale here. Also, check out reproductions of Anna Ticho's charcoal and pen-and-ink landscapes, Shalom of Safed's vibrant primitive paintings, and high-quality reproductions of Judaica and antiquities at reasonable prices. Ruppin St. ✆ **02/670-8811.** A smaller Israel Museum Gift Shop is in downtown Jerusalem at Beit Ticho (p. 94).

**Jerusalem Artists' House Gallery** ★   This cooperative gallery, sponsored by the Jerusalem Municipality and the Israeli government, represents more than 500 juried Israeli artists, ranging from the famous and established to the newest and most promising. The staff of the Artists' House can put you in touch with any artist whose work interests you and will arrange for the shipping of your purchase. Open Sunday to Thursday 10am to 1pm and 4 to 7pm, Friday 10am to 1pm, and Saturday 11am to 2pm. 12 Shmuel Ha-Nagid St. ✆ **02/625-2636.**

### BOOKSTORES
Most bookstores carrying a selection of books in English are within 2 blocks of Zion Square. Look for the well-stocked **Steimatzky** chain, with its main branch at 39 Jaffa Road (at Zion Square). It sells a good selection of new and remaindered English- and foreign-language periodicals, books, and guidebooks to various regions of the country. Prices are high, but look for interesting remainder tables.

For used books, **Sefer Ve Sefel Bookshop** (4 Yavetz St., upstairs; ✆ **02/624-8237**) has the largest selection of English-language fiction in town, and current guidebooks.

The **Book Gallery/Books on Schatz** (6 Schatz St., off King George St., a block south of Hillel St.) is extremely well stocked, with vast subterranean browsing rooms and provides a few armchairs to encourage reading while you browse. **Clal Center Bookstore** (97 Jaffa Rd.) has a good, interesting stock of quality used English books. **Tmol Shilshom Bookstore Café** (in a rear courtyard off 5 Yoel Salomon St.; ☏ 02/623-2758) has a small, eclectic collection of new and used books and magazines and remains open until midnight; it's mainly a cafe/restaurant with a wonderful program of readings and live music. The **Bookshelf** (2 Jewish Quarter Rd.; ☏ 02/627-3889), in the Jewish Quarter of the Old City, has especially helpful management. **Stein Books** (52 King George St.; ☏ 02/624-7877) specializes in Jewish studies. The **American Colony Hotel Bookshop,** at the American Colony Hotel, stocks works by many Middle Eastern writers and hosts publishing parties and talks by Palestinian, Israeli, and international writers.

## CERAMICS

The outer walls of the Dome of the Rock are covered with turquoise and cobalt-blue ceramic tiles in the Persian tradition. Two world-famous Armenian pottery workshops, the Karakashian family's **Jerusalem Pottery** and the Balian family's **Palestinian Armenian Pottery,** listed below, were brought to Jerusalem at the start of the British Mandate in order to maintain the Dome of the Rock's lavish facade. Their traditional Anatolian hand-painted ceramics have come to be regarded as a national treasure: They've had exhibitions in Israeli and world museums, and in 2004 the State of Israel honored them with a series of commemorative postage stamps.

**Jerusalem Pottery** ★★   Near the sixth Station of the Cross (p. 78) in the Old City, this shop, run by the renowned Karakashian family, is notable for individual plates and tiles decorated with lovely traditional bird, animal, and floral designs, as well as for its interpretations of ancient Jewish and Christian motifs. Standards of craftsmanship are the highest, with the careful hand painting (tile designs are incised) and vibrant colors. There's also a selection of plates, cups, and even ceramic mezuzah cases for doorposts. Jerusalem Pottery is open Monday to Saturday from 9:30am to 5pm; always call to check. 15 Via Dolorosa. ☏ **02/626-1587.** www.jerusalempottery.biz.

**Palestinian Armenian Pottery** ★★   This workshop's chief artist, Marie Balian, is famous for her rich, multi-tile ceramic panels, which are hand-painted visions of Persian gardens, desert oases, and Middle Eastern motifs. In 1992, the Smithsonian Museum in Washington, D.C., mounted *Views of Paradise,* a special exhibit of 22 of Balian's creations; her panels also adorn the Succot Patio at the house of the President of Israel. Palestinian Pottery produces a steady stream of traditional plates, bowls, teapots, pitchers, name and address tiles, and smaller panels. Monday to Saturday from 9am to 4pm; call ahead and check on hours. 14 Nablus Rd. ☏ **02/628-2826.** www.armenianceramics.com.

**Darian Armenian Ceramics** ★ Arman Darian, who emigrated from the former Soviet Armenia, where he studied traditional calligraphy and design, is a relative newcomer to the field of Armenian ceramics. Here you'll find soup tureens, cups and plates, tiles, and lamp bases, all hand-painted in the Armenian tradition but with new color combinations and graceful designs that are uniquely Darian's. He'll also design to your specifications. Open Sunday to Thursday 10am to 6pm and Friday 10am to 3pm. 12 Shlomzion HaMalka St. ℂ **02/623-4802.**

## CHOCOLATE

**Sweet 'N Karem** ★ For handmade chocolates (and ice cream), this little gem, run by Ofer and Sima (who taught themselves), is reason enough to come out and explore the already charming western fringe neighborhood of Ein Kerem (p. 98). In addition to being rich and filled with exotic ingredients, the chocolates here are all certified kosher. Open daily 9am to 6pm. At the crossroads in the center of Ein Kerem. ℂ **050/202-4481.** Bus: 17.

## CRAFTS

**Cadim Gallery** ★ This cooperative gallery displays the work of award-winning potters and a range of excellent functional pottery and inventive Judaica by some of the country's best ceramists. 4 Yoel Salomon Mall. ℂ **02/623-4869.**

**8 Ceramists Altogether** ★ For contemporary handmade ceramics, this pottery cooperative in West Jerusalem will give you a good idea of the current Israeli ceramics scene. Look for beautiful ceramic Chanukah menorahs and Passover Seder plates as well as functional and decorative pottery made by the cooperative's artists. 11 Yoel Salomon Mall. ℂ **02/624-7250.**

**Guild of Ceramists** ★ Eleven ceramists are represented in this cooperative shop at the Hillel Street end of the Yoel Salomon Mall. Among other things, many of these artisans will custom design tiles. 27 Salomon St. ℂ **02/624-4065.**

**House of Quality** ★ Across the street from and midway between the Mount Zion Hotel and the Cinémathèque, this conglomeration of craft workshops offers all sorts of delights. Keep an eye out for the witty, unique ceramic Judaica of Gaia Smith and the silver creations of Oded Davidson, but all of the craftspeople at this center are of very high caliber. Craftspeople are in their workshops at varying times. Just around the corner, in Saint Andrew's Guest House, you can also visit **Sunbula,** which sells traditional Palestinian crafts and embroidery. Hours vary for each individual artist's studio. 12 Hebron Rd. No phone. Bus: 4, 5, 6, 7, 8, 18, 21, or 48 and walk to Hebron Rd.

## GIFTS

**Lifeline for the Old** ★ This shop sells toys, needlework, clothing, jewelry, Judaica, and crafts handmade by Jerusalem's senior citizens, and is a source of pleasure for both craftspeople and customers. Sales and donations keep this remarkable institution afloat. The workshops, which help provide a meaningful creative outlet for Jerusalem's elderly, can be visited Sunday to Thursday from 8:30am to 11:30pm. Prices are very reasonable and the items are guaranteed to charm. Open Sunday to Thursday 9am to 4pm and Friday 9 to 11am. 14 Shivtei Israel St. ℂ **02/628-7829.**

## FOOD

**Machane Yehuda Produce Market** ★★ One of the great traditional food markets left in the western world, Machane Yehuda is labyrinths and caves filled with mountains of edible wonders: luscious Israeli tangerines, grapes, tomatoes, and freshly picked basil; polished aubergines; hundred of varieties of olives; freshly baked breads and pastries; ladies plucking chickens; and dozens of tiny holes-in-the-walls serving authentic market snacks. It's also becoming dotted with great little fashion boutiques, gourmet food shops, and both simple and expensive eateries. Sun-Thurs early morning to dusk; Friday early morning to early afternoon. Closed only for Shabbat and holidays. Btw. Jaffa Rd. and Agrippas St. Light Rail: Machane Yehuda.

## GLASS

**Nekker Glass Company** ★ This workshop, near the Mirrer Yeshiva on the northern fringe of Mea Shearim, revived the ancient glass-blowing traditions that began in this part of the world more than 2,000 years ago. The Nekker family arrived in Jerusalem from Baghdad in the early 1950s and set up a small glass factory with both Arab and Jewish glass blowers who now create designs and techniques from ancient times. They have even developed ways to reproduce soft, ancient patinas in a variety of colors. At Nekker's tiny workshop, you can watch the glass blowers creating delicate, affordable objects. The stock is on sale for a fraction of what it costs in retail shops. A special line of museum reproductions based on the shapes and patinas of delicate Roman glass is a bit higher in price. Staff will pack your purchases securely for travel. Call ahead to be sure it's open. 6 Bet Israel St. ✆ **02/582-9683.**

## JEWELRY

**Hedya Jewelers and the Sarah Einstein Collection** ★ Here you'll find jewelry, often made from small, exquisite component pieces of antique objects such as Yemenite wedding necklaces or Persian headdresses. Hedya's own custom-made jewelry, Hands of Fatima, and Judaica are exquisite. Special orders are welcome. 23 Hillel St. (in the passageway between Hillel and Shamai sts.). ✆ **02/622-1151.**

**Ophir** ★★ For a half-century, Jerusalemites and visitors have been fans of this shop's delicate jewelry designs that echo Victorian, Edwardian, Art Deco, and Middle Eastern styles, all created by the owner, Avraham Lor. Prices are extremely reasonable, and Lor's stock is augmented by many unusual antique and semi-antique items. Much of the jewelry collection is still to be seen in the tiny "backroom" workshop. Open Sunday, Monday, Wednesday, and Thursday 9am to 1pm and 4 to 7pm and Tuesday and Friday 9am to 1pm only. 38 Jaffa Rd. ✆ **02/624-9078.** www.ophir-jewelry.com.

## JUDAICA

**Archie Granot, Papercuts** ★★ Traditional Jewish paper cuts began to develop as a folk art in Europe and North Africa. In many homes it was the custom to hang a delicately cut piece of paper (called a *mizrach,* from the Hebrew word for "east") on the eastern wall of a room, to indicate the direction of Jerusalem. Archie Granot has raised this folk tradition to new levels with his extraordinary multi-layer contemporary designs. Prices can range from a few hundred dollars to several thousand dollars. Granot's works are in the collections of the Israel Museum, the Victoria and Albert Museum, the Jewish Museum of New York, and the Philadelphia Museum of Judaica. 1 Agron St. ✆ **02/625-2210.** www.archiegranot.com.

**Danny Azoulay** ★ A highly skilled craftsperson who came to Israel from Morocco as a small child, Danny Azoulay specializes in porcelain and fine ceramic Judaica, and his tiny shop is filled with hand-painted Chanukah menorahs, charity boxes laced with brass or silver designs, mezuzahs, spice boxes, and dreidels. The shop also sells illuminated manuscripts and *ketubbot* (marriage contracts) by some of **Israel's finest scribal** artists, such as **Amalya Nini Goldstein.** 5 Yoel Salomon St. ✆ **02/623-3918.**

EXPLORING JERUSALEM | The Shopping Scene

# THE ART OF bargaining

If you find something you like you must bargain for it. The main rules are to be courteous and keep your cool. Appear politely unsure the object is something you really want. It often helps if you're with a friend who pretends you're late for a bus or an appointment—you might even pretend to walk away. If a merchant doesn't come down on his price, don't panic and pay full price. On the other hand, never back a merchant into a corner: Never argue: "$25? I saw the same thing on Ben-Yehuda Street for $5!" This leaves the merchant no honorable alternative but to say, "Okay, go to Ben-Yehuda Street!" The chance is that you'll find the same thing or something similar close by; if not, if you leave gracefully, you can always come back and try again. Much depends on how badly the merchant needs to convert some of his stock to cash on the day of your visit. If nothing else, after a few hours of browsing and bargaining, you'll have a new appreciation for the intricacies of the Middle East peace process.

**Judaicut ★**   In this small shop, you can find a selection of papercuts, calligraphy, and *ketubbot* (marriage contracts) by leading Israeli calligraphers and artists. Prices are reasonable. Special orders can be commissioned. 21 Yoel Salomon St. ℂ **02/623-3634.** www.judaicut.co.il.

## THE OLD CITY MARKETS

A major attraction for visitors, the Old City markets have many shops offering such local products as olive-wood chess and nativity sets, rosaries, carved camels, boxes, and olive-wood Christmas tree ornaments—a great buy at about two for NIS 16. You'll also find heavy, hand-blown, bubble-filled glassware from Hebron, inlaid wooden boxes from Egypt and Syria, mother-of-pearl objects from Jordan, dramatic Palestinian embroidery, new and inexpensive imitations of antique Bedouin, Yemenite, and Bedouin-style jewelry, and locally made leather goods. *Tip:* The markets are filled with all kinds of Arabic desserts, spices, and snacks, all of which should be part of the Old City experience!

   **Old tribal Bedouin flat-weave rugs and weavings** can be found in a few shops in the Arab bazaar around the Christian Quarter Road. In older, more expensive pieces, look for bold diamond patterns and rich, subdued reds, browns, yellows, and oranges made from natural dyes of henna, pomegranate, saffron bark, and leaves from desert plants. Newer pieces tend to bright reds and other hard colors, but are still attractive. The shop of **Mr. Maazen Kaysi** (no sign), with a plate-glass show window and a recessed entrance on the right side of the Christian Quarter Road (just past the first pedestrian street turning on the right as you come from David St.), has the finest and largest selection of Bedouin weavings and other rugs. The shops dealing in **ancient antiquities** are fascinating, but unless you're an expert, judge any object you may want to purchase in terms of its decorative value rather than its alleged age or rarity.

   In the Jewish Quarter of the Old City, a good shop for **old objects and Judaica** is **Mansour Saidian** (sign may say Old City Antiques), opposite the Mizrachi Bank on the corner of Tiferet Israel Street. There's always a selection of real 19th-century European and Iranian kiddush cups and old menorahs stashed away among the cases of newer objects and jewelry. These treasures are often a bargain.

## PALESTINIAN EMBROIDERY

Antique Palestinian embroidered robes (among the world's great still-existing national costumes) hang from the doors of many shops in the Old City bazaar. Red, rose, and scarlet on hand-woven black cloth are the preferred colors, stemming from a tradition that goes back almost 3,000 years to the centuries when the prophets warned against women who sewed with scarlet threads of vanity. Many embroidery designs can be traced back to patterns introduced by the Crusaders. Prices for a caftan will range into the hundreds of dollars. The shop of **Maher Natsheh** (10 Christian Quarter Rd.) is noted for antique and old textiles. Here are some other outlets:

In addition, the following two church-supported nonprofit shops offer a dazzling array of **freshly made, exotic new embroideries** all done by specially trained women who are working to support their families. Quality is assured, and prices at these shops are extremely fair.

**Melia** ★   Melia offers many beautiful traditional pieces, as well as some imaginative decorative items. In addition to the classic divan pillowcases, there are embroidered mirror frames as well as designer-embroidered women's jackets and embroidered T-shirts. Also on sale: Western-style tablecloths and embroideries. Arab Orthodox Society Art and Training Center, Frere's St., inside the New Gate, Old City. ✆ **02/628-1377.**

**Sunbula** ★   This nonprofit shop sells a magnificent collection of densely embroidered divan pillowcases, wall hangings, and shawls, all alive with traditional motifs and colors. Many superb pieces are less than NIS 600. Other good buys here include: heavy woven Bedouin tent rugs, embroidered linen tablecloths and napkins, and a good selection of inexpensive handmade crafts and gift items. Custom-tailored jackets and other fashion items can be ordered. Open Monday to Saturday from 9am to 6pm and Sunday from 11am to 1pm. The shop is in the Saint Andrew's complex, on a hill between the train station and the Cinémathèque, and is close to the House of Quality (see House of Quality, above), with its many artists' studios. www.sunbula.org. Saint Andrews Guest House, King David and Remez sts. ✆ **02/672-1707.**

## PHOTOGRAPHS

A number of venerable, family-run photography studios on Al Khanka Street in the Old City have gone through their archives and are now selling fascinating, often very beautiful reprints of views of Jerusalem (and the entire region) from the first half of the 20th century. Kevork Kahvedjian, of **Elia Photo Service** (14 Al Khanka St.), has published a striking book, "Jerusalem Through My Father's Eyes," containing over a half-century of his father's photographic work at the Elia Studio. A few doors down, you'll find the **Varouj Photography Studio,** also selling remarkable matted reproductions of Old Jerusalem scenes from their archives for about NIS 80, many taken with an eye for the poetry of Old Jerusalem. To get to Al Khanka Street, enter Jaffa Gate and continue straight on David Street into the bazaar. At Christian Quarter Road, turn left and continue to the end. Turn right (downhill) onto Al Khanka Street at the end of Christian Quarter Road. The shops with antique photo collections for sale are all on the right side of the street.

**Vision Gallery** ★★   Neil Folberg, noted for his landscapes and photographs of the Jewish world, is the owner of this world-class gallery that handles the works of international contemporary photographers. Wonderful temporary exhibits, and vintage photographs of the Middle East and of Jewish subjects are also featured. Prices begin at NIS 400 and continue to hundreds and thousands of dollars. Israel's other gallery of note specializing in photography is the **Silver Print Gallery** in Ein Hod. 18 Rivlin St. ✆ **02/622-2253.** www.visiongallery.com.

# wineries IN THE HILL COUNTRY

West of Jerusalem are a number of interesting small wineries. The **Latrun Monastery** (📞 **08/922-0065**) is a gardened enclave founded by Trappist monks in 1890 just where the Judean hills begin to rise from the coastal plain 20km (12 miles) west of Jerusalem. A shop at the entrance gate sells Domaine de Latrun wines, liqueurs, and spirits as well as honey and olive oil produced at the monastery. Visitors are welcome to explore the gardens, vineyards, and orchards. From Hwy. 1, the Tel Aviv–Jerusalem Highway, get off at the Latrun interchange. Follow Hwy. 3 briefly in the direction of Ashkelon, and you'll come to the Latrun Monastery, opposite the large Armoured Forces Monument. No entrance fee. Monday to Saturday 9am to 1pm and 2 to 5pm.

The **Soreq Winery** (📞 **08/934-0542**) is a relatively new boutique vineyard located 40 minutes south of Tel Aviv at Kibbutz Tal Shahar. Opened in 1994, it produces cabernet sauvignons, chardonnays, and merlots. Call ahead to arrange a private tour of the winery. You can buy wine and cheese at the winery shop, and there is a picnic area on the premises. From Hwy.1, exit at the Latrun interchange. Take Hwy. 3 south toward Ashkelon for approximately 9km (5⅔ miles). The winery is located 2km (1¼ miles) after the Nachshon interchange. No entrance fee. Open Sunday to Thursday from 10am to 5pm.

The **Tzora Winery** (📞 **02/990-8261**) is a boutique winery with a rising reputation for cabernet sauvignon, sauvignon blanc, and chardonnay wines. It is located on Kibbutz Tzora in the mountains between Beit Shemesh and Jerusalem, and they will arrange private tours if you call ahead. There is a wine and cheese store and picnic area on the premises. From Hwy. 1 exit at the Beit Shemesh (Sha'ar Hagai) interchange, take Rte. 38 south toward Beit Shemesh. From Rte. 38 (about 8km/5 miles from Hwy. 1) take Rte. 3835 to Kibbutz Tzora. There is no entrance fee. Open Sunday to Thursday 9am to 5pm, Friday 9am to 2pm, and Saturday 10am to 5pm.

The **Cremesan Winery** is run by members of the Italian Salisian monastic order. The beautiful winery can be visited (when security allows) daily at Beit Jalla, near Bethlehem on the West Bank. You can also purchase the Italian-style wines produced at Beit Jalla at the **Bet Jimal Monastery** (📞 **02/991-7671**), inside Israel, near the town of Beit Shemesh from Monday to Saturday 8:30am to 5pm. There are picnic tables overlooking a fine view behind the monastery, where you may visit until dusk. This lovely place is located 2km (1¼ miles) south of Beit Shemesh (left turn off Rte. 38).

## SHOES & SANDALS

**Khalifa Shoes** ★   This shop is packed with Naot Teva footwear (the Birkenstock-like sandals and shoes of Israel), as well as with international brands known for comfort, such as Clarke's and Ecco. If you need great walking shoes this is the place. 44 Jaffa Rd. (corner of Rav Kook St., opposite Zion Sq.). 📞 **02/625-7027.**

**Sharabati Shops** ★   With two locations in the Old City bazaar near Jaffa Gate, the Sharabati family stocks the largest collection of very reasonably priced, stylish leather sandals (as well as walking and sport sandals) in the market and is known for fair, unexaggerated opening prices. A second branch is on Christian Quarter Road, in the third store on the left from the intersection with David Street. On the left side of David St. as you descend the steps into the bazaar, midway between the Petra Hotel and Christian Quarter Rd. No phone.

# SIDE TRIPS OUTSIDE JERUSALEM

**Kennedy Memorial** ★ MEMORIAL    Eleven kilometers (6¾ miles) from downtown Jerusalem, in the same general direction of Hadassah Medical Center, Yad Kennedy is reached by following the winding mountain roads past the Aminadav Moshav. Opened in May 1966, the 18m-high (59-ft.) memorial to President John F. Kennedy is designed in the shape of a cut tree trunk, symbolizing a life cut short. The mountaintop memorial is encircled by 51 columns, each bearing the emblem of a state of the Union, plus the District of Columbia. The view from the parking lot is breathtaking—a never-ending succession of mountains and valleys. The monument and adjoining picnic grounds are part of the John F. Kennedy Peace Forest.

**Abu Ghosh** ★ HISTORIC SITE    The Israeli-Arab town of Abu Ghosh (biblical Kiriath Yearim), 13km (8 miles) west of Jerusalem, can easily be reached from Jerusalem by car. Abu Ghosh is one of the few Arab villages that decided to side with Israel in the 1948 War of Independence. Israelis love to flock to Abu Ghosh on Saturday to enjoy hummus and other Arabic-style foods at the town's numerous restaurants. A number of hummus places call themselves "Abu Shukri"; most are good, but have no connection to the *real* Abu Shukri in Jerusalem's Old City. On the other hand, Abu Ghosh's **Lebanese Restaurant** is the best of the wall-to-wall dining choices in town, and serves some of the most fabulous lamb in Israel.

Abu Ghosh's great treasure is the 12th-century **Crusader Church of the Resurrection** ★, now under the guardianship of the Lazarist fathers. Like the Crusader Church of Saint Anne in Jerusalem's Old City, the Church of the Resurrection was designed to create marvelous acoustics for Gregorian chants, but it's less heavily restored and more atmospheric. It is built over an ancient cistern and well that was in use from early Canaanite times. It's open Monday to Wednesday and Friday and Saturday from 8:30 to 11:30am and 2:30 to 5:30pm. The 20th-century **Church of Notre Dame of the Ark,** built on the site of a Byzantine church, marks the last place the Ark of the Covenant rested before it was brought to Jerusalem by King David. It's open daily from 8:30 to 11:30am and 2:30 to 5:30pm.

**Neot Kedumim Biblical Landscape Reserve** ★★ NATURE RESERVE   Located in between Jerusalem and Tel Aviv on Rte. 443 (✆ **08/977-0777;** www.neot-kedumim.org.il), Neot Kedumim is a living museum of the farming, harvesting, and shepherding techniques of ancient times, laid out across 250 hectares (618 acres) of land carefully planted with flora of the biblical period. An explanatory text brings the landscape vividly to life. Expert guides explain references to nature in Judeo-Christian scriptures; you'll find an olive press and a *succa* (harvesters' shelter), and see how ancient ink was made from resin, ground pomegranates, and oak gallnuts. With an advance reservation, you may be able to join a group of 15 or more for a vegetarian buffet of reconstructed ancient recipes. Admission is NIS 35; last admission 2 hours before closing. Open Sunday to Thursday from 8:30am to sunset and Friday and holiday eves from 8:30am to 1pm. Telephone for driving or bus instructions. Guided tours in English are given Friday at 9:30am; reserve ahead to arrange other times. There are also self-guided tours; trails are wheelchair-accessible, and electric carts and wheelchairs are available on advance reservation.

**Soreq Stalactite Cave/Avshalom Nature Reserve** ★ NATURE RESERVE   Located 20km (12 miles) west of Jerusalem, along the road out of Ein Kerem toward Bar Giora (✆ **02/991-1117**), this nature reserve, with its unusual, delicate, and varied stalactites, is a favorite excursion for tour groups. Set in the limestone region, the caves

# excursions TO BETHLEHEM

*Note:* At press time the governments of most Western countries are advising their citizens not to travel in the West Bank.

That being said, in recent years, more and more travelers have ventured into Bethlehem, especially on Christian-organized tour groups for visits to the holy sites in the center of town. For those who decide to visit Bethlehem, we advise reading the news, and getting background on what's going on. Political conditions can change from day to day. **The Christian Information Centre** (p. 26) inside Jerusalem's Jaffa Gate is a good place to get up-to-date advice on political conditions and information about possible organized tours or pilgrimage groups, as well as information about how to use public transportation, or arrange for a private taxi or guide to facilitate your excursion. Travelers from Israel into the Palestinian Authority must be in possession of their foreign passports and show them at the checkpoints that separate Israel from the West Bank. Remember: You cannot drive an Israeli rental car into the West Bank.

The highlight of a visit to Bethlehem, the **Basilica of the Nativity** marking the birthplace of Jesus, was built by order of the Roman Emperor Constantine in A.D. 326. It's the oldest surviving church in the Holy Land, a wondrous place scented with incense and decorated with Byzantine art. It was spared the general destruction of churches during the

Persian Invasion of A.D. 614, because it was adorned by images of the Magi, whom the Persian soldiers recognized as fellow Persians.

A tour of Bethlehem should also take in the churches and chapels adjacent to the Basilica; the nearby **Milk Grotto Church;** the two possible sites of the **Shepherds' Field;** and **Manger Square,** in front of the Church, with its cafes and shops filled with olive-wood items and souvenirs. The **Visitor Information Office** (℃ **02/276-6677;** www.visit-palestine.com) is in the Peace Center on Manger Square and is open Sunday to Thursday from 8:30am to 3:30pm (but hours can be irregular). It offers maps and information about museums and sites in Bethlehem.

8 Kilometers (5 Miles) South of Jerusalem, in the Palestinian Authority/West Bank. Transportation: Public busses do go between Jerusalem (from the bus station near the Jaffa Gate, cost: NIS6) and Bethlehem, but they don't drop passengers near the Church of the Nativity, meaning you'll have to take a taxi from the drop off point to the historic sights. For this reason, many travelers opt for a tour. Recommended tour companies include Eg'ged Tours (www.eggedtours. com), Viator (www.viator.com), and City Discovery (www.city-discovery.com). Prices vary according to length of tour and inclusions and range from half- to full-day offerings, which include highlights in Jerusalem.

are full of incredible formations. The scenery along the road from Ein Kerem to the moshav of Nes Harim, 1.6km (1 mile) from the caves, is by itself quite beautiful; admission to the park is NIS 25 (children NIS 13) and includes a lecture with slides and a tour. *Note:* English-language tours are generally scheduled for early in the morning. Exploring the Soreq Cave entails climbing down (and up) 140 steps. The cave is NOT wheelchair-accessible. Hours are Sunday to Thursday from 8:30am to 4:30pm (to 3:30pm in winter) and Friday from 8:30am to noon; no slide show Friday. Direct service is by tour bus only. Egged will take you on a tour to the caves and nearby sights for about NIS 100.

**Mini Israel** ★★ THEME PARK   This 3-hectare (7½-acre) tourist park is impressive in its scope and detail. It re-creates many of the country's most important landmarks in the form of miniature models built to a scale of 1:25. The park separates Israel into geographic regions and features landmarks from all faiths and cultures. The models are impressive in their detail: The planes at the mock-up of Ben-Gurion Airport actually taxi on runways, and praying pilgrims at the Western Wall sway back and forth. Notable re-creations include the Old City of Jerusalem (including the Western Wall and the Dome of the Rock), the Baha'i Temple Gardens at Haifa, and the Cave of the Patriarchs in Hebron. The park is especially delightful at twilight, when the interiors of buildings are lit. The family-friendly park has a restaurant/cafe food court on the premises and a little play area for children. It takes about 2 hours to see everything. Mini Israel is accessible to those with disabilities. The exhibits are outdoors, so avoid coming on a cold, rainy winter day, or in midday summer heat. It's hard to get here without a car unless you're coming via bus tour. Regular tours to Mini Israel and other nearby sites are operated by Egged Tours (✆ **700/707-577**) on Tuesday and Thursday.

Latrun Junction, off Hwy. 1. ✆ **700/559-559.** www.minisrael.co.il. Admission NIS 72 adults, NIS 60 children 6–18. Look for coupons and discounted rates at Tourist Information and hotel desks. Nov–Mar Sun–Thurs and Sat 10am–6pm; Fri 10am–2pm; Apr and Sept–Oct Sun–Thurs 10am–8pm; Fri 10am–2pm; May–June Sun–Thurs 10am–9pm; Fri 9am–2pm; July–Aug 10am–10pm; Fri 10am–2pm.

# THE DEAD SEA & MASADA

| srael has many dramatic sights. But these two—one an unparalleled natural wonder, the other the site of extraordinary courage and tragedy—may well top the list. And happily, they can be seen in easy day trips from Jerusalem, either separately or in tandem.

## THE DEAD SEA ★★★

The Dead Sea, so dense with salt and other minerals that it's impossible to sink, is the lowest point by far on the face of the earth. It's also the most otherworldly body of water on the planet.

The southern part of the Dead Sea, where travelers like to experience the floating sensation, can have a metallic sheen in soft daylight, while in noon sunlight, it can be sky blue with miragelike white "saltbergs" floating on its surface. The northern coast (along Hwy. 1) is rugged and beautiful. At Ein Gedi and the spa hotel strip at Ein Bokek, the water is the most dense and helpful for skin diseases such as psoriasis. These were Cleopatra's favorite waters for her beauty needs, and today the water and the mud are said to be cleansing for the skin and scalp, improving skin texture and even smoothing wrinkles.

### Essentials

**GETTING THERE   By Tour Bus**   Public transport is difficult and infrequent, especially in the blazing summer weather. Both **Egged** (www.egged tours.com) and **United Bus Tours** (www.unitedtours.co.il) run affordable half-day and full-day tours to Masada and the Dead Sea, usually allowing time for a quick dip and brief stops along the way at interesting sites and vista points. Although convenient, just note that the tour buses can spend a big chunk of time collecting passengers at various hotels and drop off points in Jerusalem before heading out. **Abraham Tours** (abrahamtours.com), run by Jerusalem's Abraham Hostel also operates bus tours to the area; check with them about middle of the night departures for hikers who want to climb to the top of Masada in the cool, pre-dawn hours and catch the sunrise (a cable car carries non-climbing visitors up to Masada after 8am).

**By Car**   A **rental car** allows you to explore at your leisure and make an overnight trip. There are parking lots at Ein Gedi Beach, and at all historic sites and nature reserves along the way. From Jerusalem take Hwy. 1, east to its intersection with Hwy. 90. Turn right (south) onto Hwy. 90 (the main road along the coast of The Dead Sea) and continue following the signs to Qumran, Ein Gedi, and Masada. Highway 1 from the heights of Jerusalem to the Dead Sea (1200 feet below sea level) is a steady 4000 foot downhill run. Along the way, you'll pass black goat hair Bedouin tent encampments, and a sign noting that you've passed sea level.

## WHAT TO SEE & DO

Visitors come here, primarily, to look, float and repair. The Dead Sea contains the highest mineral content of any waters in the world: 300 grams per liter. As you bathe in The Dead Sea, you'll also be breathing the dense air of the below-sea-level atmosphere, which contains over 10 percent more oxygen than at sea level. This is helpful for people with respiratory problems and heart disease. In addition, bromides evaporating into the air from The Dead Sea contribute to a relaxed feeling of well being. Many tired and anxious people come here for at least a week in order to unwind. The dense atmosphere also filters out harmful sun rays—psoriasis sufferers can stay out in the sun a bit longer without burning. Large tour groups and long-term residents fill the area's rows of high-rise, all-inclusive hotels and spas—therapeutic colonies that don't really give you a feel for Israel. An alternative to the big hotels is Kibbutz Ein Gedi's beautiful holiday village, in an amazing desert botanical garden on a hill overlooking the Dead Sea (p. 119).

*Note:* Because the Dead Sea is drying up and water levels are falling, many of the Dead Sea spa hotels that once enjoyed beachfronts, now find themselves as much as a quarter of a mile from the water line. Sinkholes caused by the falling underground water table have become a recent danger around the region. Do not venture into areas that are barricaded off or marked as dangerous.

**The Inn of the Good Samaritan** ★ HISTORIC SITE   Located 20 km (13 miles) east of Jerusalem, just off Highway 1, this recently restored old caravan stop and inn houses a collection of ancient mosaic floors from synagogues, churches, and Roman era edifices, transported from excavations throughout Israel and reassembled here. Tradition holds that this is the site of the New Testament's parable of the Good Samaritan, who helped an injured traveler ignored by others on the Jerusalem-Jericho Road. Among the floors on display is one from a synagogue of Samaritans, who follow a Torah-based religion, but in ancient times, were rivals of their Jewish neighbors. In Byzantine times, Samaritans numbered at least several hundred thousand. The present day Samaritan community numbers only several hundred.

Highway 1, 20 km (13 miles east of Jerusalem. ℓ **02/541-7555.** Sun-Thurs 9am-3pm. Admission free.

**Qumran** ★ HISTORIC SITE According to some archeologists, the ruins of Qumran may have been a trading post; others believe that at the time of the First Jewish Revolt against Rome (A.D. 66-73) it was a communal settlement of the Essenes, an ascetic Jewish sect that may have influenced the earliest Christians. The Dead Sea Scrolls (the oldest existing copies of Jewish holy scriptures, plus other hitherto unknown extra Biblical writings) were discovered in 1947 in caves overlooking Qumran, leading many to believe the scrolls may have been written by Essene scribes. Others believe the scrolls may have been brought from libraries in Jerusalem and hidden in the caves in advance of the Roman destruction of Jerusalem in A.D. 70. Check out the stone platforms in the ruins of Qumran's "Scriptorim," where some scholars postulate scribes labored over the scrolls. Others feel these low structures could not possibly have been writing tables for normal size human beings. A video and brochures at the modern, air-conditioned Visitor's Center and cafe explain the mysteries of the site.

Rte. 90 (13km/8 miles south of junction with Hwy. 1). ℓ **02/994-2235.** Daily 8am–4pm (to 5pm in summer). Admission NIS 20.

## WHERE TO STAY & DINE

The in-house hotel restaurants offer the best possibilities for a major meal. Many visitors staying here hotel-hop to try out the different lunch or dinner buffets; they're all vast, and you're sure to find something interesting. Prices range from NIS 100 to NIS

200. In the shopping mall at Ein Bokek, there are a number of cafes and restaurants where you can get inexpensive meals and light snacks. None of the choices, however, are standouts. There's a frantically busy McDonald's. **Aroma Café,** with it's great Israeli coffee, fresh salads, and free Wi-Fi is one of the better choices.

## Expensive

### Hod Hamidbar Resort and Spa Hotels ★★
None of the hotels in the Dead Sea area come up to international five-star standards. Having a built-in clientele, here to "test the waters", they don't have to try that hard. That being said, this one likely comes to the closest, with its location right on its own beach, its lovely pool areas, top-notch spa, and better-than-usual dining options. Rooms are large and very clean, recently renovated (they have a somewhat Scandinavian look with lots of blond wood), and boast huge windows, comfortable beds and free wifi. Search online for a discount, as the hotel often offers special deals which drop it into the moderate category.

Ein Bokek. ℗ **972-8-6688222.** www.hodhotel.co.il. 203 units. $215–$359 double. Rates include breakfast. Free parking. **Amenities:** Restaurant; bar; children's activities in season; playground; fitness center; Internet (fee); several pools; room service; spa; beauty salon; free loaner bikes; free Wi-Fi and international phone calls.

## Moderate

### Kibbutz Ein Gedi Resort Hotel ★★★
Dramatically located on a hill overlooking The Dead Sea, this kibbutz and its low-rise accommodations are set amid the exotic plantings of the only internationally registered botanical garden in which people live. For visitors to this Eden, it's hard to believe that before 1949 there was nothing but barren rock here. This location, a 20-minute drive from Masada, makes a good base for those who want to climb Masada at dawn, explore the region at their own leisure, or just enjoy the beauty of the place with its gorgeous swimming pools. There are four kinds of accommodations at a wide range of prices. Standard rooms are basic, but set amid wonderful gardens and air-conditioned. Upgraded rooms and new mini-suites and deluxe-plus rooms are more luxurious; some offer decks that overlook dramatic vistas. Guests are offered free admission to the Spa at the Dead Sea and optional desert excursions as well as occasional Bedouin evening cookouts. A kiosk for food supplies opens twice daily. It's possible to arrive here using public transport, as the kibbutz provides a shuttle down to the Ein Gedi Dead Sea Spa and to the public beach, but a car is essential in order explore the area. Ein Gedi is heavily booked by groups, so reserve far in advance. This is a "green" hotel, and also a kibbutz community—service is basic and practical.

Kibbutz Ein Gedi. ℗ **08/659-4222.** www.ein-gedi.co.il. 153 units. $215-$265 standard double; $360 mini suite for 2. Rates include half-board. Discount available on Kibbutz Hotel Fly and Drive package. **Amenities:** Kibbutz dining room, desert excursions, botanical garden, 2 pools (indoor, outdoor), massage, Dead Sea spa, wellness center, tennis courts.

# Ein Gedi

Hwy. 90, 33km (21 miles) south of Qumran.

There is no modern town at Ein Gedi. The area is spread out along a 5-mile stretch of Highway 90 alongside the Dead Sea. It includes a **Nature Reserve,** an IYHA Association Youth Hostel, a **public beach** with lifeguards, showers, and **Kibbutz Ein Gedi.** Kibbutz Ein Gedi is the most beautiful place to stay in the area and contains a sprawling Resort Guest House and impressive botanical gardens.

This remote, canyon oasis near the Dead Sea has attracted small bands of people since prehistoric times. More than 5,000 years ago, an unknown Chalcolithic people built a sanctuary amid the waterfalls and springs here—a cache of their mysterious, elegantly wrought sacred vessels, copper wands, crowns, and scepters were discovered in the 1960s by Israeli archaeologists searching for hidden Dead Sea Scrolls (from 150 B.C.–A.D. 135) amid the crevasses of inaccessible cliffside caves. According to the Bible, it was to the isolated canyons of Ein Gedi that the young David fled from the paranoid King Saul around B.C. 1000; here David had the chance to kill his pursuer, but he would not lay a hand on his king, the anointed of God. The "Song of Songs" rhapsodizes over the exotic herbs and spices grown in Ein Gedi's rarefied atmosphere and soil. From approximately the 6th century B.C. until the A.D. late 8th century. Ein Gedi was famous throughout the ancient world for priceless incense, lotions, and perfumes. Ein Gedi's plants and formulas were carefully guarded by the Ein Gedi community until its demise in early Islamic times. Indeed, an inscription in the mosaic floor of the Byzantine-era synagogue discovered at Ein Gedi warns members of the community not to divulge the "secret of the town" to outsiders. After more than 1,000 years of complete desolation, the region was resettled in 1949 by a group of kibbutzniks who were amazed at how trees and plantings thrive at Ein Gedi. **Kibbutz Ein Gedi** is now lushly planted with 900 species of trees and shrubs from all over the world, and is the only internationally recognized botanical garden in which people live!

**Ein Gedi Public Beach** ★★    Thanks to free parking, this beach is often mobbed, but there's a lifeguard on duty, and it's a fun place to try out the Dead Sea's famous buoyancy. There are free (and very necessary) freshwater showers on the beach, and changing rooms are available for NIS 10. Remember not to get the Dead Sea water in your eyes, and do not try to submerge your head. Don't swim if you have skin cuts or sores!

The very basic **Pundak Ein Gedi Cafeteria** (© 08/659-4761), just beside the beach, is the only restaurant in the region. Main courses are less than NIS 50. It's open daily 11am to 4pm; an adjacent minimart is open daily 7:30am to 8pm.

About 3km (1¾ miles) south of Ein Gedi Beach is the public **Ein Gedi Sulfur Springs and Spa** (© 08/659-4813) that draws big crowds and is housed in a modern building. It's especially popular with pensioners, who are bussed in from all over Israel, but foreigners also come to try it out. Here you can soak in mineral-rich spring waters drawn from The Dead Sea. Admission to the spa costs NIS 79 for adults Sunday to Thursday, and NIS 85 Friday, Saturday, and holidays.

**Ein Gedi Nature Reserve** ★★ NATURE RESERVE    Spectacular waterfalls and hiking trails are within the **Ein Gedi Reserve's Nachal David and Nachal Arugot** canyons. Maps and suggested trail routes are available at the entrance; more-detailed maps and trail advice for hikes of several hours through these two neighboring canyon systems are available at the SPNI Center, near the hostel and the Nachal David entry gate. Follow the trail and the signposts, winding through tall pines and palm trees up and into the desert hills. You proceed between slits in the rock formations, under canopies of papyrus reeds, and after about 10 minutes of steady climbing, you'll hear the wonderful sound of rushing water. In another 5 minutes, your appetite whetted, you arrive at what is surely one of the wonders of the Judean desert—the **Nachal David–Ein Gedi waterfalls,** hidden in an oasis of vegetation that hangs in a canyon wall. A second trail involving a 30-minute climb takes you to the **Shulamit Spring** and then to the **Dodim Cave** at the top of the falls.

A 20- to 30-minute walk to the left brings you to the fenced-in ruins of a **Chalcolithic sanctuary** dating from about 3000 B.C. Mysterious copper wands and crowns, probably belonging to this sanctuary and hidden in nearby caves for more than 5,000 years, are displayed in the antiquities section of the Israel Museum.

Another walk leads to the ruins of Byzantine-era Ein Gedi's synagogue, with its marvelously intact mosaic floor. The reserve is open from 8am to 4pm; in summer until 5pm. You must make arrangements with the Nature Reserves Authority if you plan to do any of the 5- to 6-hour hikes into the depths of the *nachal* (canyon) systems, especially if you plan to go beyond the **Hidden Falls.** Always carry at least 5 liters (5⅓ qt.) of water with you if you're planning a major hike in summer. From autumn to spring, it is important to be aware of the possibility of flash floods caused by rain in distant places. No food or cigarettes are allowed on the grounds. Parts of the Reserve and the Antiquities Park are wheelchair-accessible. Admission to the reserve is NIS 26 and includes admission to the Antiquities Park (see below). There is a snack kiosk at the entrance. *Tip:* Ein Gedi is impossibly hot midday in the summer. Worse yet, during school holidays, it is overrun by school groups.

At the Ein Gedi National Antiquities Park are the ruins of **Ancient Ein Gedi ★**, one of Israel's most important archaeological sites. Admission is NIS 14. From the First and Second temples' times until the end of the Byzantine era, Ein Gedi was a largely Jewish outpost famous throughout the ancient world for its production of rare spices; fragrant, intoxicating balsam oil; and priceless myrrh. Perhaps Ein Gedi was permitted to survive the tumultuous decades of wars and rebellions against Rome because its secret formulas for spice and incense production were not only beyond value, but also irreplaceable. At Ein Gedi, the **mosaic floor** of an A.D. 6th-century synagogue has been uncovered. If you visit other mosaic synagogue floors discovered in the Jordan Valley and the Galilee, you'll find that a number of Byzantine-era synagogues (at Bet Alpha, Hammat Tiberias, and Zippori) contain a depiction of the zodiac as the centerpiece of their mosaic floors. Some scholars believe the zodiac was meant to represent the orderly patterns of God's universe. At Ein Gedi, in place of a zodiac circle, the mosaic floor is dominated by a central circle design of peacock chicks and adult birds, perhaps illustrating continuing patterns of birth and growth through which divine presence is revealed. It may be that the Jewish community at Ein Gedi, less influenced by outside cultures than the Jewish communities farther north, was reluctant to employ pagan motifs in the ornamentation of its synagogue.

The extraordinary personal papers, letters, and possessions found in The Dead Sea caves and dating from the Second Jewish Revolt against Rome (A.D. 135) belonged to Jewish inhabitants of Ein Gedi who attempted to escape the Roman armies by hiding in the region's almost inaccessible caves. Yigael Yadin's book "Bar Kokhba" details these dramatic finds.

Hwy. 90 (33km/21 miles south of Qumran). ✆ **08/658-4285.** www.parks.org.il. Admission NIS 35; archeological site only NIS 20. Sat–Thurs 8am–4pm, Fri 8am–3pm.

# MASADA ★★★

It's a tradition for Israelis to make the ascent to the top of Masada at least once—this is the scene of one of the most heroic and tragic incidents in Jewish history. Few non-Jews outside Israel had heard of Masada until its story was dramatized in a book and a subsequent television miniseries in 1981. The story of a small garrison that defied the Roman army, as the historian Flavius Josephus recorded and perhaps embellished, is worth retelling.

King Herod had built a magnificent palace complex and fortress atop this nearly inaccessible desert mountain plateau around 30 B.C. Underground cisterns assured the fortress of a lavish water supply for the palace's baths and gardens. Most impressive was Herod's personal winter villa, the extraordinary hanging palace on the northern tip of Masada, calculated to catch breathtaking vistas of the Dead Sea as well as refreshing breezes from the north. He furnished the luxurious place with every comfort as well as storehouses of food and arms, protecting the almost inaccessible location with impregnable walls. The audaciousness of such an undertaking tells much about Herod's personality. After Herod's death in 4 B.C., a small Roman garrison occupied the mount. However, during the Jewish Revolt against Rome in A.D. 66, a small band of Jewish zealots attacked and overtook the almost unattended fortress. They brought their families, lived off the vast storehouses of food, and used the arsenal of arms to defend themselves. They even raided the surrounding countryside.

Finally, in A.D. 73, 3 years after the fall of Jerusalem and the end of the First Jewish Revolt, the Romans decided to put an end to this last pocket of Jewish resistance. They built a siege ramp up to the mountaintop, using captured Jews as slave laborers, knowing the defenders of Masada could not bring themselves to attack or harm their enslaved countrymen. After an onslaught using siege engines, flaming torches, rock bombardments, and battering rams, Masada was still in Jewish hands. But with 10,000 Roman troops camped on the hillside and daily bombardments smashing at the walls, it became only a question of when the 900 defenders would succumb. Flaming torches thrown at the fort's wall were whipped by a wind into the midst of the defenders, and the garrison's gates caught fire. The Romans, seeing that Masada was practically defenseless, decided to wait until dawn and take it over in their own good time.

That final night, the 900 men, women, and children who inhabited Masada held a desperate meeting. Their leader, Eliezer Ben-Yair, in a dramatic speech (as reported by the historian Flavius Josephus who, of course, was not actually present), persuaded his followers to accept death bravely, on their own terms. In the darkness at Masada nearly 2,000 years ago, a great mass suicide occurred. Ten men were chosen as executioners. Members of families lay side by side and bared their throats. After all the families had been killed, 1 of the 10 executioners was chosen to kill the other nine; he then ran himself through on his own sword. Two women and five children survived, hiding in one of the caves on the plateau. The Romans, who had expected to fight their way in, were triply astonished at the eerie silence and the orderly groups of bodies where they had expected to encounter battle. Josephus recorded the "calm courage of [the defenders'] resolution . . . and utter contempt of death." So ended the Jewish resistance against Rome. Like almost everything in Israel, the meaning of Masada has become a matter of controversy, with some contending that glorification of a political stand that resulted in mass suicide is not good for the national psyche.

## The Visitor Center & Climbing the Ascent

Masada is now a UNESCO World Heritage Site, and a new, air-conditioned, state-of-the-art visitor complex has been set up at the entrance to the park. You'll find a very useful history video and a model of ancient Masada, a small snack bar, and a souvenir shop. It doesn't fit in with the isolation and antiquity of Masada, but the cool air and the chance to stock up on bottled water will be most welcome. There's also a small museum (admission NIS 25). Portable audio guides can be rented for the museum for NIS 25 and another NIS 25 for audio guides to Masada itself. Park admission includes a pamphlet with a map detailing the Masada site.

From the parking lot at the foot of **Masada National Park** you've got two choices—climb on foot or ride the cable car that carries you almost to the summit. If you climb, especially in the summer months, be sure to start (literally) at the crack of dawn, before the spectacular heat. On days when the heat is too great, park rangers ban climbing, so get to Masada before dawn if you are determined to make the climb.

Climbers have two choices: the route from The Dead Sea side or the Roman siege ramp originally built in A.D. 73 on the side of the mountain facing in the direction of Arad (this Roman ramp path is only accessible by car from Arad). The route from The Dead Sea side requires approximately 40 minutes to an hour; it's called the **Snake Path** because of the steep, hairpin curves. The Snake Path opens approximately an hour before sunrise (so climbers can catch the stunning vista) and closes at 3:30pm. Most visitors are happy to use the cable car to ascend and descend. *Note:* **Special-access pathways** have been created on top of Masada for those with disabilities, and special arrangements can be made to help transport those with special needs to the top. Call for information and special help in advance.

The **Sound and Light Show,** lasting 45 minutes, is usually given Tuesday and Thursday evenings at an outdoor theater on the Arad (western) side of Masada. The theater is not accessible from Hwy. 90, which runs along The Dead Sea, so allow 45 minutes to get there by car (your hotel will give you the best directions). For exact time schedules and reservations, call ☎ **08/995-9333.** Admission is NIS 50. A historical narrative is given in Hebrew, but simultaneous translations can be rented.

Masada National Park. ☎ **08/658-4207.** www.parks.org.il. Admission to Masada NIS 35 adults, half-price for children; combined admission plus one-way cable car NIS 70; with round-trip cable car NIS 80. Cable cars operate Sun–Thurs 8am–4pm, Fri and eves of holidays (including Sat) 8am–2pm. The cable car will deposit you steps from the fortress top.

## Where to Stay

**Masada Guest House and Youth Hostel** ★★   This new, architecturally beautiful youth hostel is a great budget base for exploring the region, and is right at the foot of Masada, so those who wish to climb to the top in the pre-dawn, don't have to drive or bus in from Jerusalem in the middle of the night. It's often mobbed with student groups, but the management tries to keep them in wings away from private guests. There are dorm rooms, as well as doubles and family rooms, all with fridges, TV, and a private bath/shower; terraces overlook the desert and a refreshing swimming pool. Towels, sheets, soap, and shampoo are provided. Full or half-board and even picnic meals can be arranged; meals are kosher. A synagogue is also on the premises.

Rte. 90 at Masada National Park. ☎ **08/995-3222,** or 599/510-511 in Israel. www.iyha.org.il. 88 units, all with private shower. $180 double; $45 dormitory bed. Rates include breakfast. Free parking. **Amenities:** Dining room, basketball court, rooms for those w/limited mobility, pool. Egged bus no. 444 from Jerusalem or Eilat; ask driver for special stop at Masada hostel.

# THE GALILEE

**7**

The Galilee, encompassing much of Northern Israel, is an inviting network of forested hills, olive groves, kibbutzim, and
Israeli Arab towns and villages. At this region's eastern edge
is Israel's greatest natural treasure: the Sea of Galilee, a 2½-hour
drive north of Jerusalem. This magical, turquoise body of water is a
jewel-like, freshwater lake, set amidst a circle of mountains, and surrounded by dramatic Old and New Testament sites.

Organized bus tours can take you through the highlights of this region,
but, if possible, the Galilee is the place to bring a rental car so you can
free-wheel and explore including a stay for a few days at a Kibbutz Guesthouse or country lodge. Beyond the circuit around the Sea of Galilee, some
of the area's highlights include:

**Safad (Tsfat):** A mountain city 33km (20 miles) drive northeast of the Sea
of Galilee, this has been a center for Jewish scholarship and mysticism
since the 15th century; the old city is filled with quaint lanes and artists'
homes.

**Nazareth:** The village of Jesus's youth, Nazareth is now a modern city and
important center for Israel's Arab community. It's the site of the Basilica
that marks the Annunciation. The recreated Nazareth Biblical Village is a
worthwhile attraction. Nearby are Zippori, the vast ruins of a Roman Jewish city, traditionally the home of Mary's family, and Mt. Tabor, a place of
mystery since prehistoric times (with views across Israel to Mt. Carmel)
and site of the Transfiguration of Jesus.

**Bar'am National Park:** A beautiful drive 40 km (25 miles) northwest of
Safad, where well-preserved ruins of the Bar'am synagogue from the A.D.
3rd and 4th century stand amid the remnants of a Maronite Christian village ordered evacuated by Israeli forces during the 1948 War of
Independence.

**GETTING AROUND**   You can approach the Galilee from the southeast
on the road that runs northward up the Jordan Valley, or there are two good
central routes for entering Galilee from the west: One is from Haifa to
Akko and east to Safed, then down to the Sea of Galilee. The other is due
east from Haifa to Nazareth and straight across to Tiberias. An offshoot of
the Haifa-Nazareth road is a route that detours down through the Jordan
Valley, south of the Sea of Galilee; at the Jordan Valley, turn north. In summer, the Jordan Valley, which is far below sea level, can be oppressively
hot. Give yourself time to enjoy the beaches of the Sea of Galilee, which
can be paradisiacal.

The Galilee is filled with so many places of natural beauty and historical
interest that it's worth it to rent a car, at least for a few days of travel. Buses
connect the major cities, but public transport to places in the countryside is
poor to nonexistent.

# Galilee

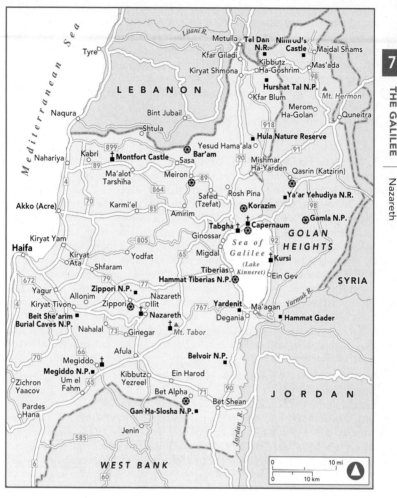

# NAZARETH ★

40km (25 miles) SE of Haifa

Nazareth, the town where Jesus grew up, and today the main city in the southern Galilee, was only a tiny hamlet in biblical times, scarcely recorded on maps or mentioned in historical works. Modern Nazareth, by contrast, is a bustling city, filled with industry and new construction. Only recently, with the restoration of Ottoman era mansions and markets in its old city, has Nazareth become more than a brief stop where visitors can check out the churches and shrines marking the life of Jesus.

The population of Nazareth is approximately 35 to 40 percent Christian and 60 to 65 percent Muslim. Along with Jerusalem, it's the headquarters of the Christian

mission movement in Israel, with more than 40 churches, convents, monasteries, orphanages, and private parochial schools. Nazareth's very name is used by Arabs and Israelis to designate Christians. Just as Jesus was also known as the Nazarene, in Arabic, Christians are called *Nasara,* and in Hebrew *Notzrim.* Because it has a more cosmopolitan, population with a high level of education, Nazareth has become the cultural and political center for the more moderate Arabic community in northern Israel. The city abounds with musicians, writers, filmmakers, local artists, small concerts and poetry readings.

The old town's crop of interesting, atmospheric guest houses, cafes and eateries can help introduce you to Nazareth's unique spirit. English is widely spoken, but the first language of most inhabitants of Nazareth is Arabic.

## Essentials
### GETTING THERE & AROUND
**BY CAR**   Nazareth is in the center of the lower Galilee, set in the largest and most fertile valley in Israel, the Yizreel Valley, often called simply Ha-Emek ("the valley"); it lies between the Galilee mountains to the north and the Samaria range to the south, midway between Haifa and Tiberias. From Tiberias, take Rte. 77, and turn south onto Rte. 754 near Kana, which will take you into Nazareth. From Haifa, take Rte. 75.

**A warning:** Nazareth has a "bypass," a road that circles the town, which explains the confusing signs that point in opposite directions for the same destination. One of these destinations is **Nazareth Elit** (or Nazarat Illit—meaning Upper Nazareth), the new, modern, mostly Jewish area to the north, planned by the government to create a Jewish community beside the city of Nazareth. Its a separate municipality.

For Nazareth itself, you'll want to go down Pope Paul VI Street and into the center of Nazareth, you follow the signs to the Basilica of the Annunciation, Nazareth's principal religious monument off Pope Paul VI Street on Casa Nova Street (also known as Bishara or Annunciation St.).

**BY BUS**   Bus service is available to Nazareth from all major cities. There is no actual bus station: Intercity buses stop on busy Pope Paul VI Street near Bank **Hapoalim. Egged Information** is just across from the bank (© **04/656-9956**), open daily 6am to 6pm. Buses to Haifa or Tiberias leave approximately every 30 minutes. It is best to ask at the information counter for the number of the most convenient bus next departing for your destination. **Nazareth Municipal Buses** have one- or two-digit numbers and can get you up the steep hill to the Salesian and Nazareth Illit neighborhoods. The web site for the excellent **Jesus Trail** organization (jesustrail.com/hike-the-jesus-trail/transportation/city-to-city-bus-schedules-timetables) provides the best information on travel in and out of Nazareth.

### ORIENTATION
**CITY LAYOUT**   Use the basilica's huge cupola, topped by a beacon, as your landmark—everything you'll need is within sight of the basilica. There are very few street signs, and building numbers are often in Arabic. Remember that it's downhill to the basilica and the center of town from most points in the city. The main roadway downhill into Nazareth (and uphill out of it) is separated into a right-hand roadway, clogged with cars parking, unloading, and waiting; and a central, less-gridlocked roadway for (we hope) moving traffic.

Casa Nova Street is the approach to the basilica, and on it you'll find restaurants, cafes, hotels, hospices, and the Tourist Information Office.

To get a feel for old Nazareth, turn into the narrow alleys that wind up and back into the terraced limestone ridges, and wander through the narrow cobbled streets of the Arab Market. Keep in mind that Nazareth is completely closed on Sunday and in full swing on Saturday. Interesting eateries, venues for small concerts, readings, and theatrical performances are opening in the beautiful, freshly restored old mansions off the main streets of the town center.

**VISITOR INFORMATION**  The **Nazareth Tourism Association Information Office** (www.nazarethinfo.org; ✆ **04/657-0555**) is on Casa Nova Street (also called El Bishara St. or Annunciation St.) near the intersection with Pope Paul VI Street, open Monday through Friday from 8:30am to 5pm, Saturday from 9am to 1pm. The Tourism Association's website is filled with excellent information on places of interest, walks, shopping, and food. The **Fauzi Azar Inn** (p. 129) gives great walking tours of the Old City many mornings at 10am for NIS 30.

## What to See & Do

There are four major things for tourists to do in Nazareth: Shop in the market, visit the New Testament sites, enjoy the many Arabic restaurants and sweet shops in the city, and visit the fascinating "Nazareth Village," a re-creation of what life was like in the tiny hamlet of Nazareth at the time of Jesus.

**New Testament Sites**  The **Basilica of the Annunciation ★★** is located on Casa Nova Street, on the spot where, according to Christian tradition, the Angel Gabriel appeared before Mary, to announce she would bear a child. The present Basilica of the Annunciation, completed in 1966, was built over earlier structures dating from 1730 to 1877. Unlike most Christian shrines in Israel, this basilica has a bold, modern design. Around the nave, on the walls, are murals that were created by artists from around the world. Note the Japanese mural of the Madonna and Child on the left (north) wall—Mary's robe is made entirely of Japanese seed pearls. Summer hours are daily from 8am to 6pm; Mass is held in the Grotto of the Annunciation at 6:30am. 11:45am and from 2 to 4:45pm. Walk out the north-side door to reach the other religious sites.

The **Church of Saint Joseph ★** is 90m (295 ft.) away, set on the site believed to have been occupied by Joseph's carpentry workshop. Open daily 7am to 6pm.

On the main street in the bazaar is the **Greek Catholic "Synagogue" Church ★**, believed to be the site of the ancient Nazareth synagogue that Jesus frequented. Farther along the road is the **Franciscan Mensa Christi Church ★**, believed to occupy the spot where Jesus ate with his disciples after the Resurrection.

**Mary's Well ★**, with its source inside the **Greek Orthodox Church of the Annunciation,** is another important holy site. The church was built at the end of the 17th century over the remains of three earlier churches. At the church entrance, on the archway above the stone staircase leading down to the well, is a mural depicting the angel Gabriel appearing to Mary,

**Our Lady of Fright Chapel ★**, sometimes called the Tremore, is on a wooded hill south of the center opposite the Galilee Hotel. It commemorates the spot where Mary watched while the people of Nazareth attempted to throw Jesus over the Precipice.

**Nazareth Village ★★**  This extraordinary re-creation of houses, farms, workshops, oil and wine presses, and terraced fields as they existed in the time of Jesus could easily have been embarrassingly hokey. It's not (we promise) because everything seen here is based on knowledge gleaned from archaeological digs in the area. Every structures in the "village" has been built in the same dimensions, and with the same

## Walking the Jesus Trail ★★★

For millions of modern travelers, walking in the footsteps of Jesus has meant taking a few steps from a tour bus to the Church of the Annunciation or to the banks of the Jordan River.

But thanks to a collaborative effort of local Christians, Muslims, and Jews—headed by the dynamic Maoz Inon and Suraida Nassar—that method of touring is changing. The group has mapped a careful, 65km (40-mile) itinerary (mainly downhill from Nazareth) of the routes Jesus would have taken as he crisscrossed the Galilee on foot from Nazareth to Zippori, Kana, and down to the Sea of Galilee. Along the way, visitors

pass olive groves, ancient springs, historic sites and ruins. Yes, modern towns and their outskirts are also passed (there's no way to avoid them), but they don't account for the majority of the trail.

The route can be hiked by independent walkers or done with organized tours. Included are places to camp, overnight lodgings, and places to eat and buy supplies. Participants can as much or as little of the trail as they like. An optional return route to Nazareth includes the ethereal Mount Tabor.

For more information, go to www.jesustrail.com.

materials and techniques, used 2,000 years ago. The same goes for the ancient costumes the cast members here wear as they perform traditional labors, such as plowing, wine and olive oil pressing, cooking, and weaving. The recreation is designed to help visitors understand the environment in which Jesus found material for his teachings and parables. Guided tours include readings from the New Testament at various points along the way, but the village should be of interest to visitors of all faiths, as it carefully delineates the nature and customs of the Jewish community that existed in Nazareth 2,000 years ago. Especially fascinating is the re-creation of a very modest A.D. 1st-century synagogue that would have existed in a Galilean village while The Temple at Jerusalem was still standing. For an additional charge, it may be possible to arrange to attend a 1st-century vegetarian meal, served in a Bedouin tent. The men, women, and children "inhabiting" the village are both Christian and Muslim residents of modern-day Nazareth.

Beside the YMCA in downtown Nazareth. © **04/645-6042.** www.nazarethvillage.com. NIS 50 adults, NIS 25 children, NIS 32 students. Additional charge for meals. Sat and Mon–Thurs 9am–5pm. Hours are flexible, and you must call ahead to schedule a tour. Additional evening tours offered Christmas, Easter, and in summer.

## Where to Stay

**Al Mutran Guest House ★**  This authentic, spacious, Ottoman-era mansion contains three apartment suites suitable for couples, families, or groups. The suites are, thankfully, air conditioned, and boast antique-studded salon/reception rooms, and modern bath and kitchenette facilities; some offer balconies. You feel as if you've rented a portion of an old semipalace in Rhodes, Marrakech, or Cairo. Great for longer-term stays, Al Mutran's staff will help plug you into a genuine Nazareth experience.

Old City, Nazareth Center. © **04/657-7947.** www.al-mutran.com. 3 units, all with bathrooms. $128–$138 double. Family suite $220 for 4 people. Rates incude breakfast. Free on street parking. **Amenities:** Lobby with free tea/coffee; free Wi-Fi.

**Fauzi Azar Inn** ★★   Both a guesthouse and a hostel—so there are accommodations here for people in all price ranges and group sizes—the inn is set in a splendid
200-year-old Nazareth mansion, replete with high, hand-painted ceilings; Ottoman
arches; splendid Turkish marble floors and a lovely garden. The private rooms have
simple, but clean wooden furnishings; and the dorm rooms have the usual hostel bunk-
beds. But one comes here more for the overall ambiance than the décor. Included in
the price of the stay is a free tour, during which the very moving history of the Inn is
detailed and Nazareth is explored including a visit to a, you guessed it, modern-day
carpenter. Other freebies include use of the communal kitchen (occasionally Arab
cooking classes are held there) and breakfast. The website offers instructions on how
to find the inn, which is hidden behind a tiny door in Nazareth's Old City. Alas, the
facilities are not handicap accessable.

Old City, Nazareth Center. ©**04/602-0469** or 054/432-2328. www.fauziazarinn.com. 10 units, most
with shared bathrooms. Private double NIS 360–NIS 450; dorm bed NIS 100. **Amenities:** Living
room; communal kitchen; patio; free tour free Wi-Fi.

## NEAR NAZARETH: ZIPPORI

Two thousand years ago, Zippori (Sepphoris) was a thriving city and Nazareth a
humble village less than 6km (3¾ miles) away. Now those roles are reversed, and Zippori is a cooperative agricultural village and the site of a fascinating archaeological
park. If you have a car, this is a placid, convenient place from which to explore.

**Zippori Village Guesthouses** ★   Built by Mitch and Suzy Pilcer (formerly
from the U.S.), these country-style units are set in a garden and contain a bedroom, a
small living room with fireplace, a sofa bed, a Jacuzzi, and a fully equipped kitchenette
that is kosher *halavi* (nonmeat only). A loft area, reached by ladder adds more sleeping
space. The nonchemical, freshwater swimming pool is a definite plus, especially in
summer. The management offers good touring advice (Mitch is a tour guide); and
wonderful breakfasts (kosher) can be ordered, left each morning beside your door. You
need a rental car in order to consider a stay here. Nearby are the ruins of Zippori,
country walks, and even donkey rides for children.

Moshav Zippori. © **04/646-2647** or 057/782-9568. www.zipori.com/en/main.htm. 7 cottages.
Sun–Thurs NIS 400 per couple; Fri NIS 650; Fri and Sat 2-night special NIS 850 per couple; NIS 80
per child. Kosher breakfast NIS 80 per couple. Rates include VAT. Discounts for large families and
long-term stays. **Amenities:** Barbecue/picnic area; pool, A/C, kosher kitchenette, Wi-Fi.

# Where to Dine

There are lots of places on Pope Paul VI Street and Casa Nova Street near the basilica
where you can grab a falafel, a *shwarma,* or a meze of Arabic salads, grilled meats,
and fresh pita bread. All have been around forever, and all serve good food, though few
have much style. If you want a small upgrade try:

**Al Rida** ★ TRADITIONAL NAZARETH   Al Rida is one of the most charming
eateries in town, serving up both traditional Nazareth ambiance and well-executed
versions of the local cuisine. That includes such exotic-for-some, but absolutely delicious oven-baked lamb neck with local seasonings and greens; artichoke hearts filled
with meat; and spicy veal sausages marinated in wine and fried with lemon and garlic.
Portions are not gigantic, so order a few dishes as you'll definitely want to share.

21 Bishara St. ©**04/608-4408.** Main courses NIS 60–NIS 140. AE, MC, V. Mon–Sat 1pm–2am; Sun
7pm–2am. Call for directions.

# Attractions near Nazareth

**Mount Tabor (or Tavor)** ★★  Like the summit of Mount Carmel, near Haifa, where the Prophet Elijah challenged the Canaanite prophets of Baal, the summit of Mount Tabor is believed to have been a Canaanite "high place," or altar, from at least the 2nd millennium B.C. The defeat of the Canaanites at such a prominent sanctuary (the mountain stands 540m or 1,772 ft. above sea level, making it the tallest of the Lower Galilee Mountains) must have had a stunning psychological effect.

Mount Tabor certainly played a crucial role in the life of Jesus Christ. Just 9.6km (6 miles) southeast of Nazareth, it must have been a dominant feature of the landscape Jesus knew in his childhood. At the summit stands the **Basilica of the Transfiguration,** which marks the traditional site where Jesus was transfigured as he spoke to Moses and Elijah in the presence of three of his disciples (Luke 9:28–36). The current Basilica was built in the 1920s over the ruins of long-destroyed Crusader and Byzantine churches (visitors can still go into the grottoes of the Crusader church). Also on the mount is the **Church of Elias** (Elijah), built in 1911 by the Greek Orthodox community. From here on a clear day you can see the Sea of Galilee, Mount Hermon, the Mediterranean Sea, and the Yizreel Valley. At this dramatic mountain, in the period of the Judges (ca. 1150 B.C.), the Prophet Deborah and her general, Barak, led the Israelite tribes to victory over the Canaanite general Sisera of Hazor (Judg. 4:12–16).

At the base of the mountain, in the Arabic **village of Shibli,** you'll find the modest but charming **Center of Bedouin Heritage** (© **04/676-7875**). It's open Saturday to Thursday from 9am to 5pm; admission is NIS 12; Shibli also hosts a number of Bedouin-style restaurants, good for an afternoon break.

Mount Tabor is accessible from Nazareth by Egged bus, private car or taxi. Although it looks close, the way is circuitous. If you're driving from the northern part of Nazareth, take Rte. 754 to Rte. 77; from Rte. 77 at the Golani Junction, turn south onto Rte. 65 to Mount Tabor. From southern Nazareth, take Rte. 60 to Afula; at Afula take Rte. 65 to Mount Tabor. If you are driving or walking, the road up Mount Tabor becomes increasingly steep the higher you ascend, with absolutely hair-raising hairpin turns. Beware of vehicles in front of you conking out and rolling downhill. The descent can seem even more horrific, but the view from the summit is magnificent.

**Zippori (Sepphoris) National Park** ★★  Now a small *moshav*, or cooperative agricultural community, the ancient city of Sepphoris dates from the era of the Maccabees in the 2nd century b.c. An enormous period of expansion and building that started in the a.d. 1st century turned the city into "the ornament of the Galilee," according to Flavius Josephus, the famed 1st-century Romano-Jewish scholar.

With its worldly, mixed population of Hellenistic pagans and Jews, it's interesting to speculate about the influence of Zippori on Jesus, who grew up in what was then the small village of Nazareth, a mere 6.5km (4 miles) away. According to some traditions, Zippori was **the birthplace of Mary.** As a city requiring the services of many skilled carpenters and builders, Zippori may have been a place often visited by Jesus; the landscapes and vistas around Zippori, unlike those of modern, urbanized Nazareth, may still resemble the countryside Jesus knew. The Crusaders built a church in Zippori, the ruins of which can still be seen, dedicated to Saint Anne and Saint Joachim, the parents of Mary. Another tradition, however, holds that although the home of Mary's family was in Zippori, Mary was born in Jerusalem.

The Jewish community in Zippori grew rapidly after the Bar Kochba revolt of A.D. 135, when thousands of refugees from Judea migrated into the Galilee. By the late 2nd century, Zippori was the seat of the Sanhedrin and the home of many great rabbinical sages, including Yehuda Ha-Nassi, who codified the Mishnah. During the Talmudic era, the city contained numerous synagogues; in 1993, archaeologists uncovered a **mosaic synagogue floor** ★ from the A.D. 5th century, decorated with an elaborate zodiac design and inscriptions in Hebrew, Aramaic, and Greek.

Other impressive finds in Zippori are the ruins of a 4,000-seat Roman amphitheater and a vast, late Roman–era Dionysian mosaic floor of a villa that includes the **"Mona Lisa of the Galilee" ★★**, a hauntingly beautiful depiction of a young woman that is one of the greatest examples of ancient mosaic portraiture ever discovered. There is also an intricate mosaic depiction of Nile landscapes, including the famous Nilometer. In other parts of the excavations, you'll find a Crusader fortress and church. A computer/multimedia program has been set up to help bring the site to life for visitors. By prior reservation a vehicle for those with disabilities can be ordered without charge.

6.5km (4 miles) northwest of Nazareth, on Rte. 79. www.parks.org.il. ℂ **04/656-8272.** Admission NIS 27 adults, NIS 14 children. Sat–Thurs 8am–5pm (in winter to 4pm); Fri 8am–3pm. Last admission an hour before closing. No public transportation.

**Beit She'arim Burial Caves National Park** ★   Somewhat reminiscent of the Sanhedrin Tombs in Jerusalem, these catacombs are located on the main road from Haifa that heads toward Afula (the principal town of the Jordan Valley).

In the late 2nd and early 3rd centuries, the town of Beit She'arim was the home of the Supreme Religious Council, the Sanhedrin, as well as headquarters of the famous Rabbi Yehuda Ha-Nassi (Judah the Prince), the compiler of the Mishnah. Many learned and famous Jews were laid to rest in this, the town's cemetery, a network of caves beneath a tranquil grove of cypress and olive trees. Over the centuries, however, the tombs were destroyed and the caves looted. The town was abandoned, and earth and rock covered the entrances to the catacombs as if they had never existed. They were unearthed in 1926 but only fully explored after the War of Independence.

Enter the burial chambers through an opening in the rock or a stone door. Inside you'll see sarcophagi carved with rams' horns and lions' heads, menorahs, and other examples of Roman-era Jewish folk art. We think catacomb 20 is the most interesting, with its legible inscriptions, carvings, and interesting relics.

The entire site here is well tended, with a parking lot, visitor facilities, and an outdoor cafe. To better understand what you'll be seeing, take in the introductory film before heading down into the catacombs.

Off Rte. 75 and Rte. 722, near HaTishbi Junction. ℂ **04/983-1643.** www.parks.org.il. Admission NIS 21 adults, NIS 9 children. Sat–Thurs 8am–5pm (to 4pm in winter); Fri 8am–3pm.

**Megiddo (Armageddon) National Park** ★   In the Old Testament, the name Megiddo appears in a number of places, mostly in relation to war. In the New Testament, the book of Revelation names Armageddon (a corruption of the Hebrew *Har Megiddo*—Mount Megiddo) as the place where the last great battle will be fought when the forces of good triumph over the forces of evil.

Which shouldn't be surprising as this UNESCO World Heritage site has always been a place of blood and swords, a crucial fortress, thanks to its strategic position on the major route leading from Egypt to Syria and Mesopotamia. Archaeologists have uncovered the remains of cities of more than 20 distinct historical periods on this *tel* (Hebrew for an archaeological mound or hill), dating from 4000 B.C. to after A.D. 500.

In fact, Megiddo has been a place of battle continuing right down into the 20th century. General Allenby launched his attack against the Turks from the Megiddo Pass in 1917, and in 1948 the Israeli forces used the fortress site as a base of operations against entrenched Arab armies.

## sweet TREATS

Several stores in Nazareth are named **Mahroum's Sweets**—pass them by! They "borrowed" the name because the concoctions at the original store—at Paul IV and El-Bishara Streets near the Basilica of the Annunciation—are so delectable, they've become a necessary late afternoon stop for tourists and locals alike. If you're like us, you'll start drooling just at the sight of the shop windows, which are filled with Israel's best baklava, Turkish delight (*maajoun*) with nuts, and *Esh el-Bulbul* ("Hummingbird's Nest," a nest of shredded wheat filled with nuts laced with honey). Dessert and Turkish coffee costs about NIS 30 or less. Trust us, the calories (and cost) are worth it. Mahroum's is open daily from 7am to 9pm.

As you enter the Megiddo National Park there is a **museum** with detailed information about the excavations, the artifacts found there, the biblical and historical references relating to its past, and a model of the site as it now exists. Many more artifacts discovered here have been removed, and may now be found in Jerusalem's Israel and Rockefeller museums.

You can walk among the ruins, including what may be a **palace** from the time of King Solomon, **King Ahab's "Chariot City,"** and what some archaeologists call **stables** with a capacity for almost 500 horses (other archaeologists claim that the structures are not stables, though exactly what they were is a matter of controversy). There is also a large **grain silo** from the reign of Jeroboam Ben Joash, king of Israel in the 8th century B.C., and a building some attribute to the time of King David (1006 B.C.–970 B.C.). On strata way down below the later buildings, you can see excavated ruins of temples 5,000 and 6,000 years old, constructed during the Chalcolithic period.

Most amazing of all is the **water tunnel ★★** dating from the reign of King Ahab in the 9th century B.C. You enter it by walking 183 steps 36m (118 ft.) down into a large pit in the earth (the collection pool inside the city walls), from which you can walk along the tunnel extending 65m (213 ft.) to a spring located outside the city, which was camouflaged by a wall covered with earth, designed to assure a constant supply of fresh water to the city even when it was under siege. (Read "The Psalm of the Hoopoe," in James Michener's "The Source," to learn how tunnelers, digging from both ends, managed to meet underground using simple engineering techniques.) *Note:* The water tunnel is wheelchair-accessible with advance arrangement by phone. It closes 30 minutes before the rest of the park.

20km (12 miles) from Haifa. ✆ **04/659-0316.** Admission NIS 27 adults, NIS 14 children. Apr–Sept Sat–Thurs 8am–5pm, Fri 8am–3pm; Oct–Mar Sat–Thurs 8am–4pm, Fri 8am–3pm. Located just north of junction of Rte. 65 and Rte. 66.

# TIBERIAS ★

330km (205 miles) N of Jerusalem; 116km (72 miles) E of Haifa

For centuries, what little industry existed in Tiberias was built around pilgrimage and veneration of ancient tombs, some with very dubious traditions. All this has been overwhelmed by Tiberias's new incarnation as a center for discos, party boats, fish restaurants, and international tour groups. The beaches are full during the hot weather months and pubs and restaurants along the Waterfront Promenade pound with techno and heavy metal on summer evenings.

At the same time, many large and small hotels in Tiberias have come to cater especially to a religious Jewish clientele, giving the city a decidedly split personality.

Little of the town's splendid history is immediately visible, though it is interesting for those who seek it out. The ancient city of Tiberias was built in A.D. 18 by Herod Antipas (son of Herod the Great), and named in honor of the Roman emperor Tiberias. With its natural hot springs and mild, far-below-sea-level climate (warm in winter; brutally hot in summer), it became one of the most elegant winter resorts in this part of the ancient world. Classical writers describe a city adorned with colonnaded streets, impressive Roman baths and temples made of imported white marble, and broad marble steps leading into the waters of the lake. Ancient and Byzantine/Talmudic-era Tiberias was larger and more spread out than the modern city; many archaeological sites are outside its present boundaries and most have not yet been excavated.

For more than a century after its founding, rabbis condemned Tiberias as a place of pagan cults and immoral activities; worse yet, it was built on a cemetery, making it forbidden to Jews as a place to live. But the healing powers of the hot springs caused the rabbinical prohibition to be rescinded, and by the late Roman era, many of the rabbinical leaders themselves were enjoying the restorative powers of the hot springs.

In the centuries after the Temple of Jerusalem had been destroyed, Tiberias developed into a new major center for Jewish learning. It was here that the Mishnah was completed in the 2nd and 3rd centuries A.D., at the direction of Rabbi Yehuda Ha-Nassi, "Judah the Prince." Here the Jerusalem Talmud was compiled in the A.D. 4th century, and the standardized rules for vowel and punctuation grammar were introduced into the Hebrew language by the scribes of Tiberias. Mystics, academicians, and men believed to have magic powers have been drawn to Tiberias throughout its history. Both the town and the towering scholarship declined after the A.D. 5th century, due to the many wars fought here by the Persians, Arabs, Crusaders, and Turks. A medieval Arab historian recorded that the residents of the town led a life of decadence—dancing, feasting, playing the flute, running around naked in the summer heat, and swatting green flies, the eternal plague of the region until modern times.

Tiberias lies on one of the earth's major geological fault lines, the Syrian/African Rift, and in 1837 the city was virtually destroyed by an earthquake. A few portions of the city's medieval walls and older buildings, composed of volcanic rock called black basalt, survived that catastrophe, but almost nothing else of medieval or ancient Tiberias can be seen today outside of the archaeological sites open to the public.

It is this rift that has given shape to the mountains and valleys, and it is the reason why you can stand at the Sea of Galilee, 210m (689 ft.) below sea level, and look up toward the north and see Mount Hermon towering 2,700m (8,858 ft.) above sea level. It's also the reason for the earthquakes and volcanic eruptions over the eons, as well as the mineral hot springs around the shores of Lake Kinneret and The Dead Sea.

Another interesting feature of the low-lying Syrian/African Rift is that it forms an incredible highway for bird migration between Europe and Africa. Two of Israel's major wildlife reserves—Hula Valley in the north, Hai Bar in the south—serve as stopping-off points for the birds on their long journey, and are popular with bird-watchers and nature lovers. (See p. 221.)

Tiberias is considered one of Israel's four "Holy Cities" (along with Jerusalem, Hebron and Safed) and though visitors do still come here to visit the tombs of ancient sages, many simply come to party. In recent years, Tiberias has become a favored base for visiting the Sea of Galilee. Its a place of pounding discos, mass volume tourist hotels (both for secular and religious Jews; quite a split personality this town has!), spas and boardwalk strolling.

**WHEN TO VISIT**   Because Tiberias is so far below sea level, the climate is mild in the fall, winter, and spring, but torrid when Tiberias is busiest in July and August.

**SPECIAL EVENTS**   The **Ein Gev Music Festival** takes place at Kibbutz Ein Gev in spring during Passover Week. Israeli folk dance and song festivals are organized along the waterfront in summer; ask the Tiberias Tourist Information Office for details. At **Kibbutz Nof Ginosar,** the very popular autumn and spring **Jacob's Ladder Folk Festival** is held, with international and Israeli musicians performing Celtic, blues, folk, and country music (www.jlfestival.com). The **Succot Swimathon** is across the Kinneret (4.8km/3 miles). Everyone is welcome to join, but bring a medical certificate stating that you are in good health. For information, contact the Tiberias Tourism Information Office, Ha-Banim Street, Tiberias (✆ **04/672-5666**).

**ORIENTATION**   Tiberias (pop. 45,000) spreads out along the Kinneret shore and climbs the hillside to the west. The very center of Tiberias is **Kikar Ha-Atzma'ut,** or Independence Square, in the Old City. Surrounding Ha-Atzma'ut Square is what little is left of historic Tiberias.

Tiberias's main street changes names as it winds through the city. As it descends from the mountains to the lake it's called Ha-Nitzahon Road; in the residential district of Kiryat Shmuel up on the hillside it becomes Yehuda Ha-Nassi Street, and as it descends to approach the Old City its name changes to Elhadeff (or El-Hadeff or Alhadif) Street. After passing Ha-Atzma'ut Square, it becomes Ha-Banim Street, and this name serves it all the way to the southern limits of the city. South of the Old City about 1.5km (1 mile) is the section called **Hammat,** or **Tiberias Hot Springs.** Ruins of an ancient resort center and synagogue, a national park, a museum, and the Tomb of Rabbi Meir Baal Haness are located near the springs.

North of the Old City, Gdud Barak Road skirts past several beaches on its way to the newly excavated site of **Magdala** (where Mary Magdalene came from), **Tabgha** (where the miracle of the loaves and fishes took place), the **Mount of Beatitudes** (where Jesus preached the Sermon on the Mount), and **Capernaum** (Kfar Nahum), a fishing community that was the hometown of Peter and the center for Jesus' ministry.

## Getting Around

You can rent a **bicycle** at Hotel Aviv (✆ **04/672-0007** or 672-3510), at the southern end of Ha Galil Street, starting at NIS 65 for standard bikes (more for fancier bikes) for a full day, with hourly and half-day rates available. Insurance, helmet, and lock are included. It's open daily. For an additional fee, you can have pickup service at points around the lake if you don't feel up to biking back to Tiberias. You can rent a car at any of the major rent-a-car companies with offices in Tiberias. Many of them are located in the block of Elhadeff Street north of Ha-Yarden Street. If you plan to pick up a rental car in Tiberias, it's a good idea to reserve ahead by internet.

## What to See & Do

The main city on the Sea of Galilee, Tiberias has a split personality. **Ha Galil Street** is reminiscent of a tree-shaded main street in any small American town—it's lined with small shops serving the population from the surrounding countryside. If the old basalt-rock buildings, with their second-story balconies, were renovated, the street could be charming. A block to the east is the other main street, **Ha-Banim Street,** passing high-rises, megahotels, and the *Midrehov,* or Pedestrian Mall, leading to the **Waterfront Promenade,** packed with tourists during the summer and Jewish holidays, throbbing at night with wall-to-wall discos, pubs, cafes, and restaurants. The Waterfront Promenade has a magnificent view across the lake. Ninety meters (295 ft.) to the left are the remains of a **Crusader fort,** jutting up in black basalt stone from the water.

If you're frantic from boredom, consider **"The Galilee Experience"** (© 04/672-3620), inside a modern structure on the Promenade, at press time. It's a 30-minute, state-of-the-art, multimedia show, with an emphasis the life of Jesus, the rise of Christianity, and also on 20th-century Zionism. Oddly, little mention is made of the ancient Jewish history of the area, or of Israel's large Arabic community, which makes up half the population of the Galilee. We think the real reason for the shows existence is to funnel tourists into its gift shop, a virtual mini-mall for religious tourists, selling anointing oil, frankincense, menorahs and religious DVD's The entrance fee is NIS 28; free for the shopping mall. The Galilee Experience is open Saturday through Thursday, 9am to 10pm, and Friday from 9am to 3pm.

**Tiberias's Jewish Tombs** Important places of veneration for religious pilgrims over the centuries, the tombs of the city of Tiberius are varied and many.

Arguably the most important is the famed **Rambam's (Maimonides's) Tomb** (its located off Yochanan Ben-Zakkai Street). Rabbi Moses Ben-Maimon, known both as Maimonides and the Rambam, was the greatest Jewish theologian of the Middle Ages. A Sephardic Jew, he was born in Cordova, Spain, but lived most of his life in Morocco and Egypt, where he was an Aristotelian philosopher, a physician (he served as personal physician to Saladin, at his royal court in Egypt), and a leading scientist and astronomer. His principal work was "The Guide for the Perplexed." Although he didn't live in Tiberias, according to legend, as he was dying, the great Maimonides had himself strapped to a donkey and was carried northward from Egypt, toward the Holy Land, where he hoped to be buried. The inhabitants of Tiberias found his body and buried him in their city. The philosopher, who died in 1204, is now honored by a newly restored mausoleum and gardens.

Nearby is the **tomb of Rabbi Yochanan Ben-Zakkai,** founder of the Yavne Academy in the years following the destruction of Jerusalem in A.D. 70 (the Yavneh Academy was central to keeping Judaism alive in the decades after Jerusalem's destruction). And on a hillside just west of town is the **memorial to Rabbi Akiva,** a cave in which, according to tradition, he was buried. This great sage compiled the commentaries of the Mishnah before the Romans tortured him to death at Caesarea around A.D. 135 for his role in supporting the Bar Kochba revolt.

The tomb of **Rabbi Meir Baal Haness** (Meir, Master of Miracles; he also lived in the time of the Mishnas), on the hill above the hot springs, is considered one of Israel's holiest sites; pilgrims visit in search of medical cures and help with personal problems. Rabbi Meir is remembered in a white building that has two tombs. The Sephardic tomb, with the shallow dome, was built around 1873 and is believed to contain the actual grave, close to the interior western wall of the synagogue; the building with the steeper dome is the Ashkenazi synagogue, erected about 1900. Tradition has it that Rabbi Meir was brought here after his death but had willed that he be buried standing up, so that when the Messiah came he could simply walk out to greet him.

Tiberias is home to other tombs in varying states of neglect, and strong pilgrimage traditions have developed over the centuries. A marble structure beside a modern apartment building, the **Tomb of the Matriarchs** is believed, according to some traditions, to be the final resting place of a number of biblical women, including Jacob's third and fourth wives, Bilhah and Zilpah; Yocheved (the mother of Moses); Zipporah (Moses' wife); Elisheva (wife of Aaron); and Avigail (one of the wives of King David).

All the tombs are open Sunday through Thursday between 8am and 4pm and Friday from 8am to 2pm. There is direct service to Tiberias by bus from all major cities. The Central Bus Station is on Ha-Yardem Street, 2 blocks inland from Ha-Atzma'ut Square.

**Hammat Tiberias National Park ★** **Hammat Tiberias** (or Hammat) contains the ruins of one of Israel's most magnificent ancient synagogues, as befits a town that would have hosted wealthy visitors from distant Jewish communities (it was a famous spa resort for centuries and was founded well before Tiberius in the A.D. 1st century) Most spectacular is the Hammat Tiberias synagogue's well-preserved **mosaic calendar floor ★★** (A.D. 4th c.), which depicts the zodiac cycle and, in its outer corners, four women representing the seasons of the year. At the center of the zodiac, the sun god Helios rides on a chariot through the heavens. Beyond the zodiac, a separate mosaic panel depicts traditional Jewish symbols, including the Ark of the Covenant flanked by two ceremonial menorahs. The famous naive zodiac floor of the Bet Alpha synagogue (which served a Byzantine-era farming village in the Jordan Valley; see p. 7) may have drawn on this very sophisticated mosaic for inspiration.

Entrance to the ruins is through the **Ernest Lehman/Hammam Suleiman Museum,** which inventories information on regional history and the curative powers of the hot springs. *Warning:* Be aware that the open water flowing through the gardens around the ruins comes directly from the hot springs and will scald you. Up the hill from the baths is the **Tomb of Rabbi Meir Baal Haness** (Rabbi Meir, Master of Miracles), a disciple of Rabbi Akiva and one of the great sages who helped to compile the Mishnah in the A.D. 2nd century.

✆ **04/672-5287.** www.parks.org.il. Admission NIS 14 adults, half-price children. Winter daily 8am–4pm; Apr–Sept 8am–5pm. Egged bus: 2 or 5. Parts of the park and museum are wheelchair-accessible.

## ORGANIZED TOURS

The **Society for Protection of Nature in Israel** (SPNI, www.aspni.org) offers well-curated walks and hikes in the Jordan and Jezreel valleys, as well as the Galililee, exploring the flora, fauna and geology of the area. The Society's tours are mostly in English; when they aren't, there are usually others taking the tour who can translate.

## CRUISES & FERRIES

**Lido Cruises Sailing Company** (✆ **04/672-1538**) operates a ferry that runs between Lido Beach in the northern part of town and Kibbutz Ginosar, toward the northeastern corner of the lake, for NIS 28 round-trip; bicycles are free to take onboard, but there's no discount if you only travel one-way. Departures often depend on a minimum number of passengers. Lido Cruises Sailing Company also offers rides on evening party boats, and water-ski and sailboard rental. Boats leave from the docks at the parking lot for the Pagoda and the Decks Restaurants, just off Gdud Barak St., a short walk north of downtown Tiberias.

**Holyland Sailing Tiberias Marina** (www.jesusboats.com; ✆ **04/672-3006**) offers more of a pleasure cruise, with 45-minute sails on the lake in smaller boats modeled after the design of a Roman-era boat (known locally as "the Jesus Boat,") found in archeological excavations at Kibbutz Ginossar, north of Tiberias. The price depends on what kind of group you may be able to join. After each cruise, passengers receive a pilgrim certificate.

## Dancing on the Waters

In good weather, the Lido Cruises Sailing Company sends out evening party boats to cruise the Sea of Galilee in the moonlight or under the stars. On board the boats are filled with Israeli Arabs, Jews, and a smattering of tourists dancing in the wind to traditional Arabic tunes, pop Israeli music, international hits, and even a waltz or two. It's happy pandemonium: Everyone dances with everyone—Galilee Arabs with Jews from Jerusalem and Tel Aviv; men with men for traditional Arabic *debkas;* women with women for the Macarena; everyone together for golden oldies or the latest on the Israeli hit parade. It's NIS 50 to join in this vision of a deliriously happy, peaceful Middle East for an hour; and it's free with a voucher you get when you dine at Decks, the best restaurant in Tiberias.

## SPORTS & OUTDOOR ACTIVITIES

Watersports are offered on and around the lake, including water-skiing, water parachuting, sailboarding, giant waterslides, kayak trips, and more. Check at your hotel or at the Tiberias Tourist Information Office for information.

**BEACHES**    The gardened **Blue Beach,** with a large swimming area, charges NIS 75 for the use of its lake facilities and a beach-chair rental. Open daily (in season) 9am to 5pm. We'd say it's worth it. The **Quiet Beach**'s NIS 45 fee includes a noisy children's pool (oddly), and is open daily (in season) from 9:30am to 5:30pm. The **Gai Beach,** 1km (⅔ mile) south of town, beyond the Galei Kinneret Hotel, has a water park with incredible slides and a fine beach with all the requisite facilities; it charges a NIS 70 to NIS 85 admission fee. Due to drought conditions, the water line is often far from the beach, and pollution has become a serious problem, from time to time, at all the area beaches.

**HORSEBACK RIDING**    In the countryside around the lake, you can join groups for trail riding; call **Vered HaGalil Guest Farm** (© **04/693-5785;** www.veredhagalil. co.il; p. 139). Vered HaGalil offers beautiful (and beautifully tended) horses for everything from well-planed range riding to 15-minute kiddie rides.

# Where to Stay

Tiberias has everything from hostels to mega hotels geared toward tour groups, with a few religious guesthouses, as well. You should note that most hotels in Tiberias have kosher kitchens and that several especially cater to the Orthodox and have glatt kosher certification (see p. 19 for an explanation of kashrut). On summer and holiday nights, the noise level from discos and party boats can make sleep difficult. Small hotels and kibbutz accommodations in the countryside around the lake can be a good option if you have a car; they also offer a better sense of the Galilee's beauty. The Tiberias Tourism Information Office gives out lists of rooms to rent in private homes.

## DOWNTOWN TIBERIAS
### Expensive
**Leonardo Plaza Tiberias** ★    Formerly a Sheraton, and recently taken over by the Israeli Fattal Chain, this 14-story high-rise has an enviable downtown location overlooking the waterfront, although it offersno direct access to the lake. In 2006, the hotel was heavily renovated and a state-of-the-art spa, with a full range of massage programs, was added. The pool area is pleasantly sheltered from the promenade and open

all year, but closes at 6pm; in season and on weekends there's live entertainment and activities for children. The roomy junior suites are great for families; rooms with balconies overlooking the lake are especially nice.

Ha-Banim St. ℂ **04/671-3333.** www.fattal.com. 258 units. $200–$320 double. Rates include breakfast; **Amenities:** Restaurant; cafe; business lounge; bar; children's activities; health club; heated outdoor pool; spa; synagogue, parking (fee) Wi-Fi (fee)

**The Scots Hotel ★★**   Set in a large, walled garden, this hotel, composed of 19th-century stone buildings in the heart of downtown Tiberias is the loveliest and most atmospheric place to stay in town. It's affiliated with the Church of Scotland, but travelers of all religions are welcome. Room categories include the modern standard ("unique") rooms and the more expensive "antique" rooms that offer atmospheric, arched ceilings, and exposed basalt-stone architectural details, plus lake views. Pampering extras insluce spa and massage services, a swimming pool, private beach, an in-house program of evening performances and activities, truly excellent meals and a friendly staff. **Two warnings:** When booked by tour groups, the tranquility of the location can be lost, and the room rates become unusually high but this is a wonderful base to tour the region from when it's not jam-packed. Dining facilities are not kosher.

1 Gdud Barak St. ℂ **04/671-0710.** www.scotshotels.co.il. 69 units. As much as $350 standard double; from $445 antique rooms., breakfast included. Thurs–Sat. minimum 2-night stay sometimes required. Limited free parking. **Amenities:** Restaurant; dining room; bar; private beach; massage; pool; nonsmoking rooms, Wi-Fi with fee.

### Inexpensive
**Hotel Aviv Holiday Flats ★**   The modern, popular Aviv, located on a quiet street in downtown Tiberias, offers large, air conditioned no-frills rooms with kitchenettes. The rooms (called holiday flats) vary in layout, so check a few if possible. Some are one room and a separate kitchenette; others contain a living area, separate bedroom, and kitchen and are good for groups or families. All flats have balconies, and some have whirlpool tubs. The hotel arranges bicycle rentals and organizes tours of the area. On-street parking is permitted here and is usually available. Do not confuse this with the nearby Hostel Aviv. Rates can vary greatly, depending on the season.

Achva St. ℂ **04/671-2272.** www.aviv-hotel.co.il. 30 units. $90–$120; higher rates during Jewish holidays. Rates include breakfast. **Amenities:** Free street parking, free Wi-Fi.

## ACCOMMODATIONS AROUND THE LAKE
### Moderate
**Kibbutz Ein Gev Resort Village ★★**   This very simple kibbutz resort is a great base for exploring the region as it boasts the best and absolutely most beautiful beach on the lake. In fact, that may be its downfall as a lodging as you'll be tempted to stay put, as the hours warm waters, with their splendid views of the Galilee hills and the Golan Heights. The kibbutz is home to its own famous (separate) restaurant specializing in fresh St. Peter's fish—a great place to dine while watching twilight descend over the Sea. Accommodations range from simple 5 person family bungalow units to basic, modern motel-style doubles, all with fridge or kitchenettes and set amid pleasant gardens. There's an in house minimart on the grounds, and a hearty kibbutz-style dinner buffet available with advance reservation or on half-board.

Kibbutz Ein Gev. ℂ **04/665-9800.** www.eingev.com. 166 units. $165–$250 double; $240–$350 for 5-person units. Higher rates Fri–Sat, Jewish holidays, and July 15–Aug 31. Rates include breakfast. Discounts on Kibbutz Hotel 7-day package. Free parking. The Holiday Village is 1.6km (1 mile) south of Ein Gev Kibbutz. **Amenities:** Restaurant; beach; business office; massage; synagogue, fridge (some units), kitchenette (some units), free Wi-Fi.

**Vered HaGalil Guest Farm ★★★**   Located a mile north of the Sea of Galilee, with sweeping vistas of the lake, this is one of Israel's hidden secrets: a relaxing retreat of rustic cabins, and more expensive cottages and suites with separate bedrooms (many with kitchenettes and Jacuzzis), all set among gardens. Vered HaGalil is famous for its beautiful horses and riding programs (open to non-guests). A short drive or hike takes you to the fascinating ruins of Korazim, a Roman-era Jewish village abandoned in early Islamic times, with many of its houses still standing, and with an impressive synagogue adorned with finely carved details in stone as the town's centerpiece. The staff offers personal, helpful attention; a pool and a country-style restaurant make this a good base to come home to after a day's touring. The restaurant, opened in 2013, features a star chef, but does not carry kosher certification; however, breakfasts are composed of dairy kosher products, on kosher kitchenware.

Korazim. ✆ **04/693-5785.** www.veredhagalil.com. 31 units. Cabin: $147–$204 double weekdays; $175–$200 double Fri and Sat. Cottage/Studio: $181–$248. Discounts for stays of 2 nights or more. Rates are higher for Jewish holidays and July–Aug. Rates include breakfast. Free parking. Located at the Korazim-Almagor crossroad, 3.5km (2¼ miles) past the turnoff to the Mount of the Beatitudes. **Amenities:** Restaurant; bar; children's play areas; equestrian stables; horseshoes; seasonal outdoor pool; spa; table tennis.

### Inexpensive

**Poria Taiber Youth Hostel ★**   Located at Poria, in the orchard-dotted hills overlooking the lake 4km (2½ miles) to the southwest of Tiberias, this is a delightful, inexpensive base for travelers with cars (there is no public bus). Yes, it's somewhat rustic, but its expertly managed by the Israel Youth Hostel Association (IYHA), kitchen facilities are included and the setting is beyond beautiful. Because it is so high above the lake, it's a bit cooler on summer nights than Tiberias itself. Family or private rooms with A/C, TV and fridge can be arranged when the hostel is not full, but call well in advance as the hostel is often exclusively booked by large, touring groups.

Poria. ✆ **04/675-0050** or 1-599/510-511; www.hihostels.com/dba/hostels-Poriya-030037.en.htm. 58 units. $100 double with private bathroom, $34 dorm bed. Rate includes breakfast. Cash only. Free parking. **Amenities:** Dining room; A/C, free Wi-Fi.

## Where to Dine

In addition to the choices in Tiberias, many travelers who have use of a car will enjoy dining at some of the delightful restaurants in the countryside and on the shore around Kinneret; see "Country Dining Around the Sea of Galilee," below.

### ON THE WATERFRONT

The specialty in Tiberias is Saint Peter's fish, so-called because it is the very fish that swam in the Sea of Galilee when Jesus called Peter away from his nets to become a "fisher of men." It's a white fish that's indigenous to the Sea of Galilee, and its taste resembles that of bass. The main place in Tiberias to try the fish, is along the **Waterfront Promenade** in the Old City.

Three of the large, attractive waterfront restaurants have the same management, the same menu, the same prices, and the same delicious food. These are the **Nof Kinneret** (✆ **04/672-0310**), the **Galei Gil** (✆ **04/672-0699**), and the **Roast on Fire** (✆ **04/672-0310**). The indoor decor is different in each restaurant, although outdoor dining on the boardwalk is virtually the same, so stroll along and see which you like the best; if the weather is good, you'll likely want to eat by the water. All three restaurants offer their fish fried, charcoal-grilled, or in a special sauce. Plan to spend about NIS 70 for something simple to NIS 140 for a large (more than a pound) serving of Saint Peter's fish, french fries, salad, and pita bread. In summer, these places may be open 24 hours on weekends.

## DOWNTOWN

A bit away from the crush of the Waterfront Promenade, around Ha Galil and Ha-Banim streets, you'll find restaurants that are less tourist-oriented. The north end of Ha Galil Street and Ha-Yarden Street next to Shimon Park is **"Falafel Row."** The lineup starts right outside Ha-Atzma'ut Square and stretches up toward the bus station. Quality and fixings can vary, but the cost should be about NIS 20 for falafel to go. The best falafel and *shwarma* stands offer a big selection of salads to tuck inside your pita.

### Inexpensive

**Guy Restaurant ★ SEPHARDIC HOME-STYLE**  This small, kosher, family-style restaurant serves up Sephardic and Middle Eastern Jewish dishes in a utilitarian environment. No one cares, though, because the food is both well-priced and extremely fresh. Specialties vary from day to day, but can include eggplant, artichokes, tomatoes, or other vegetables stuffed with rice or rice with meat; as well as (in season) plums, dates, figs, and apricots stuffed with meat, rice, and nuts.

Ha Galil St, 1 block south of Ha-Yarden St ✆ **04/672-3036.** Main courses NIS 50–NIS 80. Cash only. Sun–Thurs noon–midnight; Fri noon–1 hr. before Shabbat; Sat after Shabbat.

## NORTH OF DOWNTOWN—THE LIDO COMPLEX

Just about a 5-minute walk up Gdud Barak Street from the downtown promenade are three lively, yet romantic restaurants, each of worth serve topnotch fare. They're worth the stroll, but offer free parking for those who don't want to hoof it.

### Moderate

**Decks ★★★ KOSHER BARBECUE**  Set on a long, curving deck that seems to float over the surface of the Sea of Galilee, Decks is famous for exquisite meats, poultry, and fish barbecued in unique ways over fires that combine citrus wood, olive wood, and American hickory. That mix gives them a unique (and memorable smokiness). Specialties, not always written on the menu, include boneless shoulder of lamb, priced according to weight and of gourmet quality; moist, juicy salmon and tuna, cooked in a traditional charcoal oven brought from the coast of Dalmatia; and carpaccio of Mediterranean tuna freshly caught by the owner's son. Dinner comes with a voucher for one of the Lido Sailing Company's daytime or evening party boats—a fun experience, with local partygoers sometimes dancing on the waters to Arabic and Israeli music. An excellent place to head if romance is on the menu.

Gdud Barak St. Tiberias. ✆ **04/672-1538;** reservations 04/671-0800. Main courses NIS 70–NIS 150. Sun–Thurs 7pm–after midnight; Sat after Shabbat. Call for possible lunch hours.

**The Pagoda ★ KOSHER CHINESE/THAI**  The Pagoda also offers a deck overlooking the water (with spectacular views) but here both the fare and the building are Asian. In fact, the airy pavilion extending over the water was designed by Chinese architects who used feng shui principals to make the best use of the lovely site. Recommended dishes include the spicy Thai chicken coconut soup and the light, healthful steamed Thai dishes, including delicate fresh fish and vegetables. On the Sabbath, The Pagoda opens its nonkosher affiliate, the charming **House Restaurant,** just across Gdud Barak Street (Fri 1pm–midnight, Sat 1–4:30pm). The menu, prices, and phone number are the same as The Pagoda's—the one difference is that it operates on the Sabbath (and is the best choice in town for Friday night and Saturday dining).

Gdud Barak St. ✆ **04/672-5513.** Reservations recommended. Main courses NIS 55–NIS 120. Sushi fixed menu for 2 NIS 85–NIS 95. Sun–Thurs 12:30–3pm and 6pm–midnight.

## COUNTRY DINING AROUND THE SEA OF GALILEE

Tiberias can become very hectic in the evening, especially during the summer. If you have a car, a drive out into the countryside for dinner can be very pleasant.

**Kibbutz Ein Gev Fish Restaurant ★** FISH   This kibbutz, founded in the the 1930s, introduced St. Peter's Fish (known locally as *musht*) into the lake, and its gigantic restaurant offers the best freshly caught St. Peter's fish in Israel, served indoors or on porches and terraces overlooking the water. Be sure to come in the evening so you avoid the noontime tour buses; it's a pleasant place for dinner and watching the sunset over the lake. The St. Peter's fish is served in two sizes: medium and slightly larger (the larger size is the better deal, especially if you share) and comes with french fries or oven-baked potatoes plus a side salad, and your choice of housemade sauces. **One note:** The St. Peter's fish is the reason to come here; the other fish and meat choices on the menu are not special. Reservations recommended.

Kibbutz Ein Gev. ✆ **04/665-8135,** or -8136. Main courses NIS 90–NIS 120. Add 10 percent service charge. Daily noon–10pm.

## Tiberias After Dark

Tiberias bustles after dark, as prodigiously as it does in the daytime. That's particularly true in summer when performers of all types (both local and foreign) make appearances at the **Bet Gabriel Amphitheater** and the majestic **Sherover Promenade ★**, both on the southern tip of the Sea of Galilee (across from the Tzemach Junction). With parklike grounds, a snack bar/restaurant, and stunning vistas of the lake, it's a memorable venue for concerts. Check with the Tiberias Tourist Information Office for a schedule of performances.

**Folklore events** are often scheduled at hotels, and everyone is welcome to attend. For details, contact the tourist office at the end of the Ha-Banim Street Pedestrian Mall.

There are also many late-night pubs, cafes, bars, and restaurants. Good places for a quiet drink with live music include the **Leonardo Plaza** and the **Jordan River** hotels at the southern end of the Old City. **Big Ben,** on the Pedestrian Mall, has a more traditional indoor pub as well as a terrace; the crowd is a bit older and less rowdy.

Many of the hotels (and even the hostels) around town have nice bars and pubs where you can relax and enjoy a drink and conversation with fellow travelers.

There are plenty of opportunities to go dancing, as well. The most unusual is the summer **disco dancing** on the boat operated by the Kinneret Sailing Company on the Sea of Galilee; call ✆ **04/665-8007,** or stop by its office at the Waterfront Promenade, for information. An evening **disco cruise** also leaves from the Lido Kinneret Beach (Lido Kinneret Cruises; ✆ **04/672-0330**) at varying times.

For a lively, tropical bar with a small dance floor, there's **Papaya,** at the intersection of the Waterfront Promenade and the Pedestrian Mall; it's open nightly 5pm to 4am.

## Day Trips

**Hot Springs of Tiberias**   Located 1.6km (1 mile) south of Tiberias, these thermal baths have been famous for their curative powers for more than 3,000 years. They are probably among the earliest-known thermal baths in the world, noted by Josephus, Pliny, church historians, and many Arabic writers. Some biblical commentators have surmised that Jesus cured the sick here. There's a local legend that Solomon got demons to heal his kingdom's ailing people at this site, tricking them into perpetually stoking the fires in the earth below to heat up the water.

The hot springs contain high amounts of sulfuric and hydrochloric acid, and calcium salts, and over the centuries they've reportedly cured skin problems and such ailments as rheumatism, arthritis, and gynecological disorders. They continue to have a following: Pharmacies across Israel keep supplies of mineral salts from these springs.

For those who want to try them in person, several treatments are available, including mineral bubble bath, physiotherapy, therapeutic massage, inhalation, and mud baths,. The older Hot Springs building is segregated by sex; the newer building is a bit more spiffy. *Note:* Bring a bathing suit and towel. There's an inexpensive restaurant on site.

To gain a better understanding of the waters, check out the **museum** next to the springs. While visiting the springs, you can also spend some time exploring the ancient ruins of Hammat.

*©* **04/672-8500.** Admission to the mineral pools NIS 70 Sun–Thurs, NIS 80 Fri–Sat; discounts after 4pm and for children. Sun–Mon and Wed 8am–11pm; Tues and Thurs 8:30am–8pm; Fri 8am–4pm; Sat 8:30am–8pm. Free shuttle bus to hotels in downtown Tiberias Sun–Fri 8am–2pm.

# AROUND THE SEA OF GALILEE ★★★

The Arabic and Aramaic poets called it "the Bride," "the Handmaiden of the Hills," and "the Silver Woman." The ancient Hebrews called it "the Harp," in honor of the soothing harplike sounds of its waves, and because it roughly resembles the shape of an ancient harp. That's the name that stuck, with Israelis still calling the Sea of Galilee Kinnor, or Kinneret (both words for harp in Hebrew), as it is popularly known. According to one lexicographer, an ancient sage wrote: "God created the seven seas, but the Kinneret is His pride and joy." It's a marvelous lake, its surface constantly changing during the day. In summer the Sea of Galilee's waters are sparkling and almost bathtub-warm; if you find a tranquil, beautiful beach for a swim, you'll emerge from the lake feeling refreshed, soothed, and cleansed.

Some 210m (689 ft.) below sea level, the Sea of Galilee is 21km (13 miles) long from the place where the Jordan flows in at the north to where it empties out in the south. It was here that Jesus preached to the crowds and fed them by multiplying the bread and fishes; it is also where he restored the sick and maimed. Today, parts of the sea are filled with speedboats and water-skiers; other parts are as serene and mysterious as in ancient times.

Kinneret's waters are a vast reservoir of sardine, mullet, catfish, and the unusual combfish. They are the same fish once caught by the disciples, and they are caught in the same manner today, though some of the kibbutzim have developed careful methods of farming fish.

## Touring the Area

To tour the Sea of Galilee, head north, starting a circle that will bring you back to Tiberias before heading into the Upper Galilee region. As of this writing there is no regular bus route that completely circles the lake, so you'll have to depend on a tour bus, rental car, bicycle, or boat.

### MAGDALA (MIGDAL)

Just more than 3km (1¾ miles) north of Tiberias along the lakeside road, you'll come to the newly excavated ruin of the New Testament village of Magdala, the birthplace of Mary Magdalene. This is one of the most active archeological digs in Israel. Fresh discoveries are being made almost daily amid the lovely scenery. The town stretched right down by the water's edge. On the hill just to the south of old Magdala, along the far (west) side of the highway, you can still see the sarcophagi (stone coffins) carved out of the rocks in the place that was Magdala's cemetery. The modern town of Migdal, founded in the 20th century, is about 1.6km (1 mile) to the north of the site of ancient Magdala.

## THE GINOSAR VALLEY

A little farther on, about 10km (6¼ miles) north of Tiberias, you'll find yourself in a lush valley with many banana trees. These are part of the agriculture of **Kibbutz Nof Ginosar,** one of the larger kibbutzim, with a vast and busy kibbutz hotel. In the kibbutz, you'll find the multimedia **Yigal Alon Museum of the Galilee** (© **04/672-7700;** www.jesusboatmuseum.com). More a learning experience about the area than a museum, it offers only one genuine antiquity, **a Galilee fishing boat from approximately the** A.D. **1st century,** preserved in the muddy sediment of the lake floor and revealed in the 1980s when, because of drought, the lake receded to record-low levels. The boat is touted by some guides as "the Jesus boat." Although it may be typical of fishing boats from the time of Jesus, there is, of course, no evidence that ties it to any specific persons. Still, it's an amazing discovery, and of special interest to pilgrim groups. The wooden frame of the boat is preserved in a climate-controlled boathouse structure. The museum is open Sunday to Thursday 8:30am to 5:30pm, Friday from 8:30am to 3:30pm; closed Saturdays.

## TABGHA ★★

14km (8⅔ miles) N of Tiberias.

To reach Tabgha, where Jesus miraculously multiplied the loaves and fishes, proceed northward along the shoreline from Migdal, passing Minya, a 7th-century Arabian palace that is one of the most ancient and holy Muslim prayer sites. It's open daily from 8am to 4pm.

At Tabgha, you'll find the beautifully restored **Benedictine monastery** and the **Church of the Multiplication of the Loaves and Fishes ★★** (© **04/672-1061**). When the ancient church ruins, hidden for 1,300 years, were excavated, the **mosaic basilica floor** of a Byzantine-era church that once stood on this site was found. The floor is one of the most lyrical and skillfully made ever discovered in Israel. The section of the floor in front of the ancient altar is starkly unadorned, rather primitive, and interesting mainly for what it depicts: two fish and a humble basket filled with loaves of bread. In contrast, the main section of the mosaic is a skillfully executed, colorful tapestry of all the birds that once thrived in this area: swans, cranes, ducks, wild geese, and storks. The mosaic artist has captured the liveliness, humor, and grace of these creatures with a style rarely seen in this art form. The Nilometer, used to measure the flood levels of the Nile and famous throughout the ancient world, is also represented, leading some to speculate that the talented mosaic designer might have been Egyptian.

Be sure to read the history of this church posted just inside the entrance, in the church's courtyard. The early Judeo-Christians of nearby Capernaum (Kfar Nahum) venerated a large rock, upon which Jesus is said to have placed the bread and fish when he fed the 5,000. The rock, a natural **dolmen,** is believed by historians to have been a sacred place since prehistoric times, and was used as the altar in a Byzantine church erected over the spot in about A.D. 350. The church is open Monday to Saturday from 8:30am to 5pm and on Sunday only for Mass; modest dress required. Admission is free, but donations are accepted. There's a bookstore and souvenir shop on site..

Just east of the Multiplication Church is the **Heptapegon** ("Seven Springs" in Greek), also called the **Church of the Primacy of Saint Peter,** or Mensa Christi. It was here on the shores of Galilee that Jesus is believed to have appeared to his disciples after his crucifixion and resurrection. Peter and the others were in a boat on the lake, fishing, but with no luck. When Jesus appeared, he told them to cast their nets again. They did, and couldn't haul in the nets because they were so heavy with fish. As the disciples sat with their master having dinner, Jesus is said to have conferred the leadership of the movement on Peter. The theory of Peter's primacy, and the tradition of that primacy's being passed from one generation of disciples to the next, is the basis for the legitimacy of the Roman pontiff as leader of Christendom.

The black basalt church rests on the foundations of earlier churches. Within is a flat rock called **Mensa Christi,** or "Christ's Table," where Jesus dined that evening with his disciples. Outside the church, you can still see the stone steps said to be the place where Jesus stood when he appeared, calling out to the disciples; on the beach are seven large stones, which may once have supported a little fishing wharf.

To reach Heptapegon, you must leave the Multiplication Church, return to the highway, turn right, and climb the hill to a separate entrance. This Greek Orthodox church is open daily from 8:30am to 4:45pm; admission is free.

If it's not too hot, you can easily walk to nearby Capernaum (3km/1¾ miles) and even to the Mount of the Beatitudes (see below).

## MOUNT OF THE BEATITUDES ★★★
8km (5 miles) N of Ginosar; 3km (1¾ miles) N of Capernaum

Just beyond Tabgha, on a high hill, is the famous Mount of the Beatitudes, now the site of an Italian convent. Here Jesus preached the **Sermon on the Mount**—the site, though beautiful in itself, bears a special feeling of spirituality. As you stand on the hill, the acoustics often seem crystal-clear; you can imagine the listening crowds and the words of Jesus reverberating over the countryside. There are many good views of the Sea of Galilee and its surroundings, but the vista from this place is among the most magnificent. One odd fact about this church is the inscription on the sanctuary, which informs you that the entire project was built by Mussolini in 1937.

The domed church building itself is open daily from 8:30am to noon and 2:30 to 5pm. Admission is free, but the fee per car is NIS 10. If you go by bus from Tiberius, ask the driver to let you off at the closest stop, which is 1km (⅔ mile) from the church. There are benches along the way to rest on as you make the climb.

## CAPERNAUM (KFAR NAHUM) ★★

Known in biblical times as the village of Nahum, this is a lakeside town where Jesus preached and his disciples Peter and Andrew made their homes. During the lifetime of Jesus, in the a.d. 1st century, Kfar Nahum was a prosperous fishing community, port, and way station on the main trade route from Israel's Mediterranean coast to Damascus. It even had its own Customs House and was probably the most cosmopolitan of the lakeside towns until the founding of Tiberias, in the mid–1st century. The town was abandoned around a.d. 700 and never reconstituted.

Today, you'll find a modern Franciscan monastery, which was built on the abandoned site in 1894, as well as ancient excavations spanning 6 centuries. Among the most impressive are the ruins of **a 3rd- or 4th-century synagogue** built on the site of an even earlier synagogue—perhaps one that Jesus would have prayed in (Peter's house was nearby; see below). It's built of imported white limestone rather than native black basalt. The ruins include tall columns, marble steps, shattered statuary, a doorway facing south to Jerusalem, and many ancient Jewish symbols: carved seven-branched menorahs, palm branches, and rams' horns. Again, this structure is not the actual synagogue in which Jesus taught, since it dates from several centuries after his time, but it clearly stands on the traditional location of the town's main synagogue. It is interesting to speculate on what the proximity of Saint Peter's house to the synagogue might tell us about the position of his family in Capernaum's Jewish community. The excavations of basalt stone in the garden lead toward the sea, where you can still glimpse the remains of a small-boat basin with steps leading to the water. Admission is NIS 5. The site is open daily from 8:30am to 4:15pm.

Nearby are several houses of the period and the excavated remains of **a 5th-century octagonal church built over the ruins of the traditional site of Saint Peter's house,** in which Jesus would have stayed. Byzantine architects frequently built domed octagonal structures over places of special veneration (the octagonal Dome of the Rock in Jerusalem, built by early Muslim rulers in A.D. 691, but designed by Byzantine architects, is an example of this type of structure). Other finds include an ancient olive press and a 2nd-century marble milestone on the Via Maris (Coastal Rd.), the Roman route from Egypt to Lebanon (an inland fork of the Via Maris passed through this district en route to Damascus). It was in Kfar Nahum that Jesus began to gather his disciples around him, saying, "Follow me, and I will make you fishers of men."

### Where to Dine

**Caper Naum Restaurant** MIDDLE EASTERN   Virtually the only place to eat on the northern shore of the Sea of Galilee, this restaurant caters to pilgrim bus groups that visit the nearby Christian sites. That being said, it ain't bad, especially if you can arrange to miss the hordes. Stop by for a light meal of hummus and salads or a soup, or try the house special of Saint Peter's fish, which includes access to the salad bar, and dessert. Though a mass-production place, the fish is tasty and the location is superb.

Near Kfar Nahum. © **04/672-4805.** Reservations recommended. Complete meals NIS 70–NIS 80. Add 15 percent service. AE, DC, MC, V. Daily 9am–8pm.

## KORAZIM ★★

For a thousand years, the ruins of this village lay hidden under an ocean of impassable thistles until the land was cleared in the late 20th century. It's a hauntingly evocative site that gives the visitor a feeling for what a Jewish community in the Galilee was like 1,500 years ago. According to the New Testament, Korazim was one of the towns chastised by Jesus.

The centerpiece of this village is a large A.D. 4th- to 5th-century synagogue made of local black basalt, heavily ornamented with carved grapevines, birds, animals, and images of people harvesting the bounty of the land. You can also visit lightly reconstructed streets, houses, and a ritual bath attached to the synagogue, which was apparently destroyed either by earthquake or during civil unrest in the 7th century. A ceremonial chair carved from basalt, which served as the seat of honor for the synagogue, is especially interesting.

The national park office here (© **04/693-4982**) is open from 5am to 4pm; in summer to 5pm. Admission to the site is NIS 20 for adults and NIS 9 for children.

At the Korazim-Almagor crossroad between Tiberias and Rosh Pinna is the beautiful guest farm and dude ranch Vered HaGalil Guest Farm (see "Where to Stay Around the Sea of Galilee," below).

## KURSI ★

17km (11 miles) from Tiberias; 7km (4⅓ miles) N of Ein Gev

Kursi is on the eastern shore; according to the gospels, it is the "country of the Gergesenes" (or Gadarenes), where Jesus cast the demons out of a man who was possessed and into a herd of swine, which then plunged into the lake and drowned. For many years, speculation existed about the exact location of Kursi (also called Gergasa) and about what kind of religious structure might have been built here in commemoration of the casting out of the demons. After the Six-Day War, a bulldozer clearing the way for a new road happened to uncover the ruins of a Byzantine church complex, complete with a monastery (perhaps the largest ever built in the Holy Land), dating from the 5th to the 7th centuries. The monastery apparently contained hostel facilities for the thousands of pilgrims who came to the Galilee during Byzantine times.

Over the decades since 1967, a large basilica with an intricate mosaic floor has been uncovered, as well as a cave chapel that may have marked the place (according to the Gospel of Mark, a tomb) where Jesus encountered the possessed man. Most remarkable among the discoveries is the underground crypt where more than 30 skeletons were found, all of middle-aged men, except for one child. There is a place to buy votive candles and a snack counter.

The national park at Kursi (© **04/673-1983**) is open daily from 8am to 4pm (until 5pm in summer); admission is NIS 13 for adults and NIS 7 for children.

## KIBBUTZ EIN GEV ★

12km (7½ miles) N of Tzemach Junction; 7km (4⅓ miles) S of Kursi

About two-thirds of the way south along the lake's eastern shore brings you to **Kibbutz Ein Gev,** one of the loveliest places in Israel. Nestled between the hills of Golan and the lakefront, Ein Gev was founded in 1937 by German, Austrian, and Czechoslovakian refugees. (It was former Jerusalem Mayor Teddy Kollek's kibbutz.)

These days Ein Gev has a 5,000-seat auditorium, which has presented some of the world's greatest musicians at its annual music festival. A free mini-train tour of the kibbutz is available for visitors (ask at the office next to the Ein Gev restaurant). On the hillsides are tiers of vineyards, and elsewhere on the grounds are a banana plantation and date groves. Fishing is another big industry here; Ein Gev is home to the country's largest restaurant, serving Saint Peter's fish straight from the Sea of Galilee. The kibbutz also offers accommodations at Ein Gev Resort Village (see "Where to Stay Around the Sea of Galilee," below).

Not far from the auditorium, in a garden, is a bronze statue by the Israeli sculptress Hanna Orloff, depicting a woman holding a child aloft, in memory of a young mother-to-be from the kibbutz who was killed in the 1948 battle for Ein Gev. This settlement bore the brunt of heavy attacks in the 1948 war, and its position at the foot of the Golan Heights, below heavy Syrian military emplacements, made it a perennial target. From 1949 to 1967, Ein Gev kibbutz members depended on an endless maze of slit trenches throughout the grounds, as well as concrete underground shelters.

You can get to Ein Gev from Tiberias by bus no. 22. Farther south along the lake is a campsite, at **Kibbutz Ha-On,** with its **ostrich farm** and moderately priced Holiday Village and bed-and-breakfast accommodations; continue south along the shoreline and you'll come to **Ma'agan,** with its **Holiday Village.** Ma'agan is very near the junction for the road to the hot-spring resort of Hammat Gader. (Ask at the Tiberias Tourist Information Office or at the Tzemach Junction for information on other campsites around the lake and in the vicinity.)

## HAMMAT GADER ★

The **hot springs of Hammat Gader** (© **04/665-9999**), east of the southern tip of the Sea of Galilee, are a favorite Israeli spa and day trip for visitors to the Galilee. Nestled in the valley of the Yarmuk River, this dramatic site has been inhabited for almost 4,500 years.

The Roman city here was first constructed in the A.D. 3rd century, restored and beautified in the 7th century, and destroyed by an earthquake around 900. The **ruins**

# BED & BREAKFASTS in the galilee

One of the great pleasures of visiting the Galilee is getting closer to the people and history of the region. You do this by skipping hotels in favor of these alternative accommodations:

o **The Kibbutz Country Lodgings:** These are the less-expensive list of kibbutz accommodations compiled by the **Kibbutz Hotel Chain office** (www.kibbutz.co.il). They're less fancy than those in the more upmarket Kibbutz Hotels, but they're adequate, often in beautiful locations, and give you a closer look at kibbutz life than the more insulated Kibbutz Hotels. At some kibbutzim, the rooms are in special guest buildings; in others, you get an empty kibbutz member's room or apartment that has been especially set up for visitors. **Tip:** There are often special deals for visitors, so do ask before booking.

o **Accommodations in Israel— B&Bs, Country Lodging, Rural & Agro Tourism** (www.zimmeril. com). This is the pre-eminent source for rural tourism across a wide-spectrum of accommodations types. You might find yourself staying in a private home, with the family on site (and serving you delicious breakfasts each morning), at a kibbutz, or in a fancy B&B. Check the site for options.

o **Hostels in Israel** (www.hostels-israel.com). This is a network of 20 very good, unusual hostels throughout Israel, including the Galilee and the Golan.

All tourist information offices in major cities (including those in Tiberias, Haifa, and Safed) now are equipped with computers that let you access the current lists of bed-and-breakfast facilities available throughout the Galilee. You can telephone for reservations ahead of time, or play things by ear when you arrive in Israel.

of the Roman spa city are extensive and significant, and several important parts (the baths, the theater) have been excavated and beautifully restored. The still-apparent elegance of the Oval Hall, the Hall of Fountains, and the Hall of Pillars in the Spring Area point to the magnificence of this Roman resort in ancient times. Don't miss the wonderful lions on the mosaic synagogue floor (5th c. A.D.). The ruins are set up as a **self-guided tour** (ask at the park office about guided tours of the park).

The spa was known as El-Hamma to the Arabs and Turks, and the site is dominated by the minaret of a mosque that has fallen into disuse and been disfigured by graffiti.

**For present-day hot-springs fans,** there are modern swimming pools, hot pools, hot sulfur springs, and baths for medical therapy and beauty treatments. Just to keep you tranquil as you relax in the baths, there is also an **alligator farm in a jungle setting** with elevated walkways. For the kids, the park has trampolines and water slides. You will also find showers, changing rooms, a bar, and a Thai restaurant. Admission Sunday to Thursday NIS 75; Friday, Saturday, and holidays NIS 80; daily admission after 6pm NIS 45. Bring your own towel and bathing suit. Residents of the area as well as visitors come in droves (especially after work), often bringing picnics. The many clay oil lamps found here may indicate the ancient inhabitants of the area enjoyed night bathing after a long day of work.

The springs can be reached by bus from Tiberias. Bus schedules vary according to season, so check with the bus station for a morning departure and afternoon returns.

## river jordan BAPTISMS

Kibbutz Kinneret, just west of Degania, has established a spot where Christian pilgrims can immerse themselves in the waters of Jordan in safety and tranquility. The baptismal spot, called **Yardenit** (*C* **04/675-9111**), is 180m (591 ft.) west of the lakeshore highway (follow the signs). The river seems to flow peacefully, but its currents can be dangerous, so no swimming is allowed. The area set aside for baptisms is sheltered, and there are guide railings leading into the water. Snack and souvenir stands provide refreshment and sustenance (no charge for the baptismal dip). A special lift has been installed to enable visitors with disabilities to enter the water with a minimum amount of difficulty. It's open Saturday to Thursday 8am to 6pm and Friday 8am to 5pm; the last baptismal is 1 hour before closing.

Hammat Gader is 22km (14 miles) southeast of Tiberias. If you're driving, it's on Rte. 98 about 8.5km (5¼ miles) east of the Tzemach Junction with Rte. 92 that skirts the eastern side of the lake. As you wind down the steep road into the Yarmuk Valley, you'll pass several sentry and guard posts. The steep hillside on the other side of the valley is Jordan; you are also very close to the Syrian border.

You'll find Hammat Gader's pools open Sunday to Tuesday 7am to 4pm; Wednesday to Friday 7am to 9pm; and Saturday 7am to 9pm. Hours are constantly subject to change. Antiquities and children's activities close at 4pm. As if the ruins, hot springs, and alligator farm were not enough, a good **Thai restaurant,** the Siam (*C* **04/665-9922**), housed in a Thai-style building, has also been set up on the premises (if you dine at the restaurant, your admission to Hammat Gader is free). In 1993, there were rumors that alligators, either accidentally or as a result of a deliberate act of sabotage, had escaped into the Sea of Galilee; no sightings or hunting parties have led to anything more concrete than the Loch Ness Monster!

### KIBBUTZ DEGANIA

Located at the very southern tip of the Sea of Galilee, Degania is the country's very first kibbutz, founded in 1909 by young Russian Jewish pioneers. Without any real experience in farming, this handful of self-made peasants left city jobs to fight malarial swamps and Bedouin and local marauders. Much of the philosophical basis of kibbutz life was first formulated in this Jordan Valley settlement by its leader, A. D. Gordon. Gordon believed that a return to the soil and the honesty of manual work were the necessary ingredients for creating a new spirit in people. Although never a member of the kibbutz, he farmed until his death at age 74. A natural history museum on Degania's grounds, **Bet Gordon** (*C* **04/675-0040**), contains a library and exhibition of the area's archaeology, flora, and fauna.

Degania grew so quickly that its citizens soon branched out to other settlements. The father of Moshe Dayan, the famous commander (with the eye patch) of the Sinai Campaign, left Degania to help establish Nahalal, Israel's largest *moshav* (cooperative settlement). Eventually, some of the Degania members split with the original Degania over political and philosophical issues (especially about the nature of the Stalinist-era USSR). They broke away from Degania, establishing their own kibbutz right next door, and called it simply Degania B. The older Degania is now called Degania A.

Outside the entrance to Degania, there's a small tank—a reminder of the battle the inhabitants of Degania waged against Syrian tanks in 1948 (the members fought them off with Molotov cocktails). Today, both Degania A and B are thriving.

# SAFED (ZEFAT) ★★

36km (22 miles) NW of Tiberias; 74km (46 miles) E of Haifa

Our next destination is the medieval, mystical town of Safed (Zefat, Zfat, Tsfat, Tzfat), about 40 minutes northeast of Tiberias. Beginning in the 15th century, Safed was known for its Jewish scholars and visionary mystics. At 837m (2,746 ft.), its Israel's highest town.

For a while in the 1950s and 1960s, the town became Israel's major summer mountain resort, attracting secular and religious vacationers who enjoyed Safed's quant side streets, artists' galleries and cool nights. Today Safed is once again very religiously oriented, and it can be a problematic stay for visitors, due to limited parking, restaurants and accommodations. But the beauty of Safed's mountain location and its history as a center for Jewish mysticism and Kabbalah combine to create a special aura to the town and make it memorable if you give it time and a bit of effort.

Safed's known history began in A.D. 66, during the time of the First Jewish Revolt Against Rome, when the rebel Jewish commander, Flavius Josephus (who later went over to the Romans and became a noted historian) started building a citadel on the mountaintop in the center of Safed. In 1140, the Crusaders again built a fortress on this peak, the ruins of which can be seen today. But whatever early communities existed here in those centuries were small and unimportant.

During the 16th century, the Ottoman Turks chose the town of Safed for the provincial capital, and it became the primary government, economic, and spiritual center for the entire Galilee region. It was during this period that Sephardic Jews from Spain came here. Having escaped the horrors of Spain under the Inquisition, many of these Jewish scholars and intellectuals launched into a complex and mystical interpretation of the Hebrew scriptures called kabbalah. The town became a great center of learning, with a score of synagogues and religious schools. The first printing press in the East was introduced here during this period of scholarship and mysticism, and in 1578 the first Hebrew book—a commentary on the Scroll of Esther—was printed. During this golden age of Safed, less-mystical groups of Ashkenazi Jews were also attracted to Safed, and the entire community and its rabbinical scholars became renowned and revered throughout the Jewish world. At its height, the Jewish community numbered about 10,000, but by the 18th century, Safed was in serious decline.

In 1837, the entire town was leveled by a powerful earthquake after which both the Jewish and Muslim communities of Safed struggled on in increasing poverty. The wave of anti-Jewish rioting that swept British Mandate Palestine in 1929 was particularly severe in Safed, where the Jewish population was mainly elderly and religious. During the 1948 War for Israel's Independence, control of the strategic heights of Safed was crucial to control of the Galilee. Although outnumbered, Israeli forces held the town, and the large Arab population of Safed fled amid panic and rumors. Since then, the center of Safed (pop. 30,000) has had three parts to its personality—a rather outdated resort town, an artists' colony in the abandoned Arab neighborhood, and the long-established religious community. Until the 1970s, Safed, with its cool nights, was a favorite summer resort, but as Israelis became more international in their vacation habits, Safed's tourism industry withered, and the once-vibrant Artists' Quarter is now relatively quiet, all the better for those who decide to explore the town.

# Essentials

**GETTING THERE    By Bus**    Buses run between Safed and Tiberias, Tel Aviv, and Jerusalem.

**By Car**    Follow the main but winding roads from Tiberias, Haifa, and Akko.

**GETTING AROUND**    Most city buses, such as nos. 1, 13, 14, or 3, go from the center to the hotels on Mount Canaan.

**VISITOR INFORMATION**    The **Safed/Hazor/Rosh Pinna Tourism Association Office** is unfortunately not in Safed, but in the Galilee Mall at the entrance to Rosh Pinna (© **1-800/323-223** or 04/680-1465, open Sun–Thurs 8am–4pm). In Safed itself, you'll find the **Tzfat Tourist Information Center,** 27 Alkabetz St. (© **04/692-4427**). This useful office is run by a private Jewish outreach organization, Livnot U'lehibanot, and offers a short film on the history of Safed (NIS 5), as well as maps, books, local events, and lists of bed-and-breakfast options and private guides.

July and August are the most popular months because of Safed's cool climate. In the winter, it can be windy and as much as 20° cooler than Tiberias. Year-round, especially at night, Safed is usually the coldest city in the country.

**CITY LAYOUT**    Safed is built on hilltops. The main part of town is compactly clustered atop one hill, while South Safed occupies another hilltop to the south, and Canaan perches on a hillside across the valley to the east. Although you may find occasion to go to Mount Canaan (a few hotels are there), you'll spend most of your time in the center of Safed. Jerusalem Street (Rechov Yerushalayim) is a circular street that girdles the hill, passing through the commercial street, the Artists' Quarter, and residential sections before beginning its circle again. Walking the circle should take only 15 minutes, and it is a good way to see most of Safed.

The **Egged Bus Station** (© **04/692-1122**) is at the lowest point on Jerusalem Street's circle through town, where it intersects with Derech Jabotinsky. Walk up to Jerusalem Street from the bus station and go right, and after 360m (1,881 ft.) you will come to the tourism office. But if you come up from the bus station and go left, you'll be headed toward the commercial district. In any case, once you find Jerusalem Street you can't get lost in Safed.

# What to See & Do

While there is much to see in Safed, a traveler unfamiliar with the city's crooked streets and unimpressive doorways may unknowingly pass some of the city's best sites. Consider getting taking a **guided tour.** You can arrange for an informative walking tour of Old Safed with **Aviva Minoff,** an excellent licensed tour guide. The 2½-hour tours generally leave from the Rimon Inn, Monday through Thursday at 10am and Friday at 10:30am. For information, call © **04/692-0901,** before your arrival. Note that modest dress is required when touring the religious quarter of Safed. A

Alternatively, look for the locally published book "Six Self-Guided Tours to Tzfat," by Yisrael Shalem (approx. NIS 35); it's sold at Greenbaum's bookstore on the pedestrian mall in the center of Safed.

## THE SYNAGOGUES

During Safed's golden age in the 16th century, some of the synagogues here were devoted to the study of the Kabbalah, a mystical interpretation of the Bible and other sacred writings in which every single letter and symbol in holy writ has deep, hidden significance. Hebrew words, numbers, and the names of God have mystical powers in themselves, and can be used to ward off evil and to perform miracles.

Kabbalists believed that the system originated with Abraham and was handed down by word of mouth from ancient times. Historians of religion dispute this, however, saying that Kabbalism arose only in the 600s; it continued to be a thriving belief until the 1700s. Kabbalism was, in a way, a reaction to the heavy formalism of rabbinical Judaism. It allowed for more latitude in the interpretation of holy writ and gained great popularity in the 1100s. The most significant Kabbalist text is the "Zohar," a mystical commentary on the Pentateuch (the first five books of the Hebrew scriptures). For an interesting fictionalized interpretation of what Safed was like at the height of its glory as a Jewish religious center, I recommend the chapter "The Saintly Men of Safed" in James Michener's novel **"The Source."**

It's not easy to describe exactly where the various synagogues are—the religious quarter has few street names and is really a collection of alleyways and courtyards. Ask for *"kiryat batei knesset,"* the synagogue section.

Among the most famous old synagogues here is the one named for the scholarly 16th-century **Rabbi Joseph Caro,** author of the "Shulchan Aruch" (the Set Table), which is the standard codification of practical Jewish law. Nearby is another named in honor of **Rabbi Moshe (Moses) Alsheich** (a renowned biblical commentator) and the only fully intact synagogue to survive the 1837 earthquake. Just a few steps away is the synagogue of **Rabbi Isaac Abuhav,** a sage of the 1400s; it contains an ancient Torah scroll said to have been written by the rabbi himself. Nearby is another, dedicated to **Rabbi Yosef Bena'a,** a famous 12th-century liturgical poet also called Ha-Lavan (the White).

The synagogue quarter has two houses of worship dedicated to the greatest of the kab-balist scholars, **Rabbi Isaac Luria** (known as Ha'Ari, or "the Lion," an acronym for Adoneinu Rabbeinu Yitzchak, "Our Master Teacher Isaac"). Although Luria lived, stud-ied, and taught in Safed for only 2½ years at the end of his life (he died here at the age of 38), his work changed the face of Judaism forever. The fortresslike Sephardic synagogue, graced by fine carved-wood doors, is built where the rabbi studied and prayed, at the edge of the cemetery. The **Ashkenazi Ha'Ari Synagogue** is closer to Jerusalem Street, at a spot where the rabbi is said to have come to welcome the Sabbath with his followers. Rabbi Luria was the author of the "Kabbalat Shabbat" (Receiving the Sabbath), the litur-gical arrangement of prayers recited at the start of the Sabbath in normative Judaism.

The original building, constructed after Rabbi Luria's death, was destroyed by an earthquake in 1852 and later restored. Its ark, done in the 1800s, is especially notable. If you come with an official guide, you will get a better sense of how every nook and cranny has a story and sometimes a supernatural occurrence connected with it.

At the end of the synagogue area is a **cemetery** containing the sky-blue tombs of many famous religious leaders; they're the ones with rocks placed upon them as sym-bols of love, respect, and remembrance. There is also a military cemetery and nearby is a third cemetery containing the graves of Israelis who served with the underground Stern Gang and Irgun groups at the time of the British Mandate. Buried here are those executed by the British in Acre prison, including Dov Gruner, who is one of the best known of the underground fighters.

Another holy site is the **Cave of Shem and Eber** (or Ever), the son and grandson of Noah. This cave, located just off Ha-Palmach Street near where the Ha-Palmach stone overpass crosses Jerusalem Street, is said to be the place where Shem and Eber lived, studied, and were buried. Legend also has it that Jacob spent 14 years here study-ing before he went to the house of Laban, and that here he immersed himself in a ritual purifying bath before he wrestled with the angel. Today, there is a synagogue opposite the cave; if the cave is locked, you can ask the caretaker of the synagogue to open it for you.

## 20TH-CENTURY MEMORIALS

Going down the hill from Jerusalem Street, in the area between the synagogues and the Artists' Quarter, is a straight stairway: **Olei Ha-Gardom.** Stand at the top of this stairway, where it intersects with Jerusalem Street, and you're within sight of a lot of Safed's 20th-century historical landmarks.

Olei Ha-Gardom was the dividing line between Safed's Jewish and Arab quarters until 1948; that's why all the synagogues are clustered on the right-hand side as you're facing down the stairway. The present Artists' Quarter is in what used to be the Arab section. Look up toward the citadel, and you'll see a small opening in the fortress from which a direct line of machine-gun fire could be sent straight down the stairway, a British attempt to keep an uneasy peace between the two communities. The same day the British withdrew, the Arab and Jewish factions went to war. Look at the walls of the old police station, and you'll see it's pocked with bullet holes from the fighting.

Down Jerusalem Street from this intersection you can also see a war memorial, with a tablet describing how the fighting favored first the Arabs, then the Jews. Poised on a stone mount is a Davidka (little David), one of those homemade Jewish mortars that, though not too accurate or damaging, made a terrific noise and gave the impression of being much more dangerous than it actually was. At the top of the hill, in the beautiful hilltop park, are the ruins of a Crusader fortress (unfortunately not well maintained at present) from which you can enjoy a fine view of Mount Meiron, Mount Tabor, the Sea of Galilee, and a smattering of tiny hill villages and settlements. A war memorial commemorates the Israelis who were killed pushing the Arabs back from the heights.

The **Artists' Quarter ★★** is the area down the hill from Jerusalem Street between the Olei Ha-Gardom stairway facing the police station and the stone overpass that crosses Jerusalem Street. Here you will find picturesque houses, tiny streets, manicured gardens, and outdoor art displays. Many artists have galleries in their homes, and the homes themselves are often so charming and atmospheric that some owners charge a small admission.

**Ascent Institute of Safed ★**   This can be a rather intense place and is specifically designed for Jewish visitors who want to renew and expand their attachment to Judaism. But even if you don't sign up for a course or stay here, it's worth checking out Ascent's program of events, concerts, and lectures, many of which are open to all travelers.

2 Ha'Ari St., Old Safed. ✆ **04/692-1364.** www.ascentofsafed.com.

**General Exhibition ★**   While many of the houses in the artists' colony may be closed in winter, the General Exhibition, which shows a wide range of work by many Safed artists, is open year-round. The galleries display everything from paintings to ceramics to silk. You can purchase objects here, or get in touch with artists whose work you find interesting. Next door is the New Immigrant Artists Exhibition.

Old Mosque, Artists' Quarter. ✆ **04/692-0087.** May–Sept Sun–Thurs 10am–6pm (until 5pm Oct–Apr); Fri–Sat 10am–2pm. Head downhill from the intersection of Jerusalem and Arlosoroff sts.

**Hameiri House ★**   Located down the hill, in south Safed, Hameiri House is the **Museum and Institute for the Heritage of Safed.** It's housed in a historic 16th-century edifice, the restoration of which was done over a 27-year period, completed in 1985. Artifacts and documents portray the history of Safed's Jewish community; photographs and videos of elderly residents are interesting, especially if a translator is available.

Old City. ✆ **04/697-1307.** Admission NIS 16. Sun–Thurs 9am–2pm; Fri 9am–1pm.

**Museum of Printing Art** ★   Safed was the site of the first Hebrew press in Israel, which was set up in 1576 and published Israel's first Hebrew book a year later. Here you can see a copy of the first newspaper printed in Israel (1863); a copy of "The Palestine Post" of May 16, 1948, announcing the birth of the State of Israel; a centuries-old kabbalistic text printed in Safed; examples of modern Israeli graphics; and many other things.

Corner of Arieh Merzer and Arieh Alwail sts. ℂ **04/692-0947.** Free admission. Sun–Thurs 10am–noon and 4–6pm; Fri–Sat 10am–noon.

# Where to Stay

**Artists' Colony Inn** ★★★   This lovely, carefully restored boutique inn is one of the most delightful places to overnight in Israel. Each room is different, but they share a design aesthetic that blends the ancient "bones" of the house—stone walls, arched ceilings and windows—with handsome modern furnishings and splashes of deep jewel-like color, either on the bed's throw or on one wall of the room (just enough to give the rooms life, but not so much that they look gaudy). Run by owners Bernay and Jeff Katz—they have a special gift for hospitality—the nighly rate includes a truly gourmet breakfast and tea and snacks throughout the day. the Inn helps you feel the magic of Safed's mysterious, sometimes elusive atmosphere. On Shabbat, when restaurants are closed in Safed, a wonderful country brunch can be ordered. Jeff is a licensed guide and so a wonderful source for what to see and do in town. Call ahead for directions and help with baggage; parking is difficult and somewhat far away. Sorry, children under 12 are not welcome.

9 Simtat Yud Zayin, Safed. ℂ **04/604-1101** or 052-348-8196. www.artcol.co.il. 4 units with baths. $200–$330 per night (rate varies by season). Rates include breakfast. Extra person $55. **Amenities:** Free Wi-Fi; on-site library; snacks throughout the day.

**Bar-El B&B** ★   This B&B offers two architecturally interesting units set in a picturesque Ottoman-era house in Safed's charming artist's quarter. Rooms have been nicely renovated and offer a kitchenette, A/C, TV, modern bathroom, and can sleep up to five people. Breakfasts are excellent—owners Genine and Rony Bar El are great cooks, have a vegetarian and fish (non-meat) catering business, and are helpful with touring information. As the B&B is in the Old City, there's no adjacent parking.

23 Yud Zayin St., Artists' Quarter. ℂ/fax **04/692-3661** www.bar-el.com. 1 unit. $175 double; $30 extra person. Rate includes breakfast. Cash only. **Amenities:** Roof terrace, kitchenette w/hot plate for Sabbath, free Wi-Fi.

## OUTSIDE SAFED

**Amirim Holiday Village** ★★   Founded in 1958 by a group of self-described "nature freaks," Amirim is a vegetarian *moshav* (cooperative village) in a peaceful forested area with magnificent vistas. Most of the *moshav* families rent out comfy guest rooms; for those who want more privacy, there are also a number of private, cabins that are in great demand (cabin Nof 10 [www.nof10.com] costs extra, but offers a fabulous view). Each unit is different in layout, but similar in their woodsy décor (the look is log cabin-esque, with knotty walls, comfy furnishings, and in some cases, such niceties as Jacuzzi tubs and private terraces). On site are a number of excellent, meat-free restaurants (and they're serious about the vegetarianism here; you can be expelled from your cabin if you use your kitchen or outdoor grill to cook meat). The moshav's in-season swimming pool is available to guests, as is a spa/massage center.

Rte. 886, 4km (2½ miles) north of junction with Rte. 89. ℂ **04/698-7346** or 698-9571. Cabins $160–$260, less for rooms in private homes. Rates include breakfast. **Amenities:** Massage and beauty treatments; rooms for those w/limited mobility; swimming pool. Free Wi-Fi in some units.

## Where to Dine

The first thing you'll notice about Safed is its multitude of kosher sandwich, snack, and falafel shops along Jerusalem Street (the main downtown road), open day and night, except for the Sabbath, when the whole town is closed up tight. Safed is not a great place for fine dining, but if you have a car, there are good choices in nearby Rosh Pinna and in the surrounding countryside.

### NEAR SAFED

These choices are possible lunch or dinner excursions from Safed, but can also be reached from such places as Rosh Pinna, Vered HaGalil, or even Akko, Nahariya, Tiberias, or Haifa. Besides the opportunity to enjoy unusual meals, these restaurants offer a chance to explore remoter parts of the countryside.

**Bat Ya'ar Ranch Steak House** ★★ STEAKS  This steak house and horse ranch, set in the rugged, wooded hills, will make you think a chunk of Wyoming somehow fell from the sky and landed in the Galilee. A good map or careful instructions from the restaurant, and strong bright lights on your car are necessary to get here. And when you see a series of rough wooden buildings, set near a beautiful viewpoint, stop: That's the restaurant! Grilled steaks, chicken and burgers are served with fries or baked potato and salad in a rugged, cowboy-style room. The quality is topnotch, and the fresh air and panoramas will invite a pre- or post-dinner stroll. There's a playground for children on the grounds. It's out of character for Safed (or even for the Middle East) but Israel is filled with surprises. Reservations necessary.

Biriya Forest 5km (3 miles) northwest of Safed. ✆ **04/692-1788.** The restaurant is not kosher, but kosher food can be arranged in advance for groups. Main courses NIS 68–NIS 160. Daily 11am–10:30pm.

## Safed After Dark

Summer is the time for most of Safed's musical events. About eight chamber music concerts are held throughout the year, mostly in the summer, as well as a summer musical workshop. The **Klezmer Festival of East European Jewish Music** is the highlight of the summer programs. Check with the tourist office for the weekly scene. For piano concerts, check out **Hemdat Yamim** (✆ 04/698-9085) on the Acre-Safed highway, which usually has concerts every Monday and Saturday evening during the summer. The **Yigal Alon Cultural Center and Theatre,** on Jerusalem Street in Safed (✆ 04/697-1990), has everything from Shakespeare to ballet and popular folk dancing. It's named for the man who led the forces that liberated Safed in the 1948 war.

## Easy Day Trips

### MEIRON ★

Eight kilometers (5 miles) west of Safed is the town of Meiron, a holy place for religious Jews for 1,700 years. When Judea fell to the Romans after the Second Revolt against Rome in A.D. 135, the mountainous northern Galilee took on many refugees. One early Meiron inhabitant, a 2nd-century Talmudist named **Shimon Bar Yochai,** was ultimately forced to hide in a cave in Peqiin, a village some distance from Meiron. There, according to legend, he wrote the mystical "Zohar," or "Book of Splendor," which is central to the kabbalist belief.

Meiron is the scene of considerable pageantry during the holiday of **Lag b'Omer,** which occurs in the spring just 3½ weeks after Passover. Thousands of Orthodox Jews pour into Safed, and there follows a torchlight parade to Meiron with singing and dancing. They burn candles on top of Rabbi Shimon's tomb and light a great bonfire into which

## A veggie PARADISE

Amirim, the same *moshav* (cooperative village) we recommended for its lodgings (see p. 153) is also an excellent place to stop for a bite to eat. We recommend it even to non-vegetarians, as the food is creative, seasonal, extremely fresh and super tasty. Among the vegetarian choices inside the village of Amirim are:

**Dalia's ★★★** (© 04-698-9349)  A shining light of traditional and contemporary vegetarian cuisine in Israel it offers freshly baked breads and huge portions all reasonably priced. Beyond the excellent food, the draw here is the balcony, which provides a stunning panorama of the valley below, including the Sea of Galilee. Reservations are a must.

**Bait 77 ★★** (© 04-698-0984)  A delightful vegetarian bakery, stop here for pastries in the morning, excellent pizzas at dusk (and after).

**Rishikesh** (© 052/578-4114)  An authentic Indian restaurant, it offers both meals on location or for take away (or if you're staying at Amirim, they'll deliver to your holiday unit).

some, overcome by emotion, throw their clothes. In the morning, after the all-night festivities, 3-year-old boys are given their first haircuts, and the cut hair is thrown into the fire.

There still exists Meron's **ruined ancient stone synagogue** of restrained but impressive architectural design from the A.D. 3rd century, as well as **Rabbi Shimon's tomb** and a rock called the **Messiah's Chair.** Reputedly, on the day the Messiah arrives, he will sit right here while Elijah blows the trumpet to announce his coming. **Mount Meiron,** the highest peak in the Galilee at 878m (2,881 ft.), dominates the rugged countryside, with vistas that sweep virtually across northern Israel. The local **SPNI Field School** (© 04/698-0022) offers trail maps and information about a number of hikes through the beautiful, wooded Meiron Nature Reserve.

### SASA & THE BAR'AM SYNAGOGUE ★★★
In the northern foothills of Mount Meiron 16km (10 miles) northwest of Safed.

In 1949, American and Canadian settlers built a Kibbutz Sasa atop a 900m-high (2,953-ft.) hill and persevered despite many problems, including a polio epidemic. The thriving kibbutz is now the center of an area of forest reservations.

Just 5km (3 miles) to the north, the A.D. 3rd- to 4th-century **Bar'am Synagogue ★★★**, which served a small, rural community, is probably the best preserved and most beautiful of all the ancient synagogues in Israel. Its location, in the wild mountains near the Lebanese border, is breathtaking.

According to some scholars, the synagogue may have been in use through early medieval times. In the style of early Galilee synagogues, the building faces south, toward Jerusalem. Beautifully carved clusters of grapes ornamenting the main entrance testify to the town's abundant vineyards and orchards. At some point the design of the synagogue was changed and the main entrance walled over with large ashlars that can be seen in a 19th-century engraving of the ruined site, made from an early photograph. Archaeologists theorize that over the centuries, it became customary for worshipers to face both the Ark of the Torah and Jerusalem while praying, and the central doorway, on the southern wall of the synagogue, was walled over in order to build a Torah shrine. By the late 19th century, the ashlars walling the entrance, as well as other chunks of the synagogue, had been carried off by locals for reuse in other buildings.

The **National Park at Bar'am** (*© **04/698-9301;*** www.parks.org.il) is open daily from 8am to 4pm (until 5pm in summer); admission is NIS 20 The park is wheelchair-accessible.

The ruins of the Maronite (Christian) Arab village of **Birim** surround the cleared areas around the synagogue. As noncombatants cooperating with Israeli forces during the 1948 War of Independence, the residents of Birim had quartered Israeli troops in their homes. Late in the war, the people of Birim were told by the Israeli army to evacuate their town for what was promised would be a short time during a possible enemy offensive. They were never allowed to return, despite a ruling by the Israeli Supreme Court in the early 1950s upholding the villagers' rights to their homes. Since then, the former inhabitants of Birim, who all possess Israeli citizenship and are now scattered throughout the Galilee, have maintained an unending legal struggle to reclaim their village.

Past the synagogue, you can follow a path to the left and uphill to the **Church of Birim,** still maintained by the people of the village for weddings and funerals. If you climb the rather difficult stairs onto the roof of the church, you will be rewarded with a dramatic panorama of countryside so intensely loved by two peoples. Arabic graffiti on the church walls promise that the members of the congregation will return.

# TEL AVIV

T el Aviv has become one of the hottest travel destinations on the planet, with rave reviews from travel magazines, TV pundits, and good old-fashioned word of mouth. "Best for Style," "Best Urban Beaches," "Best Gay Destination," "Best Foodie Scene," and "Best Nightlife"—these are just a few of the accolades heaped on the city. It's not exotic or charismatic, like Jerusalem. Nor is it a magnificent world capital, like Paris. It's not even picturesque, like Amsterdam. But the lively, creative spirit of the people of Tel Aviv, mixed with miles of easy-going beaches and Mediterranean surf, make this a city with real personality.

That being said, Tel Aviv is everything Jerusalem is not. The city was founded much later, in 1909, to be exact, along a gorgeous strip of beach on the Mediterranean. Known locally as the Big Orange, Tel Aviv has no holy sites and until its founding, it had no history. What it does have is oyster bars, nightclubs, samba sessions on the beach on summer evenings, and miles and miles of massive medium-rise apartment buildings. In summer, the heat and humidity can put New Orleans to shame, but a short walk or bus ride can always get you to the sparkling waters of the Mediterranean

As the country's commercial center and also the cultural capital, Tel Aviv buzzes with the energy of high-powered business deals from around the globe. Glass skyscrapers dot the city's landscape; and more are under construction. But Tel Avivians also love to relax and play. In the 1980s, the city's beaches were smartly renewed, and they are now among the cleanest and most easily accessible urban beaches in the world. The 1990s saw the construction of an opera house, new performing-arts centers, and the development of a rarefied luxury restaurant scene. If peace is able to develop, many envision 21st century Tel Aviv as the financial Singapore of a new Middle East, but with a glossy Miami Beach veneer.

Tel Avivians are also busy preserving, gentrifying, and recycling neglected landmarks and neighborhoods. The formerly derelict **Tel Aviv Port,** at the northern end of the city, is now the hottest spot in town, wall-to-wall with inventive eateries, market events, pubs, and shops overlooking the sea. **Restored Old Jaffa** is a romantic enclave of medieval buildings and cobblestone streets. It's great for evening dining and strolling, and it's loved by visitors and Israelis alike.

Elsewhere in Tel Aviv, you'll see the delightful 1930s and early 1940s **Bauhaus/International Style** buildings that once defined the city's ultra-modern image. In the 1930s, many refugee architects and designers from Germany sought shelter in Palestine. For them, the sands of Tel Aviv provided an opportunity to create a dazzling metropolis of the future based on clean, functional lines. By the beginning of World War II, Tel Aviv had burgeoned into a garden of ultramodern, white concrete architectural wonders—the curvilinear balconies and rounded corners of Tel Aviv's building boom were featured in architectural journals throughout the world.

But despite its architectural pizzazz, 1930s Tel Aviv was not a sleek, perfectly planned utopia. Many of the dazzlingly photographed buildings admired by the outside world were filled with old-fashioned workshops. In summer, the broad, futuristic streets (designed by architects whose hearts were still in pre-1933 Berlin) sweltered under the sun and blocked whatever evening breezes might blow in from the sea.

After Israeli independence, Tel Aviv mushroomed, first with refugee camps and temporary housing for the hundreds of thousands of Holocaust survivors who poured into the country; and later with vast, drab housing projects. During the austere 1950s, Tel Aviv, although a young city, became run-down, especially around its downtown center. The beach, one of Tel Aviv's strong points, piled up with garbage. The ultra-modern buildings of the 1930s and early 1940s, constructed of sand bricks, began to crumble. The city offered little in the way of museums, hotels, or restaurants, and word was out that Tel Aviv was a hot, humid, concrete heap, ungainly and uninteresting.

In the past 30 years, however, Tel Aviv has been undergoing a carefully nurtured revolution. The beach, only a few blocks from anywhere in the city center, has made a spectacular comeback. Performing groups, ranging from the Israel Philharmonic Orchestra and the Cameri Theater to the New Israel Opera, have put Tel Aviv on the cultural map. And innovative, lively museums abound.

Tel Aviv now incorporates the once-separate city of Jaffa, which *does* have a history going back thousands of years (the Prophet Jonah lived in this seaport before his encounter with the whale). If you climb the hill of Old Jaffa and look northward toward Tel Aviv's shoreline, you'll see a city that stands on the threshold of majesty—an amazing achievement for a metropolis that's merely 100 years old.

# BEST TEL AVIV EXPERIENCES

## Exploring Old Jaffa

On summer evenings, wander the picturesque byways overlooking the sea, explore galleries and antique shops, and dine at one of Jaffa's atmospheric restaurants. By day, there's the **Jaffa Flea Market** (p. 192); bargain mercilessly and enjoy interesting little eateries nearby!

## Museum Hopping

Each one is lively and imaginative, starting with the **Diaspora Museum** (p. 183), the sprawling **Eretz Israel Museum** (p. 183), and the daring **Tel Aviv Art Museum** (p. 184). South of Tel Aviv is the **Weizmann Institute** (p. 196) in Rehovot, with its impressive interactive science exhibits (great for adults as well as kids).

## Shopping

Brash, original designer clothes make Tel Aviv a shopaholics mecca; you'll find the best selection on **Sheinkin Street,** upper **Dizengoff Boulevard,** and the trendy **Neve Zedek** neighborhood. Those who want to experience the Tel Aviv life style, and enjoy hunting for treasures, should head to the large, chaotic daily Flea Market in Old Jaffa, the Tuesday and Friday craft bazaar on the streets of Nahalat Binyamin, the eclectic Friday flea market at the Tel Aviv Port, and the Port's daily organic Farmer's Market.

## Joining the Israeli Food Revolution

Tel Aviv is the epicenter of Israel's foodie revolution. Dine here, and you'll revel in the creations of chef-driven restaurants that would be the envy of London, New York, or Los

Angeles, often at (comparatively) bargain prices. Even for street snacks and middle range eateries, Tel Aviv is a world-class gourmand's paradise. Good restaurants are everywhere, and there are special zones, like the Tel Aviv Port, where they are virtually wall-to-wall.

## Relaxing

Superb beaches, stretching from Jaffa in the south, to the Tel Aviv Port in the north, encourage locals to chill out, and they do, spending their free time on these strands swimming, people- and sunset-watching, snoozing under an umbrella, or joining in no-holds-barred game of paddle-ball. **Chinky Beach** (p. 188) at the foot of Allenby Street (also known as **Drum Beach**) is the site of a communal drumming circle that welcomes the Sabbath as the sun sinks into the Mediterranean on Friday evenings.

# ORIENTATION
## Arriving

**BY PLANE**  Flights arrive at Ben-Gurion International Airport, on the outskirts of the city. There is a fixed daytime **taxi fare** of NIS 165 from Ben-Gurion to central Tel Aviv. This fare includes one suitcase per passenger; additional suitcases are NIS 4 each. After 9pm the fixed fare will be higher. **Trains** (www.rail.co.il) leave Ben-Gurion Airport for the Arlosoroff Street Train Station in Tel Aviv two times an hour from 3:30am to 11pm. Fare is NIS 16. From there you'll need to take a local taxi. You're not too far to most Tel Aviv hotels, but with baggage, jet lag, and brutal summer heat, it's not walkable. *Note:* The Arlosoroff Train Station is a magnet for taxis looking to cash in on exhausted, unknowing tourists arriving from Ben-Gurion Airport. Always insist that your driver use the meter.

**BY TRAIN**  The **Central Railway Station** (sometimes called North Railway Station because it's in the northern reaches of the city) stands at the intersection of several major arteries—Petach Tikva Road, Haifa Road, and Arlosoroff Street. From here, municipal buses will take you throughout the city. For Israel Railways information, schedules, and fares to points in Israel go to www.rail.co.il.

**BY BUS**  From the **New Central Bus Station** (in a southern part of town) take bus or sherut no. 4, which runs along Allenby Road and then up Ben-Yehuda Street. As you ride along Ben-Yehuda, you'll be parallel to, and a block away from, Ha-Yarkon Street, where many hotels are located. Ask the driver for the stop closest to your hotel. For the more inland Dizengoff Square area, take the no. 5 bus or sherut to Dizengoff Square. For Dan Bus Lines information, call ✆ **03/639-4444.**

**BY SHERUT**  Ten-passenger vans from Jerusalem and Haifa drop passengers off just outside the main door of the vast Tel Aviv Bus Station and leave for the return trip as soon as they're full. Sheruts cost a shekel or so more than busses do, but are less of a hassle than wending your way through the six-story bus station.

**BY CAR**  Major highways connect Jerusalem, Haifa, and Ashkelon with Tel Aviv.

## Visitor Information

The **Tel Aviv Tourist Information Office** is located at 46 Herbert Samuel Promenade (✆ **03/561-6188**). It's open Sunday through Thursday 8am to 4:30pm. Its staff distributes free information about sites in Tel Aviv and throughout Israel, as well as maps (some for a fee), useful brochures, and discount coupon books. You must come in person.

Online, **Tel Aviv Guide** (www.telavivguide.net) offers lots of good information and visitor forums; **Tel Aviv 4 Fun** (www.telaviv4fun.com) has helpful information about guided and independent tours, travel tips, and reviews of attractions, hotels, and dining.

## City Layout

Tel Aviv and Jaffa (Yafo in Hebrew) together form a large urban area. But the part of Tel Aviv–Jaffa visitors focus on is the downtown seafront section, extending east only to the thoroughfare of Ibn Givrol Street. This is a 6km (3¾-mile) long strip at least 1km (⅔ mile) wide, but only certain sections are of interest to visitors—the rest of the turf is residential or industrial.

## Main Arteries & Streets

Tel Aviv's big streets mostly run north and south, roughly parallel to the sea. **Herbert Samuel Boulevard** is right along the beach. It starts near the Dan Hotel and runs south to Jaffa, with a promenade running alongside it—great for strolling and jogging.

**Ha-Yarkon Street** is a half-block inland, and runs from the northern tip of Tel Aviv down to the border with Jaffa; it is dotted with hotels of all sizes and prices. At the northern tip of Ha-Yarkon, you'll find the **Old Tel Aviv Port,** filled with trendy cafes, pubs, and restaurants, many overlooking the sea. **Ben-Yehuda Street** is the next block inland. The streets between Ha-Yarkon and Ben-Yehuda from the Dan Hotel southward are thick with good restaurants and small hotels. Northern Ben-Yehuda is home to more exclusive design and clothing shops.

At its southern end, Ben-Yehuda curves into **Allenby Street,** which continues southwest. Allenby is an old-fashioned low-budget shopping drag. Off Allenby you'll find the **Carmel Market,** Tel Aviv's roaring outdoor labyrinth where fabulous fruits and vegetables (as well as a million other things) are sold. The **Nahalat Binyamin network of pedestrian streets,** filled with shops, eateries, and a busy Tuesday and Friday crafts fair, is right off Allenby next to the Carmel Market; farther south is the offbeat **Neve Tzedek** neighborhood.

Perpendicular to Allenby, inland from the Carmel Market, is **King George Street,** lined with bakeries, cafes, and small shops connecting to the next big north-south thoroughfare, **Dizengoff Street.** Here you'll find the big Dizengoff Tower Shopping Mall at Dizengoff and King George streets, plus lots of fast-food places up to and north of **Dizengoff Square,** which is really a raised circle.

**Ibn Givrol** is the most inland of the major north-south streets. Its northern end is close to the **Golda Meir/Tel Aviv Center for Performing Arts and the Tel Aviv Art Museum.** Farther south, Ibn Givrol is close to the Mann Auditorium and the Tel Aviv Cinémathèque. It's lined with lots of places to eat and dine.

> ### Getting Connected in Tel Aviv
>
> Tel Aviv is one of the most Web-connected places on earth. The city is in the process of turning the entire beach and downtown center into a free Wi-Fi hotspot. Cafes today have as many customers typing away on iPhones, tablets, and laptops as they do simply sipping coffee!

## Getting Around

**BY BUS** Bus no. 4 and Sherut no. 4 from the **New Central Bus Station** to the center of Tel Aviv go northward to Allenby Street and on to Ben-Yehuda Street; on Ben-Yehuda, you will be running parallel to and a block inland from the many hotels on Ha-Yarkon Street.

**Bus no. 5 and Sherut no. 5** from the **New Central Bus Station** go to the Mann Auditorium, Dizengoff Square, Dizengoff Street, and the IYHA youth hostel Bnei Dan.

*Note:* No. 4 and 5 sheruts run the 4 and 5 bus routes 7 days a week (see "By Taxi/ Sherut Within Tel Aviv," below). **Bus no. 46** runs from the **New Central Bus Station to Jaffa.** Ask to get off near the Clock Tower on Yefet Street.

**Standard bus fare is NIS 6.60,** with an additional half-shekel to and from peripheral areas.

To get to **Jaffa** from central Tel Aviv, take bus no. 10, 25, or 26 heading southward. Bus no. 10 runs along Ben-Yehuda Street, a block inland from Ha-Yarkon Street, and takes you to Jaffa's Clock Tower on Yefet Street, close to Old Jaffa and the flea market. Bus no. 25, which you can pick up on King George Street near Dizengoff Street, runs through Jaffa on Jerusalem Street, a very long block parallel to and inland from Yefet Street. If you're walking (30–45 min.), simply head south along the Tel Aviv Waterfront Promenade, which runs into Jaffa. Bus no. 25 running northward will get you to the Diaspora Museum of Jewish History and Tel Aviv University. For **intercity Egged bus information,** call ✆ **03/694-8888.** For information on **Dan Bus service,** which operates in the Tel Aviv/Sharon region, call ✆ **03/639-4444.**

**BY TAXI/SHERUT WITHIN TEL AVIV**   Ten-passenger vans run along the bus no. 4 and 5 lines. They even run on a reduced schedule on Shabbat. If a van comes along, by all means take it rather than wait for the bus. Prices are the same as bus fares on weekdays; on Shabbat there is a small surcharge.

When taxis are scarce, your best bet is to head to one of the major hotels and enlist the help of the doorman. You have the right to demand that the meter (*ha-sha-*on) be used, but many drivers will try to negotiate a fixed nonmetered fare to your destination, which may or may not be to your advantage. By law, the meter must be used, especially if you insist. There are legal surcharges above the metered fare on Shabbat and after 9pm. If you use the meter, ask for a receipt (ka-*ba*-lah).

**BY TRAIN**   For train schedules, call ✆ **03/577-4000.** The best train station for those staying in central Tel Aviv is the Arlosoroff Street Station, at the eastern end of Arlosoroff Street. There is train service up the coast to Nahariya; south to Beersheba; slow, infrequent service to the western edge of Jerusalem; and a rail link to Ben-Gurion Airport. Israel Railways is undergoing a period of revival and expansion. It's becoming more and more pleasant to use. For the most current information on schedules and fares, go to **www.rail.co.il**.

# [FastFACTS] TEL AVIV

**Currency Exchange**   There are a number of internationally connected ATMs in the hotel district along Ha-Yarkon and Ben-Yehuda streets, as well as scattered elsewhere in the city. Check with your hotel desk about which is the closest. In addition, you can use the currency exchange offices along Ha-Yarkon and Ben-Yehuda streets. They usually have exchange rates comparable to the banks. Avoid shady people offering to change money on the streets no matter what rate they quote.

**Doctors & Dentists**   You can get a list of English-speaking doctors and dentists from your embassy and often from your hotel's front desk. For First Aid SOS Doctors, call ✆ **800/225-5005.** There is an Emergency Dental Treatment Center at 18 Reines St. (✆ **03/523-9241**); or call **Dental First Aid** (✆ **800/773-773**), which operates 24 hours a day.

**Drugstores**   "The Jerusalem Post" lists under

"General Assistance" the names and addresses of duty pharmacies that stay open nights and on Shabbat for the current week.

**Emergencies** For police, dial ☏ **100.** In medical emergencies, dial ☏ **101** for Magen David Adom (Red Shield of David), Israel's emergency first-aid service and ambulance. For fire, dial ☏ **102.**

**Hospitals** Ichilov Hospital (☏ **03/697-4444**) has an emergency room, dental clinic, and Malam Traveler's Clinic for immunizations. SOS Doctors medical emergency center is at ☏ **1-800/225-5005.**

**Newspapers & Magazines** See the special Tel Aviv events supplement published on Friday in "The Jerusalem Post" (available only in the Tel Aviv region); "Haaretz" ("The New York Times" of Israel) is published each day in English inside "The International Herald Tribune." It has a great listing of events in its Friday edition. The English-language editions of "Time Out Tel Aviv" and "Time Out Israel" are available for free, bimonthly at most major hotels.

**Post Office** Tel Aviv's **Central Post Office** is at 132 Allenby Rd. General hours for all services are Sunday to Thursday from 7am to 7pm, though

limited services (telephone and telegraph) are open nights and on Shabbat.

**Telegrams** can be sent at all post offices or by phoning ☏ **171.** Check with your hotel for the closest neighborhood branch.

**Safety** Israel's largest metropolitan area has less crime than most cities its size, but there is still enough that you must observe the normal precautions. Don't walk in deserted areas, especially the beaches, after dark. Terrorism is always a concern. Get away from and report any unattended bags or packages.

# WHERE TO STAY

Most of Tel Aviv's hotels are comparatively high in price and generically modern, in keeping with a city that's less than 100 years old. That being said, some do have the advantage of being on the beach. If that's important to you, target the lodgings that are on or near Ha-Yarkon Street, which runs along the beach from Mograbi Square northward. The upper rank hotels are on the sea side of Ha-Yarkon. Most of the mid- and lower-class choices are on the inland side of Ha-Yarkon, or on Ben-Yehuda Street. The Dizengoff Square area, which is further inland, is another hotel hub.

Tel Aviv can be a very noisy city. In the more expensive, high-rise hotels, upper floors are quieter. If you're looking for a moderate or budget hotel, don't take a room facing a main street unless it has air-conditioning and soundproof windows; choose a room in the back. By international standards, many "deluxe" hotels are barely that, and many hotels claiming to be five-star properties are four stars at best.

## Along Ha-Yarkon Street

Ha-Yarkon Street runs along the Mediterranean. The major hotels are all right off the sea and have either direct access to the beach or are across a small but busy road. Because of the summer heat and humidity, a hotel with a pool can be a good investment. For a long block north of the Renaissance Hotel, Ha-Yarkon becomes a wider thoroughfare with divider barriers, meaning guests staying in moderate hotels on the inland side of the street can't just dash across the road and down to the beach. Skyscraper construction is everywhere, and accompanying noise is a daytime fact of life.

### EXPENSIVE

**Dan Tel Aviv Hotel ★★** The doyenne of the city's 5-Star hotels, the Dan Tel Aviv's central location is its top selling point: It's just steps away from good dining choices and right across the road from the popular Gordon Beach. It's also a very short block from Ben Yehuda Street, with its buses and sheruts, so guests don't need to depend on taxis to get around. Of course, it also offers the comforts of a deluxe hotel, which include careful service, dignified decor and such swank amenities as the choice of either fresh or saltwater swimming pools (indoor and outdoor respectively). The design of the hotel is conservatively modern, but the layout is eccentric. It began as a small place in the 1950s and slowly expanded into wings and sections built around inner courtyards. Rooms facing inward have no view, but they shut out the city's street noise. As this is not a high-rise, the rooms facing the sea sadly overlook a busy road, so if you're sensitive to noise you may want to sacrifice the view in favor of sleep. There are many, many room categories, so ask questions before you choose.

99 Ha-Yarkon St. ℭ **800/223-7773** in the U.S., or 03/520-2525. www.danhotels.com. 286 units. $360–$500 standard double. Rates include breakfast. Bus: 4 on Ben-Yehuda St.; ask for stop near Dan Hotel. **Amenities:** 3 restaurants, bar, business center, children's activities in summer, club-level rooms, concierge, health club, 2 pools (indoor, outdoor), sauna, steam bath, nonsmoking rooms, room service, Wi-Fi (free in lobby; 1 hr. of daily in-room use for e-Dan club members).

**Sheraton Tel Aviv** ★★ Here's another one where location is its key asset: This tall Starwood property is just across the road from Gordon Beach, just steps from cafes and restaurants. Guest rooms are bright, thanks to large windows and those in the Club and Tower areas were renovated in 2012 and 2013. All are outfitted, not surprisingly, with the super-comfortable "Sheraton Sweet Sleeper" beds. Club Rooms have access to an executive lounge where a light buffet is usually out for the taking, while Tower Rooms come with a more exclusive, separate lounge and buffet, as well as special Tower Floor reception and concierge service. The Sheraton is the only beachfront high-rise with many guest rooms squarely facing the sea (other hotels offer rooms with an angled view of the Mediterranean), a BIG plus. As well, the Sheraton's dining services are primo, especially the elegant **Olive Leaf** restaurant (see p. 171) which we count as the best luxury kosher restaurant in Israel. We also think the new swimming pool area is mighty attractive. And the staff throughout the hotel are unusually helpful.

115 Ha-Yarkon St. ℭ **800/325-3535** in the U.S. and Canada, or 03/521-1111. 346 units. $310–$430 standard double; add $80 for club rooms with access to business lounge, $120 for tower rooms. Rates include breakfast. Parking (fee). Bus: 4 to Ben-Yehuda and Gordon Sts.; walk down Gordon St. to Ha-Yarkon St. **Amenities:** 3 restaurants, disco/nightclub, lounge/bar, club lounge and tower lounge, concierge, health club, outdoor pool; free Wi-Fi and Internet in tower lounge only. Wi-Fi in room for a fee.

**Renaissance Tel Aviv** ★ The Renaissance is one of the very few hotels that offers direct access to a prime section of beach, with no streets to cross. That's the good news. Unfortunately, except for executive rooms, most guest rooms here are in serious need of a renovation (like the major renovations of public areas in 2013 that brightened the hotel's overall ambiance). We'd rank it as a second choice in this area, to be looked at if the Sheraton or Dan Tel Aviv are booked up, as it does offer lovely views of the sea from rooms on the hotel's southern side. Plus, there's an indoor pool for winter swimming and summer days when the sea is hazardous because of jellyfish. All rooms have balconies and room-only rates are available.

121 Ha-Yarkon St. ℭ **03/521-5555.** www.marriott.com/hotels/travel/tlvbr-renaissance-tel-aviv-hotel. 340 units. $250–$425 double. Rates include breakfast;. Parking (fee). **Amenities:** Restaurant, cafe, bar, children's program in season, club-level rooms, fitness room, Jacuzzi, indoor pool, sauna, nonsmoking rooms, Wi-Fi (fee).

# Tel Aviv Accommodations, Dining & Attractions

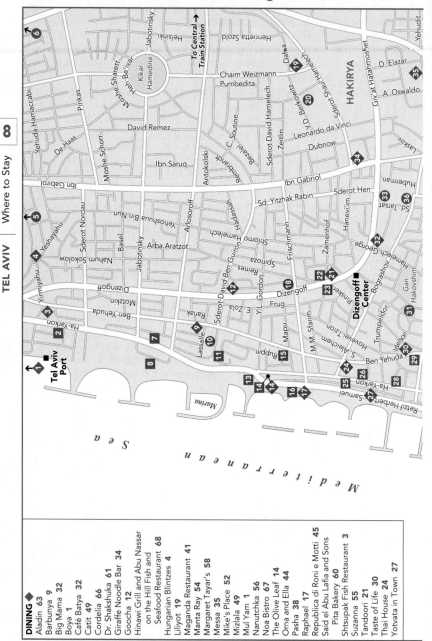

**DINING** ◆
Aladin **63**
Barbunya **9**
Big Mama **32**
Boya **1**
Café Batya **32**
Catit **49**
Cordelia **66**
Dr. Shakshuka **61**
Giraffe Noodle Bar **34**
Goocha **12**
Hinawi Grill and Abu Nassar on the Hill Fish and Seafood Restaurant **68**
Hungarian Blintzes **4**
Liliyot **19**
Maganda Restaurant **41**
Manta Ray **54**
Margaret Tayar's **58**
Messa **35**
Mike's Place **52**
Mizlala **49**
Mul Yam **1**
Nanutchka **56**
Noa Bistro **67**
The Olive Leaf **14**
Orna and Ella **44**
Pasha **38**
Raphael **17**
Republica di Roni e Motti **45**
Said el Abu Lafia and Sons Pita Bakery **60**
Shtsupak Fish Restaurant **3**
Suzanna **55**
Tandoori **21**
Taste of Life **30**
Thai House **24**
Yotvata in Town **27**

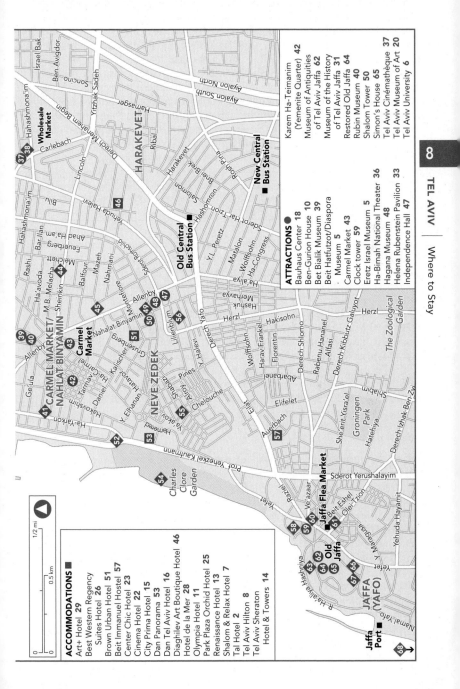

**ATTRACTIONS ●**

Bauhaus Center **18**
Ben-Gurion House **10**
Bet Bialik Museum **39**
Beit Hatfutzot/Diaspora
Museum **5**
Carmel Market **43**
Clock tower **59**
Eretz Israel Museum **5**
Ha-Bimah National Theater **36**
Hagana Museum **48**
Helena Rubenstein Pavilion **33**
Independence Hall **47**

Karem Ha-Teimanim
(Yemenite Quarter) **42**
Museum of Antiquities
of Tel Aviv Jaffa **62**
Museum of the History
of Tel Aviv Jaffa **31**
Restored Old Jaffa **64**
Rubin Museum **40**
Shalom Tower **50**
Simon's House **65**
Tel Aviv Cinémathèque **37**
Tel Aviv Museum of Art **20**
Tel Aviv University **6**

**ACCOMMODATIONS ■**

Art+ Hotel **29**
Best Western Regency
Suites Hotel **26**
Brown Urban Hotel **51**
Beit Immanuel Hostel **57**
Center Chic Hotel **23**
Cinema Hotel **22**
City Prima Hotel **15**
Dan Panorama **53**
Dan Tel Aviv Hotel **16**
Diaghilev Art Boutique Hotel **46**
Hotel de la Mer **28**
Olympia Hotel **11**
Park Plaza Orchid Hotel **25**
Renaissance Hotel **13**
Shalom & Relax Hotel **7**
Tal Hotel **2**
Tel Aviv Hilton **8**
Tel Aviv Sheraton
Hotel & Towers **14**

165

**Park Plaza Orchid Tel Aviv** ★★  With its roomy studios (equipped with kitchenettes), and one- and two-bedroom suites, this contemporary tower is an excellent choice for families (it's also right across the street from the beach). It offers standard doubles, as well, but we think it's worth the relatively small extra charge to upgrade from the small street-facing double rooms in the older wing to the larger sea view deluxe rooms (ask to stay in the newer wing above the reception area). The optional breakfast, at $50 for two people, is overpriced—you'll do better whipping something up in your kitchenette or heading to a neighboring restaurants. But the hotel's policy of offering free Wi-Fi, free international calls to land lines, and complimentary use of bicycles are all terrific, money-saving perks. The hotel is equipped with a state-of-the-art fitness room and a small pool (usually open until 7:30pm). We give it two rather than three stars because housekeeping and service are not strong points.

79 Ha-Yarkon St. ✆ **03/519-7111.** www.orchidplaza.co.il. 180 units. $250–$350 standard double. Bus: 4 to Ben-Yehuda St.; ask driver for closest stop. **Amenities:** Cafe, lobby bar, free loaner bikes, fitness room; Jacuzzi, free international calls at special phone center, outdoor pool, room service, spa, nonsmoking rooms, sauna, Wi-Fi (free).

## MODERATE

**Art+ Hotel** ★★  Five local artists were commissioned to create murals for the Art+, and their vibrant, often quirky works set the cultured yet fun tone at this relatively new hotel (it opened in 2009). They're just the beginning of the special touches here, which range from free taxis back to the airport (during certain months and for those who stay a minimum of 3 nights), to free parking to nightly, free happy hours in the hotel's book-filled lounge. We also love the snazzy sun deck, a wonderful place to gather with friends. Most guest rooms are in the back of the building, away from Ben Yehuda Street noise; all have up-to-the-minute amenities and are bright white, but with brilliant splashes of color—a blood red chair here, a lime green pillow there—that give them real elan. The only downside to these rooms is that the cheapest ones are just 110-square-feet, so they can feel a bit cramped. The location is very central and only steps away from bus and sherut lines that whisk you all over town. The staff is attentive.

35 Ben-Yehuda St. ✆ **03/797-1700.** Reservations ✆ 03/542-5555. www.atlas.co.il. 62 units. $188–$238 double. Rates include breakfast. Free nearby parking. **Amenities:** Lobby cafe, business lounge, bar, sundeck, free Wi-Fi, free parking.

**Best Western Regency Suites Hotel** ★★★  Right across from the beach and in the heart of the hotel district, this hotel, consisting entirely of one-bedroom suites, is ideal for families and long term visitors who want a bit more room and the chance to prepare their own meals. Size and set ups of the suites vary a bit; more expensive higher floor rooms are quieter and offer decks with spectacular views of the sea and sunsets. But all the suites are airy, well maintained, and contain kitchenettes, a living room with twin beds, and a living area with a sofa that can also sleep two, plus a separate bedroom for two. There's no pool, but the hotel does boast a fine rooftop deck with a Jacuzzi, free underground parking, and the option of plans with breakfast included. There are all kinds of discounts for families, long-termers, and for American AARP and AAA members. When we went to press in late 2013, the hotel was under renovation, so we expect the rooms to look extra spiffy by the time you read this. The staff is unusually helpful, and the entire building is non-smoking.

80 Ha-Yarkon St. ✆ **03/517-3939.** www.regenccysuiteshotelaviv.com. 30 units. $200–$290 suite double. Breakfast not included. 1 child 11 and under stays free with 2 paying adults. Free parking. **Amenities:** Dining room, cafe, bar, Jacuzzi, room service, kitchenette, minibar (on request), free Wi-Fi.

# private ROOMS & APARTMENTS

Internet services, like Airbnb (www.airbnb.com) can be a good way to find interesting accommodations in advance from swank beachfront pads to more modest private rooms inside a local's home. The **Tel Aviv Tourist Information Office** at 46 Herbert Samuel Promenade (ⓒ **03/561-6188**) also compiles a list of agencies and individuals who rent rooms and apartments. Though they will not make a contact or reservation for you, and they cannot guarantee the quality of service or accommodations, the tourist office staff will let you copy the list for free.

**City Prima Hotel ★**  Sometimes all you need is a quality bed and a friendly smile at the end of the day. And the City Prima certainly supplies those things. A modest property on a side street just a half-block from the beach (some rooms have lovely beach views), the hotel came under the management of the Prima Hotel chain in 2013. Happily, it looks like the chain will be retaining the hotel's crack staff; as well, the chain is known for its discounts and is currently offering great prices (as low as $120 for a double). So what do you get for your money? Standard rooms are small, but with an attempt at style (the bed headboards look a bit like beach sunsets); they vary in size and layout. The 40 studio rooms are larger and can fit up to three. Ask for a room toward the back avoid street noise. Guests who are kosher will appreciate the convenience of in-house a la carte lunch and dinner service. The hotel has limited free parking, free bike loans, and is steps away from the Number 4 and 10 buses.

9 Mapu St. ⓒ **03/524-6253.** www.prima-hotels-israel.com. 96 units. $176–$225 standard double. Rates include breakfast. **Amenities:** Dining room, cafe, bar, loaner bicycles, room service, nonsmoking rooms, fridge (on request), free Wi-Fi, free parking.

**Hotel de la Mer ★★★**  A small boutique hotel with the service of a family-run inn (read: excellent and very personal), the de la Mer is a mere ⅛ block from the beach. Opened in 2001 in a restored, historic Bauhaus building, it features restful décor; the designer used the principals of feng shui in his work and somehow that translates to lots of natural woods, oriental rugs and lovely floral coverlets in most of the rooms. A variety of guest rooms are offered; at the lowest rates are compact but pleasant digs. If you can splash out, the spacious junior suites with terraces are among the best rooms in town at any price. Breakfast is served in a friendly setting, and tea and coffee are free 24/7 in a new cafe lounge. The hotel also has a small roof terrace and a spa room for in-house massage.

62 Ha-Yarkon St. ⓒ **03/510-0011.** www.delamer.co.il. 27 units. $170–$220 double; $235–$265 suite. Rates include breakfast. **Amenities:** Dining room, cafe, room service, small spa, nonsmoking rooms, fridge or minibar, free Wi-Fi.

**Olympia Hotel ★**  This is a bland, 1970s style hotel, renovated last in 1997 and overdue for another updating. However, for a central location across the road from the beach, and for the price (especially on discounter websites), it's an affordable option in a very expensive part of town. Guest rooms are basic and there are no amenities like a pool or fitness room, but across the street near Atarim Square, a somewhat hidden outdoor staircase takes you down to a good beach beside the Herod's Hotel. Service is not great, except if you speak Russian, as many of the staff are from that part of the world. A definite second or third choice hotel (unless you get a great deal).

164 Ha-Yarkon St. ℐ **03/524-2184.** www.inisrael.com/olympia. 64 units. $90–$150 double. Rates include breakfast. **Amenities:** Dining room; cafe; bar; room service, free Wi-Fi in lobby.

# Northern Tel Aviv

This area's public beaches are more specialized in character than those further south: One area is reserved for religious beachgoers (and has separate days for men and women); the northernmost beaches attract families and students, while Hilton Beach (behind the Hilton Hotel) is popular with an easy mix of tourists, families, surfers, and the local gay community. The area is a little bit away from the Ha Yarkon Street/Ben Yehuda Street restaurant choices, but they are within walking distance, as are the restaurants in the Tel Aviv Port.

## MODERATE

**Tal Hotel ★★**   This high-rise on a sides street just off Ha-Yarkon Street, and next to one of the city's northernmost beaches, is one of the best bargains in the well-run Atlas Chain (we're constantly seeing it on discount sites, so surf the internet before booking). We also like the locale, close to the Tel Aviv Port, with its many restaurants. Guest rooms are terrifically cheery, with red chairs and brightly striped coverlets; we hear that they're going to be renovating soon, so the décor may be slightly different by the time you read this. Families with kids will appreciate the comparatively spacious guest rooms, the numerous rooms with connecting doors and the short walk to the beach, with no major streets to cross. Staff is generally very helpful. The no. 4 bus and sherut will whisk you to the more central parts of town. The Tal lends free bikes to guests. Alas, there's no on-site pool here.

287 Ha-Yarkon St. ℐ **03/542-5500.** www.atlas.co.il. 120 units. $190–$245 double. Rates include breakfast. Limited free parking. **Amenities:** Dining room, bar, room service, nonsmoking rooms, fridge, free Wi-Fi.

**Shalom & Relax Hotel ★★★**   The former Howard Johnson's has been taken over by the Atlas Chain, and we must say, they've worked miracles with this older property. Rooms are now downright chic, with "beach house" style black-and-white furnishings and lux beds. On the fifth floor is a decadent roof deck, complete with rocking chairs, sitting pods (basically, enclosed couches with lots of cushions) and, best of all, free short but relaxing massage sessions from the on-duty masseuse. Want more pampering? Special "Spa Guest Rooms" include hot tubs. Food services—which include the free afternoon snacks—use only kosher dairy/vegetarian ingredients, however the hotel does not have a "kashrut certificate." Location is primo, too, across the road from the beach in front of the Hilton Hotel (its arguably the best and most inclusive strand in this area).

216 Ha-Yarkon St. ℐ **03/542-5555.** www.atlas.co.il. 51 units. $250–$300 double. Rates include breakfast. Bus: 4 **Amenities:** Restaurant, business lounge, bar, loaner bicycles, DVD library, Jacuzzi, room service, sauna, sun deck, hot tubs in spa rooms, fridge, free Wi-Fi.

# Dizengoff Square & Ben-Yehuda Streets

This area is central but noisy. It's a good choice for a winter visit, but in summer, the beach is a hot, muggy 10-minute walk away.

## MODERATE

**Center Chic Hotel ★★**   There's a lot to live up to when you have a name that promises a good locale, as well as an up-to-the-minute look. But the Center Chic, which was redesigned in 2011, comes through, transforming a classic Bauhaus structure into the most color-saturated lodging in the city. Rooms are awash in bold patterns and deep hues; were it not for the keen eye of the designer here, the look would be quite off-putting, but somehow it all works. Much of the appeal comes from the fact that nearly every room offers its own balcony space. The staff, too, draw raves from all those who stay here, as does the spacious gardened roof terrace with sun lounges overlooking Dizengoff Square. Breakfast and complimentary late afternoon drinks and snacks are served next door at the Cinema Hotel (see below) where you can also borrow a free bike. Most rooms are very small (although fine for singles), but a few are roomier—ask if a larger room is available.

2 Zamenhoff St. (C) **03/526-6100.** www.atlas.co.il. 54 units. $163–$213 double. Rates include breakfast. **Amenities:** Breakfast served next door in Hotel Cinema; free use of hotel bicycles, fridge, free Wi-Fi.

**Cinema Hotel ★★**   Set in a white, landmark 1930s Art Deco former cinema intelligently redesigned into a hotel, this Atlas-managed property offers a central location and spiffy authentic Tel Aviv/Bauhaus style. There are lots of Atlas Hotel touches, like a friendly staff, free late afternoon drinks and snacks, a Jacuzzi on the Business Lounge's terrace, and free use of bicycles and Wi-Fi. Check in is at the ultra-modern lobby's one-time candy counter. You get a bag of popcorn with your key. Some guest rooms are getting a bit worn, but upkeep is generally good overall. A rear-facing room provides a buffer against Dizengoff Square noise. Two negatives: The 10-minute walk to the beach can be a drawback on a hot summer day. The hotel's excellent food services use only kosher dairy/vegetarian ingredients, however the hotel does not have a "kashrut certificate."

1 Zamenhoff St., at Dizengoff Sq. (C) **03/520-7100** or reservations at 03/542-5555. www.atlas.co.il. 82 units. $195–$245 double. Rates include breakfast. Long-term and Internet discounts available. Call ahead to arrange parking. **Amenities:** Dining room, cafe, bicycles, Jacuzzi, rooms for those w/limited mobility, room service, sauna. kitchenette (some rooms), minibar (some rooms), free Wi-Fi.

# Southern Tel Aviv

Across a divided thoroughfare from the sea (but a 2-block walk to a guarded swimming beach), two high-rise hotels, the Dan Panorama and the David InterContinental, hold forth alone as a tourist island in a relatively isolated, empty stretch between Tel Aviv and Jaffa, approximately 2.4km (1½ miles) south of the main Ha-Yarkon Street hotel district. Old Jaffa is a 15-minute walk along the Seaside Promenade, and the bustling **Carmel Market** (from which you can reach the restaurants and cafes of the trendy **Nahalat Binyamin, Neve Zedek,** and **Rothschild St.** areas) is a 5-minute walk across a shabby park. Note that walking through the empty Carmel Market at night is not advisable. Rates here are lower than for a comparable hotel on Ha-Yarkon Street. Further inland, the new boutique hotels offer Tel Aviv chic, but in summer, they lack the city's beach ambiance.

## EXPENSIVE

**Dan Panorama ★**   Five-star amenities, three-star pricing (thanks to not-hard-to-find internet discounts): That's the key to the popularity of this sea-facing 1980's hotel. True, the beach here isn't the best for swimming, but the hotel does have a pleasant, sunny pool overlooking the Mediterranean. And Old Jaffa, with superb restaurants and atmosphere, is only a 15-minute walk away. Guests also appreciate the enormous breakfast buffet (it outdoes those at more expensive hotels) and the well-equipped fitness room with a Jacuzzi. Now for the bad news: Except for the executive floors, most guest rooms and baths are dated and bland, though each room has a balcony and views are terrific above the 5th floor. Plus free Wi-Fi is available only in the lobby—in standard rooms it costs a whopping $20 per day and that's per device, so if you're traveling with more than one, the charges can mount up. We think the top floor executive rooms are worth the extra money, as guests have the use of a lounge that features a tasty light buffet (many sub it for dinner). The hotel gets numerous groups and families with children over holiday periods.

10 Kaufman St. ✆ **03/519-0190.** www.danhotels.com. 500 units. $270–$330 double; sea view and club level rooms add $40–$60. Rates include breakfast. Bus: 10. **Amenities:** 2 restaurants; bar, fitness center, Jacuzzi, outdoor pool, room service, synagogue, minibar, Wi-Fi (free in lobby; 1 hr. of daily in-room use for e-Dan club members).

## MODERATE

**Brown Urban Hotel** ★★  Welcome to Tel Aviv's trendiest hotel, a place so hip, its rooftop terrace attracts as many locals than guests most evening (who can resist a place with a bar, great views, "massage hut" and hot tub?). The lobby can be a scene, too, with its retro-chic rocking chairs, pop-up Souvenir design stand (featuring artsy pieces crafted by locals) and huge blown-up, vintage Playboy magazine covers for decoration. As for the rooms, they're tight at just 110-square feet for the cheapest standard ones, but so well-designed—chocolate walls, plush beds, rainfall showers in black marble bathrooms—that guests don't mind the squeeze. Especially since each floor contains a room for a variety of massage treatments, and there's a relaxing sundeck with a cooling outdoor shower. Larger (and more expensive) "Relax" rooms include their own double Jacuzzis. Though the hotel doesn't have a restaurant, guests are given a voucher for breakfast, good at a number of local restaurants. And unlike most design-savvy, boutique hotels, this one accepts children as guests.

25 Kalisher St. ✆ **03/717-0200.** www. brownhotel.co.il. 30 units $180–$235 standard room; add $80 for "Relax" room. **Amenities:** Bar, Business Center, laundry service, fitness room (outside hotel), free breakfast, spa, Jacuzzi, sundeck, free bicycle use, parking (fee), work station, free WiiFi.

**Diaghilev Art Boutique Hotel** ★★  Named for the famous Russian art critic and ballet impresario, Sergei Pavlovich Diaghilev, this boutique hotel has cannily channeled both the great man's superb sense of style and his delight in the innovative. All of the one- and two-bedroom suites are decorated with striking original art (some for sale), and set up, purposefully, to enhance sleep. There is a current theory that light disrupts sleep patterns, so it is banished from the bedrooms entirely—no blinking TV lights or glowing clocks are allowed, and even the sheets and pillowcases are black, so as to "promote restorative sleep". The separate living areas make this a good choice for business travelers as well as for tourists who want room to spread out. There's no beach atmosphere (or proximity), but you stay here to be in the zone for Tel Aviv's centers of commerce and style. Up to four people can fit into a suite.

56 Mazeh St. ✆ **03/545-3131.** www.diaghilev.com. 54 suites $190–$320 Standard double. Breakfast can be included. **Amenities:** Business center, lobby, on-site art gallery, beach shuttle in July and August, kitchenette, complete office corner on request, parking (fee), private chef on request, free Wi-Fi.

# Jaffa

## INEXPENSIVE

**Beit Immanuel Hostel** ★  Located in a neighborhood of businesses and factories on the Tel Aviv-Jaffa border, this historic and tranquil oasis is operated by a congregation of Christians and Messianic Jews, but guests of all persuasions are welcome.

A no-smoking building, the guesthouse offers basic, well-maintained, air-conditioned private rooms with bathrooms (some on the second floor have balconies) as well as beds in dorm rooms. Street-facing rooms will be noisy, and many rooms are up several steep flights of stairs; those with disabilities should ask for a ground floor room. The staff is helpful, and despite an 11pm curfew, arrangements can be made for both late night or early morning comings and departures. Breakfast in the lush garden is a special pleasure.

8 Auerbach St. ℭ **03/682-1459.** www.beitimmanuel.org. $30 per person in single-sex dorms; $110 private double with bath. Rates include breakfast. Cash only. Parking with fee. Bus: 46, ask for the Beit Immanuel Auerbach St. stop. **Amenities:** Dining room, free Wi-Fi in lobby.

# WHERE TO DINE

## Off & On Ha-Yarkon, Ben-Yehuda & Dizengoff Streets

Ha-Yarkon Street, Ben-Yehuda Street, and the side streets in between are loaded with restaurants, but don't miss dining in romantic Old Jaffa and lesser known parts of Tel Aviv, where the city's spectacular restaurant scene (among the best in the world) truly rides high. *Note:* Some non-kosher restaurants in Tel Aviv close after lunch on Friday, and then reopen Friday evening or on Saturday.

### EXPENSIVE

**The Olive Leaf** ★★ MODERN FRENCH   The most stylish Kosher eatery in all of Israel, with grand ocean views, the Olive Tree serves the sort of French food that the French themselves currently prefer. So gone are the centuries-old, heavily sauced meats and fishes. In their place is an innovative, constantly changing menu, with many unusual dishes. On one night you might tuck into sweet meats smoked with citrus and sided by mushroom and veal brain ragout. The next visit could bring a hearty Mediterranean fish soup scented with anise or Cornish hen wrapped in smoked goose breast and served on an eggplant/pesto pastry—you just never know. What doesn't change is the high quality of the ingredients, and the sure hand of star chef Charlie Fadida. One warning: The restaurant gives out a large number of free *amuse bouches* before the meal, so take that into account when ordering or you won't have room for one of the lavish desserts (and that would be tragic). Service is included in the prices, and guests of the Sheraton who pay in foreign currency and charge their meal to their room bill are exempt from the additional 18 percent VAT. If you come by to take advantage of Olive Tree's good value lunch specials, reserve a table by the window so you can watch the waves lapping the shore as you lap up whatever's in front of you.

In the Sheraton Hotel, 115 Ha-Yarkon St. ℭ **03/521-9300** or 521-1111. Reservations recommended. Main courses (priced in dollars only) $22–$45. Fixed-price lunches from $28. Sun–Thurs noon–3pm and 7:30pm–midnight. Bus 4.

**Raphael** ★★ RUSTIC FRENCH/MEDITERRANEAN   In the heart of the hotel district, Raphael offers a chance to sample the kitchen of Rafi Cohen, one of Israel's most praised chefs. The menu constantly changes, but is usually marked by earthy, hearty dishes like lamb meatballs cooked in garlic and tumeric with whole garbanzo beans and Jerusalem artichokes; or delicate North Atlantic periwinkles and herbed gnocchi in a sauce of butter, white wine, and olive oil. Raphael's is especially known for its excellent risottos, its cold seafood salads, desserts, and wine list. The recently redesigned dining room brings the décor up to the level of the food. Raphael can get crowded and noisy, so dine before 9pm if you want serenity. Reservations are key.

87 Ha-Yarkon St. ℂ **03/522-6464.** Main courses NIS 100–NIS 180; fixed-price lunch from NIS 98. Daily noon–3pm and 7pm until last customer; last order taken at 10:30pm. On lower floor of high-rise attached to the south side of the Dan Hotel. Accessible to those with disabilities. Bus 4.

## INEXPENSIVE

**Mike's Place** ★ BURGERS/PUB FOOD   A Tel Aviv institution offering free live blues, jazz, folk, or rock every night and televised sports events by day, Mike's is known for its menu of American-style comfort foods: freshly ground all-beef hamburgers, wings, grilled chicken breast, fish and chips, macaroni and cheese, baby back pork ribs, Tex-Mex, and lots more. Facing the open sea, it's a kid-friendly spot in the day and early evening; and perfect for anyone looking for an Israeli/American/Anglo atmosphere from breakfast and brunch through late-night pub crawling. Check web site for music events.

86 Herbert Samuel Promenade (next to American Embassy). ℂ **03/510-6392.** www.mikesplace bars.com. Main courses NIS 42–NIS 100. Daily 11am–after midnight. Bis 4.

**Yotvata in Town** ★★ DAIRY/VEGETARIAN   Yotvata gets its produce and dairy ingredients fresh daily from a number kibbutzim, most notably Kibbutz Yotvata, famous for dairy products. That means the food here, while simple, is extra-flavorful thanks to the fact that it may have been picked, or squeezed from a cow's udder, that very morning. The menu ranges from salads to sandwiches, to veggie pies, blintzes, pancakes, cheese platters and pizzas. Yotvata's ice cream desserts are legendary as are the fruit juice mixtures, yogurts, and milk shakes. Popular with families.

76 Herbert Samuel Promenade. ℂ **03/510-4667.** Main courses and light meals NIS 40–NIS 85. Daily 7am–4am. Bus 4.

## Along Ben-Yehuda Street

### MODERATE

**Barbunya** ★★ SEAFOOD   Few places in Tel Aviv, or the world for that matter, can boast that for *years* a line of hungry customers has snaked out the door and down the street, most every day of the week. The reason? The freshest of seafood, reasonably priced and expertly, if simply, cooked. The menu offers two categories of fixed price dinners. Each comes with an all-you-can-eat medley of Middle Eastern appetizers, chilled seltzer, and your choice of a main course from a daily list of fish or shrimp that can be ordered either grilled or fried and served with garlic, lemon, and butter. Tablecloths are sheets of packing paper, and no substitutions are permitted (or needed). Service is friendly and speedy (which kids will appreciate). Reservations are not taken.

163 Ben-Yehuda St. near Jabotinsky St. ℂ **03/527-6965.** Fixed-price meals NIS 95–NIS 115. Sat–Thurs noon–midnight; Fri noon–6pm.

### INEXPENSIVE

**Taste of Life** ★ VEGAN   This isn't your average vegan restaurant: The menu's been designed by Hebrew Israelites, an African-American group whose dietary laws prohibit any milk or meat products. So expect some unusual choices, like a barbecued twist on whole-wheat pita baked in-house with a spicy sauce, homemade mustard, and salad. Other favorites here include soy sausages, wheat burgers, tofu falafel, vegetarian *shwarma,* and faux steak sandwiches. Vegan food is always healthy, but at Taste of Life, virtue is taken to another level: The food is cholesterol-free, there's almost no salt used and nothing is fried. For drinks and dessert, try veggie coffee, fresh fruit juice, or

# kid-friendly RESTAURANTS

If your child has a sophisticated palate, feel comfortable taking him or her to most every restaurant in this chapter; none will turn you away, though you'll want to make sure they won't disturb the other diners at the more pricey places. This box really is geared towards the picky eaters among the younger set. Try any one of the restaurants below and you're sure to find at least 2 or 3 dishes that will satisfy even the most spice-averse of youngsters:

**Yotvata** (p. 172) A favorite of Tel Aviv teenagers and students, with its menu of sandwiches, pancakes, fruit shakes and other simple dishes made from farm-fresh products.

**Barbunya** (p. 172) No frills and near the hotel district, it offers fresh fish and extremely speedy service. The latter

always a blessing when traveling with impatient youngsters—just get there early at dinnertime to avoid the line.

**Said el Abu Lafia and Sons Pita Bakery** (p. 182) Wonderful Arabic pizzas and stuffed breads. Bring lots of napkins, and you're ready to have a picnic in the nearby gardens of Old Jaffa!

**Mike's Place** (p. 172) Burgers, fried chicken, mac 'n cheese and a TV constantly playing sports matches—you may have difficulty getting your kids to leave Mike's!

**Hungarian Blintzes** Who doesn't like blintzes? Well, you're children may not yet *know* they like them, but once they try these crepelike treats—which come in both sweet and savory varieties—I guarantee they'll become fans.

carob milk as well as soy ice cream, or carob cake. Prices are astonishingly low, and the cuisine goes well with Tel Aviv's torrid, muggy summer weather.

35 Ben-Yehuda St. ✆ **03/516-8906.** Main dishes NIS 26–NIS 49. Sun–Thurs 10am–9pm; Fri 10am–2pm. Bus 4.

**Thai House** ★★★ THAI    The best Asian restaurant in Israel. Period. It dazzles those who know real Thai cuisine, and makes converts of those who are new to this cuisine. The brainchild of an adventurous Israeli who spent years in Thailand living in a number of villages throughout the country, Thai House does the standard Thai dishes (so if you must, you *can* order pad thai). But it's the adventurous eaters who are rewarded here, those who sample the more exotic village fare that's rarely cooked outside of Thailand. This includes eggplant *gaeng kew wan,* aubergines simmered to perfection in a green curry coconut milk sauce; papaya salad dotted with paper-thin slices of rare roast beef and mint in a spicy sweet and sour fish sauce; and the unusual coriander shrimp rolls with bean noodles. Cocktails and wines are specially chosen to complement the menu. Ask questions and let the staff direct you.

8 Bograshov St. (corner of Ben-Yehuda St.). ✆ **03/517-8568.** Main courses NIS 55–NIS 80; business lunch specials until 5pm. Daily noon–11pm. Bus 4.

## On & Around Dizengoff Street
### MODERATE

**Goocha** ★★ SEAFOOD    For affordable seafood, plainly prepared, crowds flock to Babunya. Those who prefer their fish and shellfish with a bit more razzmatazz—in a coconut curry perhaps, or swathed in cream and chives, or in an Italian tomato sauce—come here. It's as popular as its rival, but bit more festive in atmosphere, with wine glass toting groups of diners spilling onto the streets as they await their tables and a soundtrack of rock and laughter inside. Among the many mouthwatering options, our favorites are the scallop skewers wrapped in smoked goose breast and the linguini with crab. *Note:* There are menu choices for meat eaters. A second, diner-style branch is at 14 Ibn Givrol St. This is also a great spot for late night snacks, take-aways, and tapas.

Dizengoff St. near Ben-Gurion Blvd. ✆ **03/522-2886.** Main courses NIS 50–NIS 120. Daily noon–after midnight. Bus 5.

**Tandoori ★★ INDIAN** Jews have lived for centuries in Bombay, and other Indian cities, and it is this heritage that's celebrated by owners Reena and Vinod Pushkarna. Their beautifully printed menu (it matches the serene and elegant atmosphere) carefully explains the exotic dishes and regional cuisines served here. Let the staff know if you want your choices with authentic, fiery seasonings (be careful!) or more toned down. A wide spectrum of foods from the Indian subcontinent are on offer, from banquet-style seafood, chicken and lamb courses, to lighter dinners of succulent, boneless Tandoori chicken, or chicken *tikka masala,* or an exotic (and economical) meal of vegetarian dishes with rice and wonderful Indian breads on the side. The all-you-can-eat lunch buffet here is one of the best values in town. In between courses, try refreshing *lassi,* a chilled yogurt-and-fruit drink. Reservations recommended.

2 Zamenhoff St. on Dizengoff Square. ✆ **03/629-6185.** Main courses NIS 45–NIS 90; lunch buffet (Sun–Thurs noon–3pm) NIS 69. Daily 12:30–3:30pm and 7pm–1am. Bus 5.

## INEXPENSIVE

**Big Mama ★★ ITALIAN** Famous for its thin crust pizza and delicious, affordable pasta dishes, in 2013 Big Mama reopened in this new location after a 6-year period without a home. Much rejoicing ensued (truly!). You can't go wrong here, no matter what you order—salads, focaccia, wines that taste much more expensive than they are. Main courses range from simple spaghetti laced with fresh vegetables to rich pasta dishes smothered white wine, butter, and cream and flecked with slices of roast goose or chicken. Portions are generous, and although the place is small and no frills, it's loaded with spirit.

95 HaHashmonaim St. near Dizengoff St. ✆ **03/504-8235.** Fixed menu meals NIS 39 (lunch) to NIS 59 (dinner), Sun–Fri noon to last customer; Sat noon–5pm. Bus 5.

**Café Batya ★ EUROPEAN/JEWISH** Opened by the legendary Batya Yom Tov in 1941, and personally run by the man until recently, this modest landmark of East European Jewish cooking remains a family affair with a devoted staff and following. In 2013 it moved to its new location near the Tel Aviv Cinematheque, but it continues to serve up such comforting classics as chicken soups, stuffed kishkas (intestines), chopped liver, goulash, cholent (baked Shabbat casserole), and brisket with potatoes—all of which are hard to find in trendy Tel Aviv. Desserts include simple stewed fruits, decor is utilitarian, and at the bar, you'll find plenty of vodka.

95 HaHashmonaim St., near Dizengoff St. ✆ **03/522-1335.** Main courses NIS 45–NIS 70. Daily 11am–10pm. Bus5.

# Along Allenby Street & Southward

This area is away from most hotels but contains some of the best restaurants in town.

## EXPENSIVE

**Catit ★★★ MEDITERRANEAN/FRENCH** Chef Meir Adoni's Catit offers the most justly praised menu in Tel Aviv. Born of Adoni's skill and creativity, and making

# A (usually) LOCALS-ONLY DINING EXPERIENCE

Probably Tel Aviv's best-kept restaurant secret, Hatikva is a vast area inhabited by Israeli families from such countries as Yemen and Iraq, and lengthy Etzel Street is virtually wall-to-wall with restaurants serving the foods of their heritage. That means skewered meats, Middle Eastern salads, and delicious Iraqi pita breads that the waiters obtain straight from the ovens of the many bakeries that dot the street—one of Etzel Street's mottoes is that an Iraqi pita more than 3 minutes old is stale!

The food is not only unusual and tasty, but affordable. Here you can purchase your meals by the skewer, which means you can put together a few choices like beef and turkey (about NIS 24 per skewer) plus a salad and french fries, and end up with a tasty, filling meal for around NIS 70. Or be more daring and order chicken hearts, or the *pièce de résistance* of Etzel Street restaurants: the enormously rich but delicate goose-liver skewer, barbecued to perfection and going for about NIS 40.

The street is like a food festival. Just pick out a place that looks busy and interesting (preferably next door to a bread bakery), and grab yourself a table.

**Getting there:** Pick up southbound bus no. 16 on Allenby Street near Mograbi Square, and ask the driver to let you off at Rehov Etzel in Hatikva. The ride from central Tel Aviv should take about 15 minutes.

use of traditions from around the Mediterranean, the menu's always changing but, as a constant, both appetizers and main courses contain many layers of tastes and ingredients. What do we mean? Consider a recent delight Adonis served up: grilled calamari stuffed with lamb and mozzarella then rolled into grilled eggplant and topped with goat yogurt, *techina,* roasted beans, and olive oil. A supremely complex dish, but one that worked like a charm. On that same day, foie gras was served, on grilled semolina with vanilla pastry and caramelized bananas in a sauce of veal stock and coffee (it was exquisite). Other elements of the meal are similarly flawless, including the smart wine list and the desserts, each of which looks like a work of art. The setting is simple but elegant—a background in which to savor the rich, complex dishes. Luncheon specials and prix-fixe dinners are offered. Reservations required.

57 Nahlat Binyamin. © **03/510-7001.** www.catit.co.il. Main courses at dinner NIS 170–NIS 230; lunch specials from NIS 140; 5-course menu for 2 from NIS 480. Daily noon–midnight.

**Mizlala By Meir Adoni** ★★★ CONTEMPORARY MEDITERRANEAN **Catit Restaurant** (see p. 174) offers the most praised menu in Israel. Mizlala is Adoni's younger, party-loving cousin—with an ambiance that seems more dance club than serious restaurant. But don't let the 20-something crowd, and bustling bar scene, fool you: The food is still the star here, though that star may be Lady Gaga (the fare can be quite quirky and eccentric). The daily changing, and always surprising, menu draws from many traditions. On a recent visit, *Mafroum,* a traditional North African dish of potatoes stuffed with calf sweetbreads was featured, served with gourmet hummus and pepper harissa.. Another offering was a play on Iraqi *kubbeh,* which is traditionally deep fried bulgur dumplings stuffed with ground meat. Here they were filled with shrimp and sea bass, and presented in a rustic stew of pancetta, mussels, *bamia* (okra), and beets. Some dishes nod to cuisines even farther afoot, like the very

American slow-cooked pork belly in whiskey and maple syrup that was on the menu recently. Come ready to experiment and enjoy. And if the prices at dinner are too hefty, pop by for business lunch, which tends to run between NIS 70 and NIS 95.

57 Nahalat Binyamin. ℰ **03/566-5505.** www.mizlala.co.il. Reservations necessary. Dinner for 1 NIS 300 without wine. Daily noon–4pm and 7pm–midnight. Bus 4

## MODERATE

**La Republica di Roni e Motti ★** ITALIAN   Chefs Roni Belfer and Motti Sofer preside over this benevolent "Republic", which welcomes visitors from breakfast through dinner with Italian food that is not only *molto autentico* but wonderfully fresh. That's because the chefs are also farmers, so the vegetables and herbs that enhance the dishes are all grown in the restaurant's organic garden (they make their own pasta by hand, too). After the small, complimentary antipasti, we recommend you order one of the seasonal salads, like *Fichi* (fresh figs, buffalo mozzarella, and basil-cured olives in balsamic dressing) and continue with a pasta dish, perhaps a *Tagliatelle* of mollusks and shrimps in lemon, butter, and white wine or the house special veal cannelloni. The staff is welcoming, and there are good choices of boutique Israeli wines.

3 Mazeh St. ℰ **03/647-0247.** Reservations recommended. Main Courses NIS 70–NIS 135. Sun–Fri 8:30am–midnight; Sat 9:30am–midnight.

**Nanutchka ★★** GEORGIAN/RUSSIAN   Nanutchka began as a place for tasty ethnic dishes, but has developed into a nighttime party spot, with people often dancing on the tables to Russian and Western rock, as well as traditional Georgian music, by the end of the evening. The party is fueled partly by the well-stocked bar, but also by the excellent Georgian menu of specialties like fried dumplings stuffed with goose and walnuts, lamb stews, and fresh-from-the-oven breads topped with egg and cheese.

30 Lilenblum St. ℰ **03/516-2254.** Reservations recommended. Main courses NIS 60–NIS 100; lunch (Sun–Thurs noon–5pm) NIS 48–NIS 68. Daily noon–2am. Bus 4.

# Yemenite Quarter & Carmel Market

Walk along Allenby Street from Mograbi Square, and at 54 Allenby, turn right and walk to the grid of little streets at the far end. This is the Yemenite Quarter (Karem Ha-Teimanim), a favorite of Tel Avivians and visitors alike. Built in 1909, it's one of the oldest parts of the city and its tangled streets harbor lots of scrumptious tiny eateries that might not be especially Yemenite, but do serve some of the tastiest Middle Eastern food in Tel Aviv.

## MODERATE

**Maganda ★** YEMENITE/MIDDLE EASTERN   Large and modern, Maganda nonetheless is known for a delicious, strictly kosher menu of Yemenite Middle Eastern grilled meats ranging from lamb *shashlik* (chunks of meat), kebabs (spiced ground meat), and skewered duck, livers, or fish, as well as oven-baked dishes like stuffed shoulder of lamb. It's traditional to start with an opening *meze* of Middle Eastern appetizers served with fresh Yemenite bread, followed by a calf's foot soup (a specialty, so you should try it) and baked vegetables stuffed with rice. In summer, dine on the roof terrace. Just be warned that Maganda is sometimes be overrun by tour groups. Enter the Yemenite Quarter, turn onto Najara Street and look for Maganda.

26 Rabbi Meir St. ℰ **057/934-5068.** Main courses NIS 55–NIS 90. prix fixe meals (for groups) NIS 85=NIS 145. Cash only. Sun–Thurs noon–midnight; Sat after Shabbat.

# Sheinkin Street

On the west side of Allenby Street, across from the Carmel Market, Sheinkin Street is sometimes called Tel Aviv's Greenwich Village. It's a mix of cafes, unusual shops, and family stores—a stroll and a meal here let you sample a slice of authentic Tel Aviv life away from touristy districts. King George Street, which makes a "V" with Sheinkin Street at Allenby, is home to a number of excellent and reasonably priced bakeries and nut shops—perfect if you'd like a snack for your hotel room.

**Orna and Ella ★★** CAFE   Of the many cafe/restaurants on Sheinkin Street, Orna and Ella is a longtime favorite and has the most devoted clientele. It's famous for sweet-potato pancakes, delicious cheesecakes, pastries, brioche, and espresso, but there are also sandwiches, salads, pastas, and main courses like Moroccan fish cakes and a chicken curry with basmati rice. This is a place for meetings, wine, and long conversations, so lines sometimes stretch out the door. It's both intimate and frenetic, and the waiters are charming and very Israeli.

33 Sheinkin St. ✆ **03/620-4753.** Light meals, snacks, and pastries NIS 25–NIS 88. Sun–Fri 10am–midnight; Sat 11am–midnight. Bus 4

# Neve Tzedek

After decades of neglect, this neighborhood, the oldest in the city, is coming alive with galleries, boutiques, cafes, and The Suzanne Dellal Center for Dance and Theater, the centerpiece for the revival of the area.

## INEXPENSIVE

**Suzanna ★★** MEDITERRANEAN   A charming spot that's a favorite with dancers from the nearby performance center, Suzanna is perfect for a quick bite (we especially recommend their soups and wonderful salads). If you want something more substantial, start you meal with delicious puff pastries filled with seafood in garlic cream or hearty liver and onions in pear sauce. For a main, try the chicken stuffed with couscous and dried fruits, lamb kebabs, or grilled fresh fish. You can also just stop in for coffee, dessert, or brioche. A breakfast menu is available until 1pm. Meals and drinks are served indoors in the garden or on the roof patio late into the night.

9 Shabazi St. ✆ **057/944-3060.** Main courses and light meals NIS 45–NIS 88. Daily 10am–2am.

# Near Ibn Givrol Street, Ha-Bimah & Mann Auditorium

Ibn Givrol Street runs through Tel Aviv's center of culture, from the Cinémathèque northward to Shderot Shaul Ha Melech, where you'll find the Tel Aviv Museum of Art and the Golda Meir/Tel Aviv Center for the Performing Arts. This area is lined with restaurants, including choices for fine dining as well as places for quick meals and post-theater coffee and cake. Rehov Ha'Arba'a, at the southern edge of the area, is wall-to-wall top-notch restaurants.

## EXPENSIVE

**Liliyot ★★** MODERN ISRAELI/KOSHER   A fine-dining establishment with a mission, for years Lillyot has been welcoming at risk youths into its kitchen and training them as chefs. Of course, that's not the prime reason you come here (that would be the food), but it's nice to know your money is going to such a good cause. Now, back to the food, which is always top quality, and often innovative. Recent offerings have included goose in citrus honey and cinnamon, sea bass with mango salsa, and salmon

Strategically located throughout the city, **Iceberg** is a local institution that keeps Tel Aviv cool and happy through the hotter months, with seasonal ice cream treats such as apricot or pear in wine. Our favorite two outlet of the chain is at **Tel Aviv Port**, at the **corner of Allenby Street and Rothschild Boulevard,** and at **108 Ben-Yehuda Street** (next to a wine bar called "Wineberg"). Icebergs are open daily, generally from 11am to 2am. Elsewhere in the city, look for **Aldo Ice Cream, at The Tel Aviv Port,** and at **107 Ibn Glvrol Blvd;** and **Dr. Lek on Yefet St. in Jaffa,** just 1 block north of the Clock Tower. For homemade Italian gelati and ices, our favorite is the **Yaffo Café,** 11 Olei Zion St., in the Jaffa Flea Market. They also serve wonderful apple pie, plus of salads, pastas, and frozen yogurts.

sashimi with cucumber and melon relish. The setting is as elegant as the plates, making this a good choice for a celebratory meal. Business lunch specials run from noon to 6pm. Reservations recommended.

4 Weizmann St. near Golda Meir Center. ✆ **03/609-1331.** Main courses NIS 75–NIS 205. Sun–Thurs noon–4pm and 6–11pm; Fri noon–3pm; Sat 2½ hours after Shabbat to 11:30pm.

**Messa** ★★★ MODERN ISRAELI  You dine here in white-on-white splendor right out of "Architectural Digest"—white drapes, white polished marble floors, and a long white communal table with a polished burl wood top running down the center of the dining room, surrounded by upholstered white armchairs. All the color is reserved for the food, and it *is* colorful, as well as mighty tasty. A first course might be seared portobello mushrooms served over corn polenta, tomatoes, Parmesan, truffle oil, and a poached egg. A main course could consist of seafood couscous in crab and lemon thyme sauce, or succulent lamb chops baked in focaccia with lemon butter, garlic confit, and cream of chili. Chef Moshe Aviv's is constantly changing the menu. In addition to the common banquet table, there are individual tables, a black on black bar, a fine wine list, and rich desserts. No need for black tie here, but come in your traveler's best. Reserve at least 2 days in advance.

19 Ha'Arba'a St. ✆ **03/685-6859.** Main courses NIS 88–NIS 190; some dishes available in ¾ portions; fixed-price lunches from NIS 90. Daily noon–3:30pm and 7–11:30pm.

## MODERATE

**Pasha** ★ MIDDLE EASTERN  Pasha offers a large, kosher menu of traditional Middle Eastern appetizers and main courses in a pleasant, lively setting. Go beyond the grilled skewers of meat, though, as the best dishes are the stuffed vegetables and family-style offerings like baked lamb *moussakan* (served on toasted sumac pita) or *maklouba,* a softly seasoned chicken and rice casserole. To end the meal, you'll choose from a variety of coffees (including a thick Arabic/Turkish brew) and authentic Arabic desserts. The combination of tasty food and reasonable prices has been a real hit—branches of Pasha are opening all over Israel. The house bread (extra charge) is delicious and great with first courses. Reservations recommended.

8 Ha'Arba'a St. ✆ **03/561-7778** or 057-942-8685. Main courses NIS 58–NIS 120. Sun–Thurs noon–midnight; Fri noon–4pm.

## INEXPENSIVE
**Giraffe Noodle Bar** ★★ PAN-ASIAN   It ain't all noodles (or giraffes) here, though hearty, spicy noodle plates of Pad Thai and Japanese soba noodles are quite popular. If you're with a large group, vary your order and share dim sum, Asian salads, sushi, and *gyoza* (dumplings), or perhaps calamari in red curry sauce. Indian and Afghani dishes add to the interesting choices. The menu finishes with French and Italian-style desserts. Ambiance is casual with sidewalk seating in good weather.

49 Ibn Givrol St. ℂ **03/691-6294.** Main courses NIS 45–NIS 65. Daily noon–1am.

# North by the Yarkon River

The neighborhood, just south of the Yarkon River, sometimes called Little Tel Aviv, is centered on Yirmiyahu Street, a short street near the point where Ben-Yehuda and Dizengoff streets meet, a block from the bend in the Yarkon. Take a bus or a cab north on Ha-Yarkon, Ben-Yehuda, or Dizengoff streets all the way to Yirmiyahu.

## INEXPENSIVE
**Hungarian Blintzes** ★ BLINTZES   Tel Avivians have loved this spot for almost 40 years. Choices range from blintzes filled with sweet cheese or apples to hearty, mushroom goulash blintzes in a paprika sauce. The menu also offers salads and Hungarian soups. During Shavuot, when dairy dishes are traditionally eaten, reservations are needed for this little Xanadu for blintze aficionados.

35 Yirmiyahu St. ℂ **057/943-9675.** Main courses NIS 40–NIS 60. AE, DC, MC, V. Sun–Thurs 12:30pm–1am; Fri noon–3:30; Sat after Shabbat. Bus: 4.

**Shtsupak Fish Restaurant** ★★ SEAFOOD   The food and ambiance here is very similar to, but perhaps a tiny step above, its rival, Barbunya (see p. 172). That's because Shtsupak offers a more leisurely pace at the meal, portions that are a bit more generous, and a wider range of sauces and *meze* appetizers (included in the price.) There's also a sidewalk dining terrace, a nice touch. All of which is why we think it's worth the walk or taxi ride from the hotel district. Reservations recommended.

256 Ben-Yehuda St. ℂ **03/544-1973.** Complete meals NIS 60–NIS 90. Mon–Sat noon–midnight.

# In the Tel Aviv Port

The old Tel Aviv Port used to be a derelict stretch of warehouses and garages along the northern stretch of Tel Aviv's beachfront. It's now booming with some of the city's most stylish restaurants, shops, and bars, all linked by a boardwalk promenade. The Port is bustling through the wee hours, but its also a favorite spot for a relaxing beach-front breakfast or lunch. In addition to the restaurants below, there are snack and bakery counters, bars, food markets and other restaurant for every need and interest.

Cars and taxis must stay outside the perimeter of the vast, fenced-in port, which is an added plus—pedestrians entering the entire enclave are checked by security guards at each of the port's gates.

To get here, take bus no. 4 or 5, or sherut no. 4. Taxis will let you off at the closest gate to the restaurant or bar of your choice. Most people just browse and find a restaurant they'd like to try, but after 8pm or on weekends, you'll need a reservation. After dinner, you can stroll out to the old Redding Electric Plant, which is now used as a venue for exhibitions, on a distant point at the northern end of the complex.

## EXPENSIVE

**Mul Yam** ★★★ SEAFOOD    Consistently ranked as one of the world's top seafood restaurants—it's the only Isreali listing on "Les Grandes Tables du Monde," a French honor roll of the 158 best restaurants on the planet—Mul Yam has been going strong since 1995. Chef Yoram Nitzan is no follower of the locavore movement. Several times a week, he flies in the finest seafood from all corners of the globe: lobster from Nova Scotia, mussels from Denmark, oysters from France, tuna from Sri Lanka—you get the picture. It's then crafted into perfectly composed dishes, some simple and some wildly complex, all exquisite. Not surprisingly, prices are very, very high, reflecting the cost of transporting the ingredients (and that includes the wines, which are often from boutique, small-production wineries in France). Mul Yam's 2013 cookbook, Seafoodpedia, was awarded a Gourmand World Cookbook prize, the first such win for an Israeli book.

Tel Aviv Port, Hangar 23. ℂ **03/546-9920.** www.mulyam.com/indexEn.html. Main courses NIS 170–over NIS 300; lunch specials start at NIS 170. Sun–Fri 12:30–3:30pm and 7:30–10:30pm; Sat 1–4pm and 7:30–11pm. Bus 4.

## MODERATE

**Boya** ★★ MEDITERRANEAN    Boya occupies a choice spot on the board walk overlooking the sea—on breezy nights if you dine on the deck, the spray will dust you and your dinner. The menu is gigantic and trendy, ranging from Mediterranean tapas to salmon in barbecue sauce on bok choy to darn good seafood linguine. Among desserts, Boya makes its own version of traditional Arabic sweet-cheese *kanafeh* (which you order 20 minutes in advance so it can be made fresh). If you're looking to save, go for the fixed price meals (available at breakfast, lunch, and dinner). The bar is extensive, offering more than a dozen different types of beer. Reservations are suggested.

Tel Aviv Port. ℂ **03/544-6166.** Reservations Main courses NIS 70–NIS 140. Sat–Thurs 9am–midnight; Fri 8:30am–1am. Bus 4.

# On Almah Beach North of Jaffa
## MODERATE

**Manta Ray** ★★ SEAFOOD    With a pavilion open to the sea on a quiet stretch of beach between Tel Aviv and Jaffa, this is a great place to watch the rolling waves by day, or take in the sunset while you dine. The delicious meal starts when you choose from an offering of 12 small appetizers brought around by your waiter (the fish and seafood tapas are best—make sure to have the dishes explained to you and choose a few that you like). Stars among main courses include sage-scented sea bass, the vegetarian chestnut risotto with Manchego cheese, and the seafood plate prepared in four house special styles. A seafront table is essential. Call ahead to reserve one.

Almah Beach, near Dan Panorama Hotel. ℂ **03/517-4773.** Main courses NIS 80–NIS 130. Daily 9am–midnight. Bus: 10 from Tel Aviv to Jaffa; get out at the David InterContinental Hotel stop.

# Jaffa
## EXPENSIVE

**Cordelia** ★★★ MODERN FRENCH    Set in a 1,000-year-old Crusader-era building lit by candlelight that's reflected in scores of mirrors, Cordelia is a delightfully theatrical place to dine. And that applies to Chef Nir Zook's cuisine as well as the decor. On his changing menu, the chef will often whip up a pâté of liver encrusted with black sesame seeds disguised to look like marble halvah covered with chocolate sprinkles; or set before his guests ostrich meat dusted in cocoa. The young chef (he's about 35) got his start cooking elaborate dinner parties for friends, who insisted he open his own place. To get a taste of those over-the-top feasts, order the chef's menu or the 8-course tasting menu. By the way, be sure to try anything with goat cheeses which is produced at his family's farm and is extraordinarily good. Around the corner, at Nir Zook's eccentric **Noa Bistro** you can sample a bit of Zook's simpler food for more moderate prices. He also owns the nearby **Jaffa Bar,** a temple of mixology.

30 Yefet St. www.cordelia.co.il ℂ **03/518-4668.** Main courses NIS 86–NIS 180; Mon–Sat noon–3pm and 7pm–midnight. Turn right at 30 Yefet St. into Simtat Hazhuhit, a wide, arched alley on the right as you walk up Yefet St. from the Clock Tower.

## MODERATE/EXPENSIVE

**Margaret Tayar's** ★★★ SEAFOOD   Margaret, with her tiny kitchen and gardened patio by the sea at the foot of Old Jaffa's hill, is a legend. Jaffa's fishermen bring Margaret the best of the daily catch, and after she's chosen, the gourmet restaurants of Tel Aviv can have their pick. Savvy locals, as well as Israel's most renowned chefs come here to relax and be inspired by Margaret's unforced, luscious cooking, which has won accolades from "Gourmet" and other international publications. To this day, Margaret prepares everything herself, starting with her homemade *meze* medleys of rich North African appetizers and salads. Moving on you'll find stuffed grape leaves with rice, pine nuts, and raisins drizzled with olive oil and served with a dollop of thick country yogurt, followed by a perfectly grilled whole fish with spicy quince or kumquat sauce or her signature deep-fried fillet of fresh sardines stuffed with "caviar." Non-fish dishes can include artichoke hearts stuffed with lamb or flavor-filled vegetarian or meat couscous. As the spirit moves her, Margaret may make tidbits like earthy strudel stuffed with Middle Eastern fruits, which you order early in your meal so it will be fresh from the oven in time for dessert. Ambiance is casual, made for intimate conversations as you catch the Mediterranean breezes while you dine. Always call to confirm opening hours, as they can be erratic.

4 Retsif Ha-Aliyah Shenei St. ℂ **03/682-4741.** Main courses NIS 60–NIS 120. Cash only. Oct–May Mon–Sat 1–7pm; June–Sept Mon–Fri noon–4pm and 7pm–midnight, Sat noon–7pm. Closed Sun. Bus: 10 to Jaffa Clock Tower.

## INEXPENSIVE

**Aladin** ★ MIDDLE EASTERN   The food here is standard, but the setting spectacular: a 600-year-old building with covered terraces overlooking a minaret, the sea, and the Tel Aviv coastline—fabulous for sunset watching over a leisurely dinner. As for the menu, it includes a selection of Middle Eastern salads with pita bread, followed by grilled fish or meat paired with a glass of wine. Aladin can get busy as its vista is in demand. Reservations are not accepted.

5 Mifratz Shlomo St., on hill of Old Jaffa. ℂ **03/682-6766.** Main courses NIS 50–NIS 94. Daily 11am–1am. Bus 10 to Clock Tower.

**Dr. Shakshuka** ★★ KOSHER NORTH AFRICAN   Tell an Israeli you're heading to Jaffa for the first time and he'll insist you dine at Dr. Shakshuka. Just to the side of the flea market, and with the same chaotic yet ebullient spirit, this courtyard restaurant's does the best version of its signature dish in Israel. Shakshuka, by the way, is a spicy yet comforting tomato stew, served here in a battered frying pan, and topped with a fried egg. Once you've tried it, you'll find that you crave it, even after you leave Israel. Sure this popular, family-run restaurant serves other dishes (the shwarma is just fine and the authentic Libyan-style couscous is even better than fine), but you come here for the signature dish. And for the illusion that you've stumbled into a swell street party. One note: You'll

# GOURMET GRAZING in & near jaffa

Inside the harbor of the Old Jaffa Port, **Jaffa Port Market** (Jaffamarket.co.il; open Mon-Sat 9am-11pm)is Tel Aviv's newest magnet for foodies, opened in 2012. Here, in addition to purchasing exotic ingredients and gourmet kitchen utensils, you can make a meal from food stalls, many of which are branches of some of the Tel Aviv area's best-loved local food sources. They sell a huge variety of goods: pastries, Mediterranean tapas, wines, chocolates, scrumptious deli sandwiches, hummus, bouillabaisse, you name it. You can even try traditional Arabic *kannafeh*, a sweet cheese dish

made here by a *kannafeh mayivin* in regular, sugar-free, and gluten-free.

About 2.4km (1½ miles) south of Old Jaffa and the port area is Jabalya (in Hebrew sometimes "Givat Aliya") Beach. You need a car or a taxi to get to this out-of-the-way area. Tel Avivians in the know patronize the excellent seafood restaurants here, enjoying the unobstructed views of the sunset. Long neglected, this neighborhood has become a piece of prime residential real estate. There's a public beach with safe swimming and changing rooms at the foot of the hill.

likely be seated with strangers at one of the restaurants long communal tables unless you bring a group. Take that as an opportunity. And don't miss the doctor's lemonade.

4 Beit Eshel St. ✆ **03/518-6560.** Main courses NIS 40–NIS 80. Sun–Thurs 8am–midnight; noon–4pm. Bus: 10 to Clock Tower.

**Said el Abu Lafia and Sons Pita Bakery** ★★ BAKERY   A much-loved Jaffa landmark, this aromatic bakery sells direct from-the-oven, personal-size, traditional Arabic pita-bread pizzas, stuffed breads, and Palestinian-style cheese, potato, and vegetable *burekas*. Everything is delicious (and very filling), and although there is no seating, you can take your purchases across Yefet Street up onto the hill of Old Jaffa to the sidewalk benches (there are lovely sea views up here). Bring lots of napkins. Don't confuse Abu Lafia's with neighboring imitations. Cash only.

7 Yefet St. 1 block south of the Clock Tower. ✆ **03/683-4958.** Baked goods NIS 8–NIS 18. Mon–Sat 8am–10pm. Bus: 10 to Jaffa's Clock Tower.

## MODERATE

**Hinawi Grill and Abu Nassar On The Hill Fish and Seafood Restaurant** ★★ MEAT/SEAFOOD   Abu Nassar Seafood and Hinawi Meats are two classic Tel Aviv institutions that have combined under one roof to provide the best of two worlds. The restaurant's a bit out of the way, but it's worth making the trek as the food is special without being pretentious, the setting is a spacious modern pavilion with a large dining deck overlooking the sea, and you get to experience a place that locals love. Prices are very fair, and you can dine on the freshest seafood or top-quality meats, all served in generous portions. First comes an extensive Arabic *meze*, of small dishes served with freshly toasted garlic pita. Tasty grilled fish is the staple here (including interesting catch of the day choices) but a favorite, available as a first or main course, is the house special calamari stuffed with shrimp, pine nuts, and parsley cooked in garlic and butter. At dinnertime and weekends, the eatery is filled with happy Jewish and Israeli Arab families and a cheerful spirit, and no matter how busy, service is friendly and helpful. Reservations are necessary Thursday through Saturday.

130 Kedem St., overlooking Jabalya (Givat Aliya) Beach, Jaffa. ℂ **03/507-5539** or 03/506-7132. Fixed-price meals NIS 70–NIS 120. Daily noon–midnight. 2.4km (1½ miles) south of Old Jaffa, in a residential part of the city. Taxi is best option.

# EXPLORING TEL AVIV
## The Top Attractions
### MUSEUMS

**Beit Hatfutsot/Diaspora Museum** ★★★ MUSEUM  What was the fate of the Jewish people from the time they left the Holy Land some 2500 years ago until their return after World War II? That question is at the heart of this extraordinary museum, an innovative, multi-media complex that looks at the myriad of ways Jewish culture morphed in each part of the world, developing distinctive religious rituals, modes of dress, culinary traditions and much more. Alas, until 2016, the museum's enormous "Core Exhibition,"—originally created in 1978 and the heart and soul of the museum—will be mostly closed, while a cutting-edge "New Core Exhibition" is under construction. Meanwhile, the museum will host visiting exhibits; and bits and pieces of the permanent collection will remain open, like the video archive of films about dozens of Jewish communities from the past and present, the audio library of ethno-musicology, and the Family Genealogy Center. Check the museum website for current hours and to see what's available when you visit.

Tel Aviv University campus, off Klausner St. inside the Matatia Gate (University Gate 2). ℂ **03/745-7808.** www.bh.org.il. Admission NIS 40 for core exhibit; NIS 70 for all exhibits and Family Gallery, discounts for students and seniors. Sun–Tues and Thurs 10am–4pm; Wed 10am–7pm; Fri 9am–1pm. Closed Sat and Jewish holidays; call ahead for special tour reservations. Bus: 7, 25, 274, 271, 222.

**Eretz Israel Museum** ★★★ MUSEUM  At the heart of the fascinating museum is an actual archeological site. Called **Tel Qasile,** it contains 12 layers of settlement, meaning visitors can view an excavated Canaanite temple and enter a reconstructed house from the pre-Israelite era—approximately B.C. 1100! But this dig is just the beginning of the wonders of this university-like campus, which has eight other pavil-ions dedicated to other intriguing subjects. The **Glass Pavilion** houses a rare collection of vessels, some dating back to 1500 B.C; it's one of the largest collections of ancient glass in the world. The **Ethnography pavilion** displays judaica, folk-crafts, costumes, and an exquisite collection of antique Chanukah menorahs from across the world. **The Nechustan Pavilion** explores the topics of mining and metallurgy during the biblical era. **"The Man and His Work Center"** is set up like a bazaar in which you can watch men and women engaged in ancient industries such as weaving, olive-pressing, glass-blowing, pottery-making, basketry, clothing, and tool design. There's also a garden of ancient mosaic floors from all over Israel. Covering the contemporary world are the **Lasky Planetarium** offering Hebrew-language shows of astronomy, and visiting exhibits of works by contemporary artisans—in 2013 an imaginative exhibit of modern sand art drew huge crowds; 2014 promises a remarkable exhibit of paper art. The Museum Gift shop is topnotch, featuring inventive gifts special to the Holy Land, as well as beautiful items of contemporary design. There's a good cafe on the premises.

2 Chaim Levanon St., Ramat Aviv. ℂ **03/641-5244.** www.eretzmuseum.org.il. Admission NIS 42; admission to planetarium plus museum NIS 74. Discount for students and children. Sun–Wed 10am–4pm; Thurs 10am–8pm (Ethnography and Folklore only until 4pm); Fri 10am–2pm. Bus: 13, 7, 24, 25, 27, 45, 74, 86, or 274.

**Helena Rubinstein Pavilion** ★ ART MUSEUM   This pavilion, now a part of The Tel Aviv Museum of Art, is used for visiting exhibitions and special exhibits from that museum's main collection.

6 Tarsat Blvd. ✆ **03/528-7196.** Admission NIS 45, includes admission to Tel Aviv Museum of Art. Mon, Wed, and Sat 10am–4pm; Tues and Thurs 10am–10pm; Fri 10am–2pm and 7–10pm. Bus: 5, 18, or 25.

**Tel Aviv Museum of Art** ★★ ART MUSEUM   Housing the world's largest collection of Israeli art, the Tel Aviv Museum of Art is also famed for its 20th century Russian art holdings, its strong collections of pieces from all the modernist movements, and choice works of international Impressionism and Expressionism. Always energetic and lively, the museum's architecturally exciting Herta and Paul Amir Building (added to the museum's original structure in 2011) is one of Israel's architectural masterpieces and exhibits contemporary Israeli art and design. Special treasures in the permanent collection include works by Gustav Klimt, Picasso, Kandinsky, Chagall, Modigliani, and the Roy Lichtenstein mural in the entrance lobby. The museum sponsors a superb program of concerts, films, and lectures, as well as architecture tours of Tel Aviv. The Museum Shop sells items of elegant, modern design.

27 Shaul Ha-Melekh Blvd. ✆ **03/607-7020** for info and box office. www.tamuseum.com. Admission NIS 48, includes admission to Helena Rubinstein Pavilion. Discounts for students. Mon, Wed, and Sat 10am–4pm; Tues and Thurs 10am–10pm; Fri 10am–2pm and 7–10pm. Bus: 9, 18, 28, 70, 90, or 111.

## MORE ATTRACTIONS

**Bauhaus Center** ★ GALLERY   Tel Avivians now understand the rich Bauhaus/International Style heritage of their city, and this gallery/boutique is dedicated to the architectural design and decor of these movements. The center is famous for its tours of Tel Aviv's Bauhaus treasures. Call for tour information/reservation.

99 Dizengoff St. ✆ **03/522-0249.** www.bauhaus-center.com. Free admission. Sun–Thurs 10am–7pm; Fri 10am–2pm; Sat noon–7pm. Tours given Fri 10am from Bauhaus Center' Price NIS 60.

**Ben-Gurion House** ★ HISTORIC SITE   The house and personal items remain as they were when Paula and David Ben-Gurion lived here. Ben-Gurion's impressive personal library, comprising some 20,000 books, bears witness to his knowledge and scholarship. The building itself is an interesting example of Bauhaus/International design. Most of the signs in the house are in Hebrew, but this will not detract much from your visit. In the bedroom, note a blocked-in window used as a bomb shelter.

17 Ben-Gurion Blvd. ✆ **03/522-1010.** Free admission. Sun and Tues–Thurs 8am–3pm; Mon 8am–5pm; Fri 8am–noon; Sat 11am–2pm. Bus: 4 or 5.

**Bet Bialik Museum** ★ HISTORIC SITE/MUSEUM   This was the home of Haim Nachman Bialik from 1925 to 1933. Bialik, a giant in Israeli literature, was among the first modern poets to write in Hebrew. Except for a short English brochure, there are no English explanations of the manuscripts, books, and literary artifacts displayed here, but the house (beautifully restored in 2010) is fascinating for its 1920s Tel Aviv architecture, furnishings, and feel for a cultured European world freshly transferred to the Middle East. The house is also adorned with paintings by Jewish artists from the era of British Mandate Palestine. A stop here can be combined with a visit to the nearby Rubin Museum, home of the artist Reuven Rubin (see below).

22 Bialik St. ✆ **03/525-4530.** Free admission. Sun–Thurs 9am–4:30pm; Sat 11am–2pm. Closed Sat in Aug and Fri year-round. Bus: 4.

**Haganah Museum** ★ MUSEUM   Before the establishment of the State of Israel, Haganah was the provisional organization that provided for the protection of the Jewish community in Palestine. It was the forerunner of the Israeli Defense Forces. This museum, located in the house of one of Haganah's founders, traces the history of Haganah, from the earliest defensive watch towers guarding 19th century farms, to the struggle for independence in the 1940s and its development as Israel's modern army. There is brief background information in English. It is especially interesting when troops of young Israeli soldiers are brought through on educational tours.

23 Rothschild Blvd, near Allenby St. ℰ **03/560-8624.** Admission/donation NIS 10. Sun–Thurs 8am–4pm. Bus: 4 or 5.

**Independence Hall** ★ HISTORIC SITE   Home of Meir Dizengoff, the first mayor of Tel Aviv, it was in this historic house that the independence of Israel was declared on May 14, 1948. Exhibits here detail this period of Israeli history.

16 Rothschild Blvd. ℰ **03/517-3942.** Admission NIS 12. Sun–Thurs 9am–2pm.

**Museum of the History of Tel Aviv-Jaffa** ★ MUSEUM   Tel Aviv's carefully restored old City Hall, built in 1927, now houses displays of historical photographs, documents, and a video that tell the story of Tel Aviv's early decades.

27 Bialik St. ℰ **03/517-3052.** Free admission. Sun–Thurs 9am–2pm. Bus: 4.

**Rubin Museum (Reuven House)** ★ ART MUSEUM   One of Israel's most popular and acclaimed artists, Reuven Rubin (1893–1974) painted the landscape of Mandate Palestine and the young Israeli State. Today, the modernist home of the artist, dating from 1930, houses a collection of his work, a gallery for temporary exhibits of modern Israeli art, and a multimedia presentation of Rubin's life. On the top floor, Rubin's studio and living space have been kept as he left them. Stop here after visiting the home of Israel's first great Hebrew writer, Haim Nachman Bialik (see above).

14 Bialik St. www.rubinmuseum.org.il. ℰ **03/525-5961.** Admission NIS 20, free for children. Mon and Wed–Thurs 10am–3pm; Tues 10am–8pm; Sat 11am–2pm. Call ahead: may be closed Sat July–Aug.

**Safari Park (Zoological Center)** ★ ZOO   Founded in the 1970s, this park is a wide-open plain (100 hectares/247 acres) where African animals roam free. The park has been so successful with breeding hippos, elephants, giraffes, and other animals that it exports creatures all over the world. For obvious reasons, visitors must remain in closed vehicles while traversing the 8km (5-mile) trail, but there is a shorter walking trail, as well. You'll have the opportunity to see lions, rhinos, gazelles, impalas, zebras, ostriches, storks, and much more. There's also a monkey enclosure, as well as an aviary and reptile area. Add a star to the current rating if you have children with you. The lion area closes an hour before the rest of the park. Across the street is the Ramat Gan National Park (free admission), with even more animals.

Ramat Gan. ℰ **03/631-3531.** Admission NIS 58; additional charge for Safari Bus if you don't have a car. Sat–Thurs and holidays 9am–4pm Sept–June; until 5pm July–Aug; Fri 9am–1pm year-round. Visitors may remain in the park for 1 hr. after the last entrance hour. Closed only on Holocaust Memorial Day, Israel Memorial Day, Yom Kippur Eve, and Yom Kippur. Bus: 30 (Yona Ha-Navi St.), 35 (Central Bus Station), or 67 (Central Ramat Gan).

# Jaffa ★★★

Now an integrated component in the sprawling Tel Aviv–Jaffa complex, Jaffa has a long and colorful history, dating from biblical times. This is the port, the Bible tells us, where King Solomon's ally, the Phoenician King Hiram of Tyre, landed cedars of Lebanon for the construction of Solomon's Temple. From here Jonah embarked for his adventure with the whale. The Greeks were here too, and they fostered the legend that a poor maiden named Andromeda, chained to a rock and on the verge of being sacrificed to a sea monster, was rescued by Perseus on his winged white horse. Today, visitors are shown this rock, a tourist attraction since ancient times.

But that's just the beginning of Jaffa's history: The Crusaders also came this way. And Richard the Lion-Hearted built a citadel here that was promptly snatched away by Saladin's brother, who slaughtered 20,000 Christians in the process. Napoleon passed through 600 years or so later; a few Jewish settlers came in the 1890s; and Allenby routed the Turks from the port in 1917.

One Jewish legend has it that all the sunken treasure in the world flows toward Jaffa, and that in King Solomon's day the sea offered a rich bounty, accounting for the king's wealth. Today, Jaffa still shows traces of its romantic and mysterious past. The city is built into a kind of amphitheater on the side of a hill. The old section of the city has become the starlit patio of Tel Aviv, providing an exceptional view, fine restaurants, and the most beautifully restored Old City in Israel. The flea market district, near the Clock Tower, is ramshackle but has real personality.

Tel Aviv'a Ha-Yarkon Street runs into Jaffa's Yefet Street where the landmark stone **Clock Tower** and the large Turkish mosque, Mahmudiye (1812), remind you of the city's continuing Arab community.

## A STROLL AROUND OLD JAFFA ★★★

The reclamation of Old Jaffa—only a short time ago it was a slumlike area of war ruins and crumbling Turkish palaces—has proven to be one of the most imaginative projects in Israel.

**Yefet Street,** near the landmark **Clock Tower** (built in 1896 to commemorate the reign of the Ottoman Turkish sultan) is the place to start exploring. On the west side of Yefet Street is the vast 19th century **Mahmoudiye Mosque.** Although closed to the public, you can peek past its impressive gates to see a glimpse of the courtyard and hear the calls to prayer that drift over the neighborhood five times a day. On the east side of Yefet Street (as you walk south), you'll find the streetside counters of Abulafia's bakery, famous throughout Israel for its freshly baked snacks. Just beyond Abulafia's, are the streets leading eastward into Jaffa's motley but always interesting **Flea Market and Covered Bazaars,** selling everything from old jeans and British Mandate Era detritus to old Persian tiles and reproductions of antique Hanukkah menorahs. To your right, as you walk south on Yefet Street, is an uphill road that leads to the beautifully gardened hill of Old Jaffa, with its stunning views of the Tel Aviv coastline. At the summit is the open space of **Kikar Kedumim,** the central plaza, and at one side of it, the **Franciscan Monastery of Saint Peter,** which was built above a medieval citadel. The church commemorates the visit of Saint Peter to Jaffa, and the raising from the dead of Tabitha. Opposite the church is an excavation area, surrounded by a fence, where you can inspect remnants of a **3rd-century-**B.C. **catacomb.** Facing the catacomb is a hilltop garden, **Gan Ha-Pisgah,** atop which, surrounded by trees, is a white monument depicting scenes from the Bible: the conquest of Jericho, the near-sacrifice of Isaac, and Jacob's dream.

Past the church gardens, on the sea side of the hill, you can wander through Old Jaffa for a superb all-encompassing views of Tel Aviv and the Mediterranean coastline. Incidentally, **Andromeda's Rock** is traditionally the most prominent of those blackened stones jutting up from the floor of the bay. The view is brilliant in the morning sunlight and magical at sunset and into the dark of the evening.

Returning to Kikar Kedumim, you enter the restored maze of Old Jaffa's picturesque, cobblestone market streets, filled with interesting Crusader-era architecture, eateries, artists' studios, galleries, antiques, and souvenir shops. For those interested in art and interior design, the **Ilana Goor Museum** (www.ilanagoor.com; ✆ **03/683-7676**) is a delightful stop. It's a beautifully renovated mansion/gallery of one of Israel's most successful sculptors who also specializes in furniture and jewelry design. Over the centuries, this building has been put to many uses, including a long stint as a caravansary for 19th-century Jewish pilgrims. Now each room is like a page out of fancy architecture magazine, filled with Goor's own works and her private collection of art. Before entering, ask if the rooftop cafe is open. It has good food and sweeping views. The admission fee is rather steep (NIS 35), but the building is interesting architecturally, and there are often temporary exhibits of Israeli artists. It's open Sunday to Friday from 10am to 4pm and Saturday from 10am to 6pm.

A short (.5km/⅓-mile) stroll south of Old Jaffa brings you to the old port area of **Jaffa Harbor,** now being developed into a food market and promenade of dockside restaurants and small eateries.

**Visitor's Center/Museum of Antiquities of Tel Aviv Jaffa (Jaffa Museum)** MUSEUM   This beautiful building was actually a Turkish administrative and detention center during the 19th century. Displays include objects excavated from 30 sites within the city, covering a time span beginning in the 5th millennium B.C. and ending with the Arab period.

10 Mifratz Shlomo St. ✆ **03/682-5375.** Admission NIS 20; half-price for seniors, students, and children. Sun–Thurs 9am–1pm. To get here, at the top of the hill in Old Jaffa, walk from Kikar downhill on Mifratz Shlomo St. The visitor's center/museum will be on your right.

**Simon's House** RELIGIOUS SITE   Christian tradition places the house of Simon the Tanner (venerated by Christian pilgrims for centuries) next to the lighthouse of the port, at the site of a small mosque. Acts 10 recalls St. Peter's visit to Simon's house in "Joppa."

8 Shimon Ha-Burski St. ✆ **03/683-6792.** Free admission. Daily 8–11:45am and 2–4pm; until 6:30pm in summer. To get here, walk south through Kikar Kedumim, the main square of restored Old Jaffa. At the end of the square, turn right to the steps.

See Organized Tours (below) for information on Walking Tour of Jaffa.

# ORGANIZED TOURS & SPECIAL EVENTS

**ORGANIZED TOURS**   The **Jaffa Visitor Center** (✆ **03/682-6796**) in Kikar Kedumim, right at the center of the restored section of Old Jaffa, gives out free detailed maps accompanied by historical information that makes it easy to do a self-guided tour of the area. The Jaffa Visitor Center also rents a **self-guided audio tour** for NIS 45. The helpful center is open Sunday to Thursday from 9am to 6pm. The **Association for Tourism of Tel Aviv–Jaffa** leads a free walking tour of Old Jaffa starting at the Clock Tower on Yefet Street (bus no. 10 from Tel Aviv) on Wednesday mornings at 9:30am. Call or surf to the site the **Tel Aviv Tourist Information Office** (46 Herbert Samuel St.; ✆ **03/516-6188;** www.visit-tlv.com) for current information.

Want to see Tel Aviv itself on foot? The association arranges, for a fee, excellent English-language guided tours of Neve Tzedek and of the Bauhaus areas of the city;

advance booking is required. Or enlist the help of the **Tel Aviv Tourist Information Office** (see above) which gives out municipal maps with four **"Orange" self-guided walking tours** ★★★ of Tel Aviv marked on the map. Signs along the routes mark the way as you go. Some of the routes are too long to undertake on a sweltering summer day, but if you break them up into smaller units, they are a solid itinerary of what to see in different neighborhoods. The tourist office also coordinates free walking tours of **Tel Aviv University, Art and Architecture** (Mon at 11am); **Tel Aviv By Night** (Tues at 8pm); and **Bauhaus Architecture of the White City** (Sat at 11am). Always recheck with the tourist office for times, dates, and starting points.

*Tip:* If you're a guest at the Center, Cinema, Melody, or Shalom hotels in the Atlas chain, they'll lend you free bikes for touring.

Another good source of guided tours is the **Society for the Protection of Nature in Israel (SPNI),** 85 Nahalat Binyamin St. (📞 **03/566-0960;** www.teva.org.il). Call 📞 **03/638-8625** for information on the society's English-language walking tours in the Tel Aviv area. These are highly recommended group tours that individuals can join. Day tours cost NIS 80 to NIS 300 per person, but there are longer tours and occasionally free Saturday walking tours. Go to the American Friends of SPNI website (www. aspni.org) and reserve as far in advance as possible. Most tours are given in Hebrew, but in many cases, the guide can give you a brief English translation.

**Boat Tours** from Jaffa Port to the Tel Aviv Marina and back (depending on demand and weather) run on Saturday and cost NIS 30. Call **Kef** (📞 **03/682-9070**) or **Sababa** (📞 **03/681-6739**) in Jaffa Port for schedules and reservations.

**SPECIAL/FREE EVENTS**   Many summer evenings after 8pm, there is free samba dancing on the Herbert Samuel Esplanade, beside the beach in South Tel Aviv. There is also music and dancing at other points along the beach on evenings throughout the week; free concerts are held in Yarkon Park and in Old Jaffa during the summer months. Check in person with Tel Aviv Tourist Information (see above).

**Nahalat Binyamin** Pedestrian Mall has an active, interesting outdoor **Craft Bazaar** and street performers every Tuesday and Friday from 10am to 5pm. Take bus no. 4.

# OUTDOOR PURSUITS & SPORTS

**BEACHES**   Tel Aviv's seashore is within walking distance of Dizengoff Square. A promenade runs the entire length of the beach. Most beaches have free showers and facilities for changing. **Dolphinarium Beach north to the Chinky (Drums) Beach near Mograbi Square** attracts a younger crowd, and on Friday afternoons, as the Sabbath approaches, drumming circles develop. The cleanest beaches, with the best swimming, are behind the Dan and Sheraton hotels (Frishman–Gordon sts.) northward to the Hilton hotel. The **Hilton Beach** is especially **gay friendly,** but also hosts a mix of families and surfers. Farther north, the **Nordau Beach is reserved for religious Jews,** with visitors segregated by sex according to alternate days of the week, starting with women on Sundays.

*Warning:* Swimming at Israel's Mediterranean beaches can be dangerous. The problem is riptides and whirlpools that even a strong swimmer can't fight. It's safe, however, to swim at beaches where guards are stationed. Pay attention to the safety symbols along the beaches in the form of small flags. Black flags mean absolutely no swimming in the area, red warns you to be especially cautious, and white indicates that the water's fine. Tel Aviv's city beaches are protected in many places by a system of breakwaters and are the safest in the area.

**BOATS**   Small motorboats, pedal boats, and rowboats can be rented by the hour daily from 9am to 6pm on the lake at **Yarkon Park,** near Yehoshua Gardens (✆ **03/642-0541**) at the northern end of the city. Motorboats are NIS 100 per half-hour; pedal and rowboats are NIS 65 per full hour. **Danit Tours** (✆ **052/340-0128**) does party and group boat tours from the Tel Aviv Marina. Call for information and see if you can join a group ride into the sea.

**CYCLING**   Tel Aviv is relatively flat and, in that respect, more bicycle-friendly than the mountainous cities of Jerusalem and Haifa. Drivers, however, are NOT bicycle-friendly (though new bicycle lanes should make the activity far safer than it used to be). The **Tel Aviv Municipality** has recently set up a public network of **Green Rental Bikes** with computerized pick up and return stations at strategic locations throughout the city, similar to those in many European cities. You pay by credit card, and tourists are able to participate.

*Tip:* The Green Rental Bikes are designed to promote short 30-minute rental periods to encourage Tel Avivians to get from place to place without using cars or buses. Rental rates are reasonable for the first 20 minutes, but become increasingly steep the longer you keep the bike. Worse yet, readers report problems getting the computerized rental machines to unlock or return your bike. Meanwhile, the rental rate keeps ticking away and your credit card gets billed while you fight with the machine. Maps with pick up and drop off stations can be picked up at City Hall.

For longer periods of leisurely biking, you would do better to rent a bike from one of the offices listed below, or, if you're a guest at one of the **Atlas Hotels,** reserve one of their free on-loan bikes. Serious cyclers should check ahead with the **Israeli Cycling Federation,** 6 Shitrit St., Tel Aviv (✆ **03/649-0459;** www.ofanaim.org.il). For bike rentals, try **Shuli and Mike's Bikes,** 280 Dizengoff St. (✆ **03/544-2292**), and **O-Fun,** 245 Dizengoff St. (✆ **03/544-2292**); rates run approximately NIS 40 per day from the time you rent until the day's closing time for the shop.

**JOGGING**   The long beachfront promenade, running several miles from the northern end of Jaffa to the Hilton hotel, provides an excellent stretch for urban jogging, without the inconvenience of cross streets and traffic lights. It's busy, which adds an element of safety, and you can stop for a dip in the sea or cool off at the public drinking fountains and showers that dot the beaches at various intervals.

**WATER SPORTS**   Tel Aviv Beach, midway between Mograbi Square and Jaffa, is designated for surfboarding, kayaking, wind-sailing, and kite-boarding. Contact **Surf Point** (✆ **03/517-0099;** www.surf-point.co.il) for equipment rental and lessons. Surfboard rental starts at NIS 120; the website is mostly in Hebrew.

If your hotel has no pool and you just want to swim a few laps or on the days when Tel Aviv's waters become a soup of stinging jellyfish in July and August, check out the newly rebuilt outdoor **Gordon Pool,** 14, Perry Eliezar St. ✆ **03/762-3300** (off Ha-Yarkon St, between the Tel Aviv Marina and the Carlton Hotel). Admission is NIS 65. Summer Hours: Sun 6:30am-10pm; Mon-Thurs 6am-9:30pm; Friday 6am-7pm. Phone for Saturday hours.

# SHOPPING
## Shopping Streets & Malls

**Allenby Street** is a typical bustling shopping street, filled with lower-price clothing, bakeries, bookstores, and kiosks. The **Opera Tower** is located right where Allenby

Street meets the sea. It contains a small upscale mall of shops and eateries (but there is no longer an opera house nearby). It's open standard business hours, with some cafes remaining open later in the evening.

The Dizengoff Center Shopping Mall, 2 blocks south of Dizengoff Square, toward King George Street, is a vast, multi-story mall located inside the high rise Dizengoff Tower. It contains tons of boutiques, Israeli and International chain stores, as well as a branch of the Hamashbir Department store. It's open Sunday to Thursday from 9:30am to 9pm and Friday from 9:30am to 2pm. The Dizengoff Center Shopping Mall hosts a great **Thursday and Friday Morning Fashion Fair,** filled with interesting, young local designers. Inside the Dizengoff Center, there's also a popular **Friday Morning Food Fair,** where all kinds of cakes and special dishes are offered to take home, both by professionals and by local cooks.

# Shopping A to Z
## ART
Tel Aviv's Gordon Street district is the center of serious art in Israel. Gordon Street and the cross streets, from Ha-Yarkon to Dizengoff streets, are almost wall-to-wall galleries and distinctive shops. The trendy Neve Tzedek neighborhood, in south Tel Aviv, and the nearby, shady, Rothschild Boulevard, with its superb restaurants, are also becoming art districts. Most galleries open Sunday to Thursday from 10am to 1pm and 5 to 8pm.

Heading the list of places to check out is the new **Sotheby's Auction Gallery ★★,** 11 Yehuda HaLevi St. (© **03/560-1666;** fax 03/560-8111), with exhibitions of important Israeli and international art, as well as Judaica. "Time Out" magazine, distributed free in most major hotels, will contain ads for current shows at dozens of galleries throughout the city.

## BOOKSTORES
If you're looking for English reading material, especially fiction, **Halper's Quality Used Books ★★,** 87 Allenby St. (© **03/629-9710**), is the mother lode, with at least a quarter of a mile of used, reasonably priced books on its packed shelves!

## CRAFTS
**Almaz Ethiopian Crafts ★**  On sale here are embroidered cloth amulets and hangings, clothing touched with traditional Ethiopian designs, *kipot* (yarmulkes), colorful mezuzahs, and other Judaica items, and traditional ceramics, all made by recent Jewish immigrants from Ethiopia. This store is the main outlet for a project that preserves the craft traditions of Ethiopian women and helps build self-confidence and incomes of new immigrant families. The staff can advise on other places where you can find special Ethiopian crafts. The store is open Sunday to Thursday 10am to 7pm. 71 Ibn Givrol St. © **03/539-0353.**

**Chomer Tov Ceramic Co-op ★**  You'll find decorative and functional items in this lively, contemporary ceramics gallery showing the work of 14 artists. It's in the heart of quaint, eccentric Neve Tzedek, not far from the Suzanne Dellal Dance Center. It's open Sunday to Thursday from 10am to 7pm and Friday from 10am to 2pm. 27 Shabazi St. © **03/516-6229.**

**Contemporary Crafts Market ★**  This juried outdoor craft market, held every Tuesday and Friday, offers ceramics, jewelry, Hands of Fatima, menorahs, and interesting gift items. Prices are fair and affordable. At the edge of the market, you'll often find a group of Druze women from the Galilee making delicious, freshly baked Druze-style bread. Nahalat Binyamin Pedestrian Mall.

**Shlush Shloshim Ceramics Co-op** ★   Eleven women artists sell their work here at studio prices. The co-op is in Neve Tzedek, in an appealing neighborhood of eccentric boutiques and shops. It's open Sunday to Thursday from 10am to 7pm; Friday 10am to 3pm; and Saturday 11am to 6pm. 30 Shlush (Chelouche) St., Neve Tzedek. ☎ **03/510-6067.**

## DEPARTMENT STORES

**Hamashbir Lazarchan** ★   Israel's department store chain is serviceable, though not exciting. It's a good place to pick up basics you might not have brought with you. Open Sunday to Thursday from 10am to 9pm, Friday until 2pm. Dizengoff Center, Dizengoff and King George sts. ☎ **03/528-5136.**

## FASHION

North Tel Aviv is the country's center for quality women's clothing and custom-designed fashion. **Kikar Ha Medina,** a square in the northern part of Tel Aviv, is filled with expensive international chains, but also top-of-the-line Israeli stores. The northern stretch of Dizengoff Street, starting around Gordon Street, is also home to high-style clothing shops. Worth checking are **Gideon Oberson** ★ at 8 Nirim St. (☎ **03/539-6151**) which has moved from selling just bathing suits to custom fashion; **Dorin Frankfurt** ★★, 40 Ben-Gurion St., near 164 Dizengoff St. (www.dorinf.com), an acclaimed Israeli whose designs tend toward natural textiles and easy, elegant lines; and **Gottex** ★ with an outlet shop at 62 Anilvich St (☎ **03/537-3879**). A stroll through the upper reaches of Dizengoff and Ben-Yehuda streets will reveal additional shops and designer showrooms.

The **Sheinkin Street** area and the **Neve Tzedek** neighborhood are filled with small personal places and boutiques showing the lines of younger local Israeli designers—the best in Israeli fashion is sometimes elegant, sometimes brash, often slightly insane, and made with an eye to hot, hot weather. **Naama Bezalel** ★★, 40 Sheinkin St. (☎ **03/629-3938**), is famous for touches of nostalgia, heavy on the 1950s and 1960s.

*Tip:* The **Dizengoff Center Young Designer's Bazaar** ★★ on the lower level of the Dizengoff Center Shopping Mall is a weekly festival of dynamite clothing and accessories, mostly for women. There are fitting rooms. Thursdays 4pm to 8pm and Fridays 10am to 3pm. Dizengoff Center Information (☎ **03/621-2400**). Bus 5.

## JEWELRY & JUDAICA

**Ben Zion David Yemenite Silver Art** ★★   You can see Yemenite-style silver jewelry and Judaica, with its intricate filigree patterns, at shops throughout Israel, but at Ben Zion David's elegant showroom, in the restored Old Jaffa bazaar, you'll find some of the best examples of Yemenite Jewish silversmiths. The many branches of the David family have been famous silver workers for generations. The showroom is generally open Sunday to Thursday from noon until late in the evening, Friday from 11am to 3pm, and on Saturday evenings after Shabbat. 3 Mazal Dagim St. www.yemenite-art.com. Old Jaffa. ☎ **03/681-2503,** ex 2.

## MARKETS

**Carmel Market (Shuk Ha-Carmel)** ★   At the six-sided intersection of Allenby, Nahalat Binyamin, King George, and Sheinkin streets, you enter this gigantic, throbbing, open-air, food-plus-everything-else market that's filled with sights and sounds but no tourist items. Here vendors hawk pistachios and guavas, sun hats, fresh fish, memorial candles and much more. The vendors are as interesting as the goods. Open Sunday to Thursday from 8am until dark and on Friday from 8am to 2pm. Bus 4.

**Dizengoff Center Food Fair ★**   Inside the Dizengoff Center Shopping Mall on the lower level, this is a great place to pick up cakes, pastries, and ethnic or gourmet dishes. Meals to eat on the spot average NIS 30-NIS 60. You'll meet interesting local chefs here, both professional and amateur. The fair takes place Thursdays from noon to 8pm and Fridays from 10am to 4pm. Dizengoff Center information: ☏ **03/621-2400.** Bus: 5.

**Jaffa Flea Market (Shuk Ha Pishpishim) ★**   Merchandise varies, but copper, brass, old Persian tiles, and jewelry are always to be found in these covered bazaar streets, as well as Judaica items, old family-photo albums, and tons of used jeans and mildewed clothing from India. Bargaining is the order of the day, so feel free to indulge in lengthy haggling. Combine the market with an exploration of Old Jaffa and a leisurely lunch. The flea market is open Sunday to Thursday from 10am to 6pm and on Friday from 10am to 2pm. Take bus no. 10 from Ben-Yehuda St. in Tel Aviv to the Clock Tower in Old Jaffa. Market area is 1 block east.

**Nahalat Binyamin Arts and Crafts Market ★★**   This large outdoor fair takes over the streets of the Nahalat Binyamin Pedestrian Mall (btw. Allenby St. and the Carmel Market), Tuesdays and Fridays, often with street performers and Druze ladies making freshly baked, delicious Druze bread in various corners. The crafts are uneven, but prices are fair, and there's always intriguing Judaica and jewelry that make good gifts and keepsakes. Nahalat Binyamin is lined with eateries (some of the best in the city) in all price ranges, as well as fab 1920s Tel Aviv architecture—all of which make it more than just another street fair. It is open Tuesday 10am to 5pm and Friday 10am to 3pm. Magen David Sq. (Allenby St., across from start of King George St., at the edge of the Carmel Market). Bus: 4.

**Tel Aviv Port Antiques Fair and Organic Farmer's Market ★**   This growing antiques fair and flea market in the popular Tel Aviv Port is filled with books, old vinyl records, furniture, toys, and all sorts of treasures. It's open Friday from 10am to 8pm. The organic foods market (where you can buy anything from whole-grain cookies and cakes to a fabulous mango to store in your hotel room for Shabbat) is open Monday to Thursday from 9am to 9pm; Friday from 9am to 3pm; Saturday from 9am to 7pm. Tel Aviv Port, at northern edge of Tel Aviv. Bus: 4 or 5; sherut: 4 (which runs on Sat).

## MUSEUM SHOPS

**Eretz Israel Museum Shop ★★**   Without a doubt, this is the best museum shop in the country, with well-chosen Judaica, crafts, toys, and children's books, jewelry, replicas, and gift ideas. It's open Sunday to Thursday 10am to 6pm and Friday 10am to 2pm. Eretz Israel Museum, 2 Chaim Levanon St., Ramat Aviv, Tel Aviv. ☏ **03/641-5244.**

# TEL AVIV & JAFFA AFTER DARK

No matter what season, Tel Aviv throbs with activity after sundown. Strollers are out on the boulevards, people-watchers crowd the cafes, clubs and discos bustle and crash, and restaurants are packed. Thursday, Friday, and Saturdays are the big nights out; Sunday and weekday nights are quieter.

To find out what's going on in the city, pick up a free copy of "Time Out Tel Aviv," available at many hotels, or buy "The Herald Tribune" or "The Jerusalem Post" Friday morning editions, which contain weekend magazines that list everything there is to do and see. Also pick up "Events in the Tel Aviv Region" and other free tourist publications from the travel desk of your hotel (or check out the Sheraton's well-stocked information shelves just to the left of the main entrance).

In addition to the listings below, **Hayarkon Park** (℗ **03/642-2828**), at the northern edge of Tel Aviv, hosts large outdoor concerts; there are also concerts in Hayarkon Park's Wohl Amphitheater (℗ **03/521-8210**).

# The Performing Arts

While Jerusalem has many cultural offerings, Tel Aviv is the true performance center of Israel. The Mann Auditorium is the home of the Israel Philharmonic, The Israel Ballet is also centered in Tel Aviv. Major ticket outlets are **Le'an,** 101 Dizengoff St. (℗ **03/524-7373;** www.leaan.co.il); **Hadran,** 90 Ibn Givrol St. (℗ **03/521-5200;** www.hadran.co.il); and **Castel,** 153 Ibn Givrol St. (℗ **03/604-5000;** www.eventim.co.il).

## CONCERTS, OPERA & DANCE

**Bet Lessin ★**    A multi-use venue, this theater hosts contemporary plays in Hebrew, jazz groups, and contemporary and folk musicians. If your Hebrew is snappy, head to one of their stand-up comedy nights. 101 Dizengoff St. ℗ **03/725-5300.** www.lessin.co.il.

**Israel Philharmonic Orchestra ★★★**    The **Mann Auditorium,** which can seat 3,000 concertgoers, is the home of this prestigious orchestra, founded in 1936 by Bronislaw Huberman. Concerts are also given at the Smolarz Auditorium in Tel Aviv University and in other towns, carrying on a tradition that began during the War of Independence when it played just behind the lines for the troops near Jerusalem and Beersheba. The orchestra is on vacation during August, September, and October until after the Jewish holidays. Huberman St. ℗ **1-700/703-030.** www.ipo.co.il.

**New Israeli Opera ★★★**    Housed in the architecturally interesting and controversial **Golda Meir/Tel Aviv Center for the Performing Arts,** the New Israeli Opera is the country's newest cultural gem, performing a lively program of classic and modern opera. The company draws heavily on the talent of immigrants from the former Soviet Union. The piece de resistance of the 2013-14 season is a performance of La Traviata to be held at Masada. The Tel Aviv Center for the Performing Arts hosts classical, jazz, and popular concerts. 19 Shaul Ha Melekh St. Box office for all events ℗ **03/692-7777.** www.israel-opera.co.il. Tickets NIS 120–NIS 300.

**Suzanne Dellal Center for Dance and Theater ★★★**    This complex, built in postmodern style, is the venue for visiting dance groups as well as for Israel's contemporary Bat Sheva Dance Company and the Inbal Dance Theater, which often draws upon Israel's ethnic traditions for its style. The Dellal Center hosts worthwhile modern and experimental productions, as well as a wide range of concerts and music events. It has become the heart of the effort to revive and restore the old, quaint Neve Tzedek neighborhood of Tel Aviv. Bus nos. 10 and 25 pass nearby. 6 Yehieli St. Box office ℗ **03/510-5656.** www.suzannedellal.org.il.

**Tel Aviv Museum of Art/Recanati Hall ★**    The museum hosts a wide range of afternoon and evening events, including music recitals, performances of chamber orchestras and ensembles, visiting choirs, theater and dance performances, and film screenings. There is also a cafe on the premises. Box office: 27 Shaul Ha-Melekh Blvd. ℗ **03/607-7020.**

**Tzavta ★**    This club specializes in Israeli music, both folk and popular, as well as theater productions. 30 Ibn Givrol St. ℗ **03/695-0156.** www.tzavta.co.il.

## THEATER

**Ha-Bimah National Theater** ★　Founded in Moscow in 1918 by the renowned Stanislavski and moved to British Mandate Palestine in 1928, the Ha-Bimah National Theater is the nation's first and best-known repertory theater. While performances are in Hebrew, some productions offer simultaneous translations. Kikar Ha-Bimah. ☏ **03/629-5555.** Ticket prices vary, depending on the company performing.

**New Cameri Theater** ★　This theater presents both repertory classics and new Israeli plays in Hebrew. Tuesday evenings there are simultaneous translations in English. 30 Leonardo Da Vinci St. www.cameri.co.il. ☏ **03/606-0960.** Orchestra and mezzanine seats about NIS 125, balcony seats NIS 100; earphone rental is additional.

# The Club Scene

Tel Aviv and Jaffa are the nightlife centers of Israel. Their clubs have been the breeding ground for almost all Israeli singers who have gone on to international careers. The scene changes so frequently that only a few long-term stalwarts are listed here. The monthly English edition of "Time Out Israel" (free in most major hotels) will have the best list of what's current and popular. Some discos are on tacky-looking streets, but that's no indication they'll be cheap; the atmosphere can be very different inside. Nothing starts before midnight, and most places are open daily.

## CLUBS & DANCE BARS

**Evita** ★　Tel Aviv's landmark gay bar has a packed dance floor and a management with a long involvement in the LGBT community, so this is a good place for advice and information as well as fun. There are drag and Eurovision music nights and special events for the over 30s crowd. It's open daily at 9pm until the last customer leaves. 3 Yavneh St., near Rothschild Blvd. ☏ **03/566-9559.**

**HaOman 17** ★　This is the country's iconic megaclub with top Israeli and international DJs and major parties Thursday, Friday, and Saturday nights after 1am. 88 Abarbanel St. ☏ **03/681-3636.** Admission NIS 70–NIS 120.

## BARS, PUBS & WINE BARS

Singers and pianists appear nightly at the bars in the five-star hotels such as the Dan, Hilton, Ramada Renaissance, and Sheraton.

**Chamara** ★★　As beautiful, upscale a bar as you'll find in Israel, Chamara also serves dynamite food by high-profile chef Rafi Cohen from the adjacent deluxe Raphael restaurant. 87 Ha-Yarkon St., beside Dan Hotel. ☏ **03/522-6464.**

**Gordon Inn** ★　An easygoing backpacker's hangout with a small pool table, it is attached to the popular budget hotel of the same name. 17 Gordon St. ☏ **03/523-8239.**

**Jaffa Bar** ★★　Jaffa Bar is a low-key, sprawling place with eccentric couches and armchairs scattered both in and outside an atmospheric Crusader-era building. The bar serves a creative menu of bites and tapas designed by Nir Zook, whose gourmet restaurant, **Cordelia** (p. 180), is right across the way. The cocktails are expertly mixed. It's open daily from 6pm until late. Simchat HaZchuchit, off 30 Yefet St., Jaffa. ☏ **03/518-4668.** Turn right into the covered alleyway 2 blocks south of the Clock Tower as you come from Tel Aviv.

**M.A.S.H.** ★　["]More alcohol served here" is the motto, and beer is the drink of choice. This is a haven for travelers, and it's adorned with TVs showing sports. Call for hours, as they change. 277 Dizengoff St. ☏ **03/605-1007.** Branches at 38 Allenby St., and 98 HaYarkon St.

**Mike's Place** ★★   This American-style pub, facing the sea and offering live blues, jazz, and folk music every night, is an Israeli-American institution. Students, backpackers, locals, diplomats, families, and tourists come here day and night for the friendly, laid-back atmosphere and for the burgers (ground on the spot and grilled on open fires) from the good pub menu. Sports events are shown on big projection TVs. Happy hour is 4 to 9pm daily except Saturday, when it's all day until 9pm. Open daily from noon until the last customer leaves. 86 Herbert Samuel Promenade. ✆ **03/510-6392.** www.mikesplacebars.com.

**Mishmish** ★   The name means "apricot," but the snacks here are stylish and the ambience sophisticated. Pricey drink tabs keeps out the riff-raff. 17 Lilenblum St. ✆ **03/516-8402.**

**Nanutchka** ★★   The bar at this ethnic Georgian (Caucasian Mountains, not Atlanta) restaurant with dynamite food goes from mild to totally crazy after dining hours. There's occasional dancing and live music, a friendly feel, and Georgian tapas with which to down your drinks. Every Sunday there is a Georgian party! It's open daily from noon to after midnight. 30 Lilenblum St. ✆ **03/516-2254.**

**Shalvata** ★   You can hear the sound of the wind in the thatch and palm trees on breezy nights at this fun place, set on the sands of the Tel Aviv Port. It's great for meeting people. There's dancing, with different nightly theme, DJs, and inexpensive food. It's open daily, May to November only, starting at 5pm. Tel Aviv Port. ✆ **03/602-5008.**

## GAY & LESBIAN BARS/MEETING PLACES

Bars, clubs, and meeting places abound, and there are gay nights at many bars and dance clubs. Independence Park, in front of the **Tel Aviv Hilton** on Ha-Yarkon Street, is the city's oldest cruising place, nicely landscaped and relatively safe. Hilton Beach, behind the Hilton hotel, is a mixed place with families, tourists, surfers, and some amount of beachfront cruising as well. Avoid the very seedy and dangerous (now partly disused) Old Tel Aviv Bus Station area. The English-language edition of **"Time Out Tel Aviv,"** available in many hotels, and **Tel Aviv 4 Fun** (www.telaviv4fun.com), will have a current list of the ever-changing party scene. Each June, Tel Aviv hosts the most exuberant Gay Pride Parade in the Middle East. Check websites, such as **Aguda** (www.glbt.org.il), the site for a major LGBT organization, for scheduled times as well as for advice and local information.

**Dix** ★   Dix is a hopping gay bar with an upstairs area for cruising and meeting. It's open Monday to Saturday from 10pm. 6 Dizengoff Sq. ✆ **03/525-2633.**

**Evita** ★   This is a cafe/restaurant with good food that turns into a popular gay bar after the post-dinner hour. It's open daily, but call for hours and theme nights. 31 Yavne St. ✆ **03/566-9559.**

**Shpagat Straight-Friendly Bar** ★★   This newer LGBT-oriented bar offers signs in Hebrew, Arabic, and English as well as special events like women-only nights. Lots of space and a friendly vibe make it a terrific place to hang out, and most parties and events are free. However, drinks are expensive and beer is a pricey NIS 35 for a pint. Open daily after 9pm. 43 Nahlat Binyamin. ✆ **03/560-1758.**

# Film

With a lively and popular international film scene, Tel Aviv has at least two dozen cinemas. English and American films are not dubbed (as they are in Europe), so you can sit back and enjoy the English soundtrack, otherwise check to see if foreign language films include English subtitles. Tickets run from NIS 40 to NIS 50. The commercial shorts that accompany many films are fascinating.

**Tel Aviv Cinémathèque ★★**   Located not far from the Mann Auditorium, the Cinémathèque offers a changing program of three or four films each day, ranging from international classics to rarely seen, experimental films. The Cinémathèque also hosts an annual International Film Festival at the end of March/early April as well as special festivals of Israeli films throughout the year. 2 Sprinzak St. ℂ **03/606-0800.** www.cinema.co.il.

# A SIDE TRIP FROM TEL AVIV

## Rehovot

You come to Rehovot, primarily, to pay homage to Israel's very first president Chaim Weizmann. First stop should be the **Weizmann Institute,** Israel's foremost scientific establishment and think tank, named in honor of the great man (himself a world-renowned chemist). Dedicated in 1949, the Institute conducts both fundamental and applied research and has a graduate school where about 700 students work for their master's degrees and doctorates. You enter through a gateway on Rehovot's main street, and find yourself in a beautiful compound of futuristic buildings, green lawns, lily ponds, and colorful gardens—all for the spiritual satisfaction of scientists from all over the world at work here.

The **visitor center** offers a 17-minute film about the institute and provides visitors with a self-guided walking tours to help them understand the mission and on-going work of this dynamic, world-famous institution. For a small additional fee and with advance reservation, you can also tour Weizmann House, the home of Dr. and Mrs. Weizmann, on the grounds of the institute.

The **Weizmann House ★★** (www.chaimweizmann.org.il) was built by Dr. and Mrs. Weizmann as their residence in the 1930s. It's a wonderful example of International Style architecture with a dazzling, streamlined interpretation of a Roman/Mediterranean atrium house, the masterpiece of the German refugee architect Erich Mendelssohn, who also designed the original Hadassah Hospital and Hebrew University on Mount Scopus in Jerusalem. The interior of the house is marked by an airy, sinuous staircase set in a tower lit with narrow vertical windows; private living and reception wings with French doors lead to a central pool patio. Another 1930s element, round porthole windows, brings light into the house from exterior walls. The furnishings were carefully designed by Mendelssohn, who involved Dr. and Mrs. Weizmann personally in the project. The house itself (like Washington's Mount Vernon and Jefferson's Monticello) reveals much about the personality of Dr. Weizmann, the world in which he lived, and the international visitors he entertained. A film about Dr. Weizmann's amazing life is shown in the house. The Weizmann House is open Sunday through Thursday from 10am to 3pm but only as part of a prearranged guided tour. To inquire about a house tour, call the visitor center at the Weizmann Institute (ℂ **08/934-4500** or 934-3230) before your planned visit. Be sure to specify your English-language requirement. Near the residence is a simple tomb marking the Weizmanns' resting place and a Memorial Plaza dominated by a Holocaust memorial depicting the Torah being snatched from flames.

The **Clore Science Gardens ★★** (http://davidson.weizmann.ac.il/science-garden), also on the campus of the institute, is an awe-inspiring, interactive park and science exhibit that examines natural phenomena with the spirit of verve, humor, and inventiveness that marked Dr. Weizmann's approach to scientific inquiry. The additional

# CHAIM WEIZMANN: statesman & scientist

**Chaim Weizmann** (1874–1952), biochemist, statesman, and first president of Israel, was born in a small village near Pinsk, Russia. A brilliant student, Weizmann gave lessons to earn his tuition at Berlin's Institute of Technology in Charlottenburg and at Fribourg University in Switzerland; in 1901, he began teaching at Geneva University.

In 1903, in response to pogroms in Russia, the British foreign secretary proposed a Jewish homeland in a 12,950 sq. km (5,000-sq.-mile) area of British East Africa (Uganda). The young Weizmann sided with those who would not accept Zionism without Zion. In 1906, Weizmann met with Prime Minister Balfour, who wanted to interview an anti-Ugandist. Weizmann's charm and energy impressed Balfour and won him access to the highest circles of British society. He was lionized in 1916 after developing a production process for synthesizing acetone that was crucial to the British war effort. (In his professional career, Dr. Weizmann received patents for more than 100 processes and inventions.) Moving to London, he continued to build support for a Jewish homeland in Palestine. At the end of 1917, the Balfour Declaration was issued.

Deeply convinced that the future of the Jewish people depended on the creation of a safe homeland for them, as leader of the Zionist movement in the 1920s and '30s, Weizmann worked to build the infrastructure of a modern society in Palestine "house by house and dunam by dunam." Without romantic illusion and with a passion for fairness, Weizmann cautioned the Zionist movement to understand "the truth that 600,000 Arabs live there [in Palestine] who, before the sense of justice of the world have exactly the same right to their homes in Palestine as we have to our National Home." In 1937, addressing a Royal Commission on the Partition of Palestine, he prophetically explained the plight of European Jewry: "There are six million people . . . for whom the world is divided into places where they cannot live, and places which they cannot enter."

Weizmann's eloquence could not alleviate the vast tragedy that World War II brought to his people. In 1942, his own son was killed in action with the Royal Air Force over the English Channel. Struggling through the breakdown of his health and a hostile postwar British government, Weizmann's final achievement was winning American support for the incipient Jewish state in 1948. In February 1949, he was elected president of Israel, a position he held until his death. The title of his wife, Vera Weizmann's memoirs, "The Impossible Takes Longer," summarizes the philosophy behind her husband's heavily burdened but determined optimism.

entrance fee to the science gardens is a worthwhile investment, especially for students and children.

Admission fee for the visitor center is NIS 16 for adults, NIS 12 for children. Combined admission to the visitor center and Clore Science Gardens is NIS 40 for adults and NIS 30 for children. The campus is open Sunday to Thursday from 10am to 4:45pm and Friday to 2pm.

**Rehovot** (22km/14 miles southeast of Tel Aviv; pop. 90,000) is easily reached by train or bus from Tel Aviv. Both train and bus fares are NIS 15, and the trip takes 30 minutes. The town is a rather ordinary small city, but its star attraction, the **Weizmann Institute of Science ★★** (© **08/934-4500** for the visitor center; www.weizmann.ac.il) makes an excursion very worthwhile.

# THE GOLDEN COAST

L ike the rest of the country, the Mediterranean Coast combines the old and the new in a uniquely Israeli way. Neon and chrome shopping malls and golden beaches exist side by side with biblical, Roman, and Crusader sites. The vast archaeological ruins of **Caesarea,** washed by Mediterranean waves and dotted with wonderful places to dine, is probably the most romantic ancient site in Israel. Further north, **Haifa** (Israel's third major metropolis) provides a smart base from which to explore the northern coast and the Western Galilee. Just north of Haifa, the medieval walled seaport of **Akko** (Acre), a UNESCO World Heritage Site, is one of Israel's hidden treasures.

## CAESAREA ★★

Caesarea (40km or 25 miles north of Tel Aviv) was the culminating vision of Herod the Great (37 B.C.–4 B.C.), who created a new, spectacular classical Roman city by the sea to rival Alexandria as the greatest metropolis of the Eastern Mediterranean. Since it had no natural port, he built a vast artificial harbor. On the empty sands, he constructed theaters facing the sea, temples, hippodromes, palaces, colonnaded avenues, and markets. A thousand years later, the city was reborn as a Crusader fortress, but after the Crusades, the ruins of the city were covered by sand and forgotten.

Today, the romantic ruins by the sea have become Israel's most photogenic and lively archaeological site, dotted with great eateries smack dab in the middle of the ruins. Nearby beaches, wineries, and the artists' village of Ein Hod make this a good car trip from Tel Aviv.

### Essentials

**GETTING THERE  By Tour Bus and Public Transportation**  Both **Egged** (www.eggedtours.com) and **United Bus Tours** (www.unitedtours. co.il) include stops in Caesarea on tours of the area originating in Tel Aviv, Jerusalem, and Haifa. Public transport to Caesarea National Park is virtually non-existent.

**By Car**  Highway 2 or 4 to Caesarea (sometimes Qasariyah) exit. Follow signs to Caesarea National Park, not to Caesarea City. There are free parking lots at the entrances to the park and at the old Roman Aqueduct Beach a half-mile (.6 km) north of the main park entrances. Leave no bags or valuables visible in your car.

# Exploring Caesarea

## CAESAREA NATIONAL PARK ★★

The remains of Caesarea (Qesarya, in Hebrew) are spread along a 3km (1¾-mile) stretch of Mediterranean beach. There are two separate entrances: You'll arrive at either the Roman theater or the Crusader city, which are in fact right next to each other, though the entrance gates are .5km (⅓ mile) apart. Admission to Caesarea National Park is good for both the Crusader city and the theater. You can enter the city for free after 5pm closing time to visit the restaurants that have sprung up inside the park or stroll the ruins, but special exhibits are closed at night.

At the Admission Gates, get a map showing the details of the cities that have risen at this site, both on land and in the water—the cities and harbors of Straton's Tower (the earliest settlement at the site of Caesarea), as well as the Herodian, Roman, Byzantine, and Crusader incarnations of Caesarea. There is also an excellent, inventive **Audiovisual Presentation** (© 972-2-5006261; no web info) that brings the site to life, re-creations of what Caesarea would have looked like at different times in its history. Call ahead for information, presentation schedules, and to reserve a place.

The excavations you see today are only a very small part of what's actually here, waiting to be discovered; new finds are constantly being unearthed. In recent years, ruins of a massive temple dedicated to Roman gods were uncovered and attributed to the King Herod. Other highlights include the **Roman Theater,** constructed in the time of Jesus, and used today to host summer performances). Test the acoustics by sitting in the stands and listening to someone speak on stage or clap hands.

You enter the **Crusader city** on a bridge across the deep moat, then through a gatehouse with Gothic vaulting. Emerging, you'll find yourself in the large fortified town, which covered a mere fraction of the great Herodian/Roman city. Especially noteworthy are the foundations of the **Crusader Church of Saint Paul** (1100s), down toward the sea, near the little Turkish minaret (1800s). The citadel, next to the group of shops, was badly damaged by an earthquake in 1837, as was most of the Crusader city.

The **Port of Sebastos,** a dockside part of the Crusader port, extends from the Crusader city into the sea, but King Herod's harbor at Caesarea, completed in 10 B.C. and also named Sebastos, extended at least three times as far as what you see today. It curved around to the right, where a separate northern breakwater extended to meet it, roughly where the northern Crusader fortification walls meet the sea. The breakwater was also a wide platform, with room for large quantities of cargo, housing for sailors, a lighthouse, colossi (gigantic statues), and two large towers guarding the entrance gates to the harbor. The harbor could be closed off by a chain stretched between the two towers, preventing ships from entering.

Herod's harbor was one of the largest harbors of the Roman world, mentioned by historian Flavius Josephus as an especially amazing feat of engineering because it was a total creation—built without the usual benefit of a topographical feature such as a bay or cove. Historians did not find the harbor until 1960, when a combination of aerial photography and underwater archaeological explorations revealed the ruins sunken offshore. Historians and archaeologists believe that the harbor structure probably sank vertically downward as a result of an earthquake.

The excavation of the underwater ruins is an important international project. At the **Old Caesarea Diving Center** in the Old City (© 04/626-5898; www.caesarea-diving.com), at the site of the ancient harbor, you can join a guided dive with equipment supplied starting at NIS 275 for 1 hour (you must be certified). Snorkeling tours can also be arranged. The dive explores ruins of the ancient harbor, and passes by ancient shipwrecks, classical statues, and fragments of a once-great lighthouse. Reserve ahead, although dives can't be guaranteed if sea conditions aren't good.

Admission (including the Roman Theater and Crusader city) is NIS 40 for adults, NIS 35 for children; save your ticket for the interactive audiovisual Time Trek tour. Hours are Saturday to Thursday 8am to 4pm (until 6pm Apr–Sept), and Friday from 8am to 3pm. Call ✆ **04/636-7080** for information.

## THE BYZANTINE STREET

Fifty meters (164 ft.) east of the Crusader city entrance, behind the little snack shop, is the Byzantine Street, or Street of Statues, which is actually part of a forum. The statues depict an emperor and other dignitaries.

## THE HIPPODROME

Head east from either the Byzantine Street or the Roman Theater to reach the ruined hippodrome, in the fields between the two access roads. Measuring 72×288m (236×945 ft.), the hippodrome could seat some 20,000 people. Some of the monuments in the hippodrome may have been brought from Aswan in Egypt—expense was no object when Herod built for Caesar.

## THE NEW CITY

Largely residential, the modern city of Caesarea is notable for its very worthwhile art museum, the **Ralli Museum ★**, located on Rothschild Boulevard (✆ **04/626-1013.** Mon-Tues and Thurs-Sat 10:30am-3pm. Free). The museum contains a large collection of works by Latin American and Spanish artists (including artists of Sephardic origin); is housed in a spacious, beautifully designed new building; and is one of Israel's unexpected and little-publicized surprises. The gems of the collection include sculptures by Dalí and Rodin, but the works of Latin American surrealists, representing artists from Mexico to Uruguay, are also powerful and impressive.

# Where to Stay

**Dan Caesarea ★★**  If you can't unwind at the Dan Caesarea, you may need medication. Set amidst acres of lush gardens, the Dan boasts a vast swimming pool and is right next to Israel's best golf course (guests can use it for a fee). Horseback riding, fishing, diving, bicycling, and other local activities can be easily arranged through the front desk. There is also a full program of summertime in-hotel sports including kids' basketball. The staff is attentive. And as for the hotel itself, the building is low-rise, 1980s modern, but rooms are spacious and comfy (large enough for an extra child), with terraces that take in wonderful views.

Old Caesarea Park. ✆ **04/626-9111.** www.danhotels.com. 114 units. $270–$600 double. Rates include breakfast. Free parking. **Amenities:** Restaurant; cafe; babysitting; children's activities (in season); access to golf club; health club; Jacuzzi; outdoor pool; room service; sauna; 2 lit tennis courts; Wi-Fi (fee).

**Casa Caesarea ★★**  Set right next to the 14th hole of Caesarea's golf course and surrounded by aromatic fruit trees, this chic little B&B was designed from the ground up by Anne Kleinberg, former New Yorker, cookbook author and interior designer of exquisite taste. With just two suites and a basement apartment (big enough for six and excellent for families), it can be difficult to get reservations. But make the effort, as Kleinberg the little inn is charming and the breakfasts here are stupendous.

3 Tai St. ✆ **972 4 610-0228.** www.casacaesarea.com. 3 units. $225 night double. **Amenities:** Pool, use of the golf course (fee); Wi-Fi (free); included breakfast and snacks.

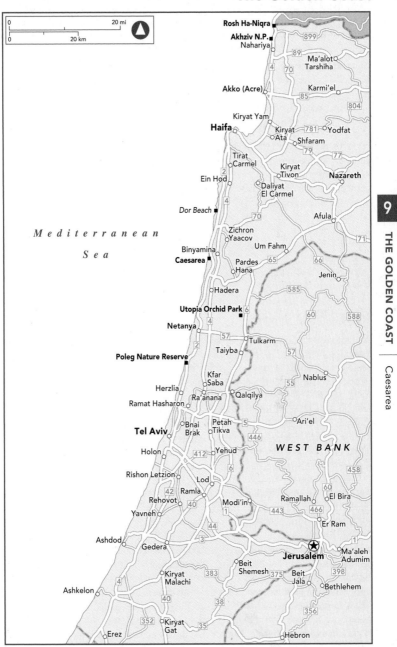

0    20 mi
0    20 km

Rosh Ha-Niqra
Akhziv N.P.
Nahariya                899
                89      Ma'alot
                        Tarshiha
        4   70
Akko (Acre)             Karmi'el
                        85          804
Kiryat Yam
Haifa       Kiryat      781    Yodfat
            Ata     Shfaram
Tirat                   79
Carmel      Kiryat          77
Ein Hod     Tivon       Nazareth
        2   Daliyat
            El Carmel
Dor Beach               Afula
        4
        70
    Zichron
    Yaacov      Um Fahm         71
Binyamina
Caesarea        65      66
        Pardes
        Hana                Jenin
    Hadera
            585
Utopia Orchid Park          60      588
            6
Netanya     4
        57  Tulkarm
    2   Taiyba       57
Poleg Nature Reserve
        Kfar
        Saba            Nablus
Herzlia             55
Ra'anana    Qalqilya
Ramat Hasharon
    Bnai    Petah       Ari'el
Tel Aviv    Brak    Tikva
            5
Holon               446    WEST BANK
        412 Yehud
Rishon Letzion      6           458
        Lod
    42  Ramla
Rehovot 40          Ramallah    El Bira
Yavneh      Modi'in         466
        1   443     Er Ram
        44
Ashdod              1
    Gedera          Jerusalem   Ma'aleh
                            Adumim
            Beit
    Kiryat  383 Shemesh  375 Beit
    Malachi             Jala    Bethlehem
Ashkelon                398
        40
        38
    352 Kiryat  35
Erez    Gat         Hebron

*Mediterranean*

*Sea*

**9**

THE GOLDEN COAST | Caesarea

## Where to Dine

Restaurants in Caesarea are excellent and stay open after the archaeological park has officially closed. Reservations are recommended for all locations. Those looking for kosher food can head to **Aresto,** Old Caesarea Park ((C) **057/944-4067**), the only kosher restaurant in the archeological park. It serves solid if unremarkable fare.

**Crusaders** ★★ SEAFOOD    There's little to find fault with at this beachside eatery. The fish is super-fresh and expertly prepared in hearty portions (there's also a smattering of meat dishes for those who don't like fish); service is efficient; and like so many of the restaurants here, the views can't be beat. Ask for one of the outdoor tables.

Old Caesarea Park. (C) **04/636-1931** or 04/636-1679. Main courses NIS 80–NIS 130. Daily noon–1am.

**Helena** ★★★ MEDITERRANEAN    A destination in its own right, this is one of Israel's finest gourmet restaurants. At its helm is the remarkable Amos Sion. His exciting contemporary menu takes inspiration from the cuisines of North Africa, the Mediterranean, and the Middle East. So you might find yourself dining on sautéed mussels in blue-cheese sauce with crispy seaweed and Egyptian spices, or chicken in date syrup on mustard pasta. If it's on the menu, the beef fillet demi-glace with pastry shells filled with porcini sauce is over the top delish. Desserts are light and elegant; the wine list is excellent; and the view of the sunset over the sea is simply the cherry on top of the experience.

Old Caesarea Park (C) **04/610-1018.** www.2eat.co.il/eng/helena. Reservations recommended. Main courses NIS 80–NIS 140; group tasting menu NIS 200. Sun–Sat noon–11pm.

# HAIFA ★★★

Some compare Haifa, beautifully situated on a hill overlooking a broad bay, to San Francisco or Naples. Israel's third-largest metropolitan area (pop. 300,000) and the capital of the north, Haifa is very different from either Jerusalem or Tel Aviv, and is a pleasure to visit for both its physical beauty and lifestyle. In a society unlike any other in the Middle East, Jews and Arabs live and work side by side; 25 percent of Haifa's population is either Muslim or Christian.

Haifa is also an excellent base for exploring northern Israel. You won't need to rent a car since many organized day tours originate in Haifa; or you can use public transportation to explore Akko or even Safed on your own. In the evenings, the city offers restaurants, films, concerts, and urban strolling to keep you busy.

You won't be the first to visit, of course. The prophet Elijah knew this territory well—from the top of Mount Carmel he won a major victory over 450 priests of Baal during the reign of King Ahab and his notorious Phoenician wife, Jezebel. In late biblical times, the Phoenician port of Zalemona thrived here, with predominantly Greek settlers, and the Jewish agricultural village of Sycaminos (sometimes called Shikmona) clung to the northwestern peak of Mount Carmel. However, Haifa did not become a major city until the 1930s, when the British built a vast, modern harbor here, and turned the community into a naval center and terminus for oil refineries and pipelines. Israel's important chemical and hi-tech industries are concentrated here, and the city is home to the Technion Institute of Technology, the M.I.T. of Israel. Despite its heavy industry, the city remains stunningly beautiful. Until the age of jet airliners, Haifa's harbor was the main entrance into the country.

Israelis are fond of saying: "Tel Aviv plays while Jerusalem prays. But Haifa works!" A visit here is filled with new insights into what Israel is all about.

# Essentials

**GETTING THERE** **By Train** The New Central Railway Station is in Bat Galim, near the Central Bus Station, in the southern part of the city. There are two other railroad stops in Haifa, so check which stop will be most convenient to your hotel. **From Tel Aviv:** Trains along the coast to Netanya and Haifa leave approximately every hour from 5:45am to 7pm, Sunday through Thursday; the last Friday train leaves at 2pm; there's no Saturday service. The trip on the express train to Haifa takes 1 hour, while the local is 20 minutes longer. The fare is NIS 32. Service north from Haifa to Akko and Nahariya is available. Train information can be obtained by calling © **04/856-4564** or going to www.rail.co.il.

**By Bus** The Egged Bus Terminal, with intercity buses to and from all points in Israel, is next to the Central Railway Station in Bat Galim. From here, you'll have to take a taxi or city bus to either of our recommended hotel districts in the German Colony or Central Carmel. Interurban bus information can be obtained by calling © **04/854-9555.** For buses within Haifa, call © **04/854-9131.**

**By Car** Major highway networks connect Haifa with Tel Aviv, Jerusalem, and the Galilee. The main routes are Hwy. 2 and Hwy. 4 along the coast.

**VISITOR INFORMATION** The **Haifa Information and Visitors Center,** 48 Ben-Gurion Blvd. (© **04/853-5606;** www.tour-haifa.co.il/eng. Sun-Thurs 9am-5pm, Fri 9am-1pm, Sat 10am-3pm) is located on the main street of the German Colony neighborhood far from most hotels, but it's well organized and worth visiting.

# Orientation

Think of Haifa as a city built on three levels. Whether you come by bus or train, you will arrive on the lower (or port) level of the city, dominated by Haifa's shipping and transportation hub. This lower level also contains the **German Colony** that's centered around Ben Gurion Boulevard, with charming restaurants and small hotels leading up to the dramatic Baha'I Center. The second level is **Hadar,** a downtown business area not too interesting for visitors. At the top of the Carmel Range, with panoramic views, is the **Central Carmel District,** a verdant residential neighborhood with its own busy commercial center built around Ha-Nasi Boulevard. Here you'll find numerous hotels, restaurants, small museums, and two of Haifa's brightest cultural beacons: Haifa Auditorium and Bet Rothschild (with its adjacent Haifa Cinematheque).

*Note:* Because Haifa is built up the side of a mountain, its main streets are sinuous switchbacks, curving and recurving like spaghetti to accommodate the steep slopes of Mount Carmel. If you're driving, the streets are always bewildering, and you will find it hard to orient yourself. Just remember: In Haifa, the two directions are up or down. About the only straight road in Haifa is underground—the Carmelit Subway that connects each level and climbs like an escalator, directly up the slopes of the Carmel.

# Getting Around

**BY SUBWAY** The **Carmelit** is a fast and efficient means of getting up and down Haifa's various levels. Its lower terminal station is located on Jaffa Road, a few blocks north of the port entrance and not far from the old (Merkaz) railway station. The Carmelit's upper terminal is at the Carmel Center.

Pulled on a long cable up and down the steep hill, the Carmelit resembles a sort of scale-model Métro. From bottom to the top, the stops are: (1) Paris Square (Kikar Paris, lower terminus, port area); (2) Solel Boneh (Hassan Shukri St.); (3) Ha-Nevi'im

# Haifa

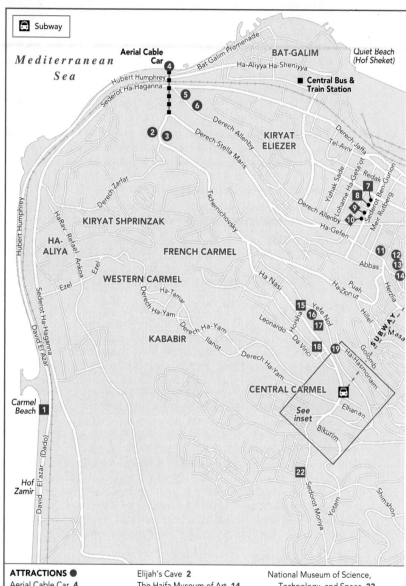

**Subway**

*Mediterranean Sea*

Aerial Cable Car **4**

BAT-GALIM

*Quiet Beach (Hof Sheket)*

Bat Galim Promenade

Ha-Aliyya Ha-Sheniyya

Hubert Humphrey

Sederot Ha-Haganna

**5**

**6**

■ Central Bus & Train Station

**2**

**3**

Derech Allenby

Derech Stella Maris

KIRYAT ELIEZER

Derech Jaffa

Tel-Aviv

Yitzhak Sade

Lohame Ha-Geta'ot

Redak

Derech Zarfat

Tschernichovsky

Derech Allenby

Ha-Gefen

Sederot Ben-Gurion

Meir Rutberg

**7**

**8**

**9**

**10**

KIRYAT SHPRINZAK

HaRav Refael Arkoa

Ezel

Ezel

**11**

**12**

**13**

**14**

Abbas

Herzlia

HA-ALIYA

FRENCH CARMEL

Ha Nasi

Puah

Ha-Zionut

Hübert Humphrey

WESTERN CARMEL

Ha-Tamar

Derech Ha-Yam

Ha-Yam

Derech Ha-Yam

Leonardo Da Vinci

Yefe Nof

Horsha

**15**

**16**

**17**

Hillel

SUBWAY

Masa

Sederot Ha-Haganna

David El Azar

KABABIR

Ilanot

Derech Ha-Yam

**18**

**19**

Ha-Hasmonaim

Golomb

CENTRAL CARMEL

Carmel Beach **1**

*See inset*

Elhanan

Bikurim

(Jaffa) David El Azar Blvd

Hof Zamir

**22**

Sederot Moriya

Yotam

Shimshon

---

**ATTRACTIONS ●**

Aerial Cable Car **4**
Baha'i Shrine & Gardens **13**
Chagall Artists' House **11**
Clandestine Immigration and Naval Museum **5**

Elijah's Cave **2**
The Haifa Museum of Art **14**
Mané Katz Museum **19**
Mitzpoor Ha-Shalom (Peace View Park) **12**
National Maritime Museum **6**

National Museum of Science, Technology, and Space **23**
Tikotin Museum of Japanese Art **16**
Stella Maris Lighthouse, Church & Carmelite Monastery **3**

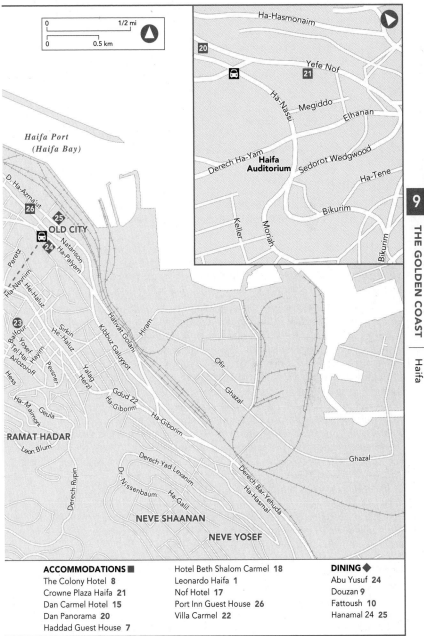

Haifa Port
(Haifa Bay)

Ha-Hasmonaim

Yefe Nof

Ha-Nassi · Megiddo

Elhanan

Derech Ha-Yam

Haifa
Auditorium

Sedorot Wedgwood

Ha-Tene

Bikurim

Keller

Moriah

Bikurim

OLD CITY

Natanson
Ha-Palyam

Peretz

Ha-Nevriim

He-Haluz

Balfour

Tel Hai · Hayim

Yosef

Arlozoroft

Pevsner

Sirkin

He-Haluz

Yalag

Herzl

Hativat Golan

Kibbuz Galuyyot

Hiram

Ofir

Ghazal

Hess

Ha-Marmon

Geula

Gdud 22

Ha-Giborim

Ha-Giborim

RAMAT HADAR

Leon Blum

Derech Rupin

Dr. Nissenbaum

Derech Yad Levanim

Ha-Galil

Derech Bar-Yehuda

Ha-Hasmal

Ghazal

NEVE SHAANAN

NEVE YOSEF

9

THE GOLDEN COAST | Haifa

**ACCOMMODATIONS** ■
The Colony Hotel **8**
Crowne Plaza Haifa **21**
Dan Carmel Hotel **15**
Dan Panorama **20**
Haddad Guest House **7**

Hotel Beth Shalom Carmel **18**
Leonardo Haifa **1**
Nof Hotel **17**
Port Inn Guest House **26**
Villa Carmel **22**

**DINING** ◆
Abu Yusuf **24**
Douzan **9**
Fattoush **10**
Hanamal 24 **25**

(Hadar business district, tourist center); (4) Masada (Masada St.); (5) Eliezer Golomb (Eliezer Golomb St.); (6) Gan Ha-Em (Central Carmel business district, upper terminus). When you take the Carmelit, don't panic—the incline is so great that the floors of the cars break into escalator-like steps.

Trains run every 10 minutes. The Carmelit operates Sunday through Thursday from 6:30am to midnight, Friday from 6:30am to 3pm, and resumes service on Saturday from 30 minutes after the end of Shabbat until midnight; it is closed during Shabbat. Ticket machines have English as well as Hebrew instructions. The fare is NIS 6.

**BY BUS**   Bus fares are charged according to your destination, so you must tell the driver where you're going. Most fares to places inside Haifa itself are NIS 6. Haifa's municipal buses operate from 5am to 11:30pm Sunday through Thursday; on Friday, bus service halts around 4:30pm; there's limited Saturday service from 9am to midnight on some lines. For info on buses inside Haifa, call ✆ **04/624-8888.** For interurban lines, call ✆ **04/854-9555.**

## Exploring Haifa

Before setting out, check with the Haifa Tourist Information Office's **"What's on in Haifa"** and the **Tourist Information Telephone Hot Line** (✆ **04/837-4253**), both of which will tell you what's happening while you're in town.

And remember too, that this is a primo beach destination. So beyond the sightseeing listed below, beachcombing can be considered a star activity. Haifa's great beaches, just south of town, are perfect for a late afternoon swim in summer, followed by fresh seafood at one of the beachside pubs. Allow time to watch the sun sink into the sea.

**The Baha'I Shrine and Gardens ★★★** LANDMARK   Haifa's most impressive sightseeing attraction is the splendid Baha'i Shrine and Gardens, reached from Zionism (Ha-Zionut) Avenue. The immaculate, majestic Baha'i gardens—with their stone peacocks and eagles and delicately manicured cypress trees—are a restful, aesthetic memorial to the founders of the Baha'i faith.

Haifa is the international headquarters for Baha'i, which began in Persia in the mid–19th century in a bloodbath of persecution. Baha'is believe in the unity of all religions and see all religious leaders—Christ, Buddha, Muhammad, Moses—as messengers of God sent at different times in history with doctrines varying to fit changing social needs but bringing substantially the same message. The most recent of these heavenly teachers, according to Baha'is, was Baha' Allah. He was exiled by the Turkish authorities to Acre, wrote his doctrines there, and died a peaceful death in Bahji House just north of Acre. See "Akko (Acre)," p. 211, for more information.

In the Haifa gardens, the huge domed **shrine** entombs the remains of the Bab, the Baha' Allah's herald. The tomb is a sight to see, with ornamental gold work and flowers in almost every nook and cranny. The Bab's remains, incidentally, were hidden for years after he died a martyr's death in front of a firing squad. Eventually, however, his followers secretly carried his remains to the Holy Land.

On a higher hilltop stands the Corinthian-style **Baha'i International Archives** building, modeled after the Parthenon, and the **Universal House of Justice,** with 58 marble columns and hanging gardens behind. These are business buildings, not open to tourists. They, and the shrine of the tomb of the Bab, all face toward Acre, the burial place of Baha' Allah.

The beautiful grounds are a geometric cascade of hanging gardens and terraces down to Ben-Gurion Boulevard—a gift of visual pleasure to the city that gave the

Baha'i religion its home. In addition to tourists, you'll see pilgrims who have come from all parts of the world to pay homage to the first leaders of this universal faith.

Off Ha-Zionut Ave. at Ben Gurion Blvd. ℂ **04/831-3131.** Reservations for admission and official tour almost always required. Free admission. Guided tours given every hour, on the hour. Modest dress required. Shrine daily 9am–noon; gardens daily 9am–5pm. Bus: 22 from the port; 23, 25, or 26 from Hadar.

**Clandestine Immigration and Naval Museum** ★★ MUSEUM This museum tells the wrenching story of those who tried to escape from Nazi-occupied Europe and of the few Holocaust survivors who made it to safety. Throughout the time of the Holocaust, when Jews desperately needed a haven, admission to British Mandate Palestine was largely denied to them by the British. Nevertheless, Jews fleeing from the Nazis during World War II, and Jewish escapees from displaced-persons camps after the war, constantly attempted to enter Palestine on rusty, unsafe, illegal vessels. One of these ships, the *Struma,* waited for months at sea for a country to accept the 765 refugees aboard until it was torpedoed and sank off Turkey in 1942. All but one on board perished. Other ships went down in Haifa harbor, with hundreds killed in sight of safety; still others, like the *Exodus 1947* (made famous by the Leon Uris book "Exodus" and the 1960 film), ran the British blockade only to have its passengers shipped to a Cyprus detention camp or returned to detention camps in Germany. The blockade-running vessel *Af-Al-Pi Chen* (**Nevertheless**) is now a part of the museum, commemorating all the ships that defied the British blockade.

204 Allenby Rd. ℂ **04/853-6249.** Admission NIS 15 adults, half-price for students and children. Sun–Thurs 8:30am–4pm. Closed Fri–Sat. Bus: 3, 5, 43, or 44.

**Mané Katz Museum** ★ ART MUSEUM Located near the Dan Panorama hotel in Central Carmel, this was once the romantic mountaintop villa of French artist Mané Katz. The museum now houses a collection of Katz's own work and personal art collection as well as interesting, well-curated visiting exhibits of contemporary art. The Mane Katz Judaica collection is especially fine

89 Yefe Nof (Panorama Rd.). ℂ **04/838-3482.** Admission for visiting exhibits NIS 25; for Mané Katz collection free admission. Sun–Mon and Wed–Thurs 10am–4pm; Tues 2–6pm; Fri 10am–1pm; Sat 10am–2pm. Bus: 22, 23, or 31. Carmelit: Central Carmel.

**Mitzpoor Ha-Shalom (Peace View Park)** ★★ PARK The grounds of the Baha'i gardens are split by Zionism Avenue. Farther up the hill is the lovely Mitzpoor Ha-Shalom (Peace View Park), also called the Ursula Malbin Sculpture Garden. Amid trees, flowers, and sloping lawns you'll find 18 bronze sculptures by Ursula Malbin of men, women, children, and animals at play. The view from here is magnificent—you can see all of Haifa's port area, Haifa Bay, Acre, Nahariya, and up to Rosh Ha-Niqra at the Lebanese border, plus all the surrounding mountains.

Zionism Ave., at the corner of Shnayim Be-November St. Free admission. Bus: 22 from the port; 23, 25, or 26 from Hadar.

**Stella Maris Lighthouse, Church and Carmelite Monastery** ★★ CHURCH During the Crusades, groups of religious hermits began to inhabit the caves of the Carmel District in emulation of Elijah the Prophet, whose life was strongly identified with this mountain. These monastic hermits were organized into the Carmelite order, which spread throughout Europe. However, the founders on the Carmel range were exiled at the end of the Crusades. The present Carmelite monastery and basilica dates from 1836. With a magnificent view of the sea, the entire ensemble of buildings, including the lighthouse, is known as "Stella Maris." An earlier monastery complex on this site served as a hospital for Napoleon's soldiers during his unsuccessful siege of Acre in 1799. The pyramid in front of the church is a memorial to the many abandoned French soldiers who were slaughtered by the Turks after Napoleon's retreat. The church is a beautiful structure, with Italian marble so vividly patterned that visitors mistakenly think the walls have been painted. Colorful paintings on the dome, done by Brother Luigi Poggi (1924–28), depict episodes from the Old Testament, the most dramatic being the scene of Elijah swept up in a chariot of fire; the statue of the Virgin Mary, carved from cedar of Lebanon, is also notable. The cave, situated below the altar, is believed to have been inhabited by Elijah. From Stella Maris, Haifa's little aerial cable car can take you down to the Bat Galim Beach Promenade, where you can walk in the Mediterranean or dine at waterfront eateries.

Stella Maris Rd. © **04/833-7758.** Daily 8am–12:30pm and 3–6pm. Modest dress required. Free admission. Bus: 25, 26, or 31.

**Tikotin Museum of Japanese Art** ★★ ART MUSEUM   As aficionados know, Israel plays host to one of the finest collections of Japanese art in the world. Collected originally by architect Felix Tikotin in the years prior to World War II, this exceptional museum owns some 7000 traditional and modern works, from antique swords to painted screens to fine ceramics. The museum is located in a handsome, Japanese-inspired building (with sliding doors and a zen garden) in Central Carmel.

89 Ha-Nassi Blvd. © **04/838-3554.** www.tmja.org.il. Joint admission to Haifa Museum of Art, Tikotin Museum of Japanese Art, and National Maritime Museum NIS 35. Mon–Thurs 10am–4pm; Fri–Sat 10am–1pm. Bus: 22 or 23. Carmelit: Gan Ha-Em Station.

**Technion** ★ CULTURAL INSTITUTION   The Technion Israel Institute of Technology is Israel's version of MIT. Founded in 1912, the 120-hectare (297-acre) campus is a most impressive university complex, offering views of the city, the coastline clear to Lebanon, and the snow-topped Syrian mountains. The Coler-California Visitor Center greets visitors with a working robot and a free 20-minute video about the school, as well as high-tech multimedia touch-screen videos, Internet kiosks, and laser-disc productions. Grab a pamphlet for a self-guided campus tour.

Technion City. © **04/829-3863.** www.technion.ac.il; Visitor's Center pard.technion.ac.il/coler/FramesColerE.html. Free admission. Visitor center hours Sun–Thurs 8:30am–3:30pm; closed Fri-Sat. Bus: 17 from Central Bus Station; Bus 31 from Central Carmel.

**Haifa University and Hecht Museum** ★★ CULTURAL INSTITUTION   With a dramatic location on the Carmel heights and many buildings designed by Oscar Niemeyer (of Brazilia fame, the superfuturistic capital city of Brazil), Haifa University is dazzling and quintessentially "Haifa." The views from the 30th floor observatory of the university's **Eshkol Tower** are not-to-be-missed, and the **Hecht Museum** contains an impressive collection of archaeological finds, as well paintings by Impressionists and artists of the Jewish School of Paris.

Hecht Museum Haifa University, Mt Carmel. © **04/824-0097.** www.mushecht.haifa.ac.il. Free admission. For a free **guided tour** of the campus; you must call in advance to reserve a spot. Sun–Mon, Wed–Thurs 10am–4pm; Tues 10am–7pm; Fri 10am–1pm; Sat 10am–2pm.

## Where to Stay

**The Colony Hotel** ★   This boutique hotel is set in a stylish, newly restored 19th-century building on a picturesque pedestrian mall leading up to the dramatic Baha'i Gardens and Center. Rooms vary so ask to look around; those at the back of the hotel are significantly quieter. A roof deck, garden, and small in-house spa are quality perks. Rooms have fridges and TVs. Look for off-season Internet deals.

28 Ben-Gurion Blvd. ℂ **04/851-3344.** www.colonyhaifa.com. 40 units. $170–$270 double. Rates include breakfast. On street parking. **Amenities:** Cafe, bar, spa, free Wi-Fi. Carmelit: Paris Square.

**Dan Carmel Hotel ★★** For 50 years, this has been Haifa's prestige hotel. Today, it's better than ever partially because, in 2012, all deluxe rooms on upper floors were totally reconstructed and now include super-luxurious bathrooms with sunken Jacuzzis and separate stall showers. As we go to press, standard rooms are in the process of being updated (alas, no sunken Jacuzzis for them, but they'll get the same chic, modern décor). A large pool and good children's programs help make this a relaxing base, as does the location, near dozens of excellent restaurants (it's also just a 5-minute walk to the Gan Ha-Em Carmelit stop). Final perk: The dazzling views.

85–87 Ha-Nassi Blvd. ℂ **04/830-3030.** www.danhotels.com. 219 units. $300–$350 double. Rates include breakfast. Parking (fee). Carmelit: Gan Ha-Em. **Amenities:** Restaurants, cafe, bar, children's activities, health club, pool and children's pool, sauna, nonsmoking rooms. Wi-Fi (free in lobby; 1 hr. of daily in-room use for e-Dan club members). Carmelit: Gan Ha-Em.

**Dan Panorama ★** Located in a 1980s high rise tower right at the Carmelit's Central Carmel subway stop, this is the most convenient place to stay in town, and its rooms offer tremendous views of the city. Other than that, it's bland-looking but efficient. We'd say the quality service and food here, along with the seasonal roof-level pool, and proximity to the Central Carmel's bustling well-priced restaurant scene, make it a still-worthy pick.

107 Ha-Nassi Blvd. ℂ **04/835-2222.** www.danhotels.com. 267 units. $205–$275 double. Rates include breakfast. Parking (fee). Carmelit: Gan Ha-Em. **Amenities:** 2 restaurants, cafe, business lounge, bar, concierge, outdoor swimming pool and children's pool, sauna. Wi-Fi (free in lobby; 1 hr. of daily in-room use for e-Dan club members).

**Loui M Apartments ★★** It's the little things that show someone cares when it comes to hotel stays. And at the Loui, those "tiny" items are myriad, including the good quality bedding (often done up in pretty floral coverlets); the inclusion of a fridge and kitchenette in each room; the swell roof deck; the way the staff seem eager to answer questions and help travelers; and the happy tchotchkes in the hallways—they give the place character. Small, too, are the prices, always a good thing. We consider the Loui a real find, especially for those who want to stay in the heart of the bustling downtown area (but well away from the noise).

35 Hechaluth ℂ **972 54-837-1342.** http://louihotelhaifa.com. 18 units. $65–$95 studio apartment. **Amenities:** Roofdeck; kitchenettes; free Wi-Fi.

**Port Inn Guest House ★** A friendly backpacker's hostel/guesthouse, this is Haifa's best super low budget choice (for digs just a step up, try the Loui; see above). It's close to the Carmelit, bus stops, and not far from the gentrified German Colony, with its many cafes and restaurants. There are well-maintained dorm beds, private singles and doubles (some with shared bathrooms), plus a garden terrace, a TV room, breakfast room, and free use of the kitchen. The helpful management also can arrange private apartment and room rentals.

34 Jaffa Rd. ℂ **04/852-4401.** www.portinn.nrt. 10 units, some with shared bathroom (3 dormitories with shared bathrooms). NIS 200 double with shared bathroom; NIS 90 dormitory bed. Breakfast is NIS 30. Cash only. **Amenities:** Breakfast room, lounge, use of kitchen, Wi-Fi with fee.

# Where to Dine

No-nonsense Haifa is not a gourmand's paradise, although it does have some finds (see below). The major dining scenes are in the Port area, Central Carmel and German Colony's **Ben Gurion Blvd Pedestrian Promenade.**

**Abu Yusuf ★ ARABIC**   A Haifa landmark for decades, no-frills Abu Yusuf serves a menu of classic appetizers, grilled meats, and oven baked dishes. The hummus here is particularly celebrated. Main courses include one trip to the buffet bar of 20 Middle Eastern salads. Ask about the fresh fish catch of the day.

1 Ha-Meginim St. ✆ **04/866-3723.** Main courses NIS 50–NIS 110. Sat–Thurs 9am–midnight; Fri 7am–4pm. Carmelit: Paris Sq.

**Douzan ★ MODERN MIDDLE EASTERN**   With an eclectic menu that combines French and Arabic traditions, plus a good wine list, Douzan is a step above its compatriots in this restaurant-jammed part of town. Partially that has to do with the service, which is unusually warm and gracious (this is a family owned place). And the food is always solid, particularly if you stick with the Middle Eastern specialties. Like Fattoush (below), Douzan offers a terrace on the Ben Gurion Pedestrian Mall with lovely vistas of the Baha'i Center and Gardens stretching up Mt. Carmel.

35 Ben Gurion Blvd. ✆ **057/944-3301.** Main courses and salads NIS 50–NIS 100. Daily 9am–after midnight.

**Fattoush ★★ MODERN MIDDLE EASTERN**   Two words: halvah ice cream. OK, that's three words, but this innovative and delicious dish is the reason it's so important to save room for dessert at Fattoush. Not that that's easy to do, as the food here is primo, whether you're trying the hummus with fried garlic and mushrooms or chowing down on the roasted eggplant with tahini. An excellent choice for vegetarians, Fattoush also shines when it comes to fish and meat dishes. And as with other restaurants o the Ben Gurion pedestrian mall, the views are delightful.

38 Ben-Gurion Blvd. ✆ **04/852-4930.** Main courses and salads NIS 55–NIS 100. Daily 9am–2am.

**Hanamal 24 ★★★ MEDITERRANEAN**   "The Jerusalem Post" called this restaurant the "culinary jewel of the north"; and though we think that title could as easily apply to Uri Buri in Akko or Helena in Caesaerea (see p. 210 and 202) this is far and away Haifa's finest restaurant and *one* of the best in the region, if not all of Israel. Helmed by chef Ran Rosh, the food has a distinctively French flare to it, not surprising as Rosh studied under Gallic legend Paul Bocuse. The menu changes daily but always includes such luxury items as foie gras, lobster and Valhrona chocolate. Don't let the location put you off (it's in a non-descript building in the warehouse district, right next to the railroad track); once inside, you'll feel like you've jetted off to an elegant mansion in Tuscany. Be sure to consult the sommelier, as the restaurant has sourced some unusual, small-production Israeli wineries for its vino. Reservations are necessary, there's no handicap access, and it's best visited by taxi.

24 Hanamal St. ✆ **057/944-2262.** www.namal24.rest-e.co.il. Main courses NIS 92–NIS 150; Business lunch menu served Mon–Fri noon–5pm; prix-fixe dinner served Mon–Thurs only NIS 150. Mon–Sat noon–midnight.

# Nightlife & Entertainment

Except when the American Fleet is in, Haifa is not a late-night town. Highlights include concerts and performances at the **Haifa Auditorium,** the film programs at the **Cinematheque,** and smaller folk and rock performances at **Haifa University.** Local pubs also buzz with activity for those looking for a fun, low-key night on the town.

# AKKO (ACRE) ★★★

Akko's Old Walled City, a true architectural gem (and a UNESCO World Heritage Site), is in the process of becoming one of Israel's new overnight destinations. That may be because it's a natural base for touring the northwest quadrant of the country. But we're guessing that many find it difficult to leave Akko itself. With romantic minarets, authentic bazaars, adorable boutique hotels, unusual shops and eateries, an impressive ramparts, Akko (23km or 14 miles north of Haifa) has undeniable charm.

It also is loaded with history. Akko has been a port city for over 4,000 years. It flourished for centuries under the Phoenicians, Romans, and Byzantines and became the capital and last stronghold of the Crusader Kingdom before it finally fell in A.D. 1291. The Crusader city and fortifications lay in ruins until Akko was rebuilt in the late 1700s by the notorious Ottoman governor, El Jezzer (The Butcher) Pasha, who constructed a walled city filled with mosques, labyrinthine markets, travelers' inn, bathhouses, and mansions, all on top of the monumental structures of the forgotten Crusader city. Akko is divided into the New City, mainly built after 1948 and home to a mixed Israeli Arab and Jewish population, and the walled **Old City,** which is the main attraction inhabited mostly by Christian and Muslim Israelis.

**GETTING THERE** **By Tour Bus and Public Transportation:** Both **Egged** (www. eggedtours.com) and **United Bus Tours** (www.unitedtours.co.il) include stops in Caesarea on tours of the area.

**By Railroad and Bus:** There is regular train and bus service from Tel Aviv and Haifa to the Akko Train and Bus Stations in the New City of Akko. From there, it's a short taxi ride to the Weizmann Street entrance to Akko's Old City.

**By Car:** From Haifa, follow signs northward to Akko. The driving distance on the Haifa-Akko road is not long, but heavy traffic can make it an hour trip. Follow signs to Akko, then to Old City. Inside the Weizmann Street entrance to the Old City walls is a pay parking lot.

**VISITOR INFORMATION** Located just inside the Weitzman St. entrance to the Old City, the excellent **Akko Visitor's Center** (𝄬 **04/995-6707;** www.akko.org.il; Sat–Thurs 8:30am–5pm) is the place to buy a detailed map of the entire city of Akko and rent a self-guided audio walking tour, which includes exploration of the Subterranean Crusader City. **Important:** A combined admission ticket to all sites and museums in the city may also be purchased here, and its an excellent value at NIS125.

## Exploring Old Akko

Allow yourself at least a half-day to wander through Old Akko's medieval streets. Unlike the restored Old City of Jaffa, which is filled with tourist galleries, Old Akko is both charming and genuine, and its streets teem with real life. The best place to start your tour is at the **Jezzar Pasha Mosque.** Right across the street from Al-Jezzar Pasha's mosque is the marvelous **Subterranean Crusader City,** and just a few steps farther is the Municipal Museum (exhibits sometimes closed for renovations) housed in Ahmed al Jezzar Pasha's **Turkish bath.**

Next you'll wander through the pleasant and colorful streets of the **bazaar.** Be sure to see the most picturesque shop in the bazaar, **Kurdy and Berit's Coffee and Spices,** at no. 13/261 (ask around, it's deep in the market). The showcases here are filled with exotic objects and herbal remedies. If you make a purchase at Kurdy and Berit's, the very hospitable owner may invite you to try a cup of thick Arabic coffee. Also look for **Abu Nassar's Oriental Sweets** and **Hummus Said,** both located in the market near the **Khan el Shwardia** and each a legend throughout northern Israel. Akko's "formal" market is **Suq El-Abiad,** but numerous streets within Old Akko serve as shopping areas. You'll pass the **El-Zeituneh Mosque** to the **Khan El-Umdan** caravansary, marked by a tall, segmented tower. A **caravansary,** or khan, was a combination travelers' inn, warehouse, banking center, stable, and factory traditionally built around a lightly fortified courtyard to house caravans, pilgrims, and other visitors.

At the port, you can hire a boat to take you on a **sea tour** of the city walls (about NIS 50 per person). Don't be afraid to bargain. Many boat operators will be glad to take you on a motor- or fishing-boat cruise around Old Akko. Settle on a price in advance (about NIS 125 for an hour is average), and get a boat that looks comfortable.

In Venezia Square (Ha-Dayagim in Hebrew), facing the port, is the **Sinian Pasha Mosque,** and behind it the **Khan El-Faranj** caravansary. Yet another khan, named **El-Shwarda,** is a short distance to the northeast. A few steps back is the Jezzar Pasha Mosque. You'll also want to visit the dreaded **Al-Jezzar Wall,** where barbaric punishments were meted out, and the outer wall of the Akko prison, scene of a massive prisoner escape in 1947 (during the British Mandate) engineered by the Jewish underground and dramatized in the film "Exodus."

## THE TOP ATTRACTIONS

**Treasures in the Walls Ethnographic Museum** ★★ MUSEUM   As you might have guessed from the name, this atmospheric museum is located right in the city walls, in an ancient tunnel. This placement gives the exhibits—all of which explore daily life from the Ottoman period through the founding of Israel—added weight, though even if they were to be housed in a warehouse, the reproduction of a 19th-century market (the museum's showpiece) would be fascinating. A second section of the museum displays exquisite antique furniture (including pieces inlaid with mother of pearl in the old Damascus tradition) and decorative items.

In the eastern wall of the Old City (left turn inside the wall at Weitzman St. entrance. ✆ **04/991-1004.** Admission NIS 15, children NIS 12. Sat–Thurs 10am–5pm; Fri 10am–2pm; curtailed hours in winter.

**Jezzar Pasha Mosque** ★ RELIGIOUS SITE   Ahmed al Jezzar ("the Butcher") Pasha was the Ottoman-Turkish governor of Akko during the late 1700s and notorious for his habit of mutilating both those in his government and those he governed. According to legend, on Al-Jezzar Pasha's whim, faithful chamberlains and retainers were ordered to slay their own children as signs of loyalty to him, and the Pasha rewarded government officials and loyal subjects with amputations of hands, arms, eyes, and legs to test their willingness to submit to his desires. If this was how he treated his friends, you can imagine the fate of his enemies. When Napoleon invaded Egypt, the English joined the Ottomans in trying to drive him out. Al-Jezzar Pasha marshaled the defenses of Akko, and the city withstood Napoleon's assault in 1799. Napoleon's forces never recovered, and Napoleon's dream of conquering Egypt died outside the walls of Akko. The Pasha died in Akko in 1804, to everyone's relief.

Ahmed al Jezzar Pasha's contributions to Akko included building fountains, a covered market, a Turkish bath, and the harmonious mosque complex that bears his name. Begun in 1781, it's an excellent example of classic Ottoman-Turkish architecture and stands among the Pasha's most ambitious projects. It also illustrates how the traditional mosque complex worked.

As you approach the mosque area, Al-Jezzar Street turns right off Weizmann Street. The mosque entrance is a few steps along Al-Jezzar Street on the left. Before you

# Akko (Acre)

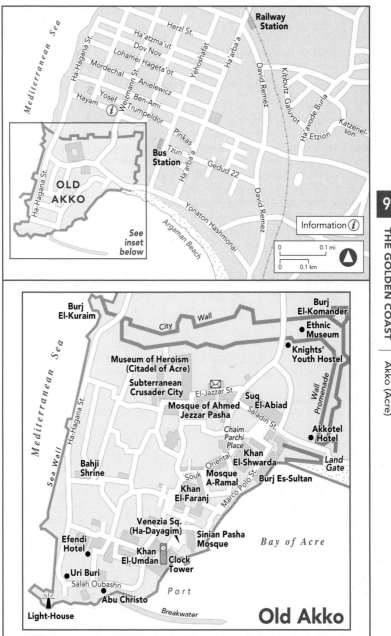

## A private GUIDE

Akko's own **Abdu Abu Tufan** knows the complex history and local legends of his city like few others. A licensed, innovative guide, he's also a professional storyteller and is great at bringing the stones and buildings of Akko to life. Contact him at www.abdu-matta.com or ✆ **04/981-3719.** Many enjoy his services so much they hire him to guide them through the entire region.

mount the stairs to the mosque courtyard, notice the ornate little building to the right of the stairs. It's a *sabil,* or cold-drinks stand, from which pure, refreshing drinking water, sometimes mixed with fruit syrups, was distributed—a part of the mosque complex's services. Note especially the fine tile fragments mounted above the little grilled windows just beneath the *sabil*'s dome. Tile-making was an Ottoman specialty.

Up the stairs, you enter the mosque courtyard. Your ticket will enable you to explore the complex of Crusader buildings, including a church (now flooded and used as cisterns) over which the mosque was built. Just inside the entry is a marble disc bearing the *tughra,* or monogram, of the Ottoman sultan. It spells out the sultan's name, his father's name, and the legend "ever-victorious."

The arcaded courtyard around the mosque can be used for prayers during hot days of summer, as can the arcaded porch at the front of the mosque. The *shadirvan,* or ablutions fountain, opposite the mosque entry, is used for ritual cleansing five times a day before prayers. You must slip off your shoes before entering the mosque proper.

Inside you'll notice the mihrab, or prayer niche, indicating the direction of Mecca, toward which worshipers must face when they pray. The galleries to the right and left of the entrance are reserved for women, the main area of the floor for men. The *minbar,* a sort of pulpit, is that separate structure with a curtained entry, stairs, and a little steeple. Around to the right are a mausoleum and a small graveyard that hold the tombs of Ahmed al Jezzar Pasha and his successor, Suleiman Pasha, and members of their families. The mosque is still used by Akko's Muslim population, so when it's in service for prayer, you must wait until the prayers are over to enter the mosque.

Al-Jezzar St. Call in advance to request hours and admission (which change; the tourist office can also help you). Modest dress required.

**Hammam al-Basha (Turkish Bath)** ★ Down at the end of Al-Jezzar Street, just around the corner, these handsome baths were built by Ahmed al Jezzar Pasha as part of his mosque complex in the 1780s. Along with a rather silly multi-media show about the baths, the museum's collections include antiquities, an exhibit on Napoleon's attack, the Museum of Heroism, and a folklore exhibit. For architecture fans only.

Al-Jezzar St. Admission $5 for adults, discounts for students and children; includes admission to Crusader City. Sun–Thurs and Sat 8:30am–6pm; Fri 8:30am–2pm; Sat 9am–5pm. Closings are 1 hr. earlier in winter.

**Museum of Underground Prisoners** ★★ The complex of buildings, in the Citadel of Akko, was used as a prison in Ottoman and British Mandate times. Part of the prison has been set aside in honor of the Jewish underground fighters imprisoned here by the British. With the help of Irgun forces, 251 prisoners staged a mass escape in May 1947. If you saw the movie "Exodus," that was the breakout featured in the film and this was the prison. The prison is also revered by Arab Israelis and by

Palestinians, whose own national fighters were detained and, in many cases, executed here during the British Mandate.

Among the exhibits are the entrance to the escape tunnel and displays of materials showing the British repression of Zionist activity during the Mandate. Not all prisoners were lucky enough to escape, however. Eight Irgun fighters were hanged here in the 10 years before Israel's independence. You can visit the death chamber, called the Hanging Room, complete with noose.

Inmates here included Zeev Jabotinsky and Dov Gruner, among other leaders of Israel's independence movement. Before the Mandate, the prison's most famous inmate was Baha' Allah (1817–92), founder of the Baha'i faith (see "Bahji," below).

Just north of Crusader City. © **04/991-1375.** Admission NIS 15 adults, discounts available for students and children. Sun–Thurs 9am–5pm; Fri 8:30am–1pm.

**Subterranean Crusader City (Hospitalers' Fortress)** ★★★ Virtually across the street from the Mosque of Ahmed al Jezzar Pasha is this Subterranean Crusader City, the town's unmissable site. In the entrance is a tourism information kiosk, where you can buy a city map and an entrance ticket.

The Crusaders built their fortified city atop what was left of the Roman city. The Ottomans, and especially Ahmed al Jezzar Pasha, built their city on top of the largely intact buildings of the Crusaders. In Ottoman times, the cavernous chambers here were used as a caravansary until Napoleon's attack. In preparation for the defense of his city, Al-Jezzar Pasha ordered the walls heightened, and the Crusader rooms partially filled with sand and dirt, to better support the walls. Today, you get a good look at how the Crusaders lived and worked in the late 1100s, from the ruined Gothic church to the dungeons and massive gathering halls. A highlight is the **Knights' Halls,** once occupied by the Knights Hospitalers of Saint John. In the ceiling of the hall, a patch of concrete marks the spot where Jewish underground members, imprisoned by the British in the citadel (directly above the hall), attempted to break out. Be sure to pick up a headset at the entrance so you understand the significance of what you're seeing.

Across from Jezzar Pasha Mosque. Admission NIS 28 adults, discounts for students and children; admission includes entrance to Municipal Museum. Sun–Thurs 8:30am–6pm; Fri 8:30am–2pm; Sat 9am–5pm. Closings are 1 hr. earlier in winter.

## AL-JEZZAR'S WALL

To appreciate the elaborate system of defenses built by Ahmed al Jezzar Pasha to protect against Napoleon's fleet and forces, turn right as you come out of the Municipal Museum/Museum of Heroism onto Ha-Hagana Street and walk a few steps north. You'll see the double system of walls with a moat in between. Jutting into the sea is an Ottoman defensive tower called the Burj El-Kuraim. You're now standing at the northwestern corner of the walled city. Walk east (inland) along the walls, and you'll pass the citadel, the Burj El-Hazineh (Treasury Tower), and cross Weizmann Street to the Burj El-Komander, the strongest point in the walls. The land wall system continues south from here all the way to the beach.

## BAHJI

To Baha'is, this shrine to their prophet Baha' Allah is the holiest place on earth. Baha'i followers believe that God is manifested to men and women through prophets such as Abraham, Moses, Jesus, and Muhammad, as well as the Bab (Baha' Allah's predecessor) and Baha' Allah himself. The Baha'i faith proclaims that all religions are one, that men and women are equal, that the world should be at peace, and that education should be universal. Baha'i followers are encouraged to live simply and to dedicate themselves to helping their fellow men and women. They look forward to a day when there will be a single world government and one world language.

The Baha'i faith grew out of the revelation of the Bab, a Persian Shiite Muslim teacher and mystic who flourished from 1844 to 1850, and was executed by the Persian shah for insurrection and radical teachings. In 1863, Mirza Husein Ali Nuri, one of the Bab's disciples, proclaimed himself Baha' Allah, the Promised One, whose coming had been foretold by the Bab. Baha' Allah was exiled by the Persian government in cooperation with the Ottoman leaders to Baghdad, Constantinople, Adrianople, and finally to Akko, where he arrived in August 1868. He and several of his followers were imprisoned for 2½ years at the Akko Citadel. The authorities later put him under house arrest, and he was eventually brought to Bahji, where he remained until his death in 1892. He is buried here in a peaceful tomb surrounded by magnificent gardens. Baha'is are still persecuted, especially in Iran where the faith was born; the Shiite Muslims in authority today look upon them as blasphemers and heretics.

You can visit the shrine at **Bahji (Delight),** where Baha' Allah lived, died, and is buried, on Friday, Saturday, and Sunday only, from 9am to noon. The house's beautiful gardens are open to visitors every day, from 9am to 4pm. Catch a no. 271 bus heading north toward Nahariya, and make sure it stops at Bahji.

Going north from Akko, you'll see an impressive gilded gate on the right-hand side of the road after about 2km (1¼ mile). This gate is not open to the public. Go past it until you are almost 3km (about 1¾ miles) from Akko, and you'll see a sign, SHAM-ERAT. Get off the bus, turn right here, and go another short distance to the visitors' gate. The Ottoman-Victorian house holds some memorabilia of Baha' Allah, and the lush gardens are a real treat.

## Where to Stay

**Akkotel ★★** This warmly welcoming boutique hotel, run by the very helpful Morani family, is set in a lovingly restored building right inside the walls of the Old City. Everything is comfy and feels like an old inn. Larger rooms (some with sleeping lofts) can fit families; bathrooms have either a tub or a shower. The breakfast is generous and the coffee is strong. What more could you ask?

1 Saladin St., Akko. Near Weitzman St. entrance to Old City. ℰ **04/987-7100.** www.akkotel.com. 16 units. $175–$237 double. Rate includes breakfast. Free limited parking. Amenities: Restaurant, fridge/minibar, free Wi-Fi.

**Efendi Hotel ★★★** Few other hotels in Israel match the grace and beauty of this luxury boutique hotel, set in a a pair of conjoined majestic Ottoman-era mansions on a byway deep in the Old City. Opened in 2012 by the owner of Akko's gourmet Uri Buri Restaurant (see below), it's a true standard setter. Many of the 12 rooms are palatial in size, some with traditional hand-painted, Ottoman-style ceilings; exquisite wooden latticework; and massive windows with exquisite views. Massages can be had in the 400-year-old on-site hammam though some find lazing on the rooftop deck with its tremendous sea views to be relaxation enough. Use of the pool at a hotel just outside the old city can be arranged. Arriving guests can phone from the Uri Buri Restaurant and arrange for directions and a baggage porter, because the hotel is not car accessible.

Louis IX St.. ℰ **074-729-9799.** www.efendi-hotel.com. 14 units. $330–$730. Free on street parking. Rates include breakfast. Amenities: Dining room, roof terrace; Turkish sauna, wine bar, free Wi-Fi.

**Knights' Youth Hostel and Guest House ★**   This brand new, efficient and spotlessly clean Israel Youth Hostel Association hostel is housed in a building that blends in with Old City architecture. It's located just inside the main entrance to the walled Old City. The hostel is heavily booked by international groups or Israeli students, however, double or family rooms can be arranged. Meals are kosher.

Weitzman St., Old Akko ✆ **02/594-5711;** nationwide reservations 1-599-510-511. www.iyha.org.il. 76 hostel units; 6 private units. $133 private double with shower, $35 for dorm bed. Rate includes half-board. **Amenities:** Dining room, TV, fridge, free Wi-Fi, nearby parking (fee).

## Where to Dine

**Humus Said ★★★** MIDDLE EASTERN   It's a strong claim, but the devotees of this 35-plus year old restaurant claim it serves the best hummus in the Middle East. Clearly the folks who line up outside the door every day agree, and I think you will too after you taste the tangy, creamy hummus that's hand mashed here and seasoned with just the right amount of cumin. The other specialty here is *makhlouta,* a Lebanese stew made with carmelized onions, lentils, chickpeas, rice, cracked and whole wheat and pinto beans, and it, too, is scrumptious.

In the Old City market—ask any local for directions; hours vary. ✆ **972-4-9913945.** A meal will be approximately $2.50–$3.50.

**Savida Seafood Bar ★★** SEAFOOD   What the fishermen bring, you will eat—that's the successful formula at this popular local eatery, but it makes the food here sound simpler than it is. In truth, the cooks at Savida are quite creative, and will often add a dash of this spice or a dollop of that sauce to liven up their dishes. Yes, the space is cramped, but the atmosphere is so festive and the service to warm-hearted, few mind. For a restaurant that opened just in 2013, it already has quite the following.

Located in the Turkish Bazaar. No phone or website. Meals about $15–$20. Hours vary.

**Uri Buri ★★★** SEAFOOD   This gourmet, but relaxed restaurant's secret ingredient is owner/chef Uri Yirmias, who knows how to prepare seafood and fish to perfection. Uri's coquilles St. Jacques, pan-seared according to his special recipe, are like the filet mignon of the sea; his delicate carpaccios are exquisite; and the restaurant's tiny, tender calamari with kumquats and pink grapefruit are among the best dishes I've ever had. All of this extraordinary food is served in a handsome (and ancient) Turkish home, by a staff that knows how to make a meal feel like a special occasion. Our advice: If you go as a couple, share one tasting menu, and order another main course, just so nobody goes away hungry.

93 Haganah St., near the lighthouse (Miidal Or) in the Old City. ✆ **04/955-2212.** Reservations necessary. Main courses NIS 60–NIS 180. Wed–Mon noon–11pm.

# EILAT & PETRA

At the southern tip of Israel, a 4-hour drive across the Negev from Tel Aviv or Jerusalem, the **Red Sea resort of Eilat** is a world apart from the rest of the country. It's a place where Israelis and tourists love to come for a few days to unwind and relax. There's no history to absorb, just easily accessible coral reefs to snorkel and plenty of beaches. Even in winter, when Jerusalem can be cold and raw and Tel Aviv can be chilly, Eilat's beaches are usually warm enough for sunbathing and at least a quick swim in the Red Sea. There are tons of hotels in every price range, and although most are not directly on the town's beachfronts, most have large swimming pools with many of them heated for winter. Summers in Eilat are blazing hot and usually filled with vacationing Israeli families.

Eilat is also the closest and most convenient border crossing into Jordan if you plan to visit Petra—unlike the busy Allenby Bridge Crossing from the West Bank into Jordan (where you must have a visa issued at a Jordanian embassy ahead of time), visas are issued on the spot at the Eilat-Aqaba Crossing, and there are far fewer crowds and processing delays.

Petra (in Jordan), the legendary and extraordinary, long lost ancient city carved from the walls of a hidden canyon, has become a must-see destination for thousands of world travelers. Although 1-day package bus tours from Eilat can give you a 2-hour glimpse of Petra, this amazing site and the dramatic landscape of southern Jordan are well worth several days of your attention.

## EILAT

Eilat's chief claims to fame for the tourist are busy beaches with almost no wave action, coral reefs filled with exotic fish, and year-round sunshine. What was once a small, relaxed desert and Red Sea resort town now hosts 50 gargantuan upscale hotels, vast shopping malls, and a downtown waterfront lined with jewelry shops, sneaker stores, and hawker's booths where visitors can while away their evenings. It's easygoing, fun, and Israelis, both Jewish and Arab, flock here to forget the pressures of daily life. Lots of European package tourists jet directly into Eilat (and see nothing else in Israel). Eilat's planners have not emphasized the desert and Bedouin traditions of the region—instead they've aimed for the generic look of a gleaming white international resort, such as Cancún. During Israeli school holidays, Eilat is usually overrun with families and kids.

Eilat is also a military outpost and a major shipping port—you'll see ample evidence of this all along the shoreline. The city's hotel area is less than a mile from the Jordanian border, and you can see the Jordanian port city of Aqaba, with a population of 30,000, across the bay in a haze of desert sand, ringed by date palms. Until Israel and Jordan signed a peace treaty in 1994, Aqaba seemed as unattainable as a mirage. There is now a border crossing for tourists just north of Eilat, and from Eilat you can also book excursions to Jordan's fabulous lost canyon city of Petra. Saudi Arabia is 20km (12 miles) south of Aqaba—you can see it from the beaches in Eilat.

During summer, the outdoor afternoon heat in Eilat can exceed 110°F (43°C); it's best to stay in the shade between noon and 4pm. In winter, the weather can be cool to chilly and dry, but the Red Sea is warm enough for swimming, especially if you're used to the waters of the North Atlantic. Pools in better hotels are often heated.

## Essentials

**GETTING THERE   By Plane   Arkia Airlines** (www.arkia.com) flies to Eilat from points in north and central Israel and offers great **flight plus hotel packages.** The downtown airport is right in the heart of Eilat, next to the hotel district, and can receive only smaller aircraft; larger planes and international flights land at **Ouvda airport,** 60km (37 miles) north of Eilat. One-way flights from Tel Aviv are approximately $180. The bus ride from Ouvda to town can take an hour. Add in the hassle of getting to and from local airports, and the option of flying to Eilat from Tel Aviv may not save that much time.

If you arrive from inside Israel at Eilat's little **downtown airport,** you will be right in the center of town, at the bottom of the hill where Hatmarim Boulevard meets Ha-Arava Road (the road north to Beersheba or the Dead Sea). It will be a quick, inexpensive taxi ride to hotels. All the local city buses (no. 1, 2, or 15) run every 20 to 30 minutes or so, from early morning until about 7 or 8pm, daily except Saturday, stopping early on Friday (about 3 or 4pm).

**By Bus**   There are a number of daily buses (except on Shabbat) from Jerusalem and Tel Aviv to Eilat. The trip takes about 4½ hours. If you arrive by bus, there's a baggage checkroom at the bus station in case you have to seek out a hotel room. It is best not to carry luggage even short distances in Eilat's hot weather. Space on buses from Jerusalem and Tel Aviv to Eilat must be reserved through Egged Buses (✆ **08/636-5111**); reserve your bus seat leaving Eilat at least 2 days ahead; on weekends, holidays, and summer vacations, 4-day advance reservations are necessary.

**By Car**   The trip takes approximately 4 hours by direct road from Tel Aviv or Jerusalem.

**VISITOR INFORMATION**   The **Eilat Tourist Information Center** (✆ **08/630-9111**; www.goisrael.com.) is located in a small building called Bridge House, on the North Beach Promenade. It's open Sunday-Thursday 8am-5pm, Friday and Jewish holiday eves 8am-1pm. Pick up English-language maps and free copies of other tourist brochures filled with discount coupons. You can also get help and advice on booking accommodations and tours, bus schedules, events in the region, diving and snorkeling information, and travel to Jordan.

### Getting to Jordan

Bus and taxi service are now available from Eilat to Aqaba, Jordan border crossing. From the Jordanian side of the border, or in Aqaba itself, you can arrange for a private or shared taxi for the 2 hour drive to Petra. Cost: $60 to $80 for a shared taxi depending on your bargaining skills.

Eilat has no VAT, but because many supplies have to be shipped in, prices tend to be higher. *Tip:* Gasoline for your car will be 18 percent cheaper in Eilat than in the rest of Israel, so fill up before heading back north.

**ORIENTATION**    There are three easily distinguishable areas in Eilat. First is the inland, amorphous town itself, built atop hills that roll toward the sea. **Coral Beach,** with its great snorkeling and smattering of hotels, is about 6km (3¾ miles) south of town on the western shore of the harbor, served by Bus 15. The **North Beach** district, a 10-minute walk from the center of town on the eastern shore of the harbor, is where the hotel and beach action lives. It is also the site of an elaborate marina system and artificial lagoon, cutting several hundred yards inland. Around this lagoon are hotels, restaurants, and a promenade filled with pubs, discos, shops, and miles of street vendors—a fun way to spend a hot summer evening.

## Sports & Outdoor Activities

**BEACHES**    The waters around Eilat are relatively wave-free and safe. The small sharks are not particularly hungry for you, however, stepping on spiny sea urchins can be a major danger.

North Beach ★ is a stony and sandy beach that starts in front of the Leonardo Eilat Hotel and extends as far eastward as the Dan Eilat Hotel and Herods Palace Hotel complex. Because it's relatively free of coral and sea urchins, this is a good beach for swimming. The nicer part of the beach is at the end near the Dan and Herods Palace hotels. Water skis and boats can be rented, but make sure you know where you're going, because you don't have to ski very far to get into Jordanian or Egyptian territory and hot water.

Coral Beach ★★, which is a short drive or a no. 15 bus ride around the curve of the bay, is the best beach for **snorkeling** and **diving.** It's blessed with coral reefs just offshore and lots of fish. Snorkeling equipment can be rented. Much of Coral Beach is now a nature preserve, perfect for both first-time and intermediate snorkeling and scuba diving. The best snorkeling is inside the actual **Coral Beach Nature Reserve** (see below).

Dolphin Reef ★★ is certainly the prettiest beach in Eilat, dotted with palm trees and thatched-roof *palapa* structures for shade. With its sandy floor, it's the best beach in Eilat for swimming. The dolphins are an added attraction. The reef's institute believes in informal, personal relationships between humans and dolphins. The dolphins are free to come and go to the open sea as they like, but for years have chosen to attach themselves to Dolphin Reef. As you swim and sun, you can watch them frolicking and being fed just beyond the roped-off human swimming zone; you can also walk out to a wooden observation pier in the dolphins' free-swimming area for a closer look. For about NIS 280 per person, you can join a guided group of snorkelers for a 25-minute **swim among the dolphins.** (Advance reservations are necessary.) Snorkeling equipment is included in the fee. For qualified divers, guided dives can also be arranged. Sometimes, these swims can bring close encounters, while at other times, the free-swimming dolphins keep their distance. You must be a good swimmer, and there are no guarantees, refunds, or rain checks. Or, you can sit right on a raft while dolphins come up to the trainers for snacks and play sessions. Dolphin Reef also hosts a program of scientific studies and therapy sessions for people with medical or emotional problems.

Also offered are sessions in the Dolphin Reef's three secluded **Relaxation Pools**—one is fresh water, one Red Sea water, and one heavy mineral water not unlike The

Dead Sea. Sessions for up to 20 people last 2 hours and include New Age music, refreshments, and a botanical habitat for resting. The price is NIS 160 per person weekdays, 190 per person weekends, and reservations are necessary. General admission to Dolphin Reef is waived for those entering with reservations for snorkeling and diving with dolphins and for the Relaxation Pools.

There is a reasonably priced cafeteria serving hot and cold drinks, snacks, and full meals on the premises, as well as a pub and a program of films on dolphins. Many evenings, when admission to the beach is free, there is live or disco music and dancing at the beach's pub. This is one of the best places in Eilat to spend a day or an evening.

Dolphin Reef is midway between North Beach and Coral Beach (© **08/630-0111** for activity reservations; www.dolphinreef.co.il). It's open Sunday to Thursday from 9am to 5pm; Fridays, Saturdays, and holidays 9am to 4:30pm. Admission is NIS 70 for adults over 15 and NIS 44 for children 5 to 15. There's no admission fee after 7pm, when the pub/restaurant and beach stay open, but the dolphin sessions finish for the day. Take bus no. 15.

**BIRD-WATCHING ★★★**    Eilat is one of the best places on earth for bird-watching, due to its prime location on the Jordan Valley–Red Sea–Great African Rift Valley migration path between Europe and Africa. Migration times are twice a year: From **September through November,** the birds head south to Africa, and from **March through May,** they head back north to Europe.

Eilat's **International Birding and Research Centre** (© **08/633-5339** or 050/211-2498 to reserve tours; fax 08/633-5319; www.birdsofeilat.com) is a clearinghouse for information and activities. It conducts a guided 2-hour bird-watching tours for NIS 150 and 4-hour tours for NIS 220. Full-day tours can also be arranged for NIS 400, between February 15 and May 15, when a general spring census of birds is conducted and is open to the public.

Each year in March, the Center hosts an **International Birdwatchers' Festival** that has been growing in reputation. Check the website for information about the many special programs and discounts on accommodations and car rentals at the time of the festival.

**BOATING**    You can hire boats 24 hours a day at the North Beach marina and lagoon—boats for water-skiing and water parachuting, sailboats, fishing boats, paddleboats, motor sea-cycles, sailboards, and kayaks are all available.

**GLASS-BOTTOM BOATS ★**    Boats leave from the jetty just north of Coral Beach or from North Beach. **Israel Yam** (© **08/633-2325**) operates daily 1½-hour glass-bottom boat trips, leaving North Beach several times during the day for NIS 70 for adults and NIS 50 for children. Look for a 15 percent discount coupon, often available in the free Hebrew- and English-language tourist brochures.

**SNORKELING & SCUBA DIVING ★★★**    *Note:* If you want to scuba dive, you must bring your certification from abroad or obtain a license in Israel.

The best-equipped firms for snorkeling and scuba diving are Aqua-Sport and Red Sea Sports Club. **Aqua-Sport** (© **08/633-4404;** ) is located across the highway from the Isrotel Yam Suf Hotel on Coral Beach. Aqua-Sport also has a program of weeklong adult diving lessons and summer camps for kids ages 10 to 15 during July and August. Aqua-Sport is open every day from 8:30am to 12:30am.

**Red Sea Sport Club's Manta Dive Center,** located at the Isrotel Yam Suf Hotel (© **08/633-3666;** www.redseasports.co.il), is another recommended diving center at

Coral Beach. It offers facilities similar to those at Aqua-Sport, plus sailing, windsurfing, boating, desert safaris, water-skiing, and bike rental. There is even a special sauna facility for divers. It's open daily from 8:30am to 4:30pm in winter and until 6pm in summer.

**Snuba diving,** tethered to an oxygen tank on a raft over the coral reef, is an easy, enjoyable way to dive without any extensive training. The **Snuba Diving Center** (℡ **08/637-2722;** www.snuba.co.il) will arrange a variety of excursions for you. Prices start at NIS 200 for 1½ hours and include training. Look for a discount coupon on the Snuba website.

## Sightseeing

### Coral Beach Nature Reserve ★★ NATURE RESERVE

A small but fascinating chunk of the Red Sea's reef system, teeming with colorful, exotic fish and sea creatures, this nature reserve is a swimmable treasure. Because the wind and current usually move southward, all you have to do is drift and paddle a bit to observe the reef through your mask. At the southern end of the reef, you can head for shore and walk back to the starting point for another round of drifting over the reef!

On-site are comfortable changing rooms with showers, and an open-air snack bar (buy an illustrated guide to the swimming trails there). The reserve also rents snorkels, masks, and fins; there is a refundable deposit of NIS 100 for each snorkel set.

*Warning:* Wear some sort of foot covering every time you enter the water here. Spiny sea urchins lurk almost everywhere you might want to stand.

Bus no. 15 runs from downtown Eilat to Coral Beach and back every half-hour. ℡ **08/637-6829.** www.parks.org.il. Park Admisssion NIS 40 adults, NIS 20 children. Mask, snorkel, and fins rental NIS 40. Daily 9am–5pm. Closed Yom Kippur. Bus: 15.

### Coral World Underwater Observatory and Marine Park ★★★ AQUARIUM

Located just south of Coral Beach, this complex includes two underwater observatories beside a busy, picturesque reef called the Japanese Gardens. In addition to the underwater observatories, you'll also find the **Maritime Museum and Aquarium.** The aquarium is built so that you stand in the middle and the fish swim around you in a huge circular tank. There are also large outdoor observation pools—one for big sharks and another for sea turtles and rays. For an additional NIS 10, you can visit the Oceanarium, a high-tech simulated "dive" in a small theater that offers the sights and feel of going underwater. Glass-bottom boat cruises are NIS 30. *Tip:* The best time to visit is between 10am and 1pm, when the light is good and the water is usually calm and clear. Be sure not to miss feeding time at 11:30am.

Off Derech Mitzraim. ℡ **08/636-4200.** www.coralworld.com. Admission NIS 79 adults, NIS 69 children 5–16. Sat–Thurs 8:30am–4:30pm; Fri 8:30am–3:30pm. Bus: 15.

## Where to Stay

Eilat has an oversupply of comfy, but predictable modern hotels in various price ranges. Most are not directly on Eilat's beachfront, but are short walks to the sea. During holiday periods, Eilat hotels can be mobbed and overpriced, but at other times, at least some of the city's hotels will be offering great Internet deals. A lot of Eilat's hotels are all inclusive, which means a running medley of meals and snacks is included in the rate.

### EXPENSIVE

**Dan Eilat Hotel ★★** This is the most unusual of Eilat's top rank hotels. Along with its neighbor, the Herod's Palace, it's right on the nicest stretch of beach on the

North Beach waterfront and offers a wide variety of rooms and suites, some with spacious terraces and fabulous Red Sea panoramas. Interior design by Adam Tihany is not the usual 5-star hotel generic, instead it plays with lively interpretations of 1940s, '50s and '60s décor. Food services are strong, and the dinner buffet is the best of any hotel in town. The gardened pools are large and attractive. Ask for a recently renovated room.

North Beach, Eilat. ℭ **08/636-2222.** www.danhotels.com. 378 units. $440–$650 standard double; surcharge for pool/sea view. Rates include breakfast. Specials from $233. Parking (fee). **Amenities:** 5 restaurants, café, nightclub, children's programs, concierge, fitness center, heated pool and children's pool, spa, squash courts, synagogue. Wi-Fi (free in lobby; 1 hr. of daily in-room use for e-Dan club members).

## INEXPENSIVE

**Isrotel Riviera Club** ★ Part of the well-managed Isrotel chain, this low rise affordable hotel set around a pool offers no-frills rooms and suites last renovated in 2012. But it's a pleasant place to stay, mostly because it boasts a good location, not far from the beach. All units contain kitchenettes and poolside patios or balconies, so it's a great choice for families. There's also a minimart and nearby mall for supplies, and it's close to the many eateries on North Beach Promenade.

North Beach, Eilat. ℭ **888/669-5700** in the U.S. and Canada or 08/630-3666. www.isrotel.com/riviera_club. 172 units. $147–$190 for 2–4 persons; specials as low as $100 double. Prices higher Jewish and Christian holidays. Rates do not include breakfast. **Amenities:** Children's club, pool, kitchenette, Wi-Fi (fee).

# Where to Dine

## INLAND, NORTH OF HATMARIM BOULEVARD

These choices are away from the almost wall-to-wall restaurants and fast-food places in North Beach, but it's worth the effort to get to them.

### Moderate

**Casa do Brasil** ★★ BRAZILIAN This is the best all-you-can-eat South American meat restaurant in Israel, so bring an appetite. The menu is a carnivore's dream: beef ribs and baby lamb to chicken wings, goose liver, Brazilian meatballs, sausages, and duck basted in a honey soy sauce. Appetizers and side dishes are included in the all-you-can-eat deal, or you can order a la carte. Some nights there's Brazilian entertainment, and if you can still move, try the fab desserts.

3 Hativat Golani, near the Eilat Police Station. ℭ **08/632-3032.** Main courses NIS 80–NIS 160. All-you-can-eat dinner from NIS 140. Daily noon–11pm.

**Eddie's Hideaway** ★★ CONTINENTAL In a tourist town at the end of the earth, where most restaurants plan for customers they'll never see again, Eddie puts his heart into every meal and keeps coming up with Continental and Asian-influenced dishes that are delicious and inventive. If it's on the menu, we highly recommend the Nairobi shrimp cooked in butter and hot paprika with onion, fresh mushrooms, and a touch of pineapple; or delicate Shanghai fish in a spicy soybean paste. Both are excellent. There's also pasta, steaks, and barbecued ribs. Salad and side dishes come with most main courses. A 10 percent service charge, added to the bill, covers the tip. If you come by taxi, Eddie may offer to reimburse you for your return trip, an example of the genteel quality of the service here.

68 Almogim St. ℭ **057/944-4190.** www.eddieshide-away.rest-e.co.il. Main courses NIS 55–NIS 110. Mon–Sat 6pm–11:30pm; closed Sun. To find it, go up Hatmarim Street past the bus station, turn right on Almogim Street. Eddie's Hideaway is not directly on Almogim Street, entrance is at the back.

# PETRA

Petra, the legendary lost city carved into the walls of a hidden desert canyon, is the most famous of Jordan's many dazzling sites. This fascinating excursion is best reached from Israel via the Eilat/Aqaba border crossing. There are escorted bus tours that leave Eilat early in the morning, get you to Petra before noon, give you an hour to look around, and have you back at your hotel in Eilat by late afternoon. But for such a short tour, you might do better just watching a video. Petra is one of the wonders of the ancient world, and its antiquities, natural beauty, and ever-changing feel at different times of day are easily worth a stay of 1 to 3 nights or more. In addition, there are beautiful, affordable desert resorts only a few minutes from Petra, which make this a good place to relax and get away from it all.

## Essentials

A 2- to 2½-hour drive north of Aqaba, Petra is the jewel in the crown of Jordan's attractions, and the main draw for many travelers to the country. The canyon city of Petra is vast, mysterious, and really demands a 1- or 2-night stay and 2 full days of exploring to get a feel for the atmosphere, to say nothing of the contents of the ruins. You could easily spend 3 or 4 very full days exploring Petra and the surrounding countryside

## Getting There

After crossing from Eilat into Aqaba, it's easy to find taxis that will take you up to Petra. Some bargaining is required, but the general fare is around JD 50. This is the fastest, safest, and most direct way to make the journey. Splitting a taxi to Petra (or to Wadi Musa, the town at the entrance to Petra National Park) with others you may meet at the border can make the fare per person very reasonable. A taxi to the Aqaba Bus Station, plus bus fare up to Petra, will be less than JD 8, but there are few buses per day and it's hard to find a schedule.

If you want to avoid the hassle of bargaining with taxi drivers, ask your hotel in Petra to arrange for a pickup for you at the border crossing for an agreed price. Most Petra hotels in all price categories will be happy to do this—it ensures you won't be lured somewhere else. Again, the fare will be about JD 50. Such is life in the Middle East that your taxi fare back from Petra/Wadi Musa to the Aqaba/Eilat Crossing should be more like JD 36 to JD 40.

Travel agencies in Eilat can arrange for escorted, 1-, 2-, or 3-day tours, or unescorted packages to Petra that will include transportation arrangements.

## Entry Requirements

You must have a valid passport that does not have an expiration date within 6 months of your planned visit. The easiest way to get to Petra from Israel is via the Eilat/Aqaba Crossing. First take an Israel taxi from Eilat to the border (officially around NIS 35, although many drivers will demand a higher rate). Pack lightly, or carry a bag on wheels, as you will have to walk from the Israeli border across a no man's land of approximately .8km (½ mile). At press time, there was a NIS 100 departure tax you must pay at the Israel border. Travelers from the United States, Canada, the United Kingdom, Ireland, Australia, and New Zealand entering Jordan overland from Israel can get a 15-day single entry visa for JD 20 (approximately $30) at the **Eilat/Aqaba Crossing** (also known as the Yitzhak Rabin Crossing). When leaving Jordan to reenter Israel, there is a Jordanian exit fee of JD 5.

To the dismay of romantics and adventurers, Petra National Park closes at sunset or earlier, even though this mysterious, long-hidden site is especially evocative in the evenings. In fact, it was once a great place to camp at night, but now camping is forbidden.

At times, the park service has been offerred escorted candlelight tours for an additional fee—a great way to spend the evening if you plan to be in Petra when the tours are available. Night tours are generally available when there's a full moon. Check with the park authorities and reserve in advance. In good weather, a Bedouin camp dinner in the mountains is another evening option. Not only do you get a traditional meal, but you also get a feel for the beautiful, wild countryside at night. Check with your hotel or the visitor center. The price is approximately JD 30 for two people.

**Bedouin guides** can be arranged through the visitor center. The official fee 4 hours of guiding is JD 50. Or, once inside the park, if you feel you need a guide, you can easily find one to escort you to specific places. *Tip:* If you have hired a Jordanian guide before entering the park and the price of his admission is included in the arrangement, you should know that the admission price for Jordanian citizens is only JD 1; don't let your guide add a JD 50 entrance fee

for himself to the price of your tour. Many of the guides are colorful, and although they may not have had formal training, most know their stuff (and have picked up great multilingual skills). It's a good idea to hire a guide, at least for your first foray into Petra, especially if you plan to do a hike to some of the more remote parts of the city. A standard 2½-hour Petra city tour costs JD 15.

At the Visitor Center, you'll also find a variety of books and maps of Petra for sale. A good guidebook and map are very useful investments, even if you hire a guide; most books make a basic self-guided tour of Petra quite easy, especially if you have a chance to read up before your visit. Officially, the park is open daily until 6pm, but in summer the guards may let visitors stay a bit later in order to take in the sunset and twilight.

*Tip:* To avoid dehydration, bring your own bottle of water when you enter Petra; as the day progresses you'll need to buy more bottled water from the Bedouins who until recently inhabited the site. A number of stands inside Petra sell refreshments and food, though prices will be high. Don't hesitate to shell out for water: It's important to keep drinking even if you're not especially thirsty to avoid the dangers of dehydration. In summer, you'll need four 1.5-liter bottles of water to get through the day.

---

*Important:* If you entered Jordan via the Eilat/Aqaba Crossing, you can reenter Israel at the Eilat/Aqaba crossing or at the Sheik Hussein crossing in northern Jordan near the Israeli town of Beit She'an, but you *cannot reenter Israel via the Allenby Bridge/King Hussein Crossing* into the West Bank near Jericho. No entry visas are issued at the Allenby Bridge Crossing from the West Bank into Jordan; if you plan to use this route, you must obtain your Jordanian visa ahead of time from a Jordanian Consulate or Embassy. If you have your Jordanian visa ahead of time, and you exited Israel via the Allenby/King Hussein Bridge (*not* to be confused with the Sheik Hussein Bridge in the north), then you *can* reenter Israel via the Allenby Bridge. *Note:* The Allenby Bridge Crossing involves travel through the currently unstable West Bank, and can involve very long delays at the Allenby Bridge due to security. We don't recommend using this route. All border crossings are closed on Yom Kippur and on Eid al Adha.

Good travel agents and reputable tour companies can generally handle the arrangements for their clients' visas. To find the nearest Jordanian diplomatic mission to your location, go to the Jordanian Foreign Ministry website at **www.mfa.gov.jo**.

## Money

The Jordanian dinar is valued at approximately $1.40, 92p, So $1 = JD 0.70 and £1 = JD 1.07.

The **Jordanian dinar** (JD) is divided into 1,000 **fils:** 10 fils are 1 piaster; 500 fils are generally referred to as 50 **piasters.** Paper currency comes in denominations of JD 1, 5, 10, 20, as well as 500 fils (half a JD); there are silver coins for 25 fils, 50 fils, 100 fils, and 250 fils; copper coins are 5 and 10 fils.

## Visitor Information

The **Jordan Tourism Board** website (www.visitjordan.com) offers very thorough information about touring Jordan and Petra. Excellent information on Petra can also be found at www.go2petra.com.

The **Royal Society for the Conservation of Nature** website (www.rscn.org.jo) has specific information about eco-tourism and hiking in **Petra; Wadi Rum ★★**, south of Petra; the wild, mountainous **Dana Reserve ★**, north of Petra; as well as to other nature and wildlife reserves in the Kingdom of Jordan.

The **visitor center** at the entrance to Petra (✆ 03/215-6029; www.petrapark.com) is open daily from 6am to 4pm in wintertime; 6am to 6pm during summer time. Admission to Petra is JD 50 for 1 day; JD 55 for 2 days; and JD 60 for 3 days. A fourth day is free of charge. If your passport indicates you are only visiting Jordan for a 1-day excursion to Petra, admission to Petra National Park is JD 90. Children under 15 are half-price. The fee may seem high, but Petra is a vast area, and the money is needed to preserve and maintain the site.

## Tour Operators

Reputable tour operators that run excursions to Petra (among other locations in Jordan) include **Abercrombie and Kent Jordan** (✆ **962-06/566-5465** in Amman; www. abercrombiekent.com); **Desert Eco Tours** (an Israeli-based company; ✆ **972-52/276-5753** outside Israel, or 052/276-5753 from inside Israel; www.desertecotours.com); and **Petra Moon Tourism** (✆ **962-03/215-6665** in Petra; www.petramoon.com). For further options, check with the Jordan Tourism Board (www.visitjordan.com).

# [FastFACTS] PETRA

**Banks**   The Arab Bank and the Housing Bank, in the center of Wadi Musa, and the Cairo Amman Bank, in the Mövenpick Hotel just outside the entrance to Petra, both change money. They also give Visa cash advances.

Banking hours are Saturday to Thursday 8:30am to 12:30pm. The Housing Bank has an ATM connected to Cirrus and PLUS.

**Emergencies**   Throughout Jordan, for police dial ✆ **191** or 192. For an ambulance, dial ✆ **193.**

**Hospitals**   The **Petra Emergency Clinic** (✆ **03/215-6694**), across the parking lot from the Petra Forum Hotel, is not a hospital, but it has an X-ray machine, an operating room, and other modern equipment. It's open daily

8am to 8pm. In an emergency, your hotel or the police (℡ **191**) can help get you there. The Petra Polyclinic (℡ **077-733-9209**) is near the main traffic circle and is open 24 hours.

**Pharmacies** The **Wadi Musa Pharmacy** (℡ **03/215-6444**) is on the main traffic circle in Wadi Musa and is open daily 24 hours. The Modern Petra Pharmacy, a block from the Wadi Musa Traffic Circle, has an English-speaking staff and carries tampons, condoms, and other items not normally stocked by local pharmacies.

**Telephones** The country code for Jordan is **962.** The area code for Petra is **03.** The area code for Amman is **06.**

# Exploring Petra

Petra is only accessible through the Siq, a narrow crevice-canyon lined with niches that once held statues of gods and spirits that protected the city. This incredible canyon winds its way through the rocks for almost 1.6km (1 mile) before opening to Petra's wonders of rock and light. If you walk through the shadowed Siq at twilight, listen for the sound of the evening owl, once the symbol and guardian of the city.

The Nabateans, who carved the elaborate palaces, temples, tombs, storerooms, and stables of their city into the solid rock of this hidden valley, dominated the Trans-Jordan area from the 3rd century B.C. through Byzantine times. A Semitic people from northern Arabia, they moved into the Negev and the southern portions of what is now Jordan in the 6th century B.C. The Nabateans commanded the trade route from Damascus to Arabia; through Petra, caravans passed, carrying spices, silk, jewels, gold, and slaves from as far away as Yemen and East Africa. As a trading people, they developed cosmopolitan tastes and easily incorporated Hellenistic and Roman design into their architecture and into their lifestyle. The fabulous facades carved into the rose sandstone cliffs of Petra are exotically Hellenistic rather than classical Greek or even Roman, and reflect a mixture of Western and Eastern, Semitic and European influences.

**Nabatean religion** was centered on two deities: **Dushara,** the god of strength and masculine attributes, and **al-Uzza,** also known as Atargatis, the goddess of water and fertility. Slowly, these deities took on the characteristics of Greek and Egyptian gods; al-Uzza, especially, became associated with elements of Aphrodite, the Greek goddess of love; Tyche, the goddess of fortune; and the Egyptian mother goddess, Isis.

In addition to their hidden capital at Petra, the Nabateans developed lucrative trading and caravan cities at **Avdat** and **Mamshit,** in the Negev. Using careful methods of conserving dew and rainwater, and developing methods of irrigation that are being studied by modern agronomists, the Nabateans made the desert bloom and managed to sustain a population in the Negev and south Jordan far larger than the population of that region today.

Until the 1st century A.D., the Nabateans maintained their independence. Nabatean neutrality and aloofness was legendary. In 40 B.C., the young Herod, who had recently been made governor of the Galilee and Judea by the Romans, was overthrown by Jewish insurgents. Desperate and pursued, Herod made his way with a small entourage across the desert to Petra to beg for sanctuary and reinforcements. Despite the fact that Herod's mother had been a Nabatean princess, the ever-cautious rulers of Petra denied him permission to enter the Siq and the confines of the city (the indefatigable Herod eventually made his way to Rome, obtained reinforcements, put down the rebellion, and ruled as Rome's "King of the Jews" until his death in 4 B.C.). In A.D. 106, the Nabateans were finally annexed into the Roman Empire, and it continued to be the center of a profitable trading route, with connections to all parts of the ancient world.

In the early 4th century, Christianity became the dominant religion of the Nabateans. Important churches were built in every Nabatean community; the bishops of Petra participated in ecumenical councils that helped shape the development of the early Church. As the Roman Empire collapsed, and the amount of trade moving on the exotic desert routes through Petra shrank, the city's economy faltered. A series of earthquakes in late Byzantine times hastened the Nabateans' decline. After Petra's conquest by Islamic armies in A.D. 633, it became a forgotten backwater. It was briefly fortified by the Crusaders, but after its surrender to Saladin in 1189, it was abandoned and sank into oblivion. Not until 1812, when the Swiss explorer Johann Ludwig Burckhardt bribed Bedouin tribesmen to take him to Petra, was the long-forgotten, uninhabited city restored to the knowledge of the world. Only since 1958 has a careful exploration of the site been undertaken.

## WALKING TOUR: **PETRA**

| START: | **The Siq.** |
| --- | --- |
| FINISH: | **Petra Museum.** |
| BEST TIMES: | **Early morning, sunset.** |
| WORST TIME: | **Midafternoon, when heat is at its worst.** |

It is important to remember that many of the sites and buildings at Petra were given fanciful names in modern times that have nothing to do with what we now know were their original functions. Also remember that once inside Petra, a fast but reasonably inclusive tour, without hikes to the sacred high places that overlook the city, can take 5 to 6 hours. Petra deserves at least 2 full days. Give yourself time to feel the mystery and beauty of the place and to explore at your leisure. Petra changes dramatically as the light of day changes.

## 1 The Siq

Beginning just near the visitor center, the winding 1.2km (¾-mile) walk through the narrow fissure, or canyonlike Siq, that leads into Petra can take from 45 minutes to 1½ hours, depending on your pace. The journey through this mysterious, highly sculptured passageway can be one of the most memorable parts of the Petra experience (especially in the soft twilight as visitors depart from Petra as night falls).

At the entrance to the Siq and at various points throughout the passageway, you'll notice channels cut into the rock that once held pipes for the water system that carried the spring of Ain Musa into Petra. There is a modern dam to prevent flash flooding during the winter rains; it is modeled after the ruins of an ancient Nabatean dam uncovered by archaeologists at this site. According to Nabatean and local Bedouin legend, Petra's water source, Ain Musa ("the Spring of Moses"), was created when Moses, leading the Israelites through the desert after the Exodus from Egypt, struck a rock with his staff in despair as his people came close to death from thirst. The rocks burst forth with cool water. (Petra's Ain Musa is not alone in claiming to be the site of this miracle.) Niches in the walls of the Siq once held the images of gods that protected the city, and intimidated visitors entering Petra.

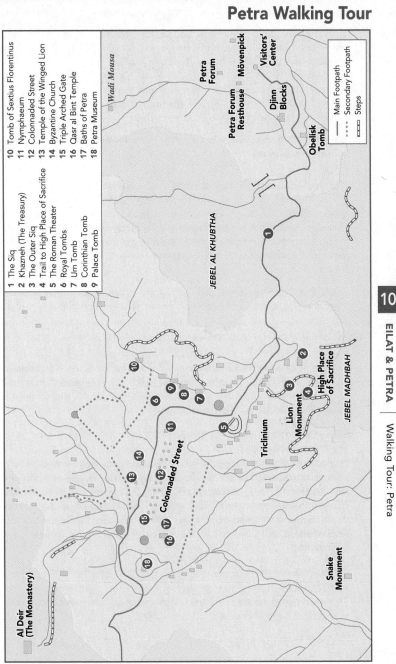

**1** The Siq
**2** Khazneh (The Treasury)
**3** The Outer Siq
**4** Trail to High Place of Sacrifice
**5** The Roman Theater
**6** Royal Tombs
**7** Urn Tomb
**8** Corinthian Tomb
**9** Palace Tomb
**10** Tomb of Sextius Florentinus
**11** Nymphaeum
**12** Colonnaded Street
**13** Temple of the Winged Lion
**14** Byzantine Church
**15** Triple Arched Gate
**16** Qasr al Bint Temple
**17** Baths of Petra
**18** Petra Museum

Main Footpath
Secondary Footpath
Steps

*Wadi Mousa*

Petra Forum

Mövenpick

Visitors' Center

Petra Forum Resthouse

Djinn Blocks

Obelisk Tomb

*JEBEL AL KHUBTHA*

High Place of Sacrifice

*JEBEL MADHBAH*

Lion Monument

Triclinium

Colonnaded Street

Snake Monument

Al Deir (The Monastery)

10

EILAT & PETRA | Walking Tour: Petra

## 2 The Khazneh (Treasury)

Suddenly, a turn in the Siq reveals the most famous structure in Petra, a royal tomb that has come to be known as the Treasury. Bedouins believed that the solid urn sculpted into the monument's facade was actually hollow and contained treasure; often they fired bullets at the urn in hopes of having the treasure spill out (you can detect their bullet marks across the magnificent facade). The Khazneh's stone facade changes color during the day: In the morning it can be a soft yellow-rose peach hue; by late afternoon, a pure, soft rose; at sunset, an intense red, before slipping into the dusty twilight.

Beyond the Khazneh (continuing to the right as you face the Khazneh), the Siq widens into what is called the:

## 3 Outer Siq

Here you'll encounter the busy modern denizens of Petra, sand artists, and water sellers. The outer Siq is lined with carved tomb facades in styles ranging from classical Roman to designs that echo Assyrian and nomadic desert influences. Honoring the dead was an important part of Nabatean culture. The outer Siq also contains caves inhabited until recently by Bedouins—the soft sandstone interiors are as wildly patterned as marbleized paper and are good spots to shelter from the hot summer sun.

To the left, opposite the Uneishu Tomb (which an inscription identifies as the tomb of the brother of a queen), is a flight of rough ancient stairs that leads to an uphill trail to the:

## 4 High Place of Sacrifice & the Tombs of Wadi Farasa

This can be an arduous hike for those out of shape, but it is a very worthwhile. A hike to the High Place of Sacrifice and back down to the colonnaded main street of ancient Petra by a different route can take 1½ to 3 hours. It's wise to invest in a guide if you decide to make the excursion.

Continuing on down what is now the main street of Petra, you come to the:

## 5 Roman Theater

Originally built by the Nabateans, who were always adapting elements of other cultures into their way of life, the theater facing cliffside facades of tombs may have been used for religious ceremonies. In the 2nd century A.D., the theater was enlarged by the Romans (who cared little for Nabatean traditions) and cut into nearby Nabatean tombs to create a vast 7,000-seat venue. The theater has been restored and, after a 1,500-year hiatus, will be used again for performances and other events.

Farther along, on the opposite side of the canyon from the theater, are the:

## 6 Royal Tombs

The tombs earned this name because of their elaborate facades, not because they were created for royal burials.

The first of these is the:

## 7 Urn Tomb

It's named for the carefully sculpted urn above its pediment. In A.D. 446, the Byzantines converted the inner chamber of this tomb into a church.

A few facades beyond is the:

## 8 Corinthian Tomb
The tomb's facade actually includes a small-scale reproduction of the **Khazneh.**

After the Corinthian Tomb is the:

## 9 Palace Tomb
Its two stories jut out from the side of the canyon. Part of the Palace Tomb was constructed of stone, rather than carved into the canyon rock.

Around to the right is the heavily eroded:

## 10 Tomb of Sextius Florentinus
The tomb was built around A.D. 130 for a Roman governor of the Province of Arabia who so admired Petra's network of tombs that he asked to be buried in a tomb of his own design in this far outpost of the Roman Empire. A faint Latin inscription and a Roman eagle mark the facade. A route of processional staircases and corridors began here and wound uphill to sacred high places on the mountain beyond.

Staying on the main path to the city center, you come to the:

## 11 Nymphaeum
This two-story fountain, dedicated to the water nymphs, is a major landmark of Petra. This lavish desert structure of flowing water, piped in from Ain Musa, must have been incredible to travelers approaching for the first time. The Nymphaeum was a place of both refreshment and worship.

The open water channel that fed the Nymphaeum continued on along the:

## 12 Colonnaded Street
The street, built after A.D. 106 by the Romans, lay over the route of an earlier Nabatean thoroughfare. It was lined with shops but also served as a civic and ceremonial route for processions.

On a rise of land to the right (north), as you walk down the Colonnaded Street, is the:

## 13 Temple of the Winged Lions
Named for the winged lions that serve as capitals for its columns, this was probably a temple dedicated to the worship of the female deity, al-Uzza. Built in A.D. 27, this was one of Petra's major temples until it was heavily damaged, apparently by fire, in the 2nd century. The structure was then used to house families until it was destroyed by an earthquake in 363. That the temple was not rebuilt as a religious structure after the fire in the 2nd century may indicate the old region of Petra had gone into decline under the Roman occupation.

Also several hundred meters to the right of the Colonnaded Street is the:

## 14 Byzantine Church
Here's a large structure with triple apses and extremely beautiful and well-preserved mosaic floors that have been uncovered by the joint Jordanian-American team excavating the site. On both sides of the Colonnaded Street are the outlines of ruined buildings. According to some theories, the Roman forum of Petra would have been among the structures to the left (south) of the Colonnaded Street.

10

EILAT & PETRA

Walking Tour: Petra

At the end of the Colonnaded Street is the:

## 15  Triple Arched Gate

The gate is adorned with carved panels containing bas-relief busts, animals, and geometric and floral designs. These monumental gateways would have borne wooden doors that opened to the *temenos*, or sacred precincts, of your next stop.

## 16  Qasr al Bint (Palace of the Pharaoh's Daughter)

Perhaps the most important temple in Petra (again, despite its romantic name, the temple has nothing to do with a Pharaoh's daughter), this massive structure was built of stone, rather than carved from rock. It is the most impressive building in Petra. It faces north, toward the Sharra mountains, from which the name of the chief Nabatean god, Dushara ("he of Sharra") is derived and may have been a sanctuary for the Dushara cult. This temple was built around the time of Jesus and was most likely destroyed late in the 3rd century.

Just to the south of the Arched Gate, but not accessible at present to visitors, were the:

## 17  Baths of Petra

These had access to a corner of the *temenos*.

Beyond the ruins of the Qasr al Bint Temple, you'll find the:

## 18  Petra Museum

There's a small collection of sculptural artifacts, jewelry, and pottery found at Petra. The museum building also houses the Petra Forum restaurant, as well as restrooms. A second part of the museum is housed in a nearby tomb.

### OTHER HIKES & EXCURSIONS AT PETRA

In addition to the hike up to the High Place of Sacrifice (see stop 4, above), a number of longer walks away from the center of Petra provide important vistas of this extraordinary place. These walks involve some amount of climbing as well as scrambling over rocks and ruined pathways; therefore, it's best to have companions with you. Guides at Petra will escort you for about JD 35 to JD 50. *Note:* You're required to have a guide when you go to more remote areas.

**Jabal Haroun** (the Mountain of Aaron, brother of Moses) is a climbing trek that can take as much as 4 to 8 hours depending on your route and requires a guide. The way passes **Ad Deir** (the Monastery), Petra's largest carved tomb, built in the 1st century A.D., with an interior adorned by carved and painted crosses from the Byzantine period. Across the canyon from Ad Deir is Jabal Haroun, the highest peak in the area. A small, white church containing the **tomb of Aaron** stands at the top of the mountain. In winter, you might ask your guide to descend on the route that passes **Wadi Siyah,** where winter rains create a waterfall. This difficult but beautiful winter hike will take at least 3 hours, and a few additional hours if you return via Wadi Siyah. **Wadi Turkimaniya** is a pleasant 45-minute round-trip walk down the wadi that starts behind and to the left of the Temple of the Winged Lions. The easy road through the wadi supports rich vegetation in winter and leads to Petra's only tomb with a Nabatean inscription.

**Qasr Habis** (the Crusader's Castle) is a climb that goes from near Petra's museum to the not very impressive ruins of Petra's Crusader stronghold; however, the pathway leads to wonderful vistas that overlook beautiful canyons. The round-trip can run from 1 to 1½ hours.

The **High Place of Sacrifice** is one of the most popular destinations for hikers, heading to the great altars carved from rock (with drainage channels for the blood of sacrificial animals) far above the city. The panorama of Petra is dazzling; the round-trip hike can take from 1½ to 2½ hours and is not for visitors who are out of shape.

Additional treks to the **Snake Monument** and to **Jebal Numair** entail a minimum of 5 or 6 hours and require guides. There are also car tours and hikes available to **Al Madras** and **Al Barid,** nearby satellite towns of Petra. Al Barid is a kind of mini-Petra, entered through a smaller version of Petra's Siq; its filled with carved canyon structures. Unlike at Petra, some of Al Barid's structures carved into cliff sides seem to have served as houses. Archaeology buffs can also take a taxi excursion (or hike with a Bedouin guide, about a 6-hr. round-trip) to the site of **El Beidha,** a Neolithic village from the 8th millennium B.C. A full-day or overnight-camping tour from Petra to the beautiful desertscapes of **Wadi Rum** is also highly recommended.

# Where to Stay

If you're staying at one of the luxury resort hotels near Petra, you can plan for a relaxing, exotic desert holiday amid marvelous surroundings, enjoying local foods, entertainment, and the opportunity to browse shops filled with tribal crafts. For those on a budget, the many less-expensive hotels at Wadi Musa, 5km (3 miles) from the entrance to Petra, are reasonably comfortable and offer the chance to meet interesting fellow travelers. A hard day of exploring Petra will work up your appetite. In the evenings, many budget hotels offer very reasonably priced buffet dinners. In fact, travelers buffet-hop and look for the most interesting and freshest deals being offered each night

*Note:* As at Israeli accommodations, hotel rates are often quoted in dollars, and bargain rates (often steeply discounted) abound.

## EXPENSIVE

**Mövenpick Resort Petra ★★★**   This is the top hotel in town, and it shares the best location with the Petra Guest House (see below)—just steps from the entrance to Petra National Park and close to local shops and eateries. Public areas of this Swiss-managed hotel are exotic in decor; dinner and lunch buffets are the best in town; and there's a library with reading material about Petra and Jordan. On the roof garden, guests can meet in the evenings over coffee or fruit-flavored hookas (waterpipes). The small pool is a blessing after the trek through Petra.

Petra. ℂ **800/344-6835** in the U.S., or 03/215-7111. www.moevenpick-petra.com. 183 units. $282–$485 double. Rates include breakfast. Add service charge, and tax. Free parking. **Amenities:** Restaurant, bar, fitness center, Internet desk (fee), library, nonsmoking rooms, heated pool, Wi-Fi (fee).

## MODERATE

**Petra Guest House ★★★**   With a perfect location right at the entrance to Petra National Park and a beautifully designed, air-conditioned ensemble of buildings that combine ancient and modern structures, this is the best mid-budget choice in the area (the atmospheric Cave Bar lounge of the Guest House is inside a Nabatean tomb). Rooms are comfy and newly redone in 2013. The staff is quite knowledgeable.

Wadi Musa, Petra. ℂ **03/215-6266.** www.guesthouse-petra.com. 73 units. JD 80 double. Rates include breakfast. Add tax, and service charge. Free parking. **Amenities:** Restaurant; bar, concierge, Wi-Fi (JD 5/hour).

**Petra Palace ★**   Located on the block of hotels and restaurants leading up to the entrance to Petra, this property is a great location and a comparative bargain. Guest rooms are nothing special but have the usual array of amenities; some overlook the mountains, others are next to the pool (useful on a hot summer day).

Wadi Musa, Petra. ⓒ **03/215-6723.** 83 units. $80–$130 double. Add tax and service charge. **Amenities:** Restaurant, bar, fitness room, heated pool, free Wi-Fi.

## INEXPENSIVE

**Al Anbat 1 Hotel**   Attracting a savvy backpacking crowd, this hotel offers screenings of Indiana Jones films, rooms with balconies, a steam room and small pool (summer only), and free shuttle to the entrance to Petra National Park, 2 miles away. There's been a lot of upgrading recently, and half the hotel was built in 2005. Breakfast and dinner buffets are good and very affordable. The newer Al Anbat 2 (ⓒ **03/215-7200**) is a small six-story tower with less expensive rooms and without the congenial atmosphere.

Wadi Musa, Petra. ⓒ **03/215-6265.** www.alanbat.com. 100 units. $44 double. Rates include tax and service. Breakfast $3 Parking. **Amenities:** Restaurant, Internet, lounge, pool, Turkish bath, Free Wi-Fi.

# Excursions South of Petra

## WADI RUM NATURE RESERVE ★★★

Also known as "The Valley of the Moon", this extraordinary valley, with its stunning sandstone and granite rock formations, was used as a background location for much of the film "Lawrence of Arabia". (It also stood in for the planet Mars in the movie "Red Planet" in 2000, which should give you some idea for how distinctive the landscape is here). Inhabited for centuries, it shelters a number of important Nabatean temples, along with ancient petroglyphs. Today Bedouins serve as guides to those who wish to explore the Valley's many wonders (or climb the rocks, an increasingly popular activity here). You can obtain information about these extraordinary reserves for camping, escorted tours, and hiking by checking the **Royal Society for the Conservation of Nature** website (www.rscn.org.jo), which contains specific information about eco-tourism to the dramatic desert landscapes of Wadi Rum, south of Petra, as well as about other nature and wildlife reserves in the Kingdom of Jordan. If you're interested in a horseback excursion through Wadi Rum, we recommend Rum Horses (www.wadirumhorses. com), but *only* to experienced riders (this is not an activity for novice riders).

Admission to the park is JD2 per person, children under 12 free, per vehicle JD5.

## AQABA ★

Aqaba can be a relaxing stop for an overnight or a day or two between Petra and Eilat If you cross the border from Eilat into Aqaba a day before your excursion up to Petra, you can avoid the morning rush hour at the border and the crush to try to get a taxi (shared or otherwise) up to Petra. Aqaba, though much quieter than Eilat, is a growing resort, and its beautiful luxury hotels are far less expensive than Israeli counterparts. If you want to splurge on a beach break, you'll get much more for you're investment in Aqaba, and arrive in Petra refreshed and rested. For the moment, the beaches are less friendly than Eilat's for women traveling alone. The town has inexpensive, interesting restaurants, and its reefs are less damaged than in Eilat.

# PLANNING YOUR TRIP TO ISRAEL

I srael is a tricky country to visit even when it's at its absolute best. Jewish, Christian, and Muslim holidays dot the calendar with accompanying high season crowds and prices. It's also a very compact country in a politically sensitive part of the world. Whenever political tensions subside for awhile, the floodgates open and the country is awash with a backlog of travelers who have been waiting to visit. Because Israel is so small, hotel rates skyrocket during these times. The minute hostilities rise or an act of terrorism occurs, tourism dips and you have the entire country to yourself. This chapter helps you get the most out of your stay with a variety of planning tools, including information on how to get there, tips on where to stay, and quick, on-the-ground resources.

# GETTING THERE

## By Plane

Israel's main international airport **Ben-Gurion (TLV)** is approximately 20 minutes by train or taxi from Tel Aviv and 45 minutes by private or shared taxi from Jerusalem. The other international airport is Eilat, at the southern tip of Israel, but it is mainly used for direct charter package flights from Europe and flights from inside the country.

### GETTING INTO TOWN FROM THE AIRPORT

**From Ben-Gurion to Jerusalem** **Sheruts** (shared taxis) will take you from the airport to any address in Jerusalem for NIS 65 per person. **Private taxis** are also available (Flat rate: NIS 270 daytime; NIS 320 night; NIS 5 surcharge for each bag); a surcharge applies for more than two passengers (see chapter 5).

**From Ben Gurion to Tel Aviv** **Trains** leave Ben-Gurion Airport for Tel Aviv every hour except in the middle of the night. The fare is NIS 15. There is no service starting 3 hours before Shabbat on Friday until after Shabbat is over Saturday night. From the railroad station you pick up a taxi to your hotel. **Private flat-rate taxis** run from the airport into Tel Aviv (see chapter 8). **Private taxi for two passengers** from the airport to your hotel runs around NIS 150 official flat rate. There are extra charges for additional passengers, for each bag, and for night or Shabbat service. Agree on the flat rate and expect around NIS 30 to pop up in additional charges. Usually, fares will be higher if you choose to pay a meter fare.

# GETTING AROUND

## By Bus

Intercity buses are the fastest and easiest way of traveling between the major cities of Israel (although traffic jams in recent years have led the country to resuscitate its almost forgotten train service along the Jerusalem–Tel Aviv–Haifa corridor). Buses between Jerusalem, Haifa, and Tel Aviv depart very frequently; at peak times as fast as each bus fills up. The Jerusalem–Tel Aviv fare is NIS 25. For less frequent buses, such as Tel Aviv or Jerusalem to Eilat (fare NIS 165 round trip) or Jerusalem to the Dead Sea (NIS 100 round trip), you must book your ticket in advance. Intercity buses do not run on the Sabbath. **Egged Bus Company** (www.egged.co.il/eng, ✆ *2800) connects most cities in Israel and operates buses within Jerusalem and Haifa, as well as working on a cooperative basis with Dan Buses in Tel Aviv.

## By Train

**Israel Railways** (www.rail.co.il) has been undergoing a revival and expansion for more than a decade. **Arlosoroff Street Central Train Station** in Tel Aviv is the rail hub of Israel. The cost of a rail ticket is slightly higher than comparable bus fares. A rail line with frequent service along the Mediterranean coast connects Tel Aviv to Haifa and Nahariya in the north; a second line connects Tel Aviv to Ben-Gurion Airport; a third line goes from Tel Aviv to Beersheba; and a fourth line goes from Tel Aviv to the western outskirts of Jerusalem. Service along the coast is fast and frequent; the Beersheba and Jerusalem lines are less frequent. Trains do not run on the Sabbath.

The **Jerusalem Train Station**, on the western edge of the city, is not a convenient place to enter Jerusalem, especially with luggage. You'd do better arriving in Jerusalem by the much faster and more frequent Egged buses or by sherut (shared taxi van), both of which bring you closer to the center of town.

## By Sherut

A sherut (shared taxi van) is a good way to travel between Jerusalem and Tel Aviv and between Tel Aviv and Haifa. Sheruts from Jerusalem leave as fast as they fill up from the corner of Rav Kook Street and Hanevi'im Street in Jerusalem (across Jaffa Rd. from Zion Square), and deposit you at the New Central Bus Station in Tel Aviv, where you can pick up local sheruts that ply the Number 4 bus route to the Ha-Yarkon St. hotel district or the Number 5 bus route to Rothschild and Dizengoff Boulevards.

Sheruts from Tel Aviv to Jerusalem or to Haifa wait just in front of the Tel Aviv Central Bus Station. Make sure the sherut you enter is going to the right destination. Sheruts to Haifa tend to fill up slowly.

*Tip*: Intercity sherut fares are virtually the same as bus fares, except on Shabbat, when they double (because no buses run). Because sheruts carry fewer passengers than buses, and there is time to scrutinize passengers, many Israelis feel sheruts are a bit less likely to be terror targets than buses.

## By Car

In the main Israeli cities, such as Tel Aviv, Haifa, and Jerusalem, a car is not only unnecessary, it's a burden. Parking is very difficult, and these cities are also cursed with such arcane driving regulations as "no left turns for 7 blocks, Sunday to Thursday 11am to 2pm." Plus, taxis, sheruts, and buses are efficient and reasonably priced, so you can easily let someone else do the driving.

**Seatbelt use** for drivers and all passengers is mandatory.

**Speed limits** are 50km (31 miles) per hour in towns and urban areas; 90km (56 miles) per hour on intercity roads unless otherwise posted.

**Age minimums** for rentals vary from company to company, but you usually must be 24 years old to rent or drive a rental car in Israel. Seniors over 75 or 80 may have some difficulty finding an agency that will rent to them. You may pay more for insurance if you're under or over a certain age.

**Road closures:** In the ultrareligious neighborhoods of Jerusalem, such as Mea Shearim or Geula, and in ultrareligious quarters of some smaller cities, public roads are closed to cars for the duration of Shabbat. Usually roads into these neighborhoods are blocked with rocks or boulders or police barriers. DO NOT TRY TO ENTER ANY ROAD BLOCKED OFF IN SUCH A WAY. Back up immediately and try to get away from the area. Drivers who inadvertently wander into such neighborhoods will have stones thrown at them and risk bodily harm.

A car becomes necessary if you want to explore the Galilee or the sites along the coast. Distances are short, so you can take in many sites. Major road signs are almost always in Hebrew and English; don't panic if on a major highway a sign is only in Hebrew—the next sign up or the one beyond will usually have the information you need in English. Your rental-car agency will provide you with GPS or maps of Israel that are sufficient for most travelers.

*Important Note:* You cannot take a rental car into or out of Israel. Cars rented in Israel are not generally insured for damages or liability if taken into the West Bank or Gaza. That being said, most companies' rental insurance does permit travel on Hwy. 1, the main east-west highway from Jerusalem to The Dead Sea and on Route 90, the main road along The Dead Sea and the Jordan Valley from near Jericho north to Tiberias. Clarify these regulations each time you rent a car and get explicit instructions as to how to get to these roads in the West Bank, making sure not to stray anywhere else in the West Bank with your rental car. Also, clarify whether your car is insured for East Jerusalem, should you be planning to drive or stay in that part of the city.

## RENTING A CAR

In general, you'll do best, money-wise, reserving a car in advance of your arrival. Car-rental agencies, both international and local, rent small cars for about $45 to $70 a day, depending on the season and size of the car. If you plan to travel in the summer, or drive to the Negev and Eilat, you'll want a car with air-conditioning that really works.

The largest Israeli car-rental firm is **Eldan** (© **800/938-5000** or 888/243-5326 in the U.S. and Canada or 08/951-5727 in the U.K.; www.eldan.co.il) and is always worth looking into. Its fleet of cars is larger and more varied than those of the international agencies, and it often has discounts. Eldan also offers more offices and service centers throughout the country than any of its noninternational, Israeli competitors, so if you have a breakdown, you have a better chance of getting a replacement quickly.

Driving is one of the best ways to see Israel, but it can be expensive. **Ways to save:**

o **Find a package** that bundles together the cost of the car with airfare or lodgings.

o **Rent** on an unlimited kilometer basis so there are no ugly surprises. Renting by the week can be cheaper, but is not a good idea unless you plan to be in countryside areas for the entire 7-day rental period.

o **Rent the cheapest class of vehicle:** There's a shortage of these cars at the rental agencies, which means there's a good chance you'll be bumped up a class, at no extra cost, if you do this. No guarantees though.

There are all kinds of Internet deals and car/hotel/airlines packages you can find, but this balance sheet will give you a general idea of what you'll actually end up paying for a lower mid-price-range car rental with automatic transmission:

| | |
|---|---|
| Basic weekly charge, unlimited kilometers $50/day | $350 |
| Collision Damage Waiver, 7 days at $18 per day | $126 |
| Mandatory Third Party Liability, 7 days at $15 per day | $105 |
| Gasoline, 100 liters at NIS 8.20 per liter (around $9.20 per gal.) | $240 |
| Total: | $781 |

These figures are an average of going rates, and the total works out to about $112 per day for a simple automatic-transmission car. Do not be misled by firms offering extremely low daily rental rates, such as $6 or $8. The daily rental rate are a small portion of the total rental bill, which includes insurance and the kilometer charge.

## PARKING, TOLLS, GASOLINE & BREAKDOWNS

There is **only one toll road** in Israel: Pan Israel Highway (Hwy. 6), which will eventually run the length of the country from north to south. At press time, only the northern and central portions of this road are open. There are no toll bridges in Israel, but there is an **optional toll tunnel under Haifa**, useful during rush hours. There are special Fast Lanes on Highway 1 for the distance between Ben Gurion Airport and Tel Aviv. The **toll for Fast Lane use** ranges from NIS 10 to NIS 75, depending on traffic congestion conditions. Check with your car rental agency as to whether your car is equipped with an automatic scanner for the Tel Aviv Fast Lane that will add the fee to your rental bill. If not, there are heavy fines for Fast Lane use.

In Jerusalem, Tel Aviv, and other main cities, **parking** can be extremely difficult. When you park on streets in downtown areas during daylight hours, you'll either pay for parking with a meter, or you'll display a parking card in the passenger window. Cards can be purchased at sidewalk dispensing machines. **Tip:** Keep a lookout for parking police who may ticket your car while you're dashing to the dispenser.

Parking is permitted where curbs are painted blue and white, although you may need to display a parking card. It's forbidden where curbs are red and white or gray. Parking on many residential streets in Jerusalem and Tel Aviv will soon be by residential sticker only. At most hotels in major cities, you'll have to pay to park in an often distant municipal lot or the hotel's limited space lot (fees are usually reasonable, but rates vary according to day or night and Shabbat). Most rural hotels have free parking.

*Note:* Do not park illegally anywhere or you will get towed; parking enforcement officials in Israel are quick and very thorough. On the Sabbath, parking meter and card regulations are not enforced in Jerusalem and in some cities. Locals may even park on the sidewalks, but unless you know what you're doing, don't follow their example.

### Sample Non–Rush Hour Driving Times in Israel

**Tel Aviv-Jerusalem:** 1 hour
**Tel Aviv-Haifa:** 1 hour 20 minutes
**Jerusalem or Tel Aviv-Eilat:** 4 hours, 30 minutes
**Jerusalem-Tiberias:** 2 hours 30 minutes
**Nazareth-Haifa:** 40 minutes
**Tiberias-Nazareth:** 30 minutes

Some smaller Israeli companies offer no rental charge on Shabbat, although you do have to pay Saturday insurance (if it is a religious company, you may be on your honor not to drive on Shabbat). Others offer free transportation from the airport to your hotel if you want to start the rental later in your trip. Companies offering such services are often more expensive, but you may find these extras worthwhile. *Warning:* Beware of companies that offer to waive rental fees and insurance on Shabbat. If your parked car is vandalized or stolen on Shabbat, you're in big trouble.

**Gasoline** comes in 91 octane and 96 octane varieties and costs about $2.10 per liter. Rental cars are often "required" to have the higher-octane gas. These gas prices fluctuate, but can work out to about $9.20per U.S. gallon. Gas stations are plentiful enough on main roads, though on Saturday some of them are closed and those that are open often add a surcharge.

**Breakdowns:** Saturday and Jewish holidays, it's near impossible to have a flat tire repaired in many areas, but your rental-car company will provide you with road service numbers to call in case of emergencies. Bigger companies usually have better service.

## By Plane

Distances in Israel are not great, and with the time you'd spend to get to the airport, pass through security, and go through the arrival process and transfers at your destination, you could probably just drive. But if traveling overland on hot days just isn't your cup of tea, then by all means use Israel's inland air service **Arkia** (✆ **09/863-3480** or *5758 for reservations in Israel; www.arkia.co.il). There are no flights on Shabbat, but otherwise daily flights connect Tel Aviv with Eilat and Rosh Pina (Safed/Tiberias), and Haifa with Eilat. Other flights are scheduled according to demand. A round-trip flight from Tel Aviv to Eilat costs approximately $160 to $280.

# TIPS ON ACCOMMODATIONS

You'll find a wide range of accommodations in Israel, ranging from hotels to kibbutz vacation guesthouses to great hostels and self-catering apartments.

There has been no official hotel rating system or hotel star system in Israel for more than 20 years, so ignore the star ratings hotels give themselves. We've included our own star ratings in this book, from 1 to 3 stars, based on recent, personal visits.

## A Note About the Seasons

Israel's hotels fill up during certain seasons and holidays, and you should be prepared with advanced reservations, secured by a deposit. Generally speaking, hotels are busiest during July and August, and on the major Jewish and Christian holidays. Rates skyrocket during these times, and rooms can be very scarce if you don't book well in advance. For detailed information, and a full list of holiday dates, see p. 21.

Off-season is generally November through February (except for Chanukah/Christmas/New Year's). It is, however, a busy season in Eilat, which has almost perfect, sunny weather when it's chilly up north.

**KIBBUTZ PACKAGES** The Kibbutz Hotels network is especially enticing. It lets you explore the real Israeli countryside while overnighting at comfortable kibbutz hotels, holiday villages, and less-pricey guesthouses and country accommodations that have swimming pools or beaches, and invariably lovely and often very dramatic settings. There are amazingly well-priced 7-night deals, which include a double room, breakfast, and a rental car (with unlimited mileage).

Although all accommodations in the kibbutz hotel and holiday village network are the equivalent of those you'd find in midrange hotels, you'll find great variety in the general setup and character of each facility. The kibbutz system also includes many less expensive **Kibbutz Country Lodgings,** a growing network of smaller kibbutz and moshav communities that run simple guest buildings, or kibbutz families who have guest-room facilities in their homes. Rates for Country Lodgings average $170 per night for a double room with a private bathroom. Best of all, you get a chance to see a bit of real kibbutz life. For further information go to www.kibbutz.co.il.

**INDEPENDENT BED & BREAKFASTS & "ZIMMERS"** Hundreds of rural accommodations in private homes, ranging from simple to luxurious, are available for tourists today. For a listing of good choices, go to the Ministry of Tourism web site: www.goisrael.com/Tourism_Eng/Articles/Accommodations/Pages/Rural Tourism - Zimmers.aspx.

The **Good Morning Jerusalem** bed-and-breakfast and holiday apartment rental office (www.accommodation.co.il) has a catalog of 130 rental apartments throughout Israel and will arrange for one that will fit your needs. There is a $50 commission for this service. For bed-and-breakfast accommodations in Jerusalem and apartments Tel Aviv, try such international sites as **AirBnB.com, Homeaway.com** and **FlipKey.com.**

At **tourist information offices** in Tel Aviv, Jerusalem, and many other Israeli cities, you can use a computer bank to access lists of accommodations in private homes for any area in the country. Ask the staff at the tourist information office for recommendations. For summers, weekends, and holidays, reserve ahead.

**YOUTH HOSTELS** Israel's wonderful network of official **Israel Youth Hostel Association Hostels,** or IYHA Hostels (✆ **1-599/510-511;** www.iyha.org.il/eng) offers simple, inexpensive accommodations in many dramatic sites throughout the country. IYHA hostels often offer the only available accommodations in remote areas of the country, or in areas along hiking routes.

In the past few years, the IYHA has been busy upgrading its network of facilities. Many hostels are in sleek new buildings set up with a maximum of four to six beds per room. A large percentage of these rooms now have private shower/bathrooms and can easily be converted into private doubles or family rooms. Dining facilities now offer meals far superior to the once-spartan youth-hostel fare.

Age is no barrier to staying at an AYHA Hostel nor is membership. Having a youth-hostel membership card, however, does give you certain advantages, such as better rates at the hostels, plus discounts at some restaurants, national parks, historical sites, museums, and on buses and trains. It is advisable to book in advance.

**Israel Hostels,** or ILH (www.hostels-israel.com), is an independent network of more than 30 interesting, independent hostels, inexpensive hotels, B&Bs, kibbutz guesthouses, and other unusual, inexpensive places to stay throughout Israel. The managements are almost always friendly, enthusiastic, well-informed, and offer personal attention. Highly recommended!

Israel is unique in that many Christian guesthouses that were originally set up for pilgrims have developed into wonderful options for travelers and most welcome guests of all faiths. Some of the best of these guesthouses are listed in detail in this guidebook, and many other excellent choices may be found on the **Christian Information Centre** website (www.cicts.org). These are among the most atmospheric and unusual accommodations in Israel, often set in historic buildings and enclaves. Rates are very reasonable; rooms are comfortable but simple; atmosphere is quiet; and the staff members are almost always polite.

# TOURS & ESCORTED TRIPS
## 1- & 2-Day Affordable Escorted Tours

**Egged Tours** (www.eggedtours.com) and **United Tours** (www.unitedtours.co.il) are the two major day tour companies in Israel. They offer identical 1- and 2-day (and longer) guided bus tours from Jerusalem and Tel Aviv to the Galilee, the Dead Sea, the Negev, the Coastal region, as well as tours of city and metropolitan areas. Some of their tours can also be taken from Haifa, Eilat, and other secondary cities. These tours can be an efficient way to visit a lot of places and fill in itineraries.

Much depends on the luck of the draw. Guides range from adequate to fabulous-- you might find yourself in a small congenial tour group that's virtually a private tour, or a busload of unruly kids. A lot of time may be consumed as your tour bus makes the round of hotels picking up and dropping off other travelers in your group before the actual tour begins. If you're thinking about taking more than two or three of these tours, it might be better to consider an organized, complete flight/hotel/package tour that will take you to all the major destinations you want to see in Israel. One-day United or Egged Tours start at around $70 per person for a bus tour of Jerusalem, while most 2-day and multiple-day tours range from $180 to $400.

Brilliant, low-budget routes were designed by **Abraham Tours** (abrahamtours.com/bus), which is affiliated with the Abraham Hostel in Jerusalem, The routes take visitors to major cities throughout Israel, with brief sightseeing stops at sites along the way that would be hard to get to by public transportation. You get off at whatever town you want to stay in, and pick up the next bus or the one after that.

## Day Tours to the West Bank

Depending on political conditions at the moment, a number of independent groups now offer escorted day tours into the West Bank/Palestinian Authority Areas. **Always check State Department and Foreign Office travel advisories before entering the West Bank.** For those who wish to see Bethlehem, Jericho, and other historic and sites under Palestinian Administration, these tours (all of which include varying degrees of emphasis on social and political conditions), can be an efficient way to explore. Most day tours range from NIS 200-NIS 400 per person.

**Abraham Tours** (www.abrahamtours.com, see above) is one recommended operator, as is **Green Olive Tours** (www.toursinenglish.com) which offers a heavier emphasis on politics. Meeting point for Green Olive tours is usually the West Jerusalem

YMCA on King David Street. **Alternative Tours** (www.alternativetours.ps/cmsms/index.php?page=jerusalem-political-tour-2), based in East Jerusalem offers tours with a more partisan Palestinian perspective.

# Private Guides

Private guides arrange all the logistics of travel during the times they are under hire and can take you to major sites as well as out-of-the-way places efficiently. For those with little time, this can be a restful way to get a great deal done and get an in-depth understanding of the country. The government licensing program has helped to raise the general quality of guides in Israel tremendously, but there's still always a risk in touring with a guide—you never know if they'll be articulate, a compelling story-teller or a complete bore. So ask for extensive references before booking and, when you can, read online reviews of the guide in question. Many good professional guides have put together a brochure or video that will give you an indication of their styles and approaches. At these (or any) prices, you don't want to be stuck with a lemon.

**Costs:** Approximate rates for a private guide are $300 to $400 per day for a Jerusalem tour by foot and taxi, $500 to $600 a day for a licensed and insured guide with a vehicle within Israel. There can be extra charges for more than 8 hours per day (the Ministry of Tourism recommends the extra charge begin at over 10 hours per day) and for off-road trips and use of off-road vehicles. If your guide accompanies you overnight, the fee should include the cost of his or her hotel room (in many places, a licensed guide will receive a discount—your guide will know where he can be put up at a discount rate). Some licensed guides are willing to offer lower rates in slow seasons, but most of the best licensed guides won't. This doesn't necessarily mean that some guides with lower rates aren't good, though they may not be as established.

If you engage an Israeli guide to arrange excursions into Jordan, the rate could be $660 to $700 per day, including a vehicle and his hotel accommodations. Israeli guides are not permitted to guide in Bethlehem or in other Palestinian administered areas.

In Israel, it's illegal for people to guide without a license. Unfortunately, if you go by car with an unlicensed guide, you're probably not insured in case of an accident.

**Recommended guides:** Following are some guides with unusual background qualifications and specialties. If they're not able to meet your time specifications or interests, they may be able to refer you to guides who will better match your needs.

o American-born **David Perlmutter** (© 054/420-1353; david@israeladventure.com) was a guide for the Society for Protection of Nature in Israel and helped design that organization's hikes and tours. He specializes in mountain-biking, hiking, and off-road tours, as well as photography, wine and culinary, cultural, and general tours.

o **Judy Stacey Goldman** (judebob@netvision.net.il) is the Tel Aviv–based coauthor of *The Underground Guide to Jerusalem* and *The Underground Guide to Tel Aviv,* two lively books. Originally from Canada, she's expert on Israeli cuisine, too.

o **Richard Woolf** (© 04/693-5377 or 050/589-4647; woolfr@netvision.net.il) specializes in the Galilee, where he has lived for almost 40 years, but guides throughout Israel. Born in the U.K., he is very patient and well-informed.

o **Sam Salem** (© 054/215-8441; guide.holy@gmail.com), a member of Jerusalem's Christian community, offers specialties that include Bethlehem, Jericho, the Old City of Jerusalem, and the Temple Mount. He has unusual access and connections to many special sites.

o **Rabbi Jeffrey Bearman** (©/fax 02/676-5197; rabbjeff@netvision.net.il), is a Reform rabbi (somewhat unusual in Israel) and a licensed guide.

- **Susan Lamdan** (lamdans@netvision.net.il) is a guide in the Jerusalem area with excellent reader feedback. She's strong on off-road hiking.
- **Madeline Lavine** (☎ 054/450-4098; madl@zahav.net.il) specializes in tours that focus on archaeology and history in Jerusalem's Old and New cities.
- **Adam Sela** (www.adamsela.com) is among the most respected guides for the Negev, southern Israel, and the rest of the country.

GoIsrael.com lists many (but not all) of the country's licensed guides.

## Escorted Tours, Packages & Trails

Israel is an unusual destination in that there are many major Jewish and Christian organizations that sponsor group tours and missions to the Holy Land. It's always worthwhile to check with your synagogue or church as to what organized group tours they can direct you to. These package tours have the added advantage of zeroing in on sites and events that are of special interest to people who share your traditions and background. For more information on escorted general-interest tours, including questions to ask before booking your trip, see www.frommers.com.

Below, we list a number of special interest tour companies.

**HIKING & NATURE TRIPS** The Society for Protection of Nature in Israel (www. teva.org.il), known as SPNI, offers a wide range of excellent nature and camping hikes and tours throughout Israel and beyond. Most tours are in Hebrew, but the guides are among the best in the business, and are generally fluent in English (as are most Israeli participants), so English speakers will not be left out. SPNI offers some tours in English.

**Israel National Trail** (www.israelnationaltrail.com) is a planned, self-guided, 1,000km (621-mile) network of hiking routes and paths that run from the northern tip of Israel to the shores of the Red Sea and take you through places of natural beauty, historic sites, and a broad range of Israel's many ethnic and religious communities. This is a wonderful resource and great for planning local hiking as well.

**Jesus Trail** (www.jesustrail.com) is a carefully planned program of walks and hikes through the area between Nazareth and the Sea of Galilee, through the areas that Jesus would have known (see p. 128).

**Desert Eco Tours** (www.desertecotours.com) offers tours and camping trips in the Negev and Jordan's Wadi Musa and Petra National Park.

**BIKING TOURS & HOLIDAYS** Jerusalem Midnight Biking (www.jerusalem biking.com) offers inventive 3-hour guided nighttime bike tours of Jerusalem's new and old cities for intermediate cyclists. In summer, tours are offered once a week; NIS 110 per person (NIS 220 including rental of mountain bike). Specially scheduled group tours can sometimes be arranged. Highly recommended.

**Israel MTB** (www.israel-mtb.com) offers escorted mountain-biking tours of varying levels of difficulty through carefully chosen landscapes ranging from a half-day to a week, and include transportation to and from biking areas, support crew, and accommodations. Prices range from $120 to $1,200. Customized tours can also be arranged. Most tours are in the desert and southern part of the country.

**CMBC,** the Carmel Mountain Bike Club (www.haifa-israel.info/velo.html), is a group of Haifa-area cycling enthusiasts, including Jon Lipman, who maintain a detailed English-language website and will be happy to share advice and infor on activities, bike rides, and tours. For further information about mountain-biking in Israel, go to the site for Israel Bike Trails (www.israelbiketrails.com).

**FOOD & WINE TRIPS** Savor Israel (www.savorisrael.com) offers a lively itinerary of day-long tours to Tel Aviv–Jaffa, Jerusalem, the Negev, and Galilee. The tours include forays into Israeli haute cuisine, ethnic cooking, visits to local wineries, dairies, and Bedouin communities, and offer great insights into the land and the people of Israel. Groups are small, and prices run from $200 to $300 per person per day.

**EatWith** (www.eatwith.com) lets travelers connect with real Israelis and share a meal in their homes. A constantly changing group of host cooks is listed and the specialties of the house are explained, ranging from a simple vegetarian meal in a grad student's apartment ($12) to a homecooked meal with a local foodie ($45 per person).

**VOLUNTEER TRIPS**   **Volunteers for Israel** (www.vfi-usa.org), arranges volunteer support positions in both civilian and military organizations in Israel. Assignments may include hospital work, repair work, and KP duty with noncombat sectors of the Israeli military. After you fulfill your 3-week obligations, you may be eligible for a special El Al discount fare. Application to this program requires a nonrefundable $100 fee.

**ARCHAEOLOGICAL DIGS**   You can volunteer to work at an archaeological dig if you are 18 or older, prepared to stay for at least 2 weeks, and capable of doing strenuous work in a hot climate. You will have to pay your own fare to and from Israel. Most excavations take place between June and October, but there are off-season digs. Lectures are given at some sites, and some offer academic credit for the work. If you'd like to join a dig, it's best to inquire as far in advance as possible.

The best summary of current digs is found each year in the January/February issue of the magazine *Biblical Archaeology Review,* available at many libraries and newsdealers. *Biblical Archaeology Review's* listings include exactly whom to contact for information about joining each specific dig, as well as estimates on expenses for volunteers and a description of each dig's recent finds. The **Israel Ministry of Tourism North American Info Center** (℡ 888/77-ISRAEL [477-235]) will also give you general, updated information about finding a suitable dig.

The **Biblical Archaeology Society** (℡ 800/221-4644 or 202/364-2636; www.bib-arch.org), which publishes the *Biblical Archaeology Review,* organizes archaeology-based study tours of Israel and the surrounding region. The **Israel Archaeological Society** (℡ 800/477-2358 or 310/472-9449; archaeology@mindspring.com), is another good resource; they will send you schedules of their tours and events.

## SPECIAL PROGRAMS

**PLANT A TREE**   If you'd like to plant a tree in Israel with your own hands, contact the Jewish National Fund (www.jnf.org/support/tree-plantingcenter) or www.trees-fortheholyland.com for more information. The cost per tree is $18.

**JEWISH-ARAB DIALOGUE PROGRAMS**   One out of every five Israeli citizens living inside the pre-1967 boundaries of Israel is Arab. There are a growing number of dialogue and intercultural-understanding projects inside Israel for Israeli Arabs and Jews. You will often find Israelis from English-speaking countries, armed with democratic traditions and experience living in multicultural societies at the forefront of these projects. Visitors to Israel may observe these organizations and participate in lectures and tours that illuminate the problems and possibilities that exist for dialogue and understanding. Short-term volunteering is also doable. This can be a good way to encounter one of the most hopeful sides of Israeli society.

**Neve Shalom/Wahat al Salaam,** 99761 Doar Na Shimshon (℡ **02/991-5621;** visitor programs 02/991-2222, ext. 101; www.nswas.com), is a unique Israeli-Palestinian cooperative village near Jerusalem that sponsors programs for visiting youth groups, including meetings with Jewish and Palestinian youth; programs for peace-oriented groups; and tours for pilgrim groups, focusing on religious sites. Neve Shalom/Wahat al Salaam (which means "Oasis of Peace") has a visitor center, guesthouse, and restaurant on its premises, and offers lecture programs.

**New Israel Fund & Shatil Volunteer Programs** (© 202/842-0900; www.nif.org), is concerned with human rights, intercultural understanding, and education programs inside Israel. It sponsors professional exchange, volunteer, and intern projects, social change fellowships, as well as village volunteer-in-residence programs for teaching English and medical, business, and other skills.

# [FastFACTS]

**ATMs** ATMs are the fastest, easiest way to change money at the best rates. Look for ATMs adorned with international flag decals that accept foreign debit cards; you'll often need a 4-digit PIN. There are fewer international ATMs in smaller towns and in the countryside, and ATMs are not restocked during Shabbat or on Jewish holidays.

**Area Codes** The telephone country code for Israel is 972. Telephone area codes are 02 for Jerusalem; 03 for Tel Aviv; 04 for Haifa, Caesarea, and the Galilee; 08 for Eilat, the Negev, The Dead Sea, and Rehovot; 09 for Netanya.

**Bugs & Wildlife Scorpions** are always something to be aware of in desert and Mediterranean regions. If bitten by a scorpion, get emergency medical treatment immediately. Scorpions do not go out of their way to attack, but they love damp, warm places, and you can get bitten if you happen to put a hand or foot where one of them is resting. Check carefully when entering showers, bathrooms, or other damp places. Always shake out towels at the beach or pool before drying yourself; shake out shoes and socks before putting them on. If you're staying in simple places in the desert, shake out your sheets before getting into bed. Orange groves may look inviting, but big, mean snakes think so, too; avoid the temptation to stroll or picnic in them. In the Jordan Valley, there is a rare but very ugly skin infection called "Rose of Sharon" that's hard to control and will scar unless you get medical treatment—don't hesitate to see a doctor about any unusual or persistent bug bites or skin eruptions.

There is rabies in the countryside, and wild animals should be avoided. Keep away from stray dogs and cats, no matter how friendly or hungry they may seem.

When snorkeling or diving in the Red Sea, remember that many coral formations are not only sharp, but can burn. It is illegal to touch or walk on any coral—not only for your safety, but for the protection of the coral, which can be easily broken and killed. Spiny sea urchins, covering the underwater floor in many parts of the Red Sea, are the bane of swimmers and snorkelers. It's best to wear foot coverings and try to avoid stepping anywhere near a sea urchin—and note that it's very easy for a wave or current to glide you right onto one. Study photo charts of fish before snorkeling, and memorize those that are poisonous to touch, especially the stonefish or rockfish, with their billowing, diaphanous fins that appear to be so delicate. From June through August, stinging and burning jellyfish plague Israel's Mediterranean waters. Do no swim on days when there is evidence of jellyfish on the beaches.

**Business Hours** Government offices are open on weekdays, usually from 7:30 or 8am. Most are closed to the public on Friday, and all are closed on Saturday. In summer, they are open until 1 or 3pm; in winter, they remain open until 2 or 4pm. Banks are open Sunday, Tuesday, and Thursday 8:30am to 12:30pm and 4 to 5:30pm; on Monday and Wednesday 8:30am to 12:30pm only; and on Friday 8:30am to noon. Remember that in Jerusalem's Old City and in places such as Nazareth

245

**Yad Sarah** (☏ **972/2-644-4633** from outside Israel; www.yadsarah.org) is Israel's largest voluntary organization. It lends medical equipment, crutches, and wheelchairs; arranges airport and intercity transportation; helps prepare and equip hotel rooms for special needs; and offers advice for travelers to Israel with special needs. All services are free, although deposits are required for equipment. Advance planning and reservations are required to get the most help from Yad Sarah, but it's also a great resource for sudden or last-minute emergencies.

and Akko's Old City, Muslim-owned shops are closed either half the day or all day on Fridays, and Christian-owned shops close on Sunday.

**Customs**   You can bring $200 worth of tax-free gifts into the country. You can also bring in 250 grams (8¾ oz.) of tobacco, one bottle (⅕ quart) of liquor, and a reasonable amount of film. When you leave, you can convert up to $3,000 back into foreign currency at the airport, so keep your bank receipts. Note that you cannot take antiquities or archaeological artifacts out of Israel unless you have a certificate identifying the object, which will be provided to you by any licensed antiquities dealer.

**Disabled Travelers**
Inside Israel, there's been an ongoing effort to provide access for visitors with disabilities—even at sites famed for their inaccessibility, such as **Masada**. Atop the dramatic plateau of Masada, a network of wheelchair-accessible pathways was completed in 2000. At least some trails in a number of Israel's national parks and nature

reserves (www.parks.org.il) have also been made wheelchair-accessible. Street crossings and public restrooms throughout the country rarely offer easy access. Some institutions located in difficult sites, such as the Israel Museum and Jerusalem Ciné-mathèque, have provisions for handicap access, but you must call in advance to be able to use these facilities.

**Doctors**   All Israeli doctors speak English. Your hotel can refer you to an appropriate physician or the nearest **Magan David Adom** (Red Star of David, Israeli equivalent of the Red Cross) emergency station.

**Drinking Laws**   The legal age for purchase of alcoholic beverages is 18; proof of age is required and often requested at bars, nightclubs, and restaurants, so it's always a good idea to bring ID when you go out. There are no closing times for bars inside Israel. Alcohol is forbidden and considered abhorrent by Islam and so is generally not available in Arabic communities inside

Israel or in Jordan or the West Bank except at hotels for tourists. Do not drink or carry alcohol in public in these areas. Carrying open containers of alcohol is against the law in Beersheva and Jerusalem. A 25 percent tax was placed on alcoholic drinks in 2013, making alcohol comparatively expensive.

**Electricity**   The electric current used in Israel is 220 volts AC (50 cycles) as opposed to the 110-volt system used in America. If your appliance doesn't have the right plug, you can buy a plug adapter in Israel quite easily for approximately NIS 3, or your hotel may have one to lend to you.

**Embassies & Consulates**   **The American Embassy** is at 71 Ha-Yarkon St., Tel Aviv (☏ **03/519-7575**). **The U.S. Consulate-General** in East Jerusalem is at 27 Nablus Rd. (☏ **02/628-7137;** http://jerusalem. usconsulate.gov).

   **The Australian Embassy** is at 23 Yehuda Ha-Levi St., Tel Aviv (☏ **03/693-5000**).

**The Irish Embassy** is at 3 Daniel Frish St., 17th floor, Tel Aviv (✆ **03/696-4166**).

**The New Zealand Embassy** is served by the British Embassy (see below).

**The British Embassy** is at 192 Ha-Yarkon St., Tel Aviv (✆ **03/725-1222**). See http://ukinisrael.fco.gov.uk/en for consulates in Jerusalem and Eilat. **The British Consulate-General** in East Jerusalem is in the Sheikh Jarrah neighborhood at 19 Nashashibi St. (✆ **02/671-7724** or 02/541-4100).

**The Canadian Embassy** is in Tel Aviv at 3 Nirim St., Beit Hasepanut, Yad Eliahu (✆ **03/636-3300**).

**Health Concerns** Sunburn and dehydration are problems throughout the region, but especially in the desert during summer. Although the air is dry, paradoxically, you often don't feel thirsty. Force yourself to drink a minimum of four 1.5-liter bottles of water a day as you travel the area in summer, more if you are in the desert. Sunscreen is a must, though you need less of it at The Dead Sea because the thicker atmosphere screens out the sun.

**Internet & Wi-Fi** Downtown West Jerusalem and Tel Aviv are heavily covered with free We-Fi zones filled with cafés and restaurants where you can bring your laptop and connect without charge, as well as Internet centers and cafes. Most budget and moderate hotels offer free Wi-Fi. More expensive

hotels charge at least $20 per day to connect. Hotels in non-urban areas generally offer Wi-Fi, either free or with a charge. Haifa has a free Wi-Fi zone along the Dado Beach Promenade and in Central Carmel.

**Language** Official languages are Hebrew and Arabic. English is very widely spoken and understood in all hotels and most restaurants. In big cities and on major roads, most signs are in Hebrew, English, and Arabic.

**LGBT Travelers** Israel has come a long way since the 1980s, when laws regarding homosexual activity were removed from the books. A decision by the government to award pensions of deceased military officers to their surviving partners, regardless of sex or marital status, was a landmark in changing attitudes. However, an open, lively gay scene has only really emerged in trendy Tel Aviv, which *Out* has called the "most gay-friendly city in the Middle East". For the past several years, Eilat, somewhat like Tel Aviv, has developed a general attitude of tolerance; mild-mannered Haifa stands somewhere between Tel Aviv and Jerusalem.

The best resource organization is the **Association for GLBT in Israel** (✆ **03/620-5590;** www.glbt.org.il. It offers advice, counseling, and updates on the social scene.

Note that in the Palestinian/Arabic communities

throughout Israel, and in East Jerusalem, the West Bank, Jordan, and Egypt, any kind of openly gay or lesbian behavior is completely forbidden both by custom and by law. Extreme caution and the lowest-possible profile are advised. Similar discretion must be observed in the ultrareligious Jewish and Hassidic neighborhoods of Jerusalem north of Jaffa Road (such as Mea Shearim); in the Old City of Jerusalem; in Safed, which has a largely religious population; and in small, less-touristed Israeli towns.

**Mail** The Israeli Postal Service is dependable. Postal rates are similar to those in the United States and the U.K. Packages must be brought to the post office unsealed for security inspection, and you must present your passport to the postal clerk.

**Mobile Phones** A number of companies will rent a phone to you for use in Israel at lower local rates, shipping it to you in advance of your trip. They include Amigo (www.amigo-us.com) and Cellular Abroad (). Saving vary, and depend on how often you use the phone and whether you'll be using it primarily for local or international calls.

At the main Arrivals Concourse at Ben-Gurion Airport, you'll see the Telecommunications Center, where all major mobile and satellite phone providers have desks. Major providers include Cellcom

(*C* **\*123;** www.cellcom. co.il/cultures/he-il/roamers_ info); Pelephone (*C* **\*166;** www.pelephone.co.il); and Orange/Partner (*C* **800/ 054-054;** www.orange. co.il). The special deals and packages you can buy or rent are constantly chang- ing, so it's best to scout around ahead of time. Orange offers a special local plus international card for NIS 130, that gives you NIS 120 of calls at an excel- lent per minute rate plus NIS 200 minutes of free calls to other phones in the Orange 054 network. Two other possibilities are Israel Phones (www.israel- phones.com) and Tikshoret Besheva (*C* **972/2-652- 2353;** yossch@netvision. net.il). Both companies will deliver a cellphone to your hotel or apartment. Daily rates (subject to change) are approximately $1 a day with an optional additional charge for insurance. With Tikshoret Besheva, incom- ing calls are free; calls within Israel to Cellcom or land phones begin at 25¢ a minute; calls to the U.S., Canada, or the U.K. begin at approximately 40¢. Prices are lower after 9pm and, with some plans, on the Sabbath.

**Note:** In the Jordan Val- ley and The Dead Sea area, which are the lowest points on earth and far below sea

level, cellphone communi- cations are not usually optimum.

**Money & Costs** From- mer's lists exact prices in the local currency. The cur- rency conversions provided were correct at press time. However, rates fluctuate, so before departing consult a currency exchange website such as **www.oanda.com/ currency/converter** to check up-to-the-minute rates.

**Currency:** The basic unit of currency is the New Israel Shekel (NIS). The shekel is divided into 100 agorot. The smallest denomination you will encounter are 10-agorot copper-colored coins, and larger, copper 50-agorot (half-shekel) coins, all useful for bus fares, but both may soon be phased out. The 1-shekel coin is a tiny silver buttonlike object that is extremely easy to lose. There are also 2-, 5- and 10-shekel coins, as well as 20-, 50-, and 100-shekel notes. **Note:** The new, small 10-shekel coins are not popular, as counterfeit 10-shekel coins abound. The real ones have fine, regular groves on the rims. If the rims are smooth or only irregularly grooved, it's bad. Get to know which is which, otherwise, you can be out a lot of money (US $2.50) for such a small coin.

**Packing Tips** Israel is a very informal country, so casual, practical clothing is acceptable everywhere. In winter, warm socks and sturdy, rubber-sole walking shoes are helpful. A folding umbrella, and fleece liners and medium-weight jackets that can be layered are essential. Women should pack a multiuse, easy-to- carry shawl for chilly nights in mountain cities such as Jerusalem, and to wrap over shorts, bare shoulders, or short sleeves when visit- ing holy sites. Men won't need ties; sport jackets are not mandatory at expensive restaurants or at perfor- mances. Sun hats are nec- essary, and men must cover their heads when entering Jewish religious places; if you don't have a head cov- ering, most synagogues will have some at the door to lend.

**Passports** It is impor- tant to check that you have at least 6 months left before your passport's expi- ration; without that cush- ion, you won't be allowed into the country.

**Pharmacies** Pharmacies are well-stocked, and you'll encounter many interna- tional name brands, but drug prices outside of Israeli insurance plans— even for nonprescription medicines—are compara- tively high.

## THE VALUE OF THE SHEKEL VS. OTHER POPULAR CURRENCIES

| NIS | Aus$ | Can$ | Euro€ | NZ$ | UK£ | US$ |
|---|---|---|---|---|---|---|
| Israeli Shekel (NIS)1 | A$0,25 | C$0.25 | €0.20 | NZ$0.31 | £0.16 | US$0.25 |

Don't wait until you're down to your last shekel if you're using ATMs to keep yourself funded. International ATM connections sometimes go down, and Israeli banks have a way of having sudden 1-day wildcat strikes. Remember that ATMs will not be restocked during Shabbat, and there's usually a run on ATMs on Friday, so stock up on Thursdays, before the Israeli weekend, and stock up a day before holidays.

**Police**   Dial 100.

**Safety**   Israel is a low-crime country. Some of the major dangers you will encounter are car-related. Israeli drivers aren't renowned for sound driving practices. Blatant tailgating is the unnerving way of life here. Car theft and theft of belongings from rental cars is also a problem. Some rental-car companies require you to use a steering wheel lock, and it is never a good idea to leave valuables in your car. When traveling in Jordan or in East Jerusalem and Arab cities inside Israel, travelers should not carry or drink alcohol (which is forbidden by Islam) in public, and modest dress is expected of both men and women. Women traveling alone must realize they are visiting Muslim societies, and the fact of being unaccompanied by a man can be regarded as suspicious and provocative. Extremely modest dress is essential.

**Security**   Terrorism is a consideration everywhere in the world, and Israelis have become experts in dealing with it. Despite the news of the past few years, the chance is actually greater that you'll be involved in a traffic mishap while in Israel. In Jerusalem, security guards now prowl the bus stops, checking and intercepting suspicious-looking people before they can board a bus. Guards conduct bag and body checks at the entrances to shopping malls, markets, shops, cafes, restaurants, transportation hubs, and hotels. You'll find security guards at most major restaurants. Always keep alert and be aware of suspicious persons, especially if they are well bundled in coats or jackets when the weather is not cold.

*Note:* Get away from and immediately report any suspicious or unattended bags or packages! Any Israeli will know how to summon the police.

**Senior Travel**   Mention the fact that you're a senior when you make your travel reservations. Some Israeli hotels, especially those in international chains, still offer lower rates for seniors, especially during off season.

**Smoking**   Smoking is against the law in all public places, including restaurants, trains, buses, and taxis.

**Student Travel**   Israel is a student-friendly country. There are all kinds of student flights and discount airfares to Israel, and if you're from a Jewish-American family, you may even be eligible for a free trip to Israel under the **Birthright (Taglit) Program** (www.birthrightisrael.com), which provides the gift of first-time, peer-group, educational tours of Israel (airfare included) to Jewish adults ages 18 to 26. More than 40,000 people have taken advantage of this program, which is designed to encourage Jewish identity and connection with the State of Israel (waiting lists are long).

Even for independent travelers, there are discounts for students at museums, national parks, and railroads, although train discounts are minimal. Check out the International **Student Travel Confederation** (ISTC; www.istc.org) website for comprehensive travel services information and details on how to get an International Student Identity Card (ISIC), which qualifies students for

PLANNING YOUR TRIP TO ISRAEL | Taxes

| WHAT THINGS COST IN ISRAEL | NIS |
| --- | --- |
| Taxi from the airport to downtown | 250 |
| Double room, moderate | US$240* |
| Double room, inexpensive | US$140* |
| Three-course dinner for one without wine, moderate | 70 |
| Bottle of beer | 18 |
| Cup of coffee | 8–14 |
| 1 liter of premium gas | NIS 8 |
| Admission to most museums | 25–50 |
| Admission to most national parks | 25–35 |

*Israeli hotel rates are quoted in dollars.

substantial savings. It also provides students with basic health and life insurance and a 24-hour help line. The card is valid for a maximum of 18 months. You can apply for the card online or in person at **STA Travel** (𝒞 **800/781-4040** in North America, 132-782 in Australia, 0871/2-300-040 in the U.K.; www.statravel.com), the biggest student-travel agency in the world. If you're no longer a student but are still under 26, you can get an International Youth Travel Card (IYTC) from the same people, which entitles you to some discounts. Travel CUTS (𝒞 **800/592-2887;** www.travelcuts.com) offers similar services for both Canadians and U.S. residents. Irish students may prefer to turn to USIT (𝒞 **01/602-1904;** www.usit.ie), an Ireland-based specialist in student, youth, and independent travel

**Taxes** At press time, there is a value-added tax (VAT) of 18 percent. This does not apply to Eilat,

which is a tax-free zone. Unless otherwise noted on the price tag, all prices automatically include the VAT. Hotel bills (including food and services charged to your room) are not subject to the VAT if you are a tourist with a tourist visa, and if you pay your bill in foreign currency or with a foreign credit or debit card. For single purchases of over $100, certain shops will give you a form you can use for refund of your VAT as you leave the country at Ben-Gurion Airport. In order to complete this transaction, you have to get to Ben-Gurion well ahead of your flight and hope that the Refund Office will be open and that the lines will not be too long. If the VAT you've paid is substantial, it could be worth the effort.

**Telephones** Israel's public telephones are mostly for phone cards only. A few public phones take 1-shekel coins, and 1-shekel coins are needed for pay phones in neighborhood

groceries and restaurants. Post offices, many hotels, and many convenience groceries and newsstands sell prepaid calling cards in denominations ranging from NIS 20 to NIS 200.

**Phoning From Within Israel:** The major city or area codes inside Israel are: 02 (for Jerusalem) 03 (for Tel Aviv) 04 (for Haifa and the Galilee) 09 (for the coast between Tel Aviv and Haifa) 08 (for the Negev and Eilat)

For calls made within the area code you're calling from, omit the area code, and just dial the local 7-digit number. For calls within Israel that are not within your area code, you must add the 2-digit city or area code to the local number (for example, from Jerusalem to Haifa, dial 04, plus the local Haifa number).

Major cellphone prefixes are 050; 052; and 054. To call a cellphone, always use the 3-digit prefix, followed by the 7-digit number.

**Phoning from Overseas:**
The international dialing prefix from Australia is 0011; from the U.S. or Canada, 011; from Ireland, New Zealand or the U.K., 00.

The country code for Israel is 972.

To call a number in Israel from overseas, dial the overseas access number (in the U.S., 011) plus 972 and then the Israeli number, omitting the initial 0 in the area code. Thus, to phone a hypothetical number in Jerusalem, you would dial 011-972-2-555-5555. To call a cellphone in Israel, again you must omit the initial 0 in the prefix. So, calling 054-666-6666, would entail dialing 011-972-54-666-6666.

**Phoning Overseas:** The international dialing code from Israel is 00. Then dial the country code, area code, and local number.

The country code for Australia is 63; for the U.S. and Canada, 1; for Ireland, 353; for New Zealand, 64; for the U.K., dial 44.

For local Israeli directory assistance ("information"), dial ✆ 144; 1-700 and 1-800 numbers are toll-free. All operators speak some English and if necessary will connect you to a special English-speaking operator.

**Time**   Israel is 2 hours ahead of Greenwich Mean Time, 7 hours ahead of Eastern Standard Time, and 10 hours ahead of Pacific Standard Time. When it's 7pm in Israel, it's noon in New York.

**Daylight Savings Time Warning**: Because Israel has its own unique dates for going on and off daylight saving time, there is often a period of 1 or 2 weeks in the spring and a month in September or October when there's only a 1-hour difference between Israel and Greenwich Mean Time and a 6-hour time difference between New York and Israel. Palestinian areas, Jordan, and Egypt keep to their own dates for daylight saving time, and those areas of the West Bank not under direct Israeli control also keep to Egyptian/Jordanian time. This can make border crossings a disaster if both countries are not synchronized. Jordan, Palestinian areas, and Egypt are normally 7 hours ahead of New York time, and 2 hours ahead of Greenwich Mean Time. In the past, because of religious and political considerations, the decision about when to begin and end Israeli daylight saving time has sometimes not been made until the last minute. For this reason, it is very important to reconfirm schedules at these times of year—you could miss your flight, or worse.

**Tipping**   Tip 10 percent in restaurants or cafes, unless a service charge is already added to your bill. Taxi drivers do not expect tips unless they have helped you load or carry luggage. An extra NIS 5 per bag is fair. Leave NIS 5 per person per day for your hotel maid, more if she has given you extra help. Barbers in Arab sectors do not expect tips; hairdressers should get 10 to 20 percent, depending on service

**Toilets**   In Israel, public toilets on the street are rare to nonexistent. Try hotel lobbies, bars, restaurants, museums, department stores, railway and bus stations, and service stations. Large hotels and fast-food restaurants are often the best bet for clean facilities. Restaurants and bars in resorts or heavily visited areas may reserve their restrooms for patrons. In each quarter of Jerusalem's Old City, there are scattered public restrooms, marked w.c., a tradition from British Mandate times. They're not 21st century, but they're better than nothing.

**Visas**   Visitors from most English-speaking countries will receive a visa for Israel on the spot at Ben-Gurion Airport or at any land border crossing (see "Entry Requirements," p. 224). There is no charge for the visa, however, there is an exit fee if you leave via a land crossing into Jordan.

Citizens of Western Europe, North America, Australia, and New Zealand are issued visas good for up to 3 months upon arrival at Israel's Ben-Gurion Airport. For security reasons, visitors whose passports indicate extensive travel to countries that are politically unstable or technically at war with Israel (such as Iran, Sudan, Afghanistan, or Lebanon) may be taken aside for questioning upon arrival in Israel, and in some cases denied entrance. Travelers with Israeli visa stamps in their passports may enter Egypt and Jordan, which have peace agreements and diplomatic relations with Israel, however, an Israeli visa stamp or any evidence of travel to Israel will generally preclude entrance into any other Arabic countries, except for Morocco and Tunisia. Travelers entering Jordan by land from Israel are issued a visa at the border for a fee. Travelers entering Sinai by land from Israel will receive a Sinai Only visa at the Taba border crossing. If you wish to travel into Egypt beyond Sinai, you must obtain an All Egypt visa from an Egyptian embassy or consulate ahead of time. If you're spending time in Eilat, the Egyptian Consulate in Eilat is most convenient. **Note:** Visas to Jordan are given on the spot at the Sheikh Hussein Crossing from northern Israel and at the Rabin Crossing from Eilat (southern Israel); however, you must obtain a visa in advance from a Jordanian embassy if you plan to enter Jordan via the Allenby–King Hussein Bridge in the West Bank.

The governments of most Western countries have advised their citizens NOT to travel to the West Bank, which includes Nablus, Ramallah, Jericho, and Bethlehem; however, depending on day-to-day political conditions, many travelers do take pilgrimage or group tours to visit Christian holy places in Bethlehem.

Travelers with Arabic-sounding surnames may also be stopped for questioning. There are some cases of travelers being turned back at the border for reasons of security or without further explanation. Such travelers are not compensated for plane tickets or for canceled hotel reservations. Unfortunately, Israel has no provision for pre-clearance visa interviews before visitors embark on their journeys.

**Water** Tap water is safe and drinkable in Israel, except at The Dead Sea. There, even luxury hotels have special taps on each floor that provide drinking water. Although Israeli water is safe, the presence of various minerals in the water may make you a bit queasy. For this reason, bottled water could be a good investment, though in small amounts and for brushing your teeth, local water is fine. In Jordan and Sinai, tap water is not drinkable. Bottled water is essential.

**Women Travelers** It's important to remember to dress modestly when visiting holy places or ultra-Orthodox Jewish neighborhoods. The penalty for immodest dress can be getting spat on, pelted with pebbles, or worse. The police generally do not take action against religious Jews who attack "immodest" visitors to their neighborhoods. The Jerusalem and Tel Aviv suburbs of Beit Shemesh and B'nai Brak should also be avoided unless you dress with **extreme** modesty. In Jerusalem, on the Number 1 and 2 bus lines, which serve Mea Shearim and the Western Wall, women are relegated to the back of the bus (so as not to tempt the gaze of ultra-religious men in the front rows). Failure to obey this rule may be met with violent protest from religious passengers.

East Jerusalem, the Old City of Jerusalem, and the West Bank are largely Arabic societies, and unless women travelers are guarded in their dress and behavior, there's a good chance there will be insults and unwanted advances. Women in Islamic societies do not venture far from their houses unless they are in the company of a husband, relatives, or at least one other woman; women travelers may seem to be breaking the rules of propriety simply by being alone. It is always best to try to have at least one traveling companion, male or female, with you if possible. Modest dress and behavior also helps to avoid unwanted attention. In Arabic communities, a woman alone, dressed in shorts or a bare midriff is not respectable, and will often not receive common courtesy. In Israel, except in religious neighborhoods, revealing dress is more common.